Kaplan Schweser's Path to Success

Level II CFA® Exam

CFA®

Welcome

As the head of Advanced Designations at Kaplan Schweser, I am pleased to have the opportunity to help you prepare for the CFA® exam. Kaplan Schweser has decades of experience in delivering the most effective CFA exam prep products in the market and I know you will find them to be invaluable in your studies.

Our products are designed to be an integrated study solution across print and digital media to provide you the best learning experience, whether you are studying with a physical book, online, or on your mobile device.

Our core product, the SchweserNotes™, addresses all of the Topics, Study Sessions, Readings, and LOS in the CFA curriculum. Each reading in the SchweserNotes has been broken into smaller, bite-sized modules with Module Quizzes interspersed throughout to help you continually assess your comprehension. Topic Assessments appear at the end of each Topic to help you assess your knowledge of the material before you move on to the next section.

All purchasers of the SchweserNotes receive online access to the Kaplan Schweser online platform (our learning management system or LMS) at www.Schweser.com. In the LMS, you will see a dashboard that tracks your overall progress and performance and also includes an Activity Feed, which provides structure and organization to the tasks required to prepare for the CFA exam. You also have access to the SchweserNotes, Module Quizzes, and Topic Assessments content as well as the Video Lectures (if purchased), which contain a short video that complements each module in the SchweserNotes. Look for the icons indicating where video content, Module Quizzes, and Topic Assessments are available online. I strongly encourage you to enter your Module Quiz and Topic Assessment answers online and use the dashboard to track your progress and stay motivated.

Again, thank you for trusting Kaplan Schweser with your CFA exam preparation. We're here to help you throughout your journey to become a CFA charterholder.

Regards,

Derek Burkett

Derek Burkett, CFA, FRM, CAIA
Vice President (Advanced Designations)

AF853288

Book 1: Ethical and Professional Standards, Quantitative Methods, and Economics

SchweserNotes™ 2019

Level II CFA®

KAPLAN® SCHWESER

SCHWESERNOTES™ 2019 LEVEL II CFA® BOOK 1: ETHICAL AND PROFESSIONAL STANDARDS, QUANTITATIVE METHODS, AND ECONOMICS

Published in 2018 by Kaplan, Inc.

Printed in the United States of America.

ISBN: 978-1-4754-7968-3

CONTENTS

STUDY SESSION 3—QUANTITATIVE METHODS

READING 6

READING 7

READING 8

READING 9

LEARNING OUTCOME STATEMENTS (LOS)

STUDY SESSION 1

The topical coverage corresponds with the following CFA Institute assigned reading:

1, 2. CFA Institute Code of Ethics and Standards of Professional Conduct Guidance for Standards I–VII

The candidate should be able to:

a. describe the six components of the Code of Ethics and the seven Standards of Professional Conduct. (page 1)
b. explain the ethical responsibilities required of CFA Institute members and candidates in the CFA Program by the Code and Standards. (page 2)
a. demonstrate a thorough knowledge of the CFA Institute Code of Ethics and Standards of Professional Conduct by applying the Code and Standards to specific situations. (page 6)
b. recommend practices and procedures designed to prevent violations of the Code of Ethics and Standards of Professional Conduct. (page 6)

STUDY SESSION 2

The topical coverage corresponds with the following CFA Institute assigned reading:

3. Application of The Code and Standards

The candidate should be able to:

a. evaluate policies and practices for a firm and an individual in relation to the CFA Institute Code of Ethics and Standards of Professional Conduct. (page 89)
b. explain the appropriate action to take in response to conduct that violates the CFA Institute Code of Ethics and Standards of Professional Conduct. (page 89)

The topical coverage corresponds with the following CFA Institute assigned reading:

4. Trade Allocation: Fair Dealing and Disclosure

The candidate should be able to:

a. evaluate trade allocation practices and determine whether they comply with the CFA Institute Standards of Professional Conduct addressing fair dealing and client loyalty. (page 101)
b. describe appropriate actions to take in response to trade allocation practices that do not adequately respect client interests. (page 102)

The topical coverage corresponds with the following CFA Institute assigned reading:

5. Changing Investment Objectives

The candidate should be able to:

a. evaluate the disclosure of investment objectives and basic policies and determine whether they comply with the CFA Institute Standards of Professional Conduct. (page 103)
b. describe appropriate actions needed to ensure adequate disclosure of the investment process. (page 104)

STUDY SESSION 3

The topical coverage corresponds with the following CFA Institute assigned reading:

6. Fintech in Investment Management

The candidate should be able to:

a. describe "fintech." (page 117)
b. describe Big Data, artificial intelligence, and machine learning. (page 118)
c. describe fintech applications to investment management. (page 119)
d. describe financial applications of distributed ledger technology. (page 120)

The topical coverage corresponds with the following CFA Institute assigned reading:

7. Correlation and Regression

The candidate should be able to:

a. calculate and interpret a sample covariance and a sample correlation coefficient and interpret a scatter plot. (page 125)
b. describe limitations to correlation analysis. (page 129)
c. formulate a test of the hypothesis that the population correlation coefficient equals zero and determine whether the hypothesis is rejected at a given level of significance. (page 130)
d. distinguish between the dependent and independent variables in a linear regression. (page 132)
e. explain the assumptions underlying linear regression and interpret regression coefficients. (page 133)
f. calculate and interpret the standard error of estimate, the coefficient of determination, and a confidence interval for a regression coefficient. (page 138)
g. formulate a null and alternative hypothesis about a population value of a regression coefficient and determine the appropriate test statistic and whether the null hypothesis is rejected at a given level of significance. (page 140)
h. calculate the predicted value for the dependent variable, given an estimated regression model and a value for the independent variable. (page 142)
i. calculate and interpret a confidence interval for the predicted value of the dependent variable. (page 143)
j. describe the use of analysis of variance (ANOVA) in regression analysis, interpret ANOVA results, and calculate and interpret the *F*-statistic. (page 144)
k. describe limitations of regression analysis. (page 149)

The topical coverage corresponds with the following CFA Institute assigned reading:

8. Multiple Regression and Issues in Regression Analysis

The candidate should be able to:

a. formulate a multiple regression equation to describe the relation between a dependent variable and several independent variables and determine the statistical significance of each independent variable. (page 160)
b. interpret estimated regression coefficients and their *p*-values. (page 161)
c. formulate a null and an alternative hypothesis about the population value of a regression coefficient, calculate the value of the test statistic, and determine whether to reject the null hypothesis at a given level of significance. (page 162)
d. interpret the results of hypothesis tests of regression coefficients. (page 162)
e. calculate and interpret 1) a confidence interval for the population value of a regression coefficient and 2) a predicted value for the dependent

variable, given an estimated regression model and assumed values for the independent variables. (page 166)

g. calculate and interpret the *F*-statistic, and describe how it is used in regression analysis. (page 167)
i. evaluate how well a regression model explains the dependent variable by analyzing the output of the regression equation and an ANOVA table. (page 169)
h. distinguish between and interpret the R^2 and adjusted R^2 in multiple regression. (page 174)
j. formulate a multiple regression equation by using dummy variables to represent qualitative factors and interpret the coefficients and regression results. (page 176)
f. explain the assumptions of a multiple regression model. (page 181)
k. explain the types of heteroskedasticity and how heteroskedasticity and serial correlation affect statistical inference. (page 181)
l. describe multicollinearity and explain its causes and effects in regression analysis. (page 188)
m. describe how model misspecification affects the results of a regression analysis and describe how to avoid common forms of misspecification. (page 190)
n. describe models with qualitative dependent variables. (page 194)
o. evaluate and interpret a multiple regression model and its results. (page 194)
p. distinguish between supervised and unsupervised machine learning. (page 198)
q. describe machine learning algorithms used in prediction, classification, clustering, and dimension reduction. (page 199)
r. describe the steps in model training. (page 202)

The topical coverage corresponds with the following CFA Institute assigned reading:

9. Time-Series Analysis

The candidate should be able to:

a. calculate and evaluate the predicted trend value for a time series, modeled as either a linear trend or a log-linear trend, given the estimated trend coefficients. (page 213)
b. describe factors that determine whether a linear or a log-linear trend should be used with a particular time series and evaluate limitations of trend models. (page 218)
c. explain the requirement for a time series to be covariance stationary and describe the significance of a series that is not stationary. (page 221)
d. describe the structure of an autoregressive (AR) model of order *p* and calculate one- and two-period-ahead forecasts given the estimated coefficients. (page 221)
e. explain how autocorrelations of the residuals can be used to test whether the autoregressive model fits the time series. (page 222)
f. explain mean reversion and calculate a mean-reverting level. (page 224)
g. contrast in-sample and out-of-sample forecasts and compare the forecasting accuracy of different time-series models based on the root mean squared error criterion. (page 225)
h. explain the instability of coefficients of time-series models. (page 226)
i. describe characteristics of random walk processes and contrast them to covariance stationary processes. (page 227)

j. describe implications of unit roots for time-series analysis, explain when unit roots are likely to occur and how to test for them, and demonstrate how a time series with a unit root can be transformed so it can be analyzed with an AR model. (page 228)
k. describe the steps of the unit root test for nonstationarity and explain the relation of the test to autoregressive time-series models. (page 228)
l. explain how to test and correct for seasonality in a time-series model and calculate and interpret a forecasted value using an AR model with a seasonal lag. (page 232)
m. explain autoregressive conditional heteroskedasticity (ARCH) and describe how ARCH models can be applied to predict the variance of a time series. (page 236)
n. explain how time-series variables should be analyzed for nonstationarity and/or cointegration before use in a linear regression. (page 238)
o. determine an appropriate time-series model to analyze a given investment problem and justify that choice. (page 239)

The topical coverage corresponds with the following CFA Institute assigned reading:

10. Probabilistic Approaches: Scenario Analysis, Decision Trees, and Simulations

The candidate should be able to:

a. describe steps in running a simulation. (page 249)
b. explain three ways to define the probability distributions for a simulation's variables. (page 249)
c. describe how to treat correlation across variables in a simulation. (page 249)
d. describe advantages of using simulations in decision making. (page 251)
e. describe some common constraints introduced into simulations. (page 252)
f. describe issues in using simulations in risk assessment. (page 253)
g. compare scenario analysis, decision trees, and simulations. (page 254)

STUDY SESSION 4

The topical coverage corresponds with the following CFA Institute assigned reading:

11. Currency Exchange Rates: Understanding Equilibrium Value

The candidate should be able to:

a. calculate and interpret the bid–offer spread on a spot or forward currency quotation and describe the factors that affect the bid–offer spread. (page 265)
b. identify a triangular arbitrage opportunity and calculate its profit, given the bid–offer quotations for three currencies. (page 267)
c. distinguish between spot and forward rates and calculate the forward premium/discount for a given currency. (page 270)
d. calculate the mark-to-market value of a forward contract. (page 272)
e. explain international parity conditions (covered and uncovered interest rate parity, forward rate parity, purchasing power parity, and the international Fisher effect). (page 273)
f. describe relations among the international parity conditions. (page 278)
g. evaluate the use of the current spot rate, the forward rate, purchasing power parity, and uncovered interest parity to forecast future spot exchange rates. (page 279)

h. explain approaches to assessing the long-run fair value of an exchange rate. (page 279)
i. describe the carry trade and its relation to uncovered interest rate parity and calculate the profit from a carry trade. (page 282)
j. explain how flows in the balance of payment accounts affect currency exchange rates. (page 283)
k. explain the potential effects of monetary and fiscal policy on exchange rates. (page 285)
l. describe objectives of central bank or government intervention and capital controls and describe the effectiveness of intervention and capital controls. (page 288)
m. describe warning signs of a currency crisis. (page 289)

The topical coverage corresponds with the following CFA Institute assigned reading:

12. Economic Growth and the Investment Decision

The candidate should be able to:

a. compare factors favoring and limiting economic growth in developed and developing economies. (page 303)
b. describe the relation between the long-run rate of stock market appreciation and the sustainable growth rate of the economy. (page 305)
c. explain why potential GDP and its growth rate matter for equity and fixed income investors. (page 305)
d. distinguish between capital deepening investment and technological progress and explain how each affects economic growth and labor productivity. (page 306)
e. forecast potential GDP based on growth accounting relations. (page 309)
f. explain how natural resources affect economic growth and evaluate the argument that limited availability of natural resources constrains economic growth. (page 310)
g. explain how demographics, immigration, and labor force participation affect the rate and sustainability of economic growth. (page 310)
h. explain how investment in physical capital, human capital, and technological development affects economic growth. (page 312)
i. compare classical growth theory, neoclassical growth theory, and endogenous growth theory. (page 315)
j. explain and evaluate convergence hypotheses. (page 317)
k. describe the economic rationale for governments to provide incentives to private investment in technology and knowledge. (page 318)
l. describe the expected impact of removing trade barriers on capital investment and profits, employment and wages, and growth in the economies involved. (page 319)

The topical coverage corresponds with the following CFA Institute assigned reading:

13. Economics of Regulation

The candidate should be able to:

a. describe classifications of regulations and regulators. (page 327)
b. describe uses of self-regulation in financial markets. (page 328)
c. describe the economic rationale for regulatory intervention. (page 329)
d. describe regulatory interdependencies and their effects. (page 329)
e. describe tools of regulatory intervention in markets. (page 330)
f. explain purposes in regulating commerce and financial markets. (page 331)
g. describe anticompetitive behaviors targeted by antitrust laws globally and evaluate the antitrust risk associated with a given business strategy. (page 332)
h. describe benefits and costs of regulation. (page 332)
i. evaluate how a specific regulation affects an industry, company, or security. (page 333)

WELCOME TO THE 2019 LEVEL II SCHWESERNOTES™

Thank you for trusting Kaplan Schweser to help you reach your goals. We are pleased that you have chosen us to assist you in preparing for the Level II CFA Exam. In this introduction, I want to explain the resources included with these SchweserNotes, suggest how you can best use Schweser materials to prepare for the exam, and direct you toward other educational resources you will find helpful as you study for the exam.

Besides the SchweserNotes themselves, there are many educational resources available at Schweser.com. Log in using the individual username and password that you received when you purchased your SchweserNotes.

SchweserNotes™

These notes consist of five volumes that include complete coverage of all 17 Study Sessions and all 471 Learning Outcome Statements (LOS). Examples and Module Quizzes (multiple-choice questions) are provided along the way to help you master the material and check your progress. At the end of each major topic area, you can take a Topic Assessment for that topic area. Topic Assessment questions are created to be exam-like in format and difficulty, to help you evaluate how well your study of each topic has prepared you for the actual exam.

Practice Questions

Studies have shown that to retain what you learn, it is essential that you quiz yourself often. For this purpose we offer SchweserPro™ QBank, which contains thousands of Level II practice questions and explanations. Questions are available for each LOS, topic, and Study Session. Build your own quizzes by specifying the topics and the number of questions. SchweserPro QBank is an important learning aid for achieving the depth of proficiency needed at Level II. It should not, however, be considered a replacement for rehearsing with "exam-type" questions as found in our Practice Exams, Volumes 1 & 2 and our Schweser Mock Exam.

Practice Exams

Schweser offers four full 6-hour practice exams: Schweser Practice Exams Volume 1 and Volume 2 each contain two complete 120-question tests. These are important tools for gaining the speed and skills you will need to pass the exam. Each book provides answers with full explanations for self-grading and evaluation. By entering your answers at Schweser.com, you can use our Performance Tracker to find out how you are performing compared to other Schweser Level II candidates.

Schweser Resource Library

We have created a number of online reference videos, which are available to all purchasers of Schweser Premium Instruction and PremiumPlus packages. Schweser Resource Library videos range from 20 to 60 minutes in length and cover such topics as: "Introduction to Item Sets," "Hypothesis Testing," "Foreign Exchange Basics," "Ratio Analysis," and "Forward Contracts."

How to Succeed

The Level II CFA exam is a formidable challenge (51 topic reviews and 471 Learning Outcome Statements), so you must devote considerable time and effort to be properly prepared. There is no shortcut! You must learn the material, know the terminology and techniques, understand the concepts, and be able to answer 120 questions quickly and mostly correctly. Fifteen hours per week for 25 weeks is a good estimate of the study time required on average, but different candidates will need more or less time, depending on their individual backgrounds and experience.

There is no way around it; CFA Institute will test you in a way that will reveal how well you know the Level II curriculum. You should begin early and stick to your study plan. Read the SchweserNotes and complete the Module Quizzes for each topic review. Prepare for and attend a live class, an online class, or a study group each week. Take quizzes often using SchweserPro Qbank and go back to review previous topics regularly. At the end of each topic area, take the online Topic Assessment to check your progress. You should try to finish reading the curriculum at least four weeks before the Level II exam so that you have sufficient time for Practice Exams and for further review of those topics that you have not yet mastered.

I would like to thank Kent Westlund, CFA Content Specialist, for his contributions to the 2019 Level II SchweserNotes for the CFA Exam.

Best regards,

Bijesh Tolia

Dr. Bijesh Tolia, CFA, CA

VP of CFA Education and Level II Manager

Kaplan Schweser

The following is a review of the Ethical and Professional Standards (1) principles designed to address the learning outcome statements set forth by CFA Institute. Cross-Reference to CFA Institute Assigned Readings #1 & #2.

READINGS 1 and 2

CFA Institute Code of Ethics and Standards of Professional Conduct Guidance for Standards I–VII

Study Session 1

EXAM FOCUS

In addition to reading this review of the ethics material, we strongly recommend that all candidates for the CFA® examination read the *Standards of Practice Handbook 11th Edition* (2014) multiple times. As a Level II CFA candidate, it is your responsibility to comply with the *Code and Standards*. The complete *Code and Standards* are reprinted in Volume 1 of the CFA Program Curriculum.

MODULE 1.1: INTRODUCTION TO THE CODE AND STANDARDS

Video covering this content is available online.

LOS 1.a: Describe the six components of the Code of Ethics and the seven Standards of Professional Conduct.

CFA® Program Curriculum, Volume 1, page 15

THE CODE OF ETHICS

Members of CFA Institute (including CFA charterholders) and candidates for the CFA designation ("Members and Candidates") must:[1]

- Act with integrity, competence, diligence, and respect, and in an ethical manner with the public, clients, prospective clients, employers, employees, colleagues in the investment profession, and other participants in the global capital markets.
- Place the integrity of the investment profession and the interests of clients above their own personal interests.

1. Copyright 2014, CFA Institute. Reproduced and republished from "The Code of Ethics," from *Standards of Practice Handbook, 11th Ed.*, 2014, with permission from CFA Institute. All rights reserved.

- Use reasonable care and exercise independent professional judgment when conducting investment analysis, making investment recommendations, taking investment actions, and engaging in other professional activities.
- Practice and encourage others to practice in a professional and ethical manner that will reflect credit on themselves and the profession.
- Promote the integrity and viability of the global capital markets for the ultimate benefit of society.
- Maintain and improve their professional competence and strive to maintain and improve the competence of other investment professionals.

THE STANDARDS OF PROFESSIONAL CONDUCT

I. Professionalism
II. Integrity of Capital Markets
III. Duties to Clients
IV. Duties to Employers
V. Investment Analysis, Recommendations, and Actions
VI. Conflicts of Interest
VII. Responsibilities as a CFA Institute Member or CFA Candidate

LOS 1.b: Explain the ethical responsibilities required of CFA Institute members and candidates in the CFA Program by the Code and Standards.

CFA® Program Curriculum, Volume 1, page 15

STANDARDS OF PROFESSIONAL CONDUCT[2]

I. PROFESSIONALISM

A. **Knowledge of the Law.** Members and Candidates must understand and comply with all applicable laws, rules, and regulations (including the CFA Institute *Code of Ethics* and *Standards of Professional Conduct*) of any government, regulatory organization, licensing agency, or professional association governing their professional activities. In the event of conflict, Members and Candidates must comply with the more strict law, rule, or regulation. Members and Candidates must not knowingly participate or assist in and must dissociate from any violation of such laws, rules, or regulations.

B. **Independence and Objectivity.** Members and Candidates must use reasonable care and judgment to achieve and maintain independence and objectivity in their professional activities. Members and Candidates must not offer, solicit, or accept any gift, benefit, compensation, or

2. Ibid.

consideration that reasonably could be expected to compromise their own or another's independence and objectivity.

C. **Misrepresentation.** Members and Candidates must not knowingly make any misrepresentations relating to investment analysis, recommendations, actions, or other professional activities.

D. **Misconduct.** Members and Candidates must not engage in any professional conduct involving dishonesty, fraud, or deceit or commit any act that reflects adversely on their professional reputation, integrity, or competence.

II. **INTEGRITY OF CAPITAL MARKETS**

A. **Material Nonpublic Information.** Members and Candidates who possess material nonpublic information that could affect the value of an investment must not act or cause others to act on the information.

B. **Market Manipulation.** Members and Candidates must not engage in practices that distort prices or artificially inflate trading volume with the intent to mislead market participants.

III. **DUTIES TO CLIENTS**

A. **Loyalty, Prudence, and Care.** Members and Candidates have a duty of loyalty to their clients and must act with reasonable care and exercise prudent judgment. Members and Candidates must act for the benefit of their clients and place their clients' interests before their employer's or their own interests.

B. **Fair Dealing.** Members and Candidates must deal fairly and objectively with all clients when providing investment analysis, making investment recommendations, taking investment action, or engaging in other professional activities.

C. **Suitability.**

1. When Members and Candidates are in an advisory relationship with a client, they must:

   a) Make a reasonable inquiry into a client's or prospective clients' investment experience, risk and return objectives, and financial constraints prior to making any investment recommendation or taking investment action and must reassess and update this information regularly.

   b) Determine that an investment is suitable to the client's financial situation and consistent with the client's written objectives, mandates, and constraints before making an investment recommendation or taking investment action.

   c) Judge the suitability of investments in the context of the client's total portfolio.

2. When Members and Candidates are responsible for managing a portfolio to a specific mandate, strategy, or style, they must make only investment recommendations or take only investment actions that are consistent with the stated objectives and constraints of the portfolio.

D. **Performance Presentation.** When communicating investment performance information, Members or Candidates must make reasonable efforts to ensure that it is fair, accurate, and complete.

E. **Preservation of Confidentiality.** Members and Candidates must keep information about current, former, and prospective clients confidential unless:

1. The information concerns illegal activities on the part of the client or prospective client,
2. Disclosure is required by law, or
3. The client or prospective client permits disclosure of the information.

IV. DUTIES TO EMPLOYERS

A. **Loyalty.** In matters related to their employment, Members and Candidates must act for the benefit of their employer and not deprive their employer of the advantage of their skills and abilities, divulge confidential information, or otherwise cause harm to their employer.

B. **Additional Compensation Arrangements.** Members and Candidates must not accept gifts, benefits, compensation, or consideration that competes with or might reasonably be expected to create a conflict of interest with their employer's interest unless they obtain written consent from all parties involved.

C. **Responsibilities of Supervisors.** Members and Candidates must make reasonable efforts to ensure that anyone subject to their supervision or authority complies with applicable laws, rules, regulations, and the Code and Standards.

V. INVESTMENT ANALYSIS, RECOMMENDATIONS, AND ACTIONS

A. **Diligence and Reasonable Basis.** Members and Candidates must:

1. Exercise diligence, independence, and thoroughness in analyzing investments, making investment recommendations, and taking investment actions.
2. Have a reasonable and adequate basis, supported by appropriate research and investigation, for any investment analysis, recommendation, or action.

B. **Communication with Clients and Prospective Clients.** Members and Candidates must:

1. Disclose to clients and prospective clients the basic format and general principles of the investment processes they use to analyze investments, select securities, and construct portfolios and must promptly disclose any changes that might materially affect those processes.

2. Disclose to clients and prospective clients significant limitations and risks associated with the investment process.

3. Use reasonable judgment in identifying which factors are important to their investment analyses, recommendations, or actions and include those factors in communications with clients and prospective clients.

4. Distinguish between fact and opinion in the presentation of investment analysis and recommendations.

C. **Record Retention.** Members and Candidates must develop and maintain appropriate records to support their investment analysis, recommendations, actions, and other investment-related communications with clients and prospective clients.

VI. CONFLICTS OF INTEREST

A. **Disclosure of Conflicts.** Members and Candidates must make full and fair disclosure of all matters that could reasonably be expected to impair their independence and objectivity or interfere with respective duties to their clients, prospective clients, and employer. Members and Candidates must ensure that such disclosures are prominent, are delivered in plain language, and communicate the relevant information effectively.

B. **Priority of Transactions.** Investment transactions for clients and employers must have priority over investment transactions in which a Member or Candidate is the beneficial owner.

C. **Referral Fees.** Members and Candidates must disclose to their employer, clients, and prospective clients, as appropriate, any compensation, consideration, or benefit received by, or paid to, others for the recommendation of products or services.

VII. RESPONSIBILITIES AS A CFA INSTITUTE MEMBER OR CFA CANDIDATE

A. **Conduct as Participants in CFA Institute Programs.** Members and Candidates must not engage in any conduct that compromises the reputation or integrity of CFA Institute or the CFA designation or the integrity, validity, or security of CFA Institute programs.

B. **Reference to CFA Institute, the CFA Designation, and the CFA Program.** When referring to CFA Institute, CFA Institute membership, the CFA designation, or candidacy in the CFA Program, Members and Candidates must not misrepresent or exaggerate the meaning or implications of membership in CFA Institute, holding the CFA designation, or candidacy in the CFA Program.

MODULE 2.1: STANDARDS I(A) AND I(B)

Video covering this content is available online.

LOS 2.a: Demonstrate a thorough knowledge of the CFA Institute Code of Ethics and Standards of Professional Conduct by applying the Code and Standards to specific situations.

LOS 2.b: Recommend practices and procedures designed to prevent violations of the Code of Ethics and Standards of Professional Conduct.

CFA® Program Curriculum, Volume 1, page 21

I Professionalism

I(A) Knowledge of the Law. Members and Candidates must understand and comply with all applicable laws, rules, and regulations (including the CFA Institute Code of Ethics and Standards of Professional Conduct) of any government, regulatory organization, licensing agency, or professional association governing their professional activities. In the event of conflict, Members and Candidates must comply with the more strict law, rule, or regulation. Members and Candidates must not knowingly participate or assist in and must dissociate from any violation of such laws, rules, or regulations.

PROFESSOR'S NOTE

While we use the term "members" in the following, note that all of the Standards apply to candidates as well.

Guidance—Code and Standards vs. Local Law

Members must know the laws and regulations relating to their professional activities in all countries in which they conduct business. Members must comply with applicable laws and regulations relating to their professional activity. Do not violate Code or Standards even if the activity is otherwise legal. Always adhere to the most strict rules and requirements (law or CFA Institute Standards) that apply.

Guidance—Participation or Association With Violations by Others

Members should dissociate, or separate themselves, from any ongoing client or employee activity that is illegal or unethical, even if it involves leaving an employer (an extreme case). While a member may confront the involved individual first, he must approach his supervisor or compliance department. Inaction with continued association may be construed as knowing participation.

Recommended Procedures for Compliance—Members

- Members should have procedures to keep up with changes in applicable laws, rules, and regulations.
- Compliance procedures should be reviewed on an ongoing basis to ensure that they address current law, CFAI Standards, and regulations.
- Members should maintain current reference materials for employees to access in order to keep up to date on laws, rules, and regulations.
- Members should seek advice of counsel or their compliance department when in doubt.
- Members should document any violations when they disassociate themselves from prohibited activity and encourage their employers to bring an end to such activity.
- There is no requirement under the Standards to report violations to governmental authorities, but this may be advisable in some circumstances and required by law in others.
- Members are strongly encouraged to report other members' violations of the Code and Standards.

Recommended Procedures for Compliance—Firms

Members should encourage their firms to:

- Develop and/or adopt a code of ethics.
- Make available to employees information that highlights applicable laws and regulations.
- Establish written procedures for reporting suspected violation of laws, regulations, or company policies.

Members who supervise the creation and maintenance of investment services and products should be aware of and comply with the regulations and laws regarding such services and products both in their country of origin and the countries where they will be sold.

Application of Standard I(A) Knowledge of the Law[3]

Example 1:

Michael Allen works for a brokerage firm and is responsible for an underwriting of securities. A company official gives Allen information indicating that the financial statements Allen filed with the regulator overstate the issuer's earnings. Allen seeks the advice of the brokerage firm's general counsel, who states that it would be difficult for the regulator to prove that Allen has been involved in any wrongdoing.

Comment:

Although it is recommended that members and candidates seek the advice of legal counsel, the reliance on such advice does not absolve a member or candidate

3. Ibid.

from the requirement to comply with the law or regulation. Allen should report this situation to his supervisor, seek an independent legal opinion, and determine whether the regulator should be notified of the error.

Example 2:

Kamisha Washington's firm advertises its past performance record by showing the 10-year return of a composite of its client accounts. However, Washington discovers that the composite omits the performance of accounts that have left the firm during the 10-year period and that this omission has led to an inflated performance figure. Washington is asked to use promotional material that includes the erroneous performance number when soliciting business for the firm.

Comment:

Misrepresenting performance is a violation of the Code and Standards. Although she did not calculate the performance herself, Washington would be assisting in violating this standard if she were to use the inflated performance number when soliciting clients. She must dissociate herself from the activity. She can bring the misleading number to the attention of the person responsible for calculating performance, her supervisor, or the compliance department at her firm. If her firm is unwilling to recalculate performance, she must refrain from using the misleading promotional material and should notify the firm of her reasons. If the firm insists that she use the material, she should consider whether her obligation to dissociate from the activity would require her to seek other employment.

Example 3:

An employee of an investment bank is working on an underwriting and finds out the issuer has altered their financial statements to hide operating losses in one division. These misstated data are included in a preliminary prospectus that has already been released.

Comment:

The employee should report the problem to his supervisors. If the firm doesn't get the misstatement fixed, the employee should dissociate from the underwriting and, further, seek legal advice about whether he should undertake additional reporting or other actions.

Example 4:

Laura Jameson, a U.S. citizen, works for an investment advisor based in the United States and works in a country where investment managers are prohibited from participating in IPOs for their own accounts.

Comment:

Jameson must comply with the strictest requirements among U.S. law (where her firm is based), the CFA Institute Code and Standards, and the laws of the country where she is doing business. In this case that means she must not participate in any IPOs for her personal account.

Example 5:

A junior portfolio manager suspects that a broker responsible for new business from a foreign country is being allocated a portion of the firm's payments for third-party research and suspects that no research is being provided. He believes that the research payments may be inappropriate and unethical.

Comment:

He should follow his firm's procedures for reporting possible unethical behavior and try to get better disclosure of the nature of these payments and any research that is being provided.

> **I(B) Independence and Objectivity.** Members and Candidates must use reasonable care and judgment to achieve and maintain independence and objectivity in their professional activities. Members and Candidates must not offer, solicit, or accept any gift, benefit, compensation, or consideration that reasonably could be expected to compromise their own or another's independence and objectivity.

Guidance

Do not let the investment process be influenced by any external sources. Modest gifts are permitted. Allocation of shares in oversubscribed IPOs to personal accounts is NOT permitted. Distinguish between gifts from clients and gifts from entities seeking influence to the detriment of the client. Gifts must be disclosed to the member's employer in any case, either prior to acceptance if possible, or subsequently.

Guidance—Investment Banking Relationships

Do not be pressured by sell-side firms to issue favorable research on current or prospective investment-banking clients. It is appropriate to have analysts work with investment bankers in "road shows" only when the conflicts are adequately and effectively managed and disclosed. Be sure there are effective "firewalls" between research/investment management and investment banking activities.

Guidance—Public Companies

Analysts should not be pressured to issue favorable research by the companies they follow. Do not confine research to discussions with company management, but rather use a variety of sources, including suppliers, customers, and competitors.

Guidance—Buy-Side Clients

Buy-side clients may try to pressure sell-side analysts. Portfolio managers may have large positions in a particular security, and a rating downgrade may have an effect on the portfolio performance. As a portfolio manager, there is a responsibility to respect and foster intellectual honesty of sell-side research.

Guidance—Fund Manager and Custodial Relationships

Members responsible for selecting outside managers should not accept gifts, entertainment, or travel that might be perceived as impairing their objectivity.

Guidance—Performance Measurement and Attribution

Performance analysts may experience pressure from investment managers who have produced poor results or acted outside their mandate. Members and candidates who analyze performance must not let such influences affect their analysis.

Guidance—Manager Selection

Members and candidates must exercise independence and objectivity when they select investment managers. They should not accept gifts or other compensation that could be seen as influencing their hiring decisions, nor should they offer compensation when seeking to be hired as investment managers. The responsibility to maintain independence and objectivity applies to all a member or candidate's hiring and firing decisions, not just those that involve investment management.

Guidance—Credit Rating Agencies

Members employed by credit rating firms should make sure that procedures prevent undue influence by the firm issuing the securities. Members who use credit ratings should be aware of this potential conflict of interest and consider whether independent analysis is warranted.

Guidance—Issuer-Paid Research

Remember that this type of research is fraught with potential conflicts. Analysts' compensation for preparing such research should be limited, and the preference is for a flat fee, without regard to conclusions or the report's recommendations.

Guidance—Travel

Best practice is for analysts to pay for their own commercial travel when attending information events or tours sponsored by the firm being analyzed.

Recommended Procedures for Compliance

- Protect the integrity of opinions—make sure they are unbiased.
- Create a restricted list and distribute only factual information about companies on the list.
- Restrict special cost arrangements—pay for one's own commercial transportation and hotel; limit use of corporate aircraft to cases in which commercial transportation is not available.

- Limit gifts—token items only. Customary, business-related entertainment is okay as long as its purpose is not to influence a member's professional independence or objectivity. Firms should impose clear value limits on gifts.
- Restrict employee investments in equity IPOs and private placements. Require pre-approval of IPO purchases.
- Review procedures—have effective supervisory and review procedures.
- Firms should have formal written policies on independence and objectivity of research.
- Firms should appoint a compliance officer and provide clear procedures for employee reporting of unethical behavior and violations of applicable regulations.

Application of Standard I(B) Independence and Objectivity

Example 1:

Steven Taylor, a mining analyst with Bronson Brokers, is invited by Precision Metals to join a group of his peers in a tour of mining facilities in several western U.S. states. The company arranges for chartered group flights from site to site and for accommodations in Spartan Motels, the only chain with accommodations near the mines, for three nights. Taylor allows Precision Metals to pick up his tab, as do the other analysts, with one exception—John Adams, an employee of a large trust company who insists on following his company's policy and paying for his hotel room himself.

Comment:

The policy of the company where Adams works complies closely with Standard I(B) by avoiding even the appearance of a conflict of interest, but Taylor and the other analysts were not necessarily violating Standard I(B). In general, when allowing companies to pay for travel and/or accommodations under these circumstances, members and candidates must use their judgment, keeping in mind that such arrangements must not impinge on a member or candidate's independence and objectivity. In this example, the trip was strictly for business and Taylor was not accepting irrelevant or lavish hospitality. The itinerary required chartered flights, for which analysts were not expected to pay. The accommodations were modest. These arrangements are not unusual and did not violate Standard I(B) so long as Taylor's independence and objectivity were not compromised. In the final analysis, members and candidates should consider both whether they can remain objective and whether their integrity might be perceived by their clients to have been compromised.

Example 2:

Walter Fritz is an equity analyst with Hilton Brokerage who covers the mining industry. He has concluded that the stock of Metals & Mining is overpriced at its current level, but he is concerned that a negative research report will hurt the good relationship between Metals & Mining and the investment-banking division of his firm. In fact, a senior manager of Hilton Brokerage has just sent him a copy of a proposal his firm has made to Metals & Mining to underwrite a debt offering.

Fritz needs to produce a report right away and is concerned about issuing a less-than-favorable rating.

Comment:

Fritz's analysis of Metals & Mining must be objective and based solely on consideration of company fundamentals. Any pressure from other divisions of his firm is inappropriate. This conflict could have been eliminated if, in anticipation of the offering, Hilton Brokerage had placed Metals & Mining on a restricted list for its sales force.

Example 3:

Tom Wayne is the investment manager of the Franklin City Employees Pension Plan. He recently completed a successful search for firms to manage the foreign equity allocation of the plan's diversified portfolio. He followed the plan's standard procedure of seeking presentations from a number of qualified firms and recommended that his board select Penguin Advisors because of its experience, well-defined investment strategy, and performance record, which was compiled and verified in accordance with the CFA Institute Global Investment Performance Standards. Following the plan selection of Penguin, a reporter from the Franklin City Record called to ask if there was any connection between the action and the fact that Penguin was one of the sponsors of an "investment fact-finding trip to Asia" that Wayne made earlier in the year. The trip was one of several conducted by the Pension Investment Academy, which had arranged the itinerary of meetings with economic, government, and corporate officials in major cities in several Asian countries. The Pension Investment Academy obtains support for the cost of these trips from a number of investment managers, including Penguin Advisors; the Academy then pays the travel expenses of the various pension plan managers on the trip and provides all meals and accommodations. The president of Penguin Advisors was one of the travelers on the trip.

Comment:

Although Wayne can probably put to good use the knowledge he gained from the trip in selecting portfolio managers and in other areas of managing the pension plan, his recommendation of Penguin Advisors may be tainted by the possible conflict incurred when he participated in a trip paid for partly by Penguin Advisors and when he was in the daily company of the president of Penguin Advisors. To avoid violating Standard I(B), Wayne's basic expenses for travel and accommodations should have been paid by his employer or the pension plan; contact with the president of Penguin Advisors should have been limited to informational or educational events only; and the trip, the organizer, and the sponsor should have been made a matter of public record. Even if his actions were not in violation of Standard I(B), Wayne should have been sensitive to the public perception of the trip when reported in the newspaper and the extent to which the subjective elements of his decision might have been affected by the familiarity that the daily contact of such a trip would encourage. This advantage would probably not be shared by competing firms.

Example 4:

An analyst in the corporate finance department promises a client that her firm will provide full research coverage of the issuing company after the offering.

Comment:

This is not a violation, but she cannot promise favorable research coverage. Research must be objective and independent.

Example 5:

An employee's boss tells him to assume coverage of a stock and maintain a buy rating.

Comment:

Research opinions and recommendations must be objective and arrived at independently. Following the boss's instructions would be a violation if the analyst determined a buy rating is inappropriate.

Example 6:

A money manager receives a gift of significant value from a client as a reward for good performance over the prior period and informs her employer of the gift.

Comment:

No violation here because the gift is from a client and is not based on performance going forward, but the gift must be disclosed to her employer. If the gift were contingent on future performance, the money manager would have to obtain permission from her employer. The reason for both the disclosure and permission requirements is that the employer must ensure that the money manager does not give advantage to the client giving or offering additional compensation, to the detriment of other clients.

Example 7:

An analyst enters into a contract to write a research report on a company, paid for by that company, for a flat fee plus a bonus based on attracting new investors to the security.

Comment:

This is a violation because the compensation structure makes total compensation depend on the conclusions of the report (a favorable report will attract investors and increase compensation). Accepting the job for a flat fee that does not depend on the report's conclusions or its impact on share price is permitted, with proper disclosure of the fact that the report is funded by the subject company.

Example 8:

A trust manager at a bank selects mutual funds for client accounts based on the profits from "service fees" paid to the bank by the mutual fund sponsor.

Comment:

This is a violation because the trust manager has allowed the fees to affect his objectivity.

Example 9:

An analyst performing sensitivity analysis for a security does not use only scenarios consistent with recent trends and historical norms.

Comment:

This is a good thing and is not a violation.

Example 10

A member whose firm is seeking to become an investment manager for a labor union contributes a large sum to the union leader's re-election campaign. After the union hires the member's firm, the member continues to spend significant amounts on entertainment for the union leader and his family.

Comment:

Offering gifts or other compensation to influence a decision to hire an investment manager is a violation of Standard I(B).

Example 11

A member who is a performance analyst notices that one of her firm's top investment managers has changed his composite construction, removing a poorly performing large account and placing it in a different composite. Knowing that the investment manager is important to the firm and a close friend of the firm's CEO, the member does not disclose this change in her performance report.

Comment:

The member violated Standard I(B) by failing to exercise independence and objectivity in her analysis. Altering composites to conceal poor performance also violates Standard III(D) Performance Presentation and may violate Standard I(C) Misrepresentation.

MODULE QUIZ 1.1, 2.1

To best evaluate your performance, enter your quiz answers online.

1. While working on a new underwriting project, Jean Brayman, CFA, has just received information from her client that leads her to believe that the firm's financial statements in the registration statement overstate the firm's financial position. Brayman should:
   A. report her finding to the appropriate governmental regulatory authority.
   B. immediately dissociate herself from the underwriting in writing to the client.
   C. seek advice from her firm's compliance department as to the appropriate action to take.

2. Karen Jones, CFA, is an outside director for Valley Manufacturing. At a director's meeting, Jones finds out that Valley Corp. has made several contributions to foreign politicians that she suspects were illegal. Jones checks with her firm's legal counsel and determines that the contributions were indeed illegal. At the next board meeting, Jones urges the board to disclose the contributions. The board, however, votes not to make a disclosure. Jones' *most appropriate* action would be to:
   A. protest the board's actions in writing to the executive officer of Valley.
   B. resign from the board and seek legal counsel as to her legal disclosure requirements.
   C. inform her supervisor of her discovery and cease attending meetings until the matter is resolved.

3. Which of the following statements is *least likely* correct? A member or candidate:
   A. can participate or assist in a violation simply by having knowledge of the violation and not taking action to stop it.
   B. is held responsible for participating in illegal acts in instances where violation of the law is evident to those who know or should know the law.
   C. must report evidence of legal violations to the appropriate governmental or regulatory organization.

4. Jack Schleifer, CFA, is an analyst for Brown Investment Managers (BIM). Schleifer has recently accepted an invitation to visit the facilities of ChemCo, a producer of chemical compounds used in a variety of industries. ChemCo offers to pay for Schleifer's accommodations in a penthouse suite at a luxury hotel and allow Schleifer to use the firm's private jet to travel to its three facilities located in New York, Hong Kong, and London. In addition, ChemCo offers two tickets to a formal high-society dinner in New York and a small desk clock with the ChemCo logo. Schleifer declines to use ChemCo's corporate jet or to allow the firm to pay for his accommodations but accepts the clock and the tickets to the dinner (which he discloses to his employer) since he will be able to market his firm's mutual funds to other guests at the dinner. Has Schleifer violated any CFA Institute Standards of Professional Conduct?
   A. Yes.
   B. No, since he is using the gifts accepted to benefit his employer's interests.
   C. No, since the gifts he accepted were fully disclosed in writing to his employer.

5. Based on the Standards of Professional Conduct, a financial analyst is *least likely* required to:
   A. report to his employer the receipt of gifts and additional compensation from clients.
   B. disclose the value of consideration to be received for referrals.
   C. pay for commercial transportation and lodging while visiting a company's headquarters.

Video covering this content is available online.

MODULE 2.2: STANDARDS I(C) AND I(D)

I(C) Misrepresentation. Members and Candidates must not knowingly make any misrepresentations relating to investment analysis, recommendations, actions, or other professional activities.

Guidance

Trust is a foundation in the investment profession. Do not make any misrepresentations or give false impressions. This includes oral, electronic, and social media communications. Misrepresentations include guaranteeing investment performance and plagiarism. Plagiarism encompasses using someone else's work (reports, forecasts, models, ideas, charts, graphs, and spreadsheet models) without giving them credit. Knowingly omitting information that could affect an investment decision or performance evaluation is considered misrepresentation.

Models and analysis developed by others at a member's firm are the property of the firm and can be used without attribution. A report written by another analyst employed by the firm cannot be released as another analyst's work.

Recommended Procedures for Compliance

A good way to avoid misrepresentation is for firms to provide employees who deal with clients or prospects a written list of the firm's available services and a description of the firm's qualifications. Employee qualifications should be accurately presented as well. To avoid plagiarism, maintain records of all materials used to generate reports or other firm products and properly cite sources (quotes and summaries) in work products. Information from recognized financial and statistical reporting services need not be cited.

Members should encourage their firms to establish procedures for verifying marketing claims of third parties whose information the firm provides to clients.

Application of Standard I(C) Misrepresentation

Example 1:

Anthony McGuire is an issuer-paid analyst hired by publicly traded companies to electronically promote their stocks. McGuire creates a website that promotes his research efforts as a seemingly independent analyst. McGuire posts a profile and a strong buy recommendation for each company on the website, indicating that the stock is expected to increase in value. He does not disclose the contractual relationships with the companies he covers on his website, in the research reports he issues, or in the statements he makes about the companies in Internet chat rooms.

Comment:

McGuire has violated Standard I(C) because the Internet site and emails are misleading to potential investors. Even if the recommendations are valid and supported with thorough research, his omissions regarding the true relationship between himself and the companies he covers constitute a misrepresentation.

McGuire has also violated Standard VI(A) Disclosure of Conflicts by not disclosing the existence of an arrangement with the companies through which he receives compensation in exchange for his services.

Example 2:

Claude Browning, a quantitative analyst for Double Alpha, Inc., returns in great excitement from a seminar. In that seminar, Jack Jorrely, a well-publicized quantitative analyst at a national brokerage firm, discussed one of his new models in great detail, and Browning is intrigued by the new concepts. He proceeds to test this model, making some minor mechanical changes but retaining the concept, until he produces some very positive results. Browning quickly announces to his supervisors at Double Alpha that he has discovered a new model and that clients and prospective clients alike should be informed of this positive finding as ongoing proof of Double Alpha's continuing innovation and ability to add value.

Comment:

Although Browning tested Jorrely's model on his own and even slightly modified it, he must still acknowledge the original source of the idea. Browning can certainly take credit for the final, practical results; he can also support his conclusions with his own test. The credit for the innovative thinking, however, must be awarded to Jorrely.

Example 3:

Paul Ostrowski runs a 2-person investment management firm. Ostrowski's firm subscribes to a service from a large investment research firm that provides research reports that can be repackaged by smaller firms for those firms' clients. Ostrowski's firm distributes these reports to clients as its own work.

Comment:

Ostrowski can rely on third-party research that has a reasonable and adequate basis, but he cannot imply that he is the author of the report. Otherwise, Ostrowski would misrepresent the extent of his work in a way that would mislead the firm's clients or prospective clients.

Example 4:

A member makes an error in preparing marketing materials and misstates the amount of assets his firm has under management.

Comment:

The member must attempt to stop distribution of the erroneous material as soon as the error is known. Simply making the error unintentionally is not a violation, but continuing to distribute material known to contain a significant misstatement of fact would be.

Example 5:

The marketing department states in sales literature that an analyst has received an MBA degree, but he has not. The analyst and other members of the firm have distributed this document for years.

Comment:

The analyst has violated the Standards, as he should have known of this misrepresentation after having distributed and used the materials over a period of years.

Example 6:

A member describes an interest-only collateralized mortgage obligation as guaranteed by the U.S. government because it is a claim against the cash flows of a pool of guaranteed mortgages, although the payment stream and the market value of the security are not guaranteed.

Comment:

This is a violation because of the misrepresentation.

Example 7:

A member describes a bank CD as "guaranteed."

Comment:

This is not a violation as long as the limits of the guarantee provided by the Federal Deposit Insurance Corporation are not exceeded and the nature of the guarantee is clearly explained to clients.

Example 8:

A member uses definitions he found online for such terms as variance and coefficient of variation in preparing marketing material.

Comment:

Even though these are standard terms, using the work of others word-for-word is plagiarism.

Example 9:

A candidate reads about a research paper in a financial publication and includes the information in a research report, citing the original research report but not the financial publication.

Comment:

To the extent that the candidate used information and interpretation from the financial publication without citing it, the candidate is in violation of the Standard. The candidate should either obtain the report and reference it directly or, if he relies solely on the financial publication, should cite both sources.

> **I(D) Misconduct.** Members and Candidates must not engage in any professional conduct involving dishonesty, fraud, or deceit or commit any act that reflects adversely on their professional reputation, integrity, or competence.

Guidance

CFA Institute discourages unethical behavior in all aspects of members' and candidates' lives. Do not abuse CFA Institute's Professional Conduct Program by seeking enforcement of this Standard to settle personal, political, or other disputes that are not related to professional ethics.

Recommended Procedures for Compliance

Firms are encouraged to adopt these policies and procedures:

- Develop and adopt a code of ethics and make clear that unethical behavior will not be tolerated.
- Give employees a list of potential violations and sanctions, including dismissal.
- Check references of potential employees.

Application of Standard I(D) Misconduct

Example 1:

Simon Sasserman is a trust investment officer at a bank in a small affluent town. He enjoys lunching every day with friends at the country club, where his clients have observed him having numerous drinks. Back at work after lunch, he clearly is intoxicated while making investment decisions. His colleagues make a point of handling any business with Sasserman in the morning because they distrust his judgment after lunch.

Comment:

Sasserman's excessive drinking at lunch and subsequent intoxication at work constitute a violation of Standard I(D) because this conduct has raised questions about his professionalism and competence. His behavior thus reflects poorly on him, his employer, and the investment industry.

Example 2:

Carmen Garcia manages a mutual fund dedicated to socially responsible investing. She is also an environmental activist. As the result of her participation at nonviolent protests, Garcia has been arrested on numerous occasions for trespassing on the property of a large petrochemical plant that is accused of damaging the environment.

Comment:

Generally, Standard I(D) is not meant to cover legal transgressions resulting from acts of civil disobedience in support of personal beliefs because such conduct does not reflect poorly on the member or candidate's professional reputation, integrity, or competence.

Example 3:

A member intentionally includes a receipt that is not in his expenses for a company trip.

Comment:

Because this act involves deceit and fraud and reflects on the member's integrity and honesty, it is a violation.

Example 4:

A member tells a client that he can get her a good deal on a car through his father-in-law, but instead gets her a poor deal and accepts part of the commission on the car purchase.

Comment:

The member has been dishonest and misrepresented the facts of the situation and has, therefore, violated the Standard.

MODULE QUIZ 2.2

To best evaluate your performance, enter your quiz answers online.

1. Jamie Hutchins, CFA, is a portfolio manager for CNV Investments Inc. Over the years, Hutchins has made several poor personal investments that have led to financial distress and personal bankruptcy. Hutchins feels that her business partner, John Smith, is mostly to blame for her situation since "he did not invest enough money in her investment opportunities and caused them to fail." Hutchins reports Smith to CFA Institute claiming Smith violated the Code and Standards relating to misconduct. Which of the following statements is *most likely* correct?
   A. By reporting Smith to CFA Institute, Hutchins has misused the Professional Conduct Program, thus violating the Code and Standards, but her poor investing and bankruptcy have not violated the Code and Standards.
   B. Hutchins's bankruptcy reflects poorly on her professional reputation and thus violates the Code and Standards, but her reporting of Smith does not.
   C. Hutchins's poor investing and bankruptcy, as well as her reporting of Smith, are both violations of the Standards.
2. In which of the following has the analyst *least likely* committed plagiarism?
   A. Julie Long takes performance projections and charts from a company she is researching, combines them with her own analysis, and publishes them under her own name.
   B. Bill Cooper finds a statistical table in the Federal Reserve Bulletin that supports the work he has done in his industry analysis and has his secretary include the table as part of his report without citing the source.
   C. Jan Niedfeldt gets a call from one of her fellow analysts stating that the analyst's research shows that XYZ Company is a buy. Niedfeldt calls up her major clients and tells them that her research shows XYZ is a buy.

3. Jamie Olson, CFA, has just started work as a trainee with Neuvo Management Corp., a small regional money management firm started six months ago. She has been told to make a few cold calls and round up some new clients. In which of the following statements has Olson *least likely* violated the Standards of Practice?
   A. "Sure, we can perform all the financial and investment services you need. We've consistently outperformed the market indexes and will continue to do so under our current management."
   B. "Sure, we can assist you with all the financial and investment services you need. If we don't provide the service in-house, we have arrangements with other full-service firms that I would be happy to tell you about."
   C. "Our firm has a long history of successful performance for our clients. While we can't guarantee future results, we do believe we will continue to benefit our clients."
4. Beth Bixby, CFA, uses a quantitative model to actively manage a portfolio of stocks with an objective of earning a greater return than the market. Over the last three years, the returns to a portfolio constructed using the model have been greater than the returns to the S&P index by between 2% and 4%. In promotional materials, Bixby states: "Through our complex quantitative approach, we select a portfolio that has similar risk to the S&P 500 Index but will receive a return between 2% and 4% greater than the index." This statement is:
   A. permissible since prior returns to the firm's model provide a reasonable and adequate basis for the promotional material.
   B. permissible since the statement describes the basic characteristics of the fund's risk and return objectives.
   C. not permissible since Bixby is misrepresenting the investment performance her firm can reasonably expect to achieve.
5. Josef Karloff, CFA, acts as liaison between Pinnacle Financial (an investment management firm) and Summit Inc. (an investment banking boutique specializing in penny stocks). When Summit underwrites an IPO, Karloff routinely has Pinnacle issue vague statements implying that the firm has cash flows, financial resources, and growth prospects that are better than is the case in reality. This action is a violation of the section of the Standards concerning:
   A. fair dealing.
   B. nonpublic information.
   C. misconduct.

MODULE 2.3: STANDARDS II(A) AND II(B)

Video covering this content is available online.

> **II Integrity of Capital Markets**
>
> **II(A) Material Nonpublic Information.** Members and Candidates who possess material nonpublic information that could affect the value of an investment must not act or cause others to act on the information.

Guidance

Information is "material" if its disclosure would impact the price of a security or if reasonable investors would want the information before making an investment decision. Ambiguous information, as far as its likely effect on price, may not be considered material. Information is "nonpublic" until it has been made available to the marketplace. An analyst conference call is not public disclosure. Selectively disclosing information by corporations creates the potential for insider-trading violations. The prohibition against acting on material nonpublic information extends to mutual funds containing the subject securities as well as related swaps and options contracts.

Some members and candidates may be involved in transactions during which they receive material nonpublic information provided by firms (e.g., investment banking transactions). Members and candidates may use the provided nonpublic information for its intended purpose, but must not use the information for any other purpose unless it becomes public information.

Guidance—Mosaic Theory

There is no violation when a perceptive analyst reaches an investment conclusion about a corporate action or event through an analysis of public information together with items of nonmaterial nonpublic information.

Guidance—Social Media

When gathering information from internet or social media sources, members and candidates need to be aware that not all of it is considered public information. Members and candidates should confirm that any material information they receive from these sources is also available from public sources, such as company press releases or regulatory filings.

Guidance—Industry Experts

Members and candidates may seek insight from individuals who have specialized expertise in an industry. However, they may not act or cause others to act on any material nonpublic information obtained from these experts until that information has been publicly disseminated.

Recommended Procedures for Compliance

Make reasonable efforts to achieve public dissemination of the information. Encourage firms to adopt procedures to prevent misuse of material nonpublic information. Use a "firewall" within the firm, with elements including:

- Substantial control of relevant interdepartmental communications, through a clearance area such as the compliance or legal department.
- Review employee trades—maintain "watch," "restricted," and "rumor" lists.
- Monitor and restrict proprietary trading while a firm is in possession of material nonpublic information.

Prohibition of all proprietary trading while a firm is in possession of material nonpublic information may be inappropriate because it may send a signal to the market. In these cases, firms should take the contra side of only unsolicited customer trades.

Application of Standard II(A) Material Nonpublic Information

Example 1:

Samuel Peter, an analyst with Scotland and Pierce, Inc., is assisting his firm with a secondary offering for Bright Ideas Lamp Company. Peter participates, via telephone conference call, in a meeting with Scotland and Pierce investment-banking employees and Bright Ideas' CEO. Peter is advised that the company's earnings projections for the next year have significantly dropped. Throughout the telephone conference call, several Scotland and Pierce salespeople and portfolio managers walk in and out of Peter's office, where the telephone call is taking place. As a result, they are aware of the drop in projected earnings for Bright Ideas. Before the conference call is concluded, the salespeople trade the stock of the company on behalf of the firm's clients, and other firm personnel trade the stock in a firm proprietary account and in employee personal accounts.

Comment:

Peter violated Standard II(A) because he failed to prevent the transfer and misuse of material nonpublic information to others in his firm. Peter's firm should have adopted information barriers to prevent the communication of nonpublic information between departments of the firm. The salespeople and portfolio managers who traded on the information have also violated Standard II(A) by trading on inside information.

Example 2:

Elizabeth Levenson is based in Taipei and covers the Taiwanese market for her firm, which is based in Singapore. She is invited to meet the finance director of a manufacturing company, along with the other ten largest shareholders of the company. During the meeting, the finance director states that the company expects its workforce to strike next Friday, which will cripple productivity and distribution. Can Levenson use this information as a basis to change her rating on the company from "buy" to "sell"?

Comment:

Levenson must first determine whether the material information is public. If the company has not made this information public (a small-group forum does not qualify as a method of public dissemination), she cannot use the information according to Standard II(A).

Example 3:

Jagdish Teja is a buy-side analyst covering the furniture industry. Looking for an attractive company to recommend as a buy, he analyzed several furniture makers by studying their financial reports and visiting their operations. He also talked to some designers and retailers to find out which furniture styles are trendy and popular.

Although none of the companies that he analyzed turned out to be a clear buy, he discovered that one of them, Swan Furniture Company (SFC), might be in trouble. Swan's extravagant new designs were introduced at substantial costs. Even though these designs initially attracted attention, in the long run, the public is buying more conservative furniture from other makers. Based on that and on P&L analysis, Teja believes that Swan's next-quarter earnings will drop substantially. He then issues a sell recommendation for SFC. Immediately after receiving that recommendation, investment managers start reducing the stock in their portfolios.

Comment:

Information on quarterly earnings figures is material and nonpublic. However, Teja arrived at his conclusion about the earnings drop based on public information and on pieces of nonmaterial nonpublic information (such as opinions of designers and retailers). Therefore, trading based on Teja's correct conclusion is not prohibited by Standard II(A).

Example 4:

A member's dentist, who is an active investor, tells the member that based on his research he believes that Acme, Inc., will be bought out in the near future by a larger firm in the industry. The member investigates and purchases shares of Acme.

Comment:

There is no violation here because the dentist had no inside information but has reached the conclusion on his own. The information here is not material because there is no reason to suspect that an investor would wish to know what the member's dentist thought before investing in shares of Acme.

Example 5:

A member received an advance copy of a stock recommendation that will appear in a widely read national newspaper column the next day and purchases the stock.

Comment:

A recommendation in a widely read newspaper column will likely cause the stock price to rise, so this is material nonpublic information. The member has violated the Standard.

Example 6:

A member trades based on information he gets by seeing an advance copy of an article that will be published in an influential magazine next week.

Comment:

This is a violation as this is nonpublic information until the article has been published.

> **II(B) Market Manipulation.** Members and Candidates must not engage in practices that distort prices or artificially inflate trading volume with the intent to mislead market participants.

Guidance

This Standard applies to transactions that deceive the market by distorting the price-setting mechanism of financial instruments or by securing a controlling position to manipulate the price of a related derivative and/or the asset itself. Spreading false rumors is also prohibited.

Application of Standard II(B) Market Manipulation

Example 1:

Matthew Murphy is an analyst at Divisadero Securities & Co., which has a significant number of hedge funds among its most important brokerage clients. Two trading days before the publication of the quarter-end report, Murphy alerts his sales force that he is about to issue a research report on Wirewolf Semiconductor, which will include his opinion that:

- Quarterly revenues are likely to fall short of management's guidance.
- Earnings will be as much as 5 cents per share (or more than 10%) below consensus.
- Wirewolf's highly respected chief financial officer may be about to join another company.

Knowing that Wirewolf had already entered its declared quarter-end "quiet period" before reporting earnings (and thus would be reluctant to respond to rumors, etc.), Murphy times the release of his research report specifically to sensationalize the negative aspects of the message to create significant downward pressure on Wirewolf's stock to the distinct advantage of Divisadero's hedge fund clients. The report's conclusions are based on speculation, not on fact. The next day, the research report is broadcast to all of Divisadero's clients and to the usual newswire services.

Before Wirewolf's investor relations department can assess its damage on the final trading day of the quarter and refute Murphy's report, its stock opens trading sharply lower, allowing Divisadero's clients to cover their short positions at substantial gains.

Comment:

Murphy violated Standard II(B) by trying to create artificial price volatility designed to have material impact on the price of an issuer's stock. Moreover, by lacking an adequate basis for the recommendation, Murphy also violated Standard V(A).

Example 2:

ACME Futures Exchange is launching a new bond futures contract. To convince investors, traders, arbitragers, hedgers, and so on, to use its contract, the exchange attempts to demonstrate that it has the best liquidity. To do so, it enters into agreements with members so that they commit to a substantial minimum trading volume on the new contract over a specific period in exchange for substantial reductions on their regular commissions.

Comment:

The formal liquidity of a market is determined by the obligations set on market makers, but the actual liquidity of a market is better estimated by the actual trading volume and bid-ask spreads. Attempts to mislead participants on the actual liquidity of the market constitute a violation of Standard II(B). In this example, investors have been intentionally misled to believe they chose the most liquid instrument for some specific purpose and could eventually see the actual liquidity of the contract dry up suddenly after the term of the agreement if the "pump-priming" strategy fails. If ACME fully discloses its agreement with members to boost transactions over some initial launch period, it does not violate Standard II(B). ACME's intent is not to harm investors but on the contrary to give them a better service. For that purpose, it may engage in a liquidity-pumping strategy, but it must be disclosed.

Example 3:

A member is seeking to sell a large position in a fairly illiquid stock from a fund he manages. He buys and sells shares of the stock between that fund and another he also manages to create an appearance of activity and stock price appreciation, so that the sale of the whole position will have less market impact and he will realize a better return for the fund's shareholders.

Comment:

The trading activity is meant to mislead market participants and is, therefore, a violation of the Standard. The fact that his fund shareholders gain by this action does not change the fact that it is a violation.

Example 4:

A member posts false information about a firm on internet bulletin boards and stock chat facilities in an attempt to cause the firm's stock to increase in price.

Comment:

This is a violation of the Standard.

MODULE QUIZ 2.3

To best evaluate your performance, enter your quiz answers online.

1. Carrie Carlson, CFA, is a citizen of Emerging Market Country (EMC) with no securities laws governing the use of material nonpublic information. Carlson has clients in Emerging Market Country and in Neighboring Country (NC), which has a few poorly defined laws governing the use of material nonpublic information. If Carlson has material nonpublic information on a publicly traded security, she:
   A. can inform her clients in EMC, but not NC.
   B. can use the information for her NC clients to the extent permitted by the laws of NC.
   C. cannot use the information to trade in either EMC or NC.

2. In order to dispel the myth that emerging market stocks are illiquid investments, Green Brothers, a "long only" emerging market fund manager, has two of its subsidiaries simultaneously buy and sell emerging market stocks. In its marketing literature, Green Brothers cites the overall emerging market volume as evidence of the market's liquidity. As a result of its actions, more investors participate in the emerging markets fund. Which of the following is *most likely* correct? Green Brothers:
   A. did not violate the Code and Standards.
   B. violated the Code and Standards by manipulating the volume in the emerging securities markets.
   C. would not have violated the Code and Standards if the subsidiaries only traded stocks not included in the fund.

3. Over the past two days, Lorraine Quigley, CFA, manager of a hedge fund, has been purchasing large quantities of Craeger Industrial Products' common stock while at the same time shorting put options on the same stock. Quigley did not notify her clients of the trades although they are aware of the fund's general strategy to generate returns. Which of the following statements is *most likely* correct? Quigley:
   A. did not violate the Code and Standards.
   B. violated the Code and Standards by manipulating the prices of publicly traded securities.
   C. violated the Code and Standards by failing to disclose the transactions to clients before they occurred.

4. Before joining Mitsui Ltd. as an analyst covering the electrical equipment manufacturing industry, Pam Servais, CFA, worked for Internet Security Systems (ISS) where she had access to nonpublic information. While at ISS, Servais learned of a severe environmental problem at two firms handling boron-based components. It is common knowledge that seven firms in the industry worldwide use the same boron handling technique. The two firms for which Servais has knowledge announced the problem last week and had immediate stock price declines of 11% and 17%, respectively. The other five firms have not made an announcement. Servais issues a report recommending Mitsui clients sell shares of the remaining five firms. Servais's issuance of this recommendation:
   A. is not a violation of CFA Institute Standards.
   B. is a violation of CFA Institute Standards because it fails to distinguish between opinion and fact.
   C. constitutes a violation of the Standard pertaining to the use of material nonpublic information.

5. Zanuatu, an island nation, does not have any regulations precluding the use of nonpublic information. Alfredo Romero has a friend and fellow CFA charterholder there with whom he has shared nonpublic information regarding firms outside of his industry. The information concerns several firms' internal earnings and cash flow projections. The friend may:
   A. trade on the information under the laws of Zanuatu, which govern her behavior.
   B. not trade on the information under CFA Institute Standards, which govern her behavior.
   C. trade on the information under CFA Institute Standards since the firms concerned are outside of Romero's industry.
6. Julia Green, CFA, has friends from her previous employer who have suggested that she receive information from them via an Internet chat room. In this way, she receives news about an exciting new product being developed by a firm in Singapore that has the potential to double the firm's revenue. The firm has not revealed any information regarding the product to the public. According to the Code and Standards, this information is:
   A. both material and nonpublic and Green may not trade on it in Singapore, but may trade on it elsewhere.
   B. both material and nonpublic and Green may not trade on it in any jurisdiction.
   C. public by virtue of its release in the chat room and Green may trade on it.
7. Will Hunter, CFA, is a portfolio manager at NV Asset Managers in Baltimore, which specializes in managing labor union pension fund accounts. A friend of Hunter's who is an investment banker asks Hunter to purchase shares in their new IPOs in order to support the price long enough for insiders to liquidate their holdings. Hunter realizes that the price of the shares will almost certainly fall dramatically after his buying support ceases. NV management "strongly suggests" that Hunter "not rock the boat" and honor the investment banker's request since NV has had a long-standing relationship with the investment bank. Hunter agrees to make the purchases. Hunter has:
   A. not violated the Code and Standards.
   B. violated the Code and Standards by attempting to distort prices.
   C. violated the Code and Standards by failing to place orders in the appropriate transaction priority.

MODULE 2.4: STANDARD III(A)

Video covering this content is available online.

III Duties to Clients

III(A) Loyalty, Prudence, and Care. Members and Candidates have a duty of loyalty to their clients and must act with reasonable care and exercise prudent judgment. Members and Candidates must act for the benefit of their clients and place their clients' interests before their employer's or their own interests.

Guidance

Client interests always come first. Although this Standard does not impose a fiduciary duty on members or candidates where one did not already exist, it does require members and candidates to act in their clients' best interest and recommend products that are suitable given their clients' investment objectives and risk tolerances.

- Exercise the prudence, care, skill, and diligence under the circumstances that a person acting in a like capacity and familiar with such matters would use.
- Manage pools of client assets in accordance with the terms of the governing documents, such as trust documents or investment management agreements.
- Make investment decisions in the context of the total portfolio.
- Inform clients of any limitations in an advisory relationship (e.g., an advisor who may only recommend her own firm's products).
- Vote proxies in an informed and responsible manner. Due to cost benefit considerations, it may not be necessary to vote all proxies.
- Client brokerage, or "soft dollars" or "soft commissions" must be used to benefit the client.
- The "client" may be the investing public as a whole rather than a specific entity or person.

Recommended Procedures of Compliance

Submit to clients, at least quarterly, itemized statements showing all securities in custody and all debits, credits, and transactions.

Encourage firms to address these topics when drafting policies and procedures regarding fiduciary duty:

- Follow applicable rules and laws.
- Establish investment objectives of client. Consider suitability of portfolio relative to client's needs and circumstances, the investment's basic characteristics, or the basic characteristics of the total portfolio.
- Diversify.
- Deal fairly with all clients in regards to investment actions.
- Disclose conflicts.
- Disclose compensation arrangements.
- Vote proxies in the best interest of clients and ultimate beneficiaries.
- Maintain confidentiality.
- Seek best execution.
- Place client interests first.

Application of Standard III(A) Loyalty, Prudence, and Care

Example 1:

First Country Bank serves as trustee for the Miller Company's pension plan. Miller is the target of a hostile takeover attempt by Newton, Inc. In attempting to ward off Newton, Miller's managers persuade Julian Wiley, an investment manager at First Country Bank, to purchase Miller common stock in the open market for the employee pension plan. Miller's officials indicate that such action would be favorably received and would probably result in other accounts being placed with the bank. Although Wiley believes the stock to be overvalued and would not ordinarily buy it, he purchases the stock to support Miller's managers, to maintain the company's good favor, and to realize additional new business. The heavy stock purchases cause Miller's market price to rise to such a level that Newton retracts its takeover bid.

Comment:

Standard III(A) requires that a member or candidate, in evaluating a takeover bid, act prudently and solely in the interests of plan participants and beneficiaries. To meet this requirement, a member or candidate must carefully evaluate the long-term prospects of the company against the short-term prospects presented by the takeover offer and by the ability to invest elsewhere. In this instance, Wiley, acting on behalf of his employer, the trustee, clearly violated Standard III(A) by using the pension plan to perpetuate existing management, perhaps to the detriment of plan participants and the company's shareholders, and to benefit himself. Wiley's responsibilities to the plan participants and beneficiaries should take precedence over any ties to corporate managers and self-interest. A duty exists to examine such a takeover offer on its own merits and to make an independent decision. The guiding principle is the appropriateness of the investment decision to the pension plan, not whether the decision benefits Wiley or the company that hired him.

Example 2:

Emilie Rome is a trust officer for Paget Trust Company. Rome's supervisor is responsible for reviewing Rome's trust account transactions and her monthly reports of personal stock transactions. Rome has been using Nathan Gray, a broker, almost exclusively for trust account brokerage transactions. Where Gray makes a market in stocks, he has been giving Rome a lower price for personal purchases and a higher price for sales than he gives to Rome's trust accounts and other investors.

Comment:

Rome is violating her duty of loyalty to the bank's trust accounts by using Gray for brokerage transactions simply because Gray trades Rome's personal account on favorable terms.

Example 3:

A member uses a broker for client-account trades that has relatively high prices and average research and execution. In return, the broker pays for the rent and other overhead expenses for the member's firm.

Comment:

This is a violation of the Standard because the member used client brokerage for services that do not benefit clients and failed to get the best price and execution for his clients.

Example 4:

In return for receiving account management business from Broker X, a member directs trades to Broker X on the accounts referred to her by Broker X, as well as on other accounts as an incentive to Broker X to send her more account business.

Comment:

This is a violation if Broker X does not offer the best price and execution or if the practice of directing trades to Broker X is not disclosed to clients. The obligation to seek best price and execution is always required unless clients provide a written statement that the member is not to seek best price and execution and that they are aware of the impact of this decision on their accounts.

Example 5:

A member does more trades in client accounts than are necessary to accomplish client goals because she desires to increase her commission income.

Comment:

The member is using client assets (brokerage fees) to benefit herself and has violated the Standard.

MODULE QUIZ 2.4

To best evaluate your performance, enter your quiz answers online.

1. Mary Herbst, CFA, a pension fund manager at GBH Investments, is reviewing some of FreeTime, Inc.'s pension fund activities over the past years. Which of the following actions related to FreeTime, Inc.'s pension fund is *most likely* to be a breach of her fiduciary duties?
   A. Paying higher-than-average brokerage fees to obtain research materials used in the management of the pension fund.
   B. Trading with selected brokers so that the brokers will recommend GBH's managers to potential clients.
   C. Selectively choosing brokers for the quality of research provided for managing FreeTime's pension.

MODULE 2.5: STANDARDS III(B) AND III(C)

Video covering this content is available online.

> **III(B) Fair Dealing.** Members and Candidates must deal fairly and objectively with all clients when providing investment analysis, making investment recommendations, taking investment action, or engaging in other professional activities.

Guidance

Do not discriminate against any clients when disseminating recommendations or taking investment action. Fairly does not mean equally. In the normal course of business, there will be differences in the time emails, faxes, etc., are received by different clients. Different service levels are okay, but they must not negatively affect or disadvantage any clients. Disclose the different service levels to all clients and prospects, and make premium levels of service available to all who wish to pay for them.

Guidance—Investment Recommendations

Give all clients a fair opportunity to act upon every recommendation. Clients who are unaware of a change in a recommendation should be advised before the order is accepted.

Guidance—Investment Actions

Treat clients fairly in light of their investment objectives and circumstances. Treat both individual and institutional clients in a fair and impartial manner. Members and candidates should not take advantage of their position in the industry to disadvantage clients (e.g., in the context of IPOs).

Recommended Procedures for Compliance

Encourage firms to establish compliance procedures requiring proper dissemination of investment recommendations and fair treatment of all customers and clients. Consider these points when establishing fair dealing compliance procedures:

- Limit the number of people who are aware that a change in recommendation will be made.
- Shorten the time frame between decision and dissemination.
- Publish personnel guidelines for pre-dissemination—have in place guidelines prohibiting personnel who have prior knowledge of a recommendation from discussing it or taking action on the pending recommendation.
- Simultaneous dissemination of new or changed recommendations to all clients who have expressed an interest or for whom an investment is suitable.
- Maintain list of clients and holdings—use to ensure that all holders are treated fairly.
- Develop written trade allocation procedures—ensure fairness to clients, timely and efficient order execution, and accuracy of client positions.
- Disclose trade allocation procedures.
- Establish systematic account review—ensure that no client is given preferred treatment and that investment actions are consistent with the account's objectives.
- Disclose available levels of service.

Application of Standard III(B) Fair Dealing

Example 1:

Bradley Ames, a well-known and respected analyst, follows the computer industry. In the course of his research, he finds that a small, relatively unknown company whose shares are traded over the counter has just signed significant contracts with some of the companies he follows. After a considerable amount of investigation, Ames decides to write a research report on the company and recommend purchase. While the report is being reviewed by the company for factual accuracy, Ames schedules a luncheon with several of his best clients to discuss the company. At the luncheon, he mentions the purchase recommendation scheduled to be sent early the following week to all the firm's clients.

Comment:

Ames violated Standard III(B) by disseminating the purchase recommendation to the clients with whom he had lunch a week before the recommendation was sent to all clients.

Example 2:

Spencer Rivers, president of XYZ Corporation, moves his company's growth-oriented pension fund to a particular bank primarily because of the excellent investment performance achieved by the bank's commingled fund for the prior 5-year period. A few years later, Rivers compares the results of his pension fund with those of the bank's commingled fund. He is startled to learn that, even though the two accounts have the same investment objectives and similar portfolios, his company's pension fund has significantly underperformed the bank's commingled fund. Questioning this result at his next meeting with the pension fund's manager, Rivers is told that, as a matter of policy, when a new security is placed on the recommended list, Morgan Jackson, the pension fund manager, first purchases the security for the commingled account and then purchases it on a pro rata basis for all other pension fund accounts. Similarly, when a sale is recommended, the security is sold first from the commingled account and then sold on a pro rata basis from all other accounts. Rivers also learns that if the bank cannot get enough shares (especially the hot issues) to be meaningful to all the accounts, its policy is to place the new issues only in the commingled account.

Seeing that Rivers is neither satisfied nor pleased by the explanation, Jackson quickly adds that nondiscretionary pension accounts and personal trust accounts have a lower priority on purchase and sale recommendations than discretionary pension fund accounts. Furthermore, Jackson states, the company's pension fund had the opportunity to invest up to 5% in the commingled fund.

Comment:

The bank's policy did not treat all customers fairly, and Jackson violated her duty to her clients by giving priority to the growth-oriented commingled fund over all other funds and to discretionary accounts over nondiscretionary accounts. Jackson must execute orders on a systematic basis that is fair to all clients. In addition, trade allocation procedures should be disclosed to all clients from the beginning. Of course, in this case, disclosure of the bank's policy would not change the fact that the policy is unfair.

Example 3:

A member gets options for his part in an IPO from the subject firm. The IPO is oversubscribed and the member fills his own and other individuals' orders but has to reduce allocations to his institutional clients.

Comment:

The member has violated the Standard. He must disclose to his employer and to his clients that he has accepted options for putting together the IPO. He should not take any shares of a hot IPO for himself and should have distributed his allocated shares of the IPO to all clients in proportion to their original order amounts.

Example 4:

A member is delayed in allocating some trades to client accounts. When she allocates the trades, she puts some positions that have appreciated in a preferred client's account and puts trades that have not done as well in other client accounts.

Comment:

This is a violation of the Standard. The member should have allocated the trades to specific accounts prior to the trades or should have allocated the trades proportionally to suitable accounts in a timely fashion.

Example 5:

Because of minimum lot size restrictions, a portfolio manager allocates the bonds she receives from an oversubscribed bond offering to her clients in a way that is not strictly proportional to their purchase requests.

Comment:

Since she has a reason (minimum lot size) to deviate from a strict pro rata allocation to her clients, there is no violation of Fair Dealing.

III(C) Suitability

1. When Members and Candidates are in an advisory relationship with a client, they must:
   a. Make a reasonable inquiry into a client's or prospective clients' investment experience, risk and return objectives, and financial constraints prior to making any investment recommendation or taking investment action and must reassess and update this information regularly.
   b. Determine that an investment is suitable to the client's financial situation and consistent with the client's written objectives, mandates, and constraints before making an investment recommendation or taking investment action.
   c. Judge the suitability of investments in the context of the client's total portfolio.
2. When Members and Candidates are responsible for managing a portfolio to a specific mandate, strategy, or style, they must make only investment recommendations or take only investment actions that are consistent with the stated objectives and constraints of the portfolio.

Guidance

In advisory relationships, be sure to gather client information at the beginning of the relationship, in the form of an investment policy statement (IPS). Consider clients' needs and circumstances and thus their risk tolerance. Consider whether or not the use of leverage is suitable for the client.

If a member is responsible for managing a fund to an index or other stated mandate, be sure investments are consistent with the stated mandate.

Guidance—Unsolicited Trade Requests

An investment manager might receive a client request to purchase a security that the manager knows is unsuitable, given the client's investment policy statement. The trade may or may not have a material effect on the risk characteristics of the client's total portfolio and the requirements are different for each case. In either case, however, the manager should not make the trade until he has discussed with the client the reasons (based on the IPS) that the trade is unsuitable for the client's account.

If the manager determines that the effect on the risk/return profile of the client's total portfolio is minimal, the manager, after discussing with the client how the trade does not fit the IPS goals and constraints, may follow his firm's policy with regard to unsuitable trades. Regardless of firm policy, the client must acknowledge the discussion and an understanding of why the trade is unsuitable.

If the trade would have a material impact on the risk/return profile of the client's total portfolio, one option is to update the IPS so that the client accepts a changed risk profile that would permit the trade. If the client will not accept a changed IPS, the manager may follow firm policy, which may allow the trade to be made in a separate client-directed account. In the absence of other options, the manager may need to reconsider whether to maintain the relationship with the client.

Recommended Procedures for Compliance

Members should:

- Put the needs and circumstances of each client and the client's investment objectives into a written IPS for each client.
- Consider the type of client and whether there are separate beneficiaries, investor objectives (return and risk), investor constraints (liquidity needs, expected cash flows, time, tax, and regulatory and legal circumstances), and performance measurement benchmarks.
- Review investor's objectives and constraints periodically to reflect any changes in client circumstances.

Application of Standard III(C) Suitability

Example 1:

Jessica McDowell, an investment advisor, suggests to Brian Crosby, a risk-averse client, that covered call options be used in his equity portfolio. The purpose would be to enhance Crosby's income and partially offset any untimely depreciation in value should the stock market or other circumstances affect his holdings unfavorably. McDowell educates Crosby about all possible outcomes, including the risk of incurring an added tax liability if a stock rises in price and is called away and, conversely, the risk of his holdings losing protection on the downside if prices drop sharply.

Comment:

When determining suitability of an investment, the primary focus should be on the characteristics of the client's entire portfolio, not on an issue-by-issue analysis. The basic characteristics of the entire portfolio will largely determine whether the investment recommendations are taking client factors into account. Therefore, the most important aspects of a particular investment will be those that will affect the characteristics of the total portfolio. In this case, McDowell properly considered the investment in the context of the entire portfolio and thoroughly explained the investment to the client.

Example 2:

Max Gubler, chief investment officer of a property/casualty insurance subsidiary of a large financial conglomerate, wants to better diversify the company's investment portfolio and increase its returns. The company's investment policy statement (IPS) provides for highly liquid investments, such as large caps, governments, and supra-nationals, as well as corporate bonds with a minimum credit rating of AA- and maturity of no more than five years. In a recent presentation, a venture capital group offered very attractive prospective returns on some of their private equity funds providing seed capital. An exit strategy is already contemplated but investors will first have to observe a minimum 3-year lock-up period, with a subsequent laddered exit option for a maximum of one third of shares per year. Gubler does not want to miss this opportunity and after an extensive analysis and optimization of this asset class with the company's current portfolio, he invests 4% in this seed fund, leaving the portfolio's total equity exposure still well below its upper limit.

Comment:

Gubler violates Standard III(A) Loyalty, Prudence, and Care as well as Standard III(C). His new investment locks up part of the company's assets for at least three and for up to as many as five years and possibly beyond. Since the IPS requires investments in highly liquid investments and describes accepted asset classes, private equity investments with a lock-up period certainly do not qualify. Even without such lock-up periods an asset class with only an occasional, and thus implicitly illiquid, market may not be suitable. Although an IPS typically describes objectives and constraints in great detail, the manager must make every effort to understand the client's business and circumstances. Doing so should also enable the manager to recognize, understand, and discuss with the client other factors that may be or may become material in the investment management process.

Example 3:

A member gives a client account a significant allocation to non-dividend paying high-risk securities even though the client has low risk tolerance and modest return objectives.

Comment:

This is a violation of the Standard.

Example 4:

A member puts a security into a fund she manages that does not fit the mandate of the fund and is not a permitted investment according to the fund's disclosures.

Comment:

This, too, is a violation of the Standard.

Example 5:

A member starts his own money management business but puts all clients in his friend's hedge funds.

Comment:

He has violated the Standards with respect to suitability. He must match client needs and circumstances to the investments he recommends and cannot act like a sales agent for his friend's funds.

MODULE QUIZ 2.5

To best evaluate your performance, enter your quiz answers online.

1. Melvin Byrne, CFA, manages a portfolio for James Martin, a very wealthy client. Martin's portfolio is well diversified with a slight tilt toward capital appreciation. Martin requires very little income from the portfolio. Recently, Martin's brother, Cliff, has become a client of Byrne. Byrne proceeds to invest Cliff's portfolio in a similar manner to James's portfolio based on the fact that both brothers have a similar lifestyle and are only two years apart in age. Which of the following statements is *most likely* correct? Byrne:
   A. violated the Code and Standards by knowingly creating a conflict of interest between James's and Cliff's portfolios.
   B. violated the Code and Standards by failing to determine Cliff's objectives and constraints prior to investing his portfolio.
   C. did not violate the Code and Standards.

2. Jessica Ellis, CFA, manages an international stock fund for a group of wealthy investors with similar investment objectives. According to the investment policy statement, the fund is to pursue an aggressive growth strategy while maintaining sufficient international diversification and is prohibited from using leverage. Ellis has just received a request from the majority of the group of investors to purchase for the fund a large position in German bonds which they believe to be significantly undervalued. Which of the following actions should Ellis take to avoid violating the Code and Standards?
   A. Purchase the bonds since it was requested by the clients to whom Ellis has a fiduciary duty.
   B. Inform the investors that she is unable to make the purchase since it is inconsistent with the international stock portfolio's investment mandate.
   C. Purchase the bonds only after receiving a written consent statement signed by the majority of the investors stating that they are aware that the investment is not suitable for the portfolio.

3. Shane Matthews, CFA, is a principal at Carlson Brothers, a leading regional investment bank specializing in initial public offerings of small to mid-sized biotech firms. Just before many of the IPOs are offered to the general public, Matthews arranges for 10% of the shares of the firm going public to be distributed to select Carlson clients. This action is *most likely* a violation of the Standard concerning:
   A. additional compensation.
   B. disclosure of conflicts of interest.
   C. fair dealing.

Video covering this content is available online.

MODULE 2.6: STANDARDS III(D) AND III(E)

> **III(D) Performance Presentation.** When communicating investment performance information, Members or Candidates must make reasonable efforts to ensure that it is fair, accurate, and complete.

Guidance

Members must avoid misstating performance or misleading clients/prospects about investment performance of themselves or their firms, should not misrepresent past performance or reasonably expected performance, and should not state or imply the ability to achieve a rate of return similar to that achieved in the past. For brief presentations, members must make detailed information available on request and indicate that the presentation has offered limited information.

Recommended Procedures for Compliance

Encourage firms to adhere to Global Investment Performance Standards. Obligations under this Standard may also be met by:

- Considering the sophistication of the audience to whom a performance presentation is addressed.

- Presenting performance of weighted composite of similar portfolios rather than a single account.
- Including terminated accounts as part of historical performance and clearly stating when they were terminated.
- Including all appropriate disclosures to fully explain results (e.g., model results included, gross or net of fees, etc.).
- Maintaining data and records used to calculate the performance being presented.

Application of Standard III(D) Performance Presentation

Example 1:

Kyle Taylor of Taylor Trust Company, noting the performance of Taylor's common trust fund for the past two years, states in the brochure sent to his potential clients that "You can expect steady 25% annual compound growth of the value of your investments over the year." Taylor Trust's common trust fund did increase at the rate of 25% per annum for the past year which mirrored the increase of the entire market. The fund, however, never averaged that growth for more than one year, and the average rate of growth of all of its trust accounts for five years was 5% per annum.

Comment:

Taylor's brochure is in violation of Standard III(D). Taylor should have disclosed that the 25% growth occurred in only one year. Additionally, Taylor did not include client accounts other than those in the firm's common trust fund. A general claim of firm performance should take into account the performance of all categories of accounts. Finally, by stating that clients can expect a steady 25% annual compound growth rate, Taylor also violated Standard I(C), which prohibits statements of assurances or guarantees regarding an investment.

Example 2:

Aaron McCoy is vice president and managing partner of the equity investment group of Mastermind Financial Advisors, a new business. Mastermind recruited McCoy because he had a proven 6-year track record with G&P Financial. In developing Mastermind's advertising and marketing campaign, McCoy prepared an advertisement that included the equity investment performance he achieved at G&P Financial. The advertisement for Mastermind did not identify the equity performance as being earned while at G&P. The advertisement was distributed to existing clients and prospective clients of Mastermind.

Comment:

McCoy violated Standard III(D) by distributing an advertisement that contained material misrepresentations regarding the historical performance of Mastermind. Standard III(D) requires that members and candidates make every reasonable effort to ensure that performance information is a fair, accurate, and complete representation of an individual or firm's performance. As a general matter, this standard does not prohibit showing past performance of funds managed at a prior firm as part of a performance track record so long as it is accompanied by appropriate disclosures detailing where the performance comes from and the person's specific role in achieving that performance. If McCoy chooses to use his past performance from G&P in Mastermind's advertising, he should make full disclosure as to the source of the historical performance.

Example 3:

A member puts simulated results of an investment strategy in a sales brochure without disclosing that the results are not actual performance numbers.

Comment:

The member has violated the Standard.

Example 4:

In materials for prospective clients, a member uses performance figures for a large-cap growth composite she has created by choosing accounts that have done relatively well and including some accounts with significant mid-cap exposure.

Comment:

This is a violation of the Standard as the member has attempted to mislead clients and has misrepresented her performance.

Example 5:

A member changes his firm's performance attribution method to one he believes is more consistent with the strategies used by the firm's investment managers.

Comment:

To avoid a violation of the Standard, the member must disclose this change to existing and new clients. He should explain the reasons for changing the method and report the managers' performance attribution using *both* the old and new methods so that clients may compare them.

> **III(E) Preservation of Confidentiality.** Members and Candidates must keep information about current, former, and prospective clients confidential unless:
>
> 1. The information concerns illegal activities on the part of the client or prospective client,
> 2. Disclosure is required by law, or
> 3. The client or prospective client permits disclosure of the information.

Guidance

If illegal activities by a client are involved, members may have an obligation to report the activities to authorities. The confidentiality Standard extends to former clients as well.

The requirements of this Standard are not intended to prevent Members and Candidates from cooperating with a CFA Institute Professional Conduct Program (PCP) investigation.

Recommended Procedures for Compliance

Members should avoid disclosing information received from a client except to authorized co-workers who are also working for the client. Members should follow firm procedures for storage of electronic data and recommend adoption of such procedures if they are not in place.

Application of Standard III(E) Preservation of Confidentiality

Example 1:

Sarah Connor, a financial analyst employed by Johnson Investment Counselors, Inc., provides investment advice to the trustees of City Medical Center. The trustees have given her a number of internal reports concerning City Medical's needs for physical plant renovation and expansion. They have asked Connor to recommend investments that would generate capital appreciation in endowment funds to meet projected capital expenditures. Connor is approached by a local business man, Thomas Kasey, who is considering a substantial contribution either to City Medical Center or to another local hospital. Kasey wants to find out the building plans of both institutions before making a decision, but he does not want to speak to the trustees.

Comment:

The trustees gave Connor the internal reports so she could advise them on how to manage their endowment funds. Because the information in the reports is clearly both confidential and within the scope of the confidential relationship, Standard III(E) requires that Connor refuse to divulge information to Kasey.

Example 2:

David Bradford manages money for a family-owned real estate development corporation. He also manages the individual portfolios of several of the family members and officers of the corporation, including the chief financial officer (CFO). Based on the financial records from the corporation, as well as some questionable practices of the CFO that he has observed, Bradford believes that the CFO is embezzling money from the corporation and putting it into his personal investment account.

Comment:

Bradford should check with his firm's compliance department as well as outside counsel to determine whether applicable securities regulations require reporting the CFO's financial records.

Example 3:

A member has learned from his client that one of his goals is to give more of his portfolio income to charity. The member tells this to a friend who is on the board of a worthy charity and suggests that he should contact the client about a donation.

Comment:

The member has violated the Standard by disclosing information he has learned from the client in the course of their business relationship.

Example 4:

A member learns that a pension account client is violating the law with respect to charges to the pension fund.

Comment:

The member must bring this to the attention of her supervisor and try to end the illegal activity. Failing this, the member should seek legal advice about any disclosure she should make to legal or regulatory authorities and dissociate herself from any continuing association with the pension account.

MODULE QUIZ 2.6

To best evaluate your performance, enter your quiz answers online.

1. In a marketing brochure, DNR Asset Managers presents the performance of several composite portfolios managed according to similar investment strategies. In constructing composites, the firm excludes individual portfolios with less than $1 million in assets, excludes terminated portfolios, and includes simulated results. DNR includes the following disclosure in the brochure: "Past performance is no guarantee of future results. Composites exclude portfolios under $1 million in assets and include results from simulated model portfolios with similar strategies." DNR's brochure:
   A. does not violate the Code and Standards.
   B. violates the Code and Standards by failing to include terminated portfolios in the performance presentation.
   C. violates the Code and Standards by excluding portfolios under $1 million from the composite performance presentation.
2. Beth Anderson, CFA, is a portfolio manager for several wealthy clients including Reuben Carlyle. Anderson manages Carlyle's personal portfolio of stock and bond investments. Carlyle recently told Anderson that he is under investigation by the IRS for tax evasion related to his business, Carlyle Concrete (CC). After learning about the investigation, Anderson proceeds to inform a friend at a local investment bank so that they may withdraw their proposal to take CC public. Which of the following is *most likely* correct? Anderson:
   A. violated the Code and Standards by failing to maintain the confidentiality of her client's information.
   B. violated the Code and Standards by failing to detect and report the tax evasion to the proper authorities.
   C. did not violate the Code and Standards since the information she conveyed pertained to illegal activities on the part of her client.

3. Which of the following is *least likely* one of the recommendations included in the Standards of Practice Handbook with regard to Performance Presentation?
   A. Include terminated accounts in past performance history.
   B. Present the performance of a representative account to show how a composite has performed.
   C. Consider the level of financial knowledge of the audience to whom the performance is presented.

MODULE 2.7: STANDARDS IV(A), IV(B), AND IV(C)

Video covering this content is available online.

IV Duties to Employers

IV(A) Loyalty. In matters related to their employment, Members and Candidates must act for the benefit of their employer and not deprive their employer of the advantage of their skills and abilities, divulge confidential information, or otherwise cause harm to their employer.

Guidance

Members must not engage in any activities which would injure the firm, deprive it of profit, or deprive it of the advantage of employees' skills and abilities. Members should always place client interests above interests of their employer but consider the effects of their actions on firm integrity and sustainability. There is no requirement that the employee put employer interests ahead of family and other personal obligations; it is expected that employers and employees will discuss such matters and balance these obligations with work obligations.

Guidance—Employer Responsibility

Members are encouraged to give their employer a copy of the Code and Standards. Employers should not have incentive and compensation systems that encourage unethical behavior.

Guidance—Independent Practice

Independent practice for compensation is allowed if a notification is provided to the employer fully describing all aspects of the services, including compensation, duration, and the nature of the activities *and* if the employer consents to all terms of the proposed independent practice before it begins.

Guidance—Leaving an Employer

Members must continue to act in their employer's best interests until resignation is effective. Activities which may constitute a violation include:

- Misappropriation of trade secrets.
- Misuse of confidential information.
- Soliciting employer's clients prior to leaving.

- Self-dealing.
- Misappropriation of client lists.

Employer records on any medium (e.g., home computer, PDA, cell phone) are the property of the firm.

Once an employee has left a firm, simple knowledge of names and existence of former clients is generally not confidential. There is also no prohibition on the use of experience or knowledge gained while with a former employer. If an agreement exists among employers (e.g, the U.S. "Protocol for Broker Recruiting") that permits brokers to take certain client information when leaving a firm, a member or candidate may act within the terms of the agreement without violating the Standard.

Guidance—Social Media

Members and candidates must adhere to their employers' policies concerning social media. When planning to leave an employer, members and candidates must ensure that their social media use complies with their employers' policies for notifying clients about employee separations. A best practice is to use separate social media accounts for personal and professional communications.

Guidance—Whistleblowing

There may be isolated cases where a duty to one's employer may be violated in order to protect clients or the integrity of the market, and not for personal gain.

Guidance—Nature of Employment

The applicability of this Standard is based on the nature of the employment—employee versus independent contractor. If Members and Candidates are independent contractors, they still have a duty to abide by the terms of the agreement.

Application of Standard IV(A) Loyalty

Example 1:

James Hightower has been employed by Jason Investment Management Corporation for 15 years. He began as an analyst but assumed increasing responsibilities and is now a senior portfolio manager and a member of the firm's investment policy committee. Hightower has decided to leave Jason Investment and start his own investment management business. He has been careful not to tell any of Jason's clients that he is leaving; he does not want to be accused of breaching his duty to Jason by soliciting Jason's clients before his departure. Hightower is planning to copy and take with him the following documents and information he developed or worked on while at Jason: (1) the client list, with addresses, telephone numbers, and other pertinent client information; (2) client account statements; (3) sample marketing presentations to prospective clients containing Jason's performance record; (4) Jason's recommended list of securities; (5) computer models to determine asset allocations for accounts with different objectives; (6) computer models for stock selection; and (7) personal computer spreadsheets for Hightower's major corporate recommendations which he developed when he was an analyst.

Comment:

Except with the consent of their employer, departing employees may not take employer property, which includes books, records, reports, and other materials, and may not interfere with their employer's business opportunities. Taking any employer records, even those the member or candidate prepared, violates Standard IV(A).

Example 2:

Dennis Elliot has hired Sam Chisolm who previously worked for a competing firm. Chisolm left his former firm after 18 years of employment. When Chisolm begins working for Elliot, he wants to contact his former clients because he knows them well and is certain that many will follow him to his new employer. Is Chisolm in violation of the Standard IV(A) if he contacts his former clients?

Comment:

Because client records are the property of the firm, contacting former clients for any reason through the use of client lists or other information taken from a former employer without permission would be a violation of Standard IV(A). In addition, the nature and extent of the contact with former clients may be governed by the terms of any non-compete agreement signed by the employee and the former employer that covers contact with former clients after employment.

But, simple knowledge of the name and existence of former clients is not confidential information, just as skills or experience that an employee obtains while employed is not "confidential" or "privileged" information. The Code and Standards do not impose a prohibition on the use of experience or knowledge gained at one employer from being used at another employer. The Code and Standards also do not prohibit former employees from contacting clients of their previous firm, absent a non-compete agreement. Members and candidates are free to use public information about their former firm after departing to contact former clients without violating Standard IV(A).

In the absence of a non-compete agreement, as long as Chisolm maintains his duty of loyalty to his employer before joining Elliot's firm, does not take steps to solicit clients until he has left his former firm, and does not make use of material from his former employer without its permission after he has left, he would not be in violation of the Code and Standards.

Example 3:

Several employees are planning to depart their current employer within a few weeks and have been careful to not engage in any activities that would conflict with their duty to their current employer. They have just learned that one of their employer's clients has undertaken a request for proposal (RFP) to review and possibly hire a new investment consultant. The RFP has been sent to the employer and all of its competitors. The group believes that the new entity to be formed would be qualified to respond to the RFP and eligible for the business. The RFP submission period is likely to conclude before the employees' resignations are effective. Is it permissible for the group of departing employees to respond to the RFP under their anticipated new firm?

Comment:

A group of employees responding to an RFP that their employer is also responding to would lead to direct competition between the employees and the employer. Such conduct would violate Standard IV(A) unless the group of employees received permission from their employer as well as the entity sending out the RFP.

Example 4:

A member solicits clients and prospects of his current employer to open accounts at the new firm he will be joining shortly.

Comment:

It is a violation of the Standard to solicit the firm's clients and prospects while he is still employed by the firm.

Example 5:

Two employees discuss joining with others in an employee-led buyout of their employer's emerging markets investment management business.

Comment:

There is no violation here. Their employer can decide how to respond to any buyout offer. If such a buyout takes place, clients should be informed of the nature of the changes in a timely manner.

Example 6:

A member is writing a research report on a company as a contract worker for Employer A (using Employer A's premises and materials) with the understanding that Employer A does not claim exclusive rights to the outcome of her research. As she is finishing the report, she is offered a full-time job by Employer B and sends Employer B a copy of a draft of her report for publication.

Comment:

She has violated the Standard by not giving Employer A the first rights to act on her research. She must also be careful not to take any materials used in preparing the report from Employer A's premises.

Example 7:

A member helps develop software for a firm while acting as an unpaid intern and takes the software, without permission, with her when she takes a full-time job at another firm.

Comment:

She is considered an employee of the firm and has violated the Standard by taking her employer's property without permission.

Example 8:

A member prepares to leave his employer and open his own firm by registering with the SEC, renting an office, and buying office equipment.

Comment:

As long as these preparations have not interfered with the performance of his current job, there has been no violation. The solicitation of firm clients and prospects prior to leaving his employer would, however, be a violation of the Standard.

Example 9:

A member is a full-time employee of an investment management firm and wants to accept a paid position as town mayor without asking his employer's permission.

Comment:

Because the member serving as mayor does not conflict with his employer's business interests, as long as the time commitment does not preclude performing his expected job functions well, there is no violation.

Example 10:

A member who has left one employer uses public sources to get the phone numbers of previous clients and solicits their business for her new employer.

Comment:

As long as there is no agreement in force between the member and his previous employer that prohibits such solicitation, there is no violation of the Standards.

> **IV(B) Additional Compensation Arrangements.** Members and Candidates must not accept gifts, benefits, compensation, or consideration that competes with or might reasonably be expected to create a conflict of interest with their employer's interest unless they obtain written consent from all parties involved.

Guidance

Compensation includes direct and indirect compensation from a client and other benefits received from third parties. Written consent from a member's employer includes email communication. Members and candidates who are hired to work part time should discuss any arrangements that may compete with their employer's interest at the time they are hired, and abide by any limitations their employer identifies.

Recommended Procedures for Compliance

Make an immediate written report to employer detailing any proposed compensation and services, if additional to that provided by employer. Details including any performance incentives should be verified by the offering party.

Application of Standard IV(B) Additional Compensation Arrangements

Example 1:

Geoff Whitman, a portfolio analyst for Adams Trust Company, manages the account of Carol Cochran, a client. Whitman is paid a salary by his employer, and Cochran pays the trust company a standard fee based on the market value of assets in her portfolio. Cochran proposes to Whitman that "any year that my portfolio achieves at least a 15% return before taxes, you and your wife can fly to Monaco at my expense and use my condominium during the third week of January." Whitman does not inform his employer of the arrangement and vacations in Monaco the following January as Cochran's guest.

Comment:

Whitman violated Standard IV(B) by failing to inform his employer in writing of this supplemental, contingent compensation arrangement. The nature of the arrangement could have resulted in partiality to Cochran's account, which could have detracted from Whitman's performance with respect to other accounts he handles for Adams Trust. Whitman must obtain the consent of his employer to accept such a supplemental benefit.

Example 2:

A member is on the board of directors of a company whose shares he purchases for client accounts. As a member of the board, he receives the company's product at no charge.

Comment:

Because receiving the company's product constitutes compensation for his service, he is in violation of the Standard if he does not disclose this additional compensation to his employer.

> **IV(C) Responsibilities of Supervisors.** Members and Candidates must make reasonable efforts to ensure that anyone subject to their supervision or authority complies with applicable laws, rules, regulations, and the Code and Standards.

Guidance

Members must make reasonable efforts to *prevent* employees from violating laws, rules, regulations, or the Code and Standards, as well as make reasonable efforts to *detect* violations.

Guidance—Compliance Procedures

Understand that an adequate compliance system must meet industry standards, regulatory requirements, and the requirements of the Code and Standards. Members with supervisory responsibilities have an obligation to bring an inadequate compliance system to the attention of firm's management and recommend corrective action. While investigating a possible breach of compliance procedures, it is appropriate to limit the suspected employee's activities.

A member or candidate faced with no compliance procedures or with procedures he believes are inadequate must decline supervisory responsibility in writing until adequate procedures are adopted by the firm.

Recommended Procedures for Compliance

A member should recommend that his employer adopt a code of ethics. Employers should not commingle compliance procedures with the firm's code of ethics—this can dilute the goal of reinforcing one's ethical obligations. Members should encourage employers to provide their code of ethics to clients.

Adequate compliance procedures should:

- Be clearly written.
- Be easy to understand.
- Designate a compliance officer with authority clearly defined.
- Have a system of checks and balances.
- Outline the scope of procedures.
- Outline what conduct is permitted.
- Contain procedures for reporting violations and sanctions.
- Structure incentives so that unethical behavior is not rewarded.

Once the compliance program is instituted, the supervisor should:

- Distribute it to the proper personnel.
- Update it as needed.
- Continually educate staff regarding procedures.
- Issue reminders as necessary.
- Require professional conduct evaluations.
- Review employee actions to monitor compliance and identify violations.
- Enforce procedures once a violation occurs.
- Review procedures and identify any changes needed to prevent violations in the future.

If there is a violation, respond promptly and conduct a thorough investigation while increasing supervision or placing limitations on the wrongdoer's activities.

Application of Standard IV(C) Responsibilities of Supervisors

Example 1:

Jane Mattock, senior vice president and head of the research department of H&V, Inc., a regional brokerage firm, has decided to change her recommendation for Timber Products from buy to sell. In line with H&V's procedures, she orally advises certain other H&V executives of her proposed actions before the report is prepared for publication. As a result of his conversation with Mattock, Dieter Frampton, one of the executives of H&V accountable to Mattock, immediately sells Timber's stock from his own account and from certain discretionary client accounts. In addition, other personnel inform certain institutional customers of the changed recommendation before it is printed and disseminated to all H&V customers who have received previous Timber reports.

Comment:

Mattock failed to supervise reasonably and adequately the actions of those accountable to her. She did not prevent or establish reasonable procedures designed to prevent dissemination of or trading on the information by those who knew of her changed recommendation. She must ensure that her firm has procedures for reviewing or recording trading in the stock of any corporation that has been the subject of an unpublished change in recommendation. Adequate procedures would have informed the subordinates of their duties and detected sales by Frampton and selected customers.

Example 2:

Deion Miller is the research director for Jamestown Investment Programs. The portfolio managers have become critical of Miller and his staff because the Jamestown portfolios do not include any stock that has been the subject of a merger or tender offer. Georgia Ginn, a member of Miller's staff, tells Miller that she has been studying a local company, Excelsior, Inc., and recommends its purchase. Ginn adds that the company has been widely rumored to be the subject of a merger study by a well-known conglomerate and discussions between them are under way. At Miller's request, Ginn prepares a memo recommending the stock. Miller passes along Ginn's memo to the portfolio managers prior to leaving for vacation, noting that he has not reviewed the memo. As a result of the memo, the portfolio managers buy Excelsior stock immediately. The day Miller returns to the office, Miller learns that Ginn's only sources for the report were her brother, who is an acquisitions analyst with Acme Industries and the "well-known conglomerate" and that the merger discussions were planned but not held.

Comment:

Miller violated Standard IV(C) by not exercising reasonable supervision when he disseminated the memo without checking to ensure that Ginn had a reasonable and adequate basis for her recommendations and that Ginn was not relying on material nonpublic information.

Example 3:

A member responsible for compliance by the firm's trading desk notices a high level of trading activity in a stock that is not on the firm's recommended list. Most of this trading is being done by a trainee, and the member does not investigate this trading.

Comment:

This is a violation of the member's responsibilities as supervisor. She must take steps to monitor the activities of traders in training, as well as investigate the reason for the heavy trading of the security by her firm's trading desk.

MODULE QUIZ 2.7

To best evaluate your performance, enter your quiz answers online.

1. Connie Fletcher, CFA, works for a small money management firm that specializes in pension accounts. Recently, a friend asked her to act as an unpaid volunteer manager for the city's street sweep pension fund. As part of the position, the city would grant Fletcher a free parking space in front of her downtown office. Fletcher is considering the offer. Before she accepts, she should *most appropriately*:
   A. do nothing since this is a volunteer position.
   B. inform her current clients in writing and discuss the offer with her employer.
   C. disclose the details of the volunteer position to her employer and obtain written permission from her employer.
2. Which of the following statements about an investment supervisor's responsibilities is *least likely* correct? A supervisor:
   A. should bring an inadequate compliance system to the attention of management and recommend corrective action.
   B. is responsible for instructing those to whom he has delegated authority about methods to detect and prevent violations of the law and standards.
   C. need only report employee violations of the Code and Standards to upper management and provide a written warning to the employee to cease such activities.
3. Robert Blair, CFA, Director of Research, has had an ongoing battle with management about the adequacy of the firm's compliance system. Recently, it has come to Blair's attention that the firm's compliance procedures are inadequate in that they are not being monitored and not carefully followed. What should Blair *most appropriately* do?
   A. Resign from the firm unless the compliance system is strengthened and followed.
   B. Send his superior a memo outlining the problem.
   C. Decline in writing to continue to accept supervisory responsibility until reasonable compliance procedures are adopted.
4. Ahmed Jamal, CFA, head of research for Valley Brokers, decided it was time to change his recommendation on D&R Company from buy to sell. He orally announced his decision during the Monday staff meeting and said his written report would be finished and disseminated to Valley's customers by the middle of next week. As a result of this announcement, Doris Smith, one of Jamal's subordinates, immediately sold her personal shares in D&R, and Martin Temple told his largest institutional customers of the change the following day. Which Standards have *most likely* been violated?
   A. Jamal violated Standard IV(C) Responsibilities of Supervisors; Smith violated Standard II(A) Material Nonpublic Information; and Temple violated Standard VI(B) Priority of Transactions.
   B. Jamal violated Standard IV(C) Responsibilities of Supervisors; Smith violated Standard VI(B) Priority of Transactions; and Temple violated Standard III(B) Fair Dealing.
   C. Smith violated Standard VI(B) Priority of Transactions, and Temple violated Standard III(B) Fair Dealing.

5. Sally Albright, CFA, works full-time for Frank & Company, an investment management firm, as a fixed-income security analyst. Albright has been asked by a business contact at KDG Enterprises to accept some analytical work from KDG on a consulting basis. The work would entail investigating potential distressed debt securities in the small-cap market. Albright should *most appropriately*:
   A. accept the work as long as she obtains consent to all the terms of the engagement from Frank & Company.
   B. not accept the work as it violates the Code and Standards by creating a conflict of interest.
   C. accept the work as long as she obtains written consent from KDG and does it on her own time.

Video covering this content is available online.

MODULE 2.8: STANDARD V

V Investment Analysis, Recommendations, and Actions

V(A) Diligence and Reasonable Basis. Members and Candidates must:

- Exercise diligence, independence, and thoroughness in analyzing investments, making investment recommendations, and taking investment actions.
- Have a reasonable and adequate basis, supported by appropriate research and investigation, for any investment analysis, recommendation, or action.

Guidance

The application of this Standard depends on the investment philosophy adhered to, members' and candidates' roles in the investment decision-making process, and the resources and support provided by employers. These factors dictate the degree of diligence, thoroughness of research, and the proper level of investigation required.

Guidance—Reasonable Basis

The level of research required to satisfy the requirement for due diligence will differ depending on the product or service offered. A list of some things that should be considered prior to making a recommendation or taking investment action includes:

- Global and national economic conditions.
- A firm's financial results, operating history, and business cycle stage.
- Fees and historical results for a mutual fund.
- Limitations of any quantitative models used.
- A determination of whether peer group comparisons for valuation are appropriate.

Guidance—Using Secondary or Third-Party Research

Members should encourage their firms to adopt a policy for periodic review of the quality of third-party research, if they have not. Examples of criteria to use in judging quality are:

- Review assumptions used.
- Determine how rigorous the analysis was.
- Identify how timely the research is.
- Evaluate objectivity and independence of the recommendations.

Guidance—Using Quantitative Research

Members must be able to explain the basic nature of the quantitative research and how it is used to make investment decisions. Members should consider scenarios outside those typically used to assess downside risk and the time horizon of the data used for model evaluation to ensure that both positive and negative cycle results have been considered.

Guidance—Developing Quantitative Techniques

The Standard requires greater diligence of members and candidates who create quantitative techniques than of those who use techniques developed by others. Members and candidates must understand the technical details of the products they offer to clients. A member or candidate who has created a quantitative strategy must test it thoroughly, including extreme scenarios with inputs that fall outside the range of historical data, before offering it to clients.

Guidance—External Advisers

Members should make sure their firms have procedures in place to review any external advisers they use or promote to ensure that, among other things, the advisers:

- Have adequate compliance and internal controls.
- Present returns information that is correct.
- Do not deviate from their stated strategies.

Guidance—Group Research and Decision Making

Even if a member does not agree with the independent and objective view of the group, he does not necessarily have to decline to be identified with the report, as long as there is a reasonable and adequate basis.

Recommended Procedures for Compliance

Members should encourage their firms to consider these policies and procedures supporting this Standard:

- Have a policy requiring that research reports and recommendations have a basis that can be substantiated as reasonable and adequate.
- Have detailed, written guidance for proper research and due diligence.
- Have measurable criteria for judging the quality of research, and base analyst compensation on such criteria.
- Have written procedures that provide a minimum acceptable level of scenario testing for computer-based models and include standards for the range of scenarios, model accuracy over time, and a measure of the sensitivity of cash flows to model assumptions and inputs.
- Have a policy for evaluating outside providers of information that addresses the reasonableness and accuracy of the information provided and establishes how often the evaluations should be repeated.
- Adopt a set of standards that provides criteria for evaluating external advisers and states how often a review of external advisers will be performed.

Application of Standard V(A) Diligence and Reasonable Basis

Example 1:

Helen Hawke manages the corporate finance department of Sarkozi Securities, Ltd. The firm is anticipating that the government will soon close a tax loophole that currently allows oil and gas exploration companies to pass on drilling expenses to holders of a certain class of shares. Because market demand for this tax-advantaged class of stock is currently high, Sarkozi convinces several companies to undertake new equity financings at once before the loophole closes. Time is of the essence, but Sarkozi lacks sufficient resources to conduct adequate research on all the prospective issuing companies. Hawke decides to estimate the IPO prices based on the relative size of each company and to justify the pricing later when her staff has time.

Comment:

Sarkozi should have taken on only the work that it could adequately handle. By categorizing the issuers as to general size, Hawke has bypassed researching all the other relevant aspects that should be considered when pricing new issues and thus has not performed sufficient due diligence. Such an omission can result in investors purchasing shares at prices that have no actual basis. Hawke has violated Standard V(A).

Example 2:

A member in the corporate finance department of a securities firm prices IPO shares without doing adequate research because she wants to get them to market quickly.

Comment:

This is a violation of Standard V(A).

Example 3:

A member screens a database of investment managers and sends a recommendation of five of them to a client. Subsequently, but before the client receives the report, one of the recommended firms loses its head of research and several key portfolio managers. The member does not update her report.

Comment:

This is a violation as the member should have notified the client of the change in key personnel at the management firm.

Example 4:

A member writes a report in which she estimates mortgage rates. After reviewing it, a majority of the investment committee vote to change the report to reflect a different interest rate forecast. Must the member dissociate herself from the report?

Comment:

The same facts may give rise to different opinions and as long as the committee has a reasonable and adequate basis for their (differing) opinion, the member is under no obligation to ask that her name be removed from the report or to disassociate from issuing the report.

Example 5:

A member makes a presentation for an offering his firm is underwriting, using maximum production levels as his estimate in order to justify the price of the shares he is recommending for purchase.

Comment:

Using the maximum possible production without acknowledging that this is not the expected level of production (or without presenting a range of possible outcomes and their relative probabilities) does not provide a reasonable basis for the purchase recommendation and is a violation of the Standard.

Example 6:

A member posts buy recommendations in an internet chat room based on "conventional wisdom" and what the public is currently buying.

Comment:

A recommendation that is not based on independent and diligent research into the subject company is a violation of the Standard.

Example 7:

A member is a principal in a small investment firm that bases its securities recommendations on third-party research that it purchases.

Comment:

This is not a violation as long as the member's firm periodically checks the purchased research to determine that it has met, and still meets, the criteria of objectivity and reasonableness required by the Standard.

Example 8:

A member selects an outside advisor for international equities based solely on the fact that the selected firm has the lowest fees for managing the international equities accounts.

Comment:

This is a violation of Standard V(A). The member must consider performance and service, not just fees, in selecting an outside advisor for client accounts.

Example 9:

A member investigates the management, fees, track record, and investment strategy of a hedge fund and recommends it to a client who purchases it. The member accurately discloses the risks involved with the investment in the hedge fund. Soon afterward, the fund reports terrible losses and suspends operations.

Comment:

The bad outcome does not mean there has necessarily been a violation of Standard V(A). A member who has performed reasonable due diligence and disclosed investment risks adequately has complied with the requirements of Standard V(A), regardless of the subsequent outcome.

V(B) Communication with Clients and Prospective Clients. Members and Candidates must:

1. Disclose to clients and prospective clients the basic format and general principles of the investment processes they use to analyze investments, select securities, and construct portfolios and must promptly disclose any changes that might materially affect those processes.
2. Disclose to clients and prospective clients significant limitations and risks associated with the investment process.
3. Use reasonable judgment in identifying which factors are important to their investment analyses, recommendations, or actions and include those factors in communications with clients and prospective clients.
4. Distinguish between fact and opinion in the presentation of investment analysis and recommendations.

Guidance

Proper communication with clients is critical to provide quality financial services. Members must distinguish between opinions and facts and always include the basic characteristics of the security being analyzed in a research report.

Members must illustrate to clients and prospects the investment decision-making process utilized.

All means of communication are included here, not just research reports.

In preparing recommendations for structured securities, allocation strategies, or any other nontraditional investment, members should communicate those risk factors specific to such investments. In all cases, members should communicate the potential gains and losses on the investment clearly in terms of total returns. Members are required to communicate significant changes in the risk characteristics of an investment or strategy and to update clients regularly about changes in the investment process, including any risks and limitations that have been newly identified.

When using projections from quantitative models and analysis, members may violate the Standard by not explaining the limitations of the model and the assumptions it uses, which provides a context for judging the uncertainty regarding the estimated investment result.

Members and candidates must inform clients about limitations inherent to an investment. Two examples of such limitations are liquidity and capacity. *Liquidity* refers to the ability to exit an investment readily without experiencing a significant extra cost for doing so. *Capacity* refers to an investment vehicle's ability to absorb additional investment without reducing the returns it is able to achieve.

Recommended Procedures for Compliance

Selection of relevant factors in a report can be a judgment call, so be sure to maintain records indicating the nature of the research, and be able to supply additional information if it is requested by the client or other users of the report.

Application of Standard V(B) Communication with Clients and Prospective Clients

Example 1:

Sarah Williamson, director of marketing for Country Technicians, Inc., is convinced that she has found the perfect formula for increasing Country Technician's income and diversifying its product base. Williamson plans to build on Country Technician's reputation as a leading money manager by marketing an exclusive and expensive investment advice letter to high-net-worth individuals. One hitch in the plan is the complexity of Country Technician's investment system—a combination of technical trading rules (based on historical price and volume fluctuations) and portfolio-construction rules designed to minimize risk. To simplify the newsletter, she decides to include only each week's top-five buy and sell recommendations and to leave out details of the valuation models and the portfolio-structuring scheme.

Comment:

Williamson's plans for the newsletter violate Standard V(B) because she does not intend to include all the relevant factors behind the investment advice. Williamson need not describe the investment system in detail in order to implement the advice effectively, but clients must be informed of Country Technician's basic process and logic. Without understanding the basis for a recommendation, clients cannot possibly understand its limitations or its inherent risks.

Example 2:

Richard Dox is a mining analyst for East Bank Securities. He has just finished his report on Boisy Bay Minerals. Included in his report is his own assessment of the geological extent of mineral reserves likely to be found on the company's land. Dox completed this calculation based on the core samples from the company's latest drilling. According to Dox's calculations, the company has in excess of 500,000 ounces of gold on the property. Dox concludes his research report as follows: "Based on the fact that the company has 500,000 ounces of gold to be mined, I recommend a strong BUY."

Comment:

If Dox issues the report as written, he will violate Standard V(B). His calculation of the total gold reserves for the property is an opinion, not a fact. Opinion must be distinguished from fact in research reports.

Example 3:

May & Associates is an aggressive growth manager that has represented itself since its inception as a specialist at investing in small-capitalization domestic stocks. One of May's selection criteria is a maximum capitalization of $250 million for any given company. After a string of successful years of superior relative performance, May expanded its client base significantly, to the point at which assets under management now exceed $3 billion. For liquidity purposes, May's chief investment officer (CIO) decides to lift the maximum permissible market-cap ceiling to $500 million and change the firm's sales and marketing literature accordingly to inform prospective clients and third-party consultants.

Comment:

Although May's CIO is correct about informing potentially interested parties as to the change in investment process, he must also notify May's existing clients. Among the latter group might be a number of clients who not only retained May as a small-cap manager but also retained mid-cap and large-cap specialists in a multiple-manager approach. Such clients could regard May's change of criteria as a style change that could distort their overall asset allocations.

Example 4:

Rather than lifting the ceiling for its universe from $250 million to $500 million, May & Associates extends its small-cap universe to include a number of non-U.S. companies.

Comment:

Standard V(B) requires that May's CIO advise May's clients of this change because the firm may have been retained by some clients specifically for its prowess at investing in domestic small-cap stocks. Other variations requiring client notification include introducing derivatives to emulate a certain market sector or relaxing various other constraints, such as portfolio beta. In all such cases, members and candidates must disclose changes to all interested parties.

Example 5:

A member sends a report to his investment management firm's clients describing a strategy his firm offers in terms of the high returns it will generate in the event interest rate volatility decreases. The report does not provide details of the strategy because they are deemed proprietary. The report does not consider the possible returns if interest rate volatility actually increases.

Comment:

This is a violation on two counts. The basic nature of the strategy must be disclosed, including the extent to which leverage is used to generate the high returns when volatility falls. Further, the report must include how the strategy will perform if volatility rises, as well as if it falls.

Example 6:

A member's firm changes from its old equity selection model, which is based on price-sales ratios, to a new model based on several factors, including future earnings growth rates, but does not inform clients of this change.

Comment:

This is a violation because members must inform their clients of any significant change in their investment process. Here, the introduction of forecast data on earnings growth can be viewed as a significant change because the old single-variable model was based on reported rather than forecast data.

Example 7:

A member's firm, in response to poor results relative to its stated benchmark, decides to structure portfolios to passively track the benchmark and does not inform clients.

Comment:

This is a significant change in the investment process and must be communicated to clients.

Example 8:

At a firm where individual portfolio managers have been responsible for security selection, a new policy is implemented whereby only stocks on an approved list constructed by the firm's senior managers may be purchased in client accounts. A member who is a portfolio manager does not inform his clients.

Comment:

This is a violation of the Standard because it represents a significant change in the investment process.

Example 9:

A member changes his firm's outside manager of real estate investments and provides information of this change only in the firm's annual report where outside advisers are listed.

Comment:

This is a violation of the Standard. The member should notify clients immediately of such a change in the firm's investment process.

Example 10:

A member discovers that an error in one of his firm's quantitative models led to a number of trades in one portfolio that should not have been made. The member corrects the error in the model and rebalances the portfolio to reverse the erroneous trades, but does not report the issue.

Comment:

The member violated the Standard by failing to disclose both the error and the corrective action to clients.

PROFESSOR'S NOTE

Remember, the argument that clients "won't care" about a process change can be turned around to "there's no reason not to disclose the change."

> **V(C) Record Retention.** Members and Candidates must develop and maintain appropriate records to support their investment analysis, recommendations, actions, and other investment-related communications with clients and prospective clients.

Guidance

Members must maintain research records that support the reasons for the analyst's conclusions and any investment actions taken. Such records are the property of the firm. If no other regulatory standards or firm policies are in place, the Standard recommends a 7-year minimum holding period. All communications with clients through any medium, including emails and text messages, are records that must be retained.

A member who changes firms must recreate the analysis documentation supporting her recommendation using publicly available information or information obtained from the company and must not rely on memory or materials created at her previous firm.

Recommended Procedures for Compliance

This recordkeeping requirement generally is the firm's responsibility.

Application of Standard V(C) Record Retention

Example 1:

One of Nikolas Lindstrom's clients is upset by the negative investment returns in his equity portfolio. The investment policy statement for the client requires that the portfolio manager follow a benchmark-oriented approach. The benchmark for the client included a 35% investment allocation in the technology sector, which the client acknowledged was appropriate. Over the past three years, the portion put into the segment of technology stocks suffered severe losses. The client complains to the investment manager that so much money was allocated to this sector.

Comment:

For Lindstrom, it is important to have appropriate records to show that over the past three years the percentage of technology stocks in the benchmark index was 35%. Therefore, the amount of money invested in the technology sector was appropriate according to the investment policy statement. Lindstrom should also have the investment policy statement for the client stating that the benchmark was appropriate for the client's investment objectives. He should also have records indicating that the investment had been explained appropriately to the client and that the investment policy statement was updated on a regular basis.

Example 2:

A member bases his research reports on interviews, his own analysis, and industry reports from third parties on his industry and related industries.

Comment:

The member must keep records of all the information that went into the research on which his reports and recommendations are based.

Example 3:

When a member leaves a firm at which he has developed a complex trading model, he takes documentation of the model assumptions and how they were derived over time with him because he will use the model at his new firm.

Comment:

Taking these materials without permission from his previous employer is a violation of his duties to his (previous) employer. While he may use knowledge of the model at the new firm, the member must recreate the supporting documents. The originals are the property of the firm where he worked on developing the model.

MODULE QUIZ 2.8

To best evaluate your performance, enter your quiz answers online.

1. Gail Stefano, CFA, an analyst for a U.S. brokerage firm that serves U.S. investors, researches public utilities in South American emerging markets. Stefano makes the following statement in a recent report: "Based on the fact that the South American utilities sector has seen rapid growth in new service orders, we expect that most companies in the sector will be able to convert the revenue increases into significant profits. We also believe the trend will continue for the next three to five years." The report goes on to describe the major risks of investing in this market, in particular the political and exchange rate instability associated with South American countries. Stefano's report:
   A. has not violated the Code and Standards.
   B. violated the Code and Standards by failing to properly distinguish factual information from opinions.
   C. violated the Code and Standards by failing to properly identify details related to the operations of South American utilities.
2. Which of the following is *most likely* a violation of Standard III(B) Fair Dealing?
   A. A firm makes investment recommendations and also manages a mutual fund. The firm routinely begins trading for the fund's account ten minutes before announcing recommendation changes to client accounts.
   B. After releasing a general recommendation to all clients, an analyst calls the firm's largest institutional clients to discuss the recommendation in more detail.
   C. A portfolio manager allocates IPO shares to all client accounts, including her brother's fee-based retirement account.
3. Eugene Nieder, CFA, has just accepted a new job as a quantitative analyst for Paschal Investments, LLP. Nieder developed a complex model while working for his previous employer and plans to recreate the model for Paschal. Nieder did not make copies of the model or any supporting documents since his employer refused to grant him permission to do so. Nieder will recreate the model from memory. Which of the following statements is *most likely* correct?
   A. Nieder can recreate the model without violating the Code and Standards as long as he also generates supporting documentation.
   B. Nieder can recreate the model without violating the Code and Standards without documentation if the model is modified from its original form.
   C. Nieder cannot recreate the model without violating the Code and Standards because it is the property of his former employer.

4. Fred Johnson, CFA, a financial analyst and avid windsurfer, has begun an investment survey of the water sports leisure industry. His brother sells windsurfing gear in Tampa and tells him that Swordfish9 is the "hottest windsurfing rig on the market and will be highly profitable for Swordfish Enterprises." Johnson had never heard of Swordfish9 previously, but after testing the board himself became very excited about the Swordfish9 and issued an investment recommendation of "buy" on Swordfish Enterprises. As a result of issuing the recommendation, Johnson has:
   A. not violated the Code and Standards.
   B. violated the Code and Standards by failing to establish a reasonable and adequate basis.
   C. violated the Code and Standards by failing to consider the suitability of the investment for his clients.
5. Which of the following actions is a *required*, rather than *recommended*, action under the Standard regarding diligence and a reasonable basis for a firm's research recommendations?
   A. Have a policy requiring that research reports and recommendations have a basis that can be substantiated as reasonable and adequate.
   B. Compensate analysts based on measurable criteria to assess the quality of their research.
   C. Review the assumptions used and evaluate the objectivity of externally generated research reports.

MODULE 2.9: STANDARD VI

Video covering this content is available online.

> **VI Conflicts of Interest**
>
> **VI(A) Disclosure of Conflicts.** Members and Candidates must make full and fair disclosure of all matters that could reasonably be expected to impair their independence and objectivity or interfere with respective duties to their clients, prospective clients, and employer. Members and Candidates must ensure that such disclosures are prominent, are delivered in plain language, and communicate the relevant information effectively.

Guidance

Members must fully disclose to clients, prospects, and their employers all actual and potential conflicts of interest in order to protect investors and employers. These disclosures must be clearly stated.

Guidance—Disclosure to Clients

The requirement that all potential areas of conflict be disclosed allows clients and prospects to judge motives and potential biases for themselves. Disclosure of broker/dealer market-making activities would be included here. Board service is another area of potential conflict.

The most common conflict which requires disclosure is actual ownership of stock in companies that the member recommends or that clients hold.

Another common source of conflicts of interest is a member's compensation/ bonus structure, which can potentially create incentives to take actions that produce immediate gains for the member with little or no concern for longer-term returns for the client. Such conflicts must be disclosed when the member is acting in an advisory capacity and must be updated in the case of significant change in compensation structure.

Guidance—Disclosure of Conflicts to Employers

Members must give the employer enough information to judge the impact of the conflict. Take reasonable steps to avoid conflicts, and report them promptly if they occur.

Recommended Procedures of Compliance

Any special compensation arrangements, bonus programs, commissions, and incentives should be disclosed.

Application of Standard VI(A) Disclosure of Conflicts

Example 1:

Hunter Weiss is a research analyst with Farmington Company, a broker and investment banking firm. Farmington's merger and acquisition department has represented Vimco, a conglomerate, in all of its acquisitions for 20 years. From time to time, Farmington officers sit on the boards of directors of various Vimco subsidiaries. Weiss is writing a research report on Vimco.

Comment:

Weiss must disclose in his research report Farmington's special relationship with Vimco. Broker/dealer management of and participation in public offerings must be disclosed in research reports. Because the position of underwriter to a company presents a special past and potential future relationship with a company that is the subject of investment advice, it threatens the independence and objectivity of the report and must be disclosed.

Example 2:

Samantha Snead, a portfolio manager for Thomas Investment Counsel, Inc., specializes in managing defined-benefit pension plan accounts, all of which are in the accumulative phase and have long-term investment objectives. A year ago, Snead's employer, in an attempt to motivate and retain key investment professionals, introduced a bonus compensation system that rewards portfolio managers on the basis of quarterly performance relative to their peers and certain benchmark indexes. Snead changes her investment strategy and purchases several high-beta stocks for client portfolios in an attempt to improve short-term performance. These purchases are seemingly contrary to the client investment policy statement. Now, an officer of Griffin Corporation, one of Snead's pension fund clients, asks why Griffin Corporation's portfolio seems to be dominated by high-beta stocks of companies that often appear among the most actively traded issues. No change in objective or strategy has been recommended by Snead during the year.

Comment:

Snead violated Standard VI(A) by failing to inform her clients of the changes in her compensation arrangement with her employer that created a conflict of interest. Firms may pay employees on the basis of performance, but pressure by Thomas Investment Counsel to achieve short-term performance goals is in basic conflict with the objectives of Snead's accounts.

Example 3:

Bruce Smith covers East European equities for Marlborough investments, an investment management firm with a strong presence in emerging markets. While on a business trip to Russia, Smith learns that investing in Russian equity directly is difficult but that equity-linked notes that replicate the performance of the underlying Russian equity can be purchased from a New York-based investment bank. Believing that his firm would not be interested in such a security, Smith purchases a note linked to a Russian telecommunications company for his own account without informing Marlborough. A month later, Smith decides that the firm should consider investing in Russian equities using equity-linked notes, and he prepares a write-up on the market that concludes with a recommendation to purchase several of the notes. One note recommended is linked to the same Russian telecom company that Smith holds in his personal account.

Comment:

Smith violated Standard VI(A) by failing to disclose his ownership of the note linked to the Russian telecom company. Smith is required by the standard to disclose the investment opportunity to his employer and look to his company's policies on personal trading to determine whether it was proper for him to purchase the note for his own account. By purchasing the note, Smith may or may not have impaired his ability to make an unbiased and objective assessment of the appropriateness of the derivative instrument for his firm, but Smith's failure to disclose the purchase to his employer impaired his employer's ability to render an opinion regarding whether the ownership of a security constituted a conflict of interest that might have affected future recommendations. Once he recommended the notes to his firm, Smith compounded his problems by not disclosing that he owned the notes in his personal account—a clear conflict of interest.

Example 4:

An investment management partnership sells a significant stake to a firm that is publicly traded. The partnership has added the firm's stock to its recommended list and approved its commercial paper for cash management accounts.

Comment:

Members are required to disclose such a change in firm ownership to all clients. Further, any transactions in client accounts involving the securities of the public firm, and any recommendations concerning the public firm's securities, must include a disclosure of the business relation between it and the partnership.

Example 5:

A member provides clients with research about a company's stock, and his wife inherits a significant amount of stock in the company.

Comment:

The member must disclose this potential conflict to his employer and in any subsequent reports or recommendations he authors. His employer may prudently choose to reassign the stock.

Example 6:

A member's investment banking firm receives a significant number of options as partial compensation for bringing a firm public. The member will profit personally from a portion of these options as well.

Comment:

In any research report on the public firm's securities, the member must disclose the fact that these options exist and include their number and the expiration date(s). Because he will profit personally from these, he must also disclose the extent of his participation in these options.

Example 7:

A member accepts an offer from a stock promoter who will provide additional compensation when the member sells Acme stock to his clients. He does not inform his clients or his employer.

Comment:

The member is in violation of the Standard because he must disclose this additional compensation to those clients to whom he recommends the stock and to his employer. Both have a right to determine for themselves the extent to which this additional compensation might affect the member's objectivity.

Example 8:

A member who is a portfolio manager for a small investment management firm serving individuals accepts a job as a trustee of an endowment fund that has over €1.5 billion in assets and does not disclose this to her employer.

Comment:

This is a significant position that may require a substantial portion of the member's time and may involve decisions on security selection and trading. The member is in violation of the Standard by not disclosing this involvement to her employer and by not discussing it with her employer before accepting the position.

Example 9:

A member replaces his firm's external manager, which has had average results, with a friend's firm.

Comment:

Taking such action without disclosing to his firm that the new manager is a personal friend is a violation of the Standards.

Example 10:

A member who is a portfolio manager participates in her employer's defined contribution pension plan through automatic contributions each pay period. The investment choices in the plan are large, diversified mutual funds, including one fund that is managed by her employer.

Comment:

The Standard does not require the member to disclose her personal investments in diversified funds unless this is her firm's policy, nor does it require preclearence for her automatic payroll deductions. The member should follow her firm's policies with regard to preclearing and disclosing her investments in firm-managed funds.

> **VI(B) Priority of Transactions.** Investment transactions for clients and employers must have priority over investment transactions in which a Member or Candidate is the beneficial owner.

Guidance

Client transactions take priority over personal transactions and over transactions made on behalf of the member's firm. Personal transactions include situations where the member is a "beneficial owner." Personal transactions may be undertaken only after clients and the member's employer have had an adequate opportunity to act on a recommendation. Note that family member accounts that are client accounts should be treated just like any client account; they should not be disadvantaged.

Information about pending trades should not be acted on for personal gain. The overriding considerations with respect to personal trades are that they do not disadvantage any clients.

Recommended Procedures for Compliance

All firms should have in place basic procedures that address conflicts created by personal investing. The following areas should be included:

- Limited participation in equity IPOs. Members can avoid these conflicts by not participating in IPOs.
- Restrictions on private placements. Strict limits should be placed on employee acquisition of these securities and proper supervisory procedures should be in place. Participation in these investments raises conflict of interest issues, similar to IPOs.
- Establish blackout/restricted periods. Employees involved in investment decision-making should have blackout periods prior to trading for clients—no "front running" (i.e., purchase or sale of securities in advance of anticipated

client or employer purchases and sales). The size of the firm and the type of security should help dictate how severe the blackout requirement should be.

- Reporting requirements. Supervisors should establish reporting procedures, including duplicate trade confirmations, disclosure of personal holdings/ beneficial ownership positions, and preclearance procedures.
- Disclosure of policies. Members must fully disclose to investors their firm's personal trading policies.

Members should encourage their firms to adopt such procedures if they have not.

Application of Standard VI(B) Priority of Transactions

Example 1:

Erin Toffler, a portfolio manager at Esposito Investments, manages the retirement account established with the firm by her parents. Whenever IPOs become available, she first allocates shares to all her other clients for whom the investment is appropriate; only then does she place any remaining portion in her parents' account, if the issue is appropriate for them. She has adopted this procedure so that no one can accuse her of favoring her parents.

Comment:

Toffler has breached her duty to her parents by treating them differently from her other accounts simply because of the family relationship. As fee-paying clients of Esposito Investments, Toffler's parents are entitled to the same treatment as any other client of the firm. If Toffler has beneficial ownership in the account, however, and Esposito Investments has preclearance and reporting requirements for personal transactions, she may have to preclear the trades and report the transactions to Esposito.

Example 2:

A brokerage's insurance analyst, Denise Wilson, makes a closed-circuit report to her firm's branches around the country. During the broadcast, she includes negative comments about a major company within the industry. The following day, Wilson's report is printed and distributed to the sales force and public customers. The report recommends that both short-term traders and intermediate investors take profits by selling that company's stocks. Several minutes after the broadcast, Ellen Riley, head of the firm's trading department, closes out a long call position in the stock. Shortly thereafter, Riley establishes a sizable "put" position in the stock. Riley claims she took this action to facilitate anticipated sales by institutional clients.

Comment:

Riley expected that both the stock and option markets would respond to the "sell" recommendation, but she did not give customers an opportunity to buy or sell in the options market before the firm itself did. By taking action before the report was disseminated, Riley's firm could have depressed the price of the "calls" and increased the price of the "puts." The firm could have avoided a conflict of interest if it had waited to trade for its own account until its clients had an opportunity to receive and assimilate Wilson's recommendations. As it is, Riley's actions violated Standard VI(B).

Example 3:

A member who is a research analyst does not recommend a stock to his employer because he wants to purchase it quickly for his personal account.

Comment:

He has violated the priority of transactions by withholding this information from his employer and seeking to profit personally at his employer's expense. The member has likely violated his duty to his employer under Standard IV(A) Loyalty as well.

Example 4:

A member who manages a fund gets hot IPO shares for her husband's account from syndicate firms, even when the fund is unable to get shares.

Comment:

The member has violated the Standard by this action. She must act in the interest of the shareholders of the fund and place allocated shares there first. She must also inform her employer of her participation in these offerings through her beneficial interest in her husband's account(s).

Example 5:

A member allows an employee to continue his duties without having signed a required report of his personal trading activity over the last three months. The employee, a CFA candidate, has been purchasing securities for his own account just before firm buy recommendations have been released.

Comment:

The employee has violated the Standard. The member has also violated Standard IV(C) Responsibilities of Supervisors by allowing the employee to continue in his regular duties.

Example 6:

A member reveals a sell rating on some securities in a broadcast to all of her firm's brokers. The changed rating is sent to clients the next day. Shortly after revealing the change to her firm's brokers and prior to dissemination to clients, she buys puts on the stock for her firm's account.

Comment:

The member did not give clients adequate opportunity to act on the change in recommendation before buying the puts for her firm's account.

> **VI(C) Referral Fees.** Members and Candidates must disclose to their employer, clients, and prospective clients, as appropriate, any compensation, consideration, or benefit received from, or paid to, others for the recommendation of products or services.

Guidance

Members must inform employers, clients, and prospects of any benefit received for referrals of customers and clients, allowing them to evaluate the full cost of the service as well as any potential partiality. All types of consideration must be disclosed.

Recommended Procedures for Compliance

Members should encourage their firms to adopt clear procedures regarding compensation for referrals. Firms that do not prohibit such fees should have clear procedures for approval, and members should provide their employers with updates at least quarterly regarding the nature and value of referral compensation received.

Application of Standard VI(C) Referral Fees

Example 1:

Brady Securities, Inc., a broker/dealer, has established a referral arrangement with Lewis Brothers, Ltd., an investment counseling firm. In this arrangement, Brady Securities refers all prospective tax-exempt accounts, including pension, profit-sharing, and endowment accounts, to Lewis Brothers. In return, Lewis Brothers makes available to Brady Securities on a regular basis the security recommendations and reports of its research staff, which registered representatives of Brady Securities use in serving customers. In addition, Lewis Brothers conducts monthly economic and market reviews for Brady Securities personnel and directs all stock commission business generated by referral accounts to Brady Securities.

Willard White, a partner in Lewis Brothers, calculates that the incremental costs involved in functioning as the research department of Brady Securities are US$20,000 annually.

Referrals from Brady Securities last year resulted in fee income of US$200,000 for Lewis Brothers, and directing all stock trades through Brady Securities resulted in additional costs to Lewis Brothers' clients of US$10,000.

Diane Branch, the chief financial officer of Maxwell Inc., contacts White and says that she is seeking an investment manager for Maxwell's profit-sharing plan. She adds, "My friend Harold Hill at Brady Securities recommended your firm without qualification, and that's good enough for me. Do we have a deal?" White accepts the new account but does not disclose his firm's referral arrangement with Brady Securities.

Comment:

White has violated Standard VI(C) by failing to inform the prospective customer of the referral fee payable in services and commissions for an indefinite period to Brady Securities. Such disclosure could have caused Branch to reassess Hill's recommendation and make a more critical evaluation of Lewis Brothers' services.

Example 2:

James Handley works for the Trust Department of Central Trust Bank. He receives compensation for each referral he makes to Central Trust's brokerage and personal financial management department that results in a sale. He refers several of his clients to the personal financial management department but does not disclose the arrangement within Central trust to his clients.

Comment:

Handley has violated Standard VI(C) by not disclosing the referral arrangement at Central Trust Bank to his clients. The Standard does not distinguish between referral fees paid by a third party for referring clients to the third party and internal compensation arrangements paid within the firm to attract new business to a subsidiary. Members and candidates must disclose all such referral fees. Therefore, Handley would be required to disclose, at the time of referral, any referral fee agreement in place between Central Trust Bank's departments. The disclosure should include the nature and the value of the benefit and should be made in writing.

Example 3:

An investment consultant conducts an independent and objective analysis of investment managers for a pension fund and selects the best one. Subsequently, the selected advisor makes a payment to the consultant.

Comment:

This is a violation of the Standard. The potential for a payment should have been disclosed to the pension fund. There are very likely regulatory or legal considerations with regard to such payment as well.

MODULE QUIZ 2.9

To best evaluate your performance, enter your quiz answers online.

1. Which of the following is *least likely* a violation of Standard VI(B) Priority of Transactions? An analyst:
   - A. trades for her own account before her firm announces a change in a recommendation.
   - B. trades for her son's trust account, which is not a firm account, on the day after her firm changes its buy/sell recommendation.
   - C. takes a position for her own outside account in a stock one week after she published a buy recommendation for the stock.

2. As part of an agreement with Baker Brokerage, Hern Investment Company, a money manager for individual clients, provides monthly emerging market overviews in exchange for prospective client referrals and European equity research from Baker. Clients and prospects of Hern are not made aware of the agreement, but clients unanimously rave about the high quality of the research provided by Baker. As a result of the research, many clients with non-discretionary accounts have earned substantial returns on their portfolios. Managers at Hern have also used the research to earn outstanding returns for the firm's discretionary accounts. Which of the following statements is *most likely* correct? Hern:
   A. has not violated the Code and Standards.
   B. has violated the Code and Standards by using third-party research in discretionary accounts.
   C. has violated the Code and Standards by failing to disclose the referral agreement with Baker.

3. Neiman Investment Co. receives brokerage business from Pick Asset Management in exchange for referring prospective clients to Pick. Pick advises clients—in writing, at the time the relationship is established—of the nature of its arrangement with Neiman. With regard to this practice, Pick has:
   A. complied with the Code and Standards.
   B. violated the Code and Standards by failing to preserve the confidentiality of the agreement with Neiman.
   C. violated the Code and Standards by inappropriately negotiating an agreement that creates a conflict of interest.

4. Daniel Lyons, CFA, is an analyst for a French firm that sells investment research to European companies. Lyons's aunt owns 30,000 shares of French National Bank (FNB). She informs Lyons that as a part of her estate planning she has created a trust in his name into which she has placed 2,000 shares of FNB. The trust is structured so that Lyons will not receive control of the assets for two years, at which time his aunt will also gift her current home to Lyons and move into a retirement community. Lyons is due to update his research coverage of FNB next week. Lyons should *most appropriately*:
   A. advise his superiors that he is no longer able to issue research recommendations on FNB.
   B. update the report without notification since the shares are held in trust and are beyond his direct control.
   C. disclose the situation to his employer and, if then asked to prepare a report, also disclose the situation in the report.

Video covering this content is available online.

MODULE 2.10: STANDARD VII

VII Responsibilities as a CFA Institute Member or CFA Candidate

VII(A) Conduct as Participants in CFA Institute Programs. Members and Candidates must not engage in any conduct that compromises the reputation or integrity of CFA Institute or the CFA designation or the integrity, validity, or security of CFA Institute programs.

PROFESSOR'S NOTE

The Standard is intended to cover conduct such as cheating on the CFA exam or otherwise violating rules of CFA Institute or the CFA program. It is not intended to prevent anyone from expressing any opinions or beliefs concerning CFA Institute or the CFA program.

Members must not engage in any activity that undermines the integrity of the CFA charter. This Standard applies to conduct which includes:

- Cheating on the CFA exam or any exam administered by CFA Institute (e.g., CIPM).
- Revealing anything about either broad or specific topics tested, content of exam questions, or formulas required or not required on the exam.
- Not following rules and policies of any CFA Institute program.
- Giving confidential information on the CFA program to candidates or the public.
- Improperly using the designation to further personal and professional goals.
- Misrepresenting information on the Professional Conduct Statement (PCS) or the CFA Institute Professional Development Program.

Members and candidates are not precluded from expressing their opinions regarding the exam program or CFA Institute but must not reveal confidential information about the CFA program.

Candidates who violate any of the CFA exam policies (calculator, personal belongings, Candidate Pledge) have violated Standard VII(A).

Members who volunteer in the CFA program may not solicit or reveal information about questions considered for or included on a CFA exam, about the grading process, or about scoring of questions.

Application of Standard VII(A) Conduct as Participants in CFA Institute Programs

Example 1:

Jose Ramirez is an investment-relations consultant for several small companies that are seeking greater exposure to investors. He is also the program chair for the CFA Institute society in the city where he works. To the exclusion of other companies, Ramirez only schedules companies that are his clients to make presentations to the society.

Comment:

Ramirez, by using his volunteer position at CFA Institute to benefit himself and his clients, compromises the reputation and integrity of CFA Institute and, thus, violates Standard VII(A).

Example 2:

A member who is an exam grader discusses with friends the guideline answer for and relative candidate performance on a specific question he graded on the CFA exam.

Comment:

He has violated his Grader's Agreement and also the Standard by compromising the integrity of the CFA exam.

Example 3:

A candidate does not stop writing when asked to by the proctor at the CFA exam.

Comment:

By taking additional time compared to other candidates, this candidate has violated the Standard, compromising the integrity of the exam process.

Example 4:

A member who is a volunteer on a CFA Institute committee tells her clients that what she learns through her committee work will allow her to better serve their interests.

Comment:

She has violated the Standard by using her CFA committee position to benefit herself personally and to any extent her "inside" knowledge has benefited her clients.

Example 5:

A candidate tells another candidate, "I'm sure glad that Bayes' formula was not on the Level I test this year."

Comment:

This is a violation of Standard VII(A). Candidates are not permitted to reveal any formulas required or not required on a CFA exam.

Example 6:

A candidate tells his beloved CFA instructor, "I really appreciate the emphasis that you put on Financial Reporting and Analysis because that was a huge part of the test this year."

Comment:

This is a violation of Standard VII(A). Candidates are not permitted to disclose the relative weighting of topics on the exam.

Example 7:

A candidate tells his mother, "There was an item set on the CFA exam on the Residual Income Model that just kicked my butt."

Comment:

This is a violation of Standard VII(A). Candidates are not permitted to disclose specific topics tested on the exam.

> **VII(B) Reference to CFA Institute, the CFA Designation, and the CFA Program.**
>
> When referring to CFA Institute, CFA Institute membership, the CFA designation, or candidacy in the CFA Program, Members and Candidates must not misrepresent or exaggerate the meaning or implications of membership in CFA Institute, holding the CFA designation, or candidacy in the CFA Program.

Guidance

Members must not make promotional promises or guarantees tied to the CFA designation. Do not:

- Over-promise individual competence.
- Over-promise investment results in the future (i.e., higher performance, less risk, etc.).

Guidance—CFA Institute Membership

Members must satisfy these requirements to maintain membership:

- Sign PCS annually.
- Pay CFA Institute membership dues annually.

If they fail to do this, they are no longer active members.

Guidance—Using the CFA Designation

Do not misrepresent or exaggerate the meaning of the designation. Use of the CFA designation by a charterholder is subject to terms of the annual Professional Conduct Statement Agreement.

Guidance—Referencing Candidacy in the CFA Program

There is no partial designation. It is acceptable to state that a candidate successfully completed the program in three years, if in fact he did, but claiming superior ability because of this is not permitted.

Recommended Procedures for Compliance

Make sure that members' and candidates' firms are aware of the proper references to a member's CFA designation or candidacy, as this is a common error.

Application of Standard VII(B) Reference to CFA Institute, the CFA Designation, and the CFA Program

Example 1:

An advertisement for AZ Investment Advisors states that all the firm's principals are CFA charterholders and all passed the three examinations on their first attempt. The advertisement prominently links this fact to the notion that AZ's mutual funds have achieved superior performance.

Comment:

AZ may state that all principals passed the three examinations on the first try as long as this statement is true and is not linked to performance or does not imply superior ability. Implying that (1) CFA charterholders achieve better investment results and (2) those who pass the exams on the first try may be more successful than those who do not violates Standard VII(B).

Example 2:

Five years after receiving his CFA charter, Louis Vasseur resigns his position as an investment analyst and spends the next two years traveling abroad. Because he is not actively engaged in the investment profession, he does not file a completed Professional Conduct Statement with CFA Institute and does not pay his CFA Institute membership dues. At the conclusion of his travels, Vasseur becomes a self-employed analyst, accepting assignments as an independent contractor. Without reinstating his CFA Institute membership by filing his Professional Conduct Statement and paying his dues, he prints business cards that display "CFA" after his name.

Comment:

Vasseur has violated Standard VII(B) because Vasseur's right to use the CFA designation was suspended when he failed to file his Professional Conduct Statement and stopped paying dues. Therefore, he no longer is able to state or imply that he is an active CFA charterholder. When Vasseur files his Professional Conduct Statement and resumes paying CFA Institute dues to activate his membership, he will be eligible to use the CFA designation upon satisfactory completion of CFA Institute reinstatement procedures.

Example 3:

A member still uses the initials CFA after his name even though his membership has been suspended for not paying dues and for not submitting a personal conduct statement as required.

Comment:

This is a violation of the Standard.

Example 4:

A member puts the CFA logo on his letterhead, his business cards, and the company letterhead.

Comment:

By putting the logo on the company letterhead (rather than the letterhead or business card of an individual who is a CFA charterholder), the member has violated the Standard.

Example 5:

A member maintains an online account on a popular internet forum using the name "Old_CFA_Charterholder." The member is not otherwise identified in the forum.

Comment:

This use of the designation violates the Standard because the name hides the member's identity.

MODULE QUIZ 2.10

To best evaluate your performance, enter your quiz answers online.

1. Paula Osgood, CFA, is promoting her new money management firm by issuing an advertisement. Which of these items is *least likely* a violation of the professional designation Standard? The advertisement states that:
   A. she passed three exams covering ethics, financial statement analysis, asset valuation, and portfolio management, and that she is a member of the local society. Osgood signs the advertisement followed by the letters CFA in oversized and bold strike letters.
   B. she passed three 6-hour exams on her first attempts over the minimum period of one and a half years. Knowledge tested included ethics, financial statement analysis, asset valuation, and portfolio management. In addition, she is a member of the local society.
   C. because of her extensive CFA training, she will be able to achieve better investment results than non-CFA managers since she is one of very few professionals to have been awarded this designation.

2. Frist Investments, Inc. has just hired Michael Pulin to manage institutional portfolios, most of which are pension related. Pulin has just taken the Level III CFA Program exam and is awaiting his results. Pulin has more than 15 years of investment management experience with individual clients but has never managed an institutional portfolio. Pulin joined the CFA Institute as an affiliate member two years ago and is in good standing with the organization. Which of the following statements would be *most appropriate* for Frist to use in advertising Pulin as a new member of the firm? Pulin:
   A. has many years of investment experience which, along with his participation in the CFA program, will allow him to deliver superior investment performance relative to other managers.
   B. is a CFA Level III and passed the first two exams on the first attempt. He is an affiliate member of the CFA Institute. We expect him to become a regular member if he passes the Level III examination.
   C. is a Level III CFA candidate and has many years of excellent performance in the investment management industry. Pulin is an affiliate member of the CFA Institute and will be eligible to become a CFA charterholder and regular member if he passes the Level III CFA Program exam.

3. Samantha Donovan, CFA, is an exam proctor for the Level II CFA Program exam. The day before the exam is to be administered, Donovan faxes a copy of one of the questions to two friends, James Smythe and Lynn Yeats, who are Level II candidates in the CFA program. Donovan, Smythe, and Yeats had planned the distribution of an exam question months in advance. Smythe used the fax to prepare for the exam. Yeats, however, had second thoughts and threw the fax away without looking at its contents. Which of the following statements is *most likely* correct?
   A. Smythe violated the Code and Standards, but Yeats did not.
   B. Donovan violated the Code and Standards, but Smythe did not.
   C. Donovan and Yeats both violated the Code and Standards.

4. After sitting for the Level I CFA exam, Cynthia White goes to Internet discussion site *CFA Haven* to express her frustration. White writes, "CFA Institute is not doing a competent job of evaluating candidates, because none of the questions in the June exam touched on Alternative Investments." White *most likely* violated the Standard related to conduct as a candidate in the CFA program by:
   A. publicly disputing CFA Institute policies and procedures.
   B. disclosing subject matter covered or not covered on a CFA exam.
   C. participating in an internet forum that is directed toward CFA Program participants.

5. After passing all three levels of the CFA Program examinations on her first attempts and being awarded her CFA Charter, Paula Osgood is promoting her new money management firm by issuing an advertisement. Which of these statements would *most likely* violate the Standard related to use of the CFA designation?
   A. "To earn the right to use the CFA designation, Paula passed three exams covering ethics, financial statement analysis, asset valuation, and portfolio management."
   B. "Paula passed three 6-hour exams on her first attempts and is a member of her local investment analyst society."
   C. "Because of her extensive training, Paula will be able to achieve better investment results than managers who have not been awarded the CFA designation."

KEY CONCEPTS

LOS 1.a, LOS 1.b

Members of CFA Institute (including CFA charterholders) and candidates for the CFA designation ("Members and Candidates") must:[4]

- Act with integrity, competence, diligence, and respect, and in an ethical manner with the public, clients, prospective clients, employers, employees, colleagues in the investment profession, and other participants in the global capital markets.
- Place the integrity of the investment profession and the interests of clients above their own personal interests.
- Use reasonable care and exercise independent professional judgment when conducting investment analysis, making investment recommendations, taking investment actions, and engaging in other professional activities.
- Practice and encourage others to practice in a professional and ethical manner that will reflect credit on themselves and the profession.
- Promote the integrity and viability of the global capital markets for the ultimate benefit of society.
- Maintain and improve their professional competence and strive to maintain and improve the competence of other investment professionals.

The Standards of Professional Conduct are organized into seven standards:

I. Professionalism

II. Integrity of Capital Markets

III. Duties to Clients

IV. Duties to Employers

V. Investment Analysis, Recommendations, and Action

VI. Conflicts of Interest

VII. Responsibilities as a CFA Institute Member or CFA Candidate

4. Copyright 2014, CFA Institute. Reproduced and republished from "The Code of Ethics," from *Standards of Practice Handbook, 11th Ed.*, 2014, with permission from CFA Institute. All rights reserved.

ANSWER KEY FOR MODULE QUIZZES

Module Quiz 1.1, 2.1

1. **C** According to Standard I(A), informing her supervisor or firm's compliance department is appropriate. Dissociating herself would be premature. She should report her suspicions to a supervisory person and attempt to remedy the situation. (Module 2.1, LOS 2: I(A))

2. **B** According to Standard I(A), since she has taken steps to stop the illegal activities and the board has ignored her, Jones must dissociate from the board and seek legal advice as to what other actions would be appropriate in this instance. She may need to inform legal or regulatory authorities of the illegal activities. (Module 2.1, LOS 2: I(A))

3. **C** According to Standard I(A), in some instances, reporting a legal violation to governmental or regulatory officials may be appropriate, but this isn't always necessary, and it isn't required under Standard I(A). (Module 2.1, LOS 2: I(A))

4. **A** Standard I(B), Independence and Objectivity, requires that members and candidates reject offers of gifts or compensation that could compromise their independence or objectivity. Schleifer has appropriately rejected the offer of the hotel accommodations and the use of ChemCo's jet. He may accept the desk clock since this gift is of nominal value and is unlikely to compromise his independence and objectivity. Schleifer cannot accept the tickets to the dinner, however. Since it is a formal high-society dinner, the tickets are most likely expensive or difficult to come by. Even though he has disclosed the gift to his employer and he plans to use the dinner as a marketing opportunity for his firm, the gift itself may influence Schliefer's future research in favor of ChemCo. Allowing such potential influence is a violation of Standard I(B). (Module 2.1, LOS 2: I(B))

5. **C** Standard I(B) recommends, but does not require, that an analyst have his firm pay for ordinary travel expenses to visit companies that are the subject of research. The other choices are required by the Standards. (Module 2.1, LOS 2: I(B))

Module Quiz 2.2

1. **A** Hutchins's personal bankruptcy may reflect poorly on her professional reputation if it resulted from fraudulent or deceitful business activities. There is no indication of this, however, and the bankruptcy is thus not a violation. Smith has not violated the Code and Standards by refusing to invest with Hutchins in what turned out to be bad investment opportunities. By reporting Smith to CFA Institute for a violation, Hutchins has misused the Professional Conduct Program to settle a dispute unrelated to professional ethics and has thus violated Standard I(D), Misconduct. (LOS 2: I(D))

2. **B** According to Standard I(C), Misrepresentation, factual data from a recognized statistical reporting service need not be cited. (LOS 2: I(C))

3. **B** In the other choices, Olson violates Standard I(C) by misrepresentating the services that she or her firm are capable of performing, her qualifications, her academic or professional credentials, or the firm's credentials. The firm is small and most likely cannot perform all investment services the client may require. The firm cannot guarantee future outperformance of the market indexes. The firm doesn't have a long history (only six months). (LOS 2: I(C))

4. **C** There can be no assurance that a premium of 2% to 4% will consistently be obtained. Bixby is in violation of Standard I(C), Misrepresentation, since she has made an implicit guarantee of the fund's expected performance. (LOS 2: I(C))

5. **C** Since the statements are vague, we have no direct evidence that a violation of securities law has occurred. However, under Standard I(D), Misconduct, members and candidates are prohibited from engaging in activities involving deceit. Karloff's action is a clear attempt to mislead the investing public regarding the value of Summit IPOs. (LOS 2: I(D))

Module Quiz 2.3

1. **C** According to Standard II(A), members and candidates are under no circumstances allowed to use material nonpublic information to trade securities. Carlson must abide by the Code and Standards, which is the most strict regulation in the scenario. (LOS 2: II(A))

2. **B** The intent of Green Brothers' actions is to manipulate market liquidity in order to attract investment to its own funds. The increased trading activity was not based on market fundamentals or an actual trading strategy to benefit investors. It was merely an attempt to mislead market participants in order to increase assets under Green Brothers' management. The action violates Standard II(B), Market Manipulation. (LOS 2: II(B))

3. **A** Quigley's trades are most likely an attempt to take advantage of an arbitrage opportunity that exists between Craeger's common stock and its put options. She is not manipulating the prices of securities in an attempt to mislead market participants, which would violate Standard II(B), Market Manipulation. She is pursuing a legitimate investment strategy. Participants in her hedge fund are aware of the fund's investment strategy, and thus Quigley did not violate the Code and Standards by not disclosing this specific set of trades in advance of trading. (LOS 2: II(B))

4. **A** There is no indication that Servais has inside information pertaining to the situation at the five firms in question—only the two firms that have already gone public with the information. It is common knowledge that the other five firms follow the same boron handing procedures. She is, therefore, in compliance with Standard II(A) concerning the use of material nonpublic information in the issuance of the investment recommendation. (LOS 2: II(A))

5. **B** Even though the laws of Zanuatu would not preclude trading on the information, as a CFA Charterholder the friend is bound by the CFA Institute Code and Standards. Standard II(A) prohibits the use of material nonpublic information, and the friend may not trade the stocks about which she has such information under any circumstances. (LOS 2: II(A))

6. **B** The release of such information to a limited circle via an Internet chat room does not cause the information to be public. The information is also clearly material. Therefore, Green is not allowed to trade on the information under Standard II(A). (LOS 2: II(A))

7. **B** NV management is asking Hunter to violate Standard II(B), Market Manipulation, which prohibits taking actions that are designed to distort prices or artificially increase trading volume. The intent of Hunter's actions is to mislead market participants and allow corporate insiders to take advantage of the artificially high prices. (LOS 2: II(B))

Module Quiz 2.4

1. **B** Standard III(A), Loyalty, Prudence, and Care. Herbst is acting as a fiduciary for the pension plan beneficiaries. Choosing brokers based on quality of services provided is reasonable. She may pay higher-than-average brokerage fees so long as doing so benefits the pension beneficiaries, not other clients. Trading with selected brokers solely to gain referrals is not likely to be in the pension beneficiaries' best interest since it does not take into account other important factors for selecting brokerage firms. (LOS 2: III(A))

Module Quiz 2.5

1. **B** Standard III(C), Suitability, requires that before taking investment action, members and candidates must make a reasonable inquiry into a client's or prospect's investment objectives and constraints as well as their prior investment experience. Byrne cannot assume that because the brothers have similar lifestyles and are close in age that they should have similarly managed portfolios. Byrne should have interviewed Cliff directly before investing his portfolio. (LOS 2: III(C))

2. **B** According to Standard III(C), Ellis must consider the suitability of each new investment (as well as the current holdings) in light of the portfolio mandate. In this given case, the client is the fund. Ellis must only make investments that are in accordance with the fund's investment policy statement. Therefore, Ellis should not purchase the unsuitable bonds as requested by her clients. (LOS 2: III(C))

3. **C** Standard III(B), Fair Dealing, requires that members not selectively disadvantage clients, specifically in the case of IPOs. Disclosure of an inequitable allocation method does not relieve the member of his obligation to fair dealing. (LOS 2: III(B))

Module Quiz 2.6

1. **B** By failing to include terminated portfolios in the performance presentation, the performance will have an inherent upward bias, making results appear better than they truly are. By excluding the terminated portfolios, DNR misleads its potential investors and thus violates Standard III(D), Performance Presentation, which prohibits any "practice that would lead to misrepresentation of a member or candidate's performance record." (LOS 2: III(D))

2. **A** Anderson must maintain the confidentiality of client information according to Standard III(E). Confidentiality may be broken in instances involving illegal activities on the part of the client, but the client's information may only be relayed to proper authorities. Anderson did not have the right to inform the investment bank of her client's investigation. (LOS 2: III(E))

3. **B** The recommended procedure in Standard III(D), Performance Presentation, is to present the performance of a composite as a weighted average of the performance of similar portfolios rather than using a single representative account. (LOS 2: III(D))

Module Quiz 2.7

1. **C** According to Standard IV(A), Loyalty, members and candidates are expected to act for the benefit of the employer and not deprive the employer of their skills. Fletcher is performing work similar to the services that her employer provides for a fee. Although the position is a volunteer position, Fletcher will receive compensation in the form of a free parking space. In light of the circumstances, Fletcher must disclose the details of the position and get written permission before accepting the volunteer position. (LOS 2: IV(A))

2. **C** According to Standard IV(C), Responsibilities of Supervisors, reporting the violation and warning the employee to cease activities that violate the law or the Code and Standards are not enough. The supervisor must take steps (such as limiting employee activity or increasing the level of employee monitoring) to prevent further violations while he conducts an investigation. (LOS 2: IV(C))

3. **C** According to Standard IV(C), because he is aware that the firm's compliance procedures are not being monitored and followed and because he has repeatedly tried to get company management to correct the situation, Blair should decline supervisory responsibility until adequate procedures to detect and prevent violations of laws, regulations, and the Code and Standards are adopted and followed. If he does not do so, he will be in violation of the Code and Standards. (LOS 2: IV(C))

4. **B** Jamal failed to properly supervise employees and provide adequate procedures and policies to prevent employee violations. Smith should not have traded her own account ahead of client accounts. Temple should not

have disclosed the recommendation change selectively but should have informed his clients fairly and objectively. No inside information was used in the question. (LOS 2: IV(C))

5. **A** Albright may accept work for which she receives outside compensation and which may compete with her employer only if she obtains her employer's consent. Under Standard IV(A), Loyalty, such consent must be obtained from her employer prior to beginning the work. (LOS 2: IV(A))

Module Quiz 2.8

1. **A** Historical growth can be cited as a fact since it actually happened. Stefano states that her firm expects further growth and profitability, which is an opinion. She does not claim that these are facts. In addition, Stefano identifies relevant factors and highlights in particular the most significant risks of investing in South American utilities. She has fully complied with Standard V(B), Communication with Clients and Prospective Clients. Under the Standard, it is not necessary to include every detail about a potential investment in a report. Members and candidates are expected to use their judgment and identify the most important factors to include. (LOS 2: V(B))

2. **A** Choice B is not necessarily a violation. Firms can offer different levels of service to clients as long as this is disclosed to all clients. The largest institutional clients would likely be paying higher fees for a greater level of service. Also note that the analyst's brother's account in choice C should be treated the same as any other client account. (LOS 2: V(B))

3. **A** Nieder must not take models or documents from his previous employer without explicit permission to do so, or he would violate Standard IV(A), Loyalty. He is allowed, however, to reproduce the model from memory but must recreate the supporting documentation to maintain compliance with Standard V(C), Record Retention. (LOS 2: V(A))

4. **B** Johnson has apparently let his recreational passion cloud his judgment. This is not to say that Swordfish Enterprises is not or will not be an excellent investment. However, if he had never heard of the firm previously, issuing an investment recommendation without conducting a thorough financial investigation indicates a failure to exercise diligence and also indicates that he lacks a reasonable and adequate basis for his recommendation. He is in violation of Standard V(A). (LOS 2: V(A))

5. **C** It is required under Standard V(A), Diligence and Reasonable Basis, that third-party research assumptions be reviewed and both the independence and objectivity of the research and recommendations be evaluated. The other choices are recommended policies and procedures under the Standard. (LOS 2: V(A))

Module Quiz 2.9

1. **C** Members and candidates must give clients adequate opportunity to act on new or changed recommendations before taking investment action in their own non-firm accounts or other non-client accounts in which they have a beneficial interest. One week is likely an acceptable waiting period. (LOS 2: VI(B))

2. **C** According to Standard VI(C), Referral Fees, Hern must disclose the referral arrangement between itself and Baker so that potential clients can judge the true cost of Hern's services and assess whether there is any partiality inherent in the recommendation of services. (LOS 2: VI(C))

3. **A** There is no violation of the CFA Institute Standards regarding this matter. The referral arrangement is fully disclosed to clients before they agree to do business with Pick. Therefore, clients can fully assess the effect of the agreement on the referral and how the agreement may affect their accounts before hiring Pick as their asset manager. (LOS 2: VI(C))

4. **C** Even though the shares are held in trust, this could still be construed as a conflict of interest. Lyons is obligated under Standard VI(A), Disclosure of Conflicts, to inform his employer of the potential conflict. If he is then authorized to issue investment recommendations on the security in question, the existence of a potential conflict must be disclosed in the report. (LOS 2: VI(A))

Module Quiz 2.10

1. **B** According to Standard VII(B), any explanation of the designation in print form should be a concise description of the requirements or of CFA Institute. The other statements contain violations of Standard VII(B), in particular the presentation of the letters CFA. Also, she may not imply superior performance as a result of being a CFA charterholder. (LOS 2: VII(B))

2. **C** Standard VII(B) governs acceptable methods of referencing the CFA Institute, CFA designation, and CFA Program. Candidates may reference their candidacy if they are enrolled for or waiting for the results of, a CFA Program exam. Pulin may also reference his membership status with the CFA Institute as well as his remaining eligibility requirements to become a CFA charterholder. (LOS 2: VII(B))

3. **C** In this situation, Donovan, Smythe, and Yeats all violated Standard VII(A), Conduct as Members and Candidates in the CFA Program. The Standard prohibits conduct that compromises the integrity, validity, or security of the CFA Program exams. Donovan clearly breached the exam security. Smythe and Yeats both compromised the integrity of the exams by planning to use the actual exam question to gain an advantage over other candidates. Even though Yeats did not ultimately use the information to study for the exam, she participated in a scheme to cheat on the CFA Program exam. (LOS 2: II(A))

4. **B** Standard VII(A) Conduct as Members and Candidates in the CFA Program prohibits candidates from revealing which portions of the Candidate Body of Knowledge were or were not covered on an exam. Members and candidates are free to disagree with the policies, procedures, or positions taken by the CFA Institute. The Standard does not prohibit participating in CFA Program-related Internet blogs, forums, or social networks. (LOS 2: VII(A))

5. **C** Standard VII(B) Reference to CFA Institute, the CFA Designation, and the CFA Program prohibits members and candidates from implying superior performance as a result of being a CFA charterholder. Concise factual descriptions of the requirements to obtain the CFA Charter are acceptable. Osgood's statement that she passed the exams on her first attempts is acceptable because it states a fact. (LOS 2: VII(B))

The following is a review of the Ethical and Professional Standards (2) principles designed to address the learning outcome statements set forth by CFA Institute. Cross-Reference to CFA Institute Assigned Reading #3.

READING 3 Application of The Code and Standards

Study Session 2

EXAM FOCUS

The cases discussed here introduce you to the obligations CFA Institute members and CFA® charterholders and candidates have under the Code and Standards. These cases will give you a sense of the types of scenarios you are likely to encounter on the Level II exam. The particulars of any case are not important in terms of test questions. However, understanding how to analyze a case and having the ability to recommend procedures to bring an illustrative firm into compliance are crucial to your success on the ethics portion of the exam.

MODULE 3.1: ETHICS CASE STUDIES

Video covering this content is available online.

LOS 3.a: Evaluate policies and practices for a firm and an individual in relation to the CFA Institute Code of Ethics and Standards of Professional Conduct.

LOS 3.b: Explain the appropriate action to take in response to conduct that violates the CFA Institute Code of Ethics and Standards of Professional Conduct.

CFA® Program Curriculum, Volume 1, page 207

1. EDVARD STARK CASE OUTLINE

The main facts of the Edvard Stark case are as follows:

- Edvard Stark, CFA, a private client adviser for Eyearne Bank, manages a globally diversified portfolio for client accounts. Stark also advises clients on their outside holdings, thereby developing strong relationships with them.

- Stark starts research into cryptocurrencies and realizes that competitive pressures make mining established digital currencies very difficult. Stark settles on Meerine, a newer cryptocurrency. To limit his risk of being wrong, he recommends Meerine to a few of his smallest clients with an initial recommended allocation of 1% of portfolio.
- After attending several conferences, Stark starts mining Meerine using his home computer without informing his employer.
- Stark realizes that the trading volume is low and volatility high for Meerine but is confident about its prospects. Meerine price appreciates since his 1% recommendation. Stark then recommended a 3% portfolio allocation to Meerine to all clients.
- In subsequent client review meetings, Stark shares the performance of Meerine, its low correlation with stocks and bonds, and discloses his mining activity. Stark offers to sell Meerine out of his own account to the firm's larger clients.

CASE RESULTS

Standard III(B) Duties to Clients: Fair Dealing

All clients should be treated fairly when taking investment actions and offering advice. Offering different levels of service is not a violation as long as it does not disadvantage a client group and is disclosed.

Violations of Standard III(B):

- It is not acceptable for Stark to fill orders of larger clients from his personal account.

Actions required to prevent these violations:

- Collect orders from all clients and fill the orders (if suitable) pro rata or not offer to sell to anybody from his personal account.

Standard III(C) Duties to Clients: Suitability

Investment actions on behalf of the client and investment advice provided to a client must be consistent with client's goals and constraints.

Violations of Standard III(C):

- Even though Stark has evaluated the risk-reduction benefit of Meerine, blanket 3% allocation may not be suitable for every client.
- The initial 1% allocation recommendation to the smallest client was driven by using those clients as "guinea pigs" (if things don't work out, Stark's and the bank's reputations would be less tarnished) and not based on suitability for those clients.

Actions required to prevent these violations:

- Properly assess the client's circumstances (including goals and constraints) to determine for which client an investment in Meerine is appropriate and, if so, what an appropriate level of investment should be for that client.

Standard IV(B) Duties to Employer: Additional Compensation Arrangements

Cryptocurrencies compete with banks for transaction completion services. Stark's mining of Meerine (even on his own computer) might conflict with Eyearne Bank's interest.

Violations of Standard IV(B):

- Failing to inform the employer before engaging in mining activities.

Actions required to prevent these violations:

- Stark should disclose to a supervisor or compliance officer of his intent to mine Meerine, what his potential earnings would be from this activity, and obtain a written permission before mining.

Standard V(A) Investment Analysis, Recommendations, and Actions: Diligence and Reasonable Basis

Even though Stark has researched Meerine, this initial recommendation to the smallest clients is not grounded in reasonable basis.

Violations of Standard V(A):

- Stark's evaluation of cryptocurrencies and Meerine in particular was not thorough.

Actions required to prevent these violations:

- Stark should document his research into Meerine, the drivers of its value, and clients for which it would be suitable.

Standard VI(A) Conflicts of Interest: Disclosure of Conflicts

Stark must disclose all conflicts of interest that could reasonably be expected to impair his independence and objectivity.

Violations of Standard VI(A):

- Stark recommending an investment with limited liquidity which he holds in his personal account would reasonably be construed as a conflict of interest. Not disclosing this conflict would be a violation of Standard VI(A).
- Stark only reveals his mining activities in client meetings *after* his 3% recommendation is made to all clients.

Actions required to prevent these violations:

- Stark should disclose the conflict created by his recommendation of Meerine to his clients and his employer which he is mining and currently holds in his personal portfolio.

2. SUBATH AGARWAY CASE OUTLINE

The main facts of the Subath Agarway case are as follows:

- Subath Agarway, CFA, recently joined CrowdWisdom as VP of due diligence. CrowdWisdom is a young, online crowdfunding company that matches venture capital investors with startups seeking capital. Fee paying applicants that satisfy CrowdWisdom's due diligence would be listed on their platform and made available to all the investors that are members of the platform.
- The founders of CrowdWisdom want to grow rapidly and want to recruit the customers of startups as potential member investors on their platform. Additionally, they created an investment club comprising those members that were very active investors on the platform. Members of the investment club received a market intelligence report in addition to generally available applicant information.
- Agarway's due diligence process includes several screens that he has successfully tested at his previous job, where he personally invested in several startups. These screens include size of the startup's potential market, accounting policies, interviews with company executives, etc.
- One of the most promising companies that passed Agarway's screen is Deko, an IT startup with impressive founders, attractive prospects, and a unique product. Deko's target customer base is pre-teens and teenagers. The company's strategy calls for soliciting investment from customers via emails. Emails specify that the investors have to be adults over the age of 18.
- Over time, Agarway's stack of applications to be reviewed grows over 300 and the founders are pressuring to have 10% acceptance rate. Agarway explains that there are time constraints in reviewing applications. Founders also recommend that two specific applicants that they met at a conference be accepted.

CASE RESULTS

Standard I(A) Professionalism: Knowledge of Law

- Members and candidates should understand and comply with all applicable laws and regulations.

Violations of Standard I(A):

- It may not be legal in many jurisdictions to solicit investments from teenagers even if the solicitations specify that it is for adults only.
- Additionally, it may be illegal in many jurisdictions to collect information about minors without the permission of their parents. Sharing of information is further governed by various privacy laws that need to be carefully evaluated.

Actions required to prevent these violations:

- Agarway needs to ensure that Deko is in compliance with all applicable laws and regulations.

Standard VI(A) Conflict of Interest: Disclosure

- Members and candidates are required to disclose all conflicts of interest that could reasonably be expected to impair their independence and objectivity.

Violations of Standard VI(A):

- Preferential access of market intelligence to members of the investment club may disadvantage other investors.
- Agarway's personal investments may be competing with potential startup applicants creating a conflict of interest.

Actions required to prevent these violations:

- Agarway's personal investments that compete with prospects as well as the preferential access to market intelligence to members of the investment club need to be disclosed to all investors.

3. PETER SHERMAN CASE OUTLINE

The main facts of the Peter Sherman case are as follows:

- Peter Sherman, CFA, was employed for five years with Pearl Investment Management as an emerging markets analyst. While he was at Pearl, he developed outside consulting positions with several Latin American companies. This outside consulting activity was disclosed to Pearl. Sherman recently switched firms and is now employed by the Glenarm Company.
- Glenarm is a small investment management firm that has been investigated, censured, and fined by the SEC for securities violations. Glenarm's partners are eager to repair the firm's reputation and hoped that hiring a CFA charterholder would help retain current clients and bring in new business.
- Before joining the firm, Glenarm asked Sherman to solicit current and prospective Pearl clients. Glenarm offered Sherman a large stake in the first-year investment management fees of any Pearl clients that Sherman could bring to Glenarm.
- While still employed at Pearl, Sherman visited socially with several Pearl clients in an attempt to woo them away from Pearl. He also contacted potential Pearl clients that Pearl has been actively soliciting. He even contacted some clients that Pearl had rejected.
- As he left Pearl, Sherman took the following items with him to his new job:
  - Pearl marketing presentations.
  - Computer stock selection models that he developed.
  - Research materials.
  - News articles on firms that he had been following.
  - A list of research ideas that were rejected by Pearl.

CASE RESULTS

Standard IV(A) Duties to Employers: Loyalty

It is acceptable for Sherman to contact prospects that Pearl decided not to pursue because of a particular size or investment objective while he is still employed at Pearl.

Violations of Standard IV(A):

- It is not acceptable for Sherman to contact Pearl's clients and potential clients (even if it is done "after hours"). Solicitation of these clients would be detrimental to Pearl's business. Sherman has an obligation to act in Pearl's best interest while still an employee of Pearl.
- Unless the employer consents, departing employees may not misappropriate property. All of the items Sherman took are the property of Pearl and there is a violation.

PROFESSOR'S NOTE

Members and Candidates must always act for the benefit of the employer. By taking confidential information and soliciting clients and prospects to benefit Glenarm, Sherman has harmed his old employer, Pearl, and is in violation of his duty of loyalty. Sherman must act in the "old" employer's best interest while still employed there.

Actions required to prevent these violations:

- Sherman should not solicit Pearl's clients or prospects until he leaves Pearl's employment.
- Sherman should not have taken Pearl property.

Standard IV(B) Duties to Employers: Additional Compensation Arrangements

Violations of Standard IV(B):

- Sherman did not disclose his consulting arrangements to Glenarm.

Actions required to prevent these violations:

- Sherman should disclose his consulting arrangements to Glenarm.

Standard VI(A) Disclosure of Conflicts, and Standard I(B) Independence and Objectivity

Violations of Standards VI(A) and I(B):

- The consulting arrangements had the potential to affect Sherman's independence and objectivity.
- Disclosures must be prominent and delivered in plain language.

Actions required to prevent these violations:

- Sherman must disclose all details about outside compensation to Glenarm and obtain written permission from Glenarm in advance of entering into any such arrangements.

4. PRESTON PARTNERS CASE OUTLINE

The following statements summarize the main facts of the Preston Partners case:

- Sheldon Preston, CFA, is president of Preston Partners. Preston Partners is a midsize investment management firm that specializes in managing large-cap portfolios for individuals and pension funds. CFA Institute's Code and Standards have been adopted as part of Preston's compliance manual.
- Preston wrote the firm's compliance manual but did a cursory job because he was in a hurry. A copy of the manual was provided to all employees upon joining the firm.
- During his daily review of Preston Partner trades, Preston found that Gerald Smithson, CFA, had added the stocks of Utah BioChemical Co. and Norgood PLC to all his clients' portfolios.
- Preston Partners manages Utah BioChemical's pension fund. In addition, the president and CEO of Utah BioChemical, Arne Okapuu, has Smithson manage his personal portfolio. Smithson and Okapuu have had a long-term business relationship.
- Smithson was vacationing in London and had seen Okapuu and the chairman of Norgood talking at a restaurant. Smithson contacted an analyst that he knew in London, Andrew Jones, and requested information on Norgood. Jones's latest research report had placed a "hold" recommendation on Norgood stock.
- Norgood is an aggressive investment and Utah BioChemical is a conservative investment.
- Smithson performed a complete analysis of the biotech industry, Norgood, and Utah BioChemical. Based on his analysis and the fact that he saw Okapuu and Norgood's chairman talking, he deduced that a merger between the two firms was possible.
- Smithson ordered block trades of 50,000 shares for each firm. The firm's compliance manual was vague on the proper allocation of shares from a block trade. Smithson decided to allocate shares based on the size of the client's account, with the largest clients receiving their shares first at the most favorable prices. Also, the needs and constraints of Smithson's clients vary widely.
- Utah BioChemical and Norgood announced that they were merging. The share price of both firms increased by 40%.

CASE RESULTS

In researching and making client investment decisions, Smithson complied with Standard V(A) Diligence and Reasonable Basis. Furthermore, Smithson did not possess or act on insider information. What he learned was assembled through the "mosaic" theory.

However, Smithson did not comply with portions of the Standards relating to suitability of investments for clients and trade allocations. Preston failed to properly exercise his supervisory responsibility.

Standard III(C) Duties to Clients: Suitability

Violations of Standard III(C):

- Smithson should have considered clients' individual risk tolerances, needs, circumstances, and goals; he should have also better matched clients with investments. Norgood is too volatile for many clients' accounts.

Actions required to prevent this violation:

- Be sure that Smithson's clients have written investment objectives and policy statements.
- For accounts which contain unsuitable investments, the shares should be sold, and Preston Partners should reimburse any loss.

Standard III(B) Duties to Clients: Fair Dealing

Violations of Standard III(B):

- The firm had no clear procedures for allocating block trades to client accounts. Large accounts were favored, disadvantaging smaller accounts.

Actions required to prevent this violation:

- Detailed guidelines covering block trades must be prepared, emphasizing fairness to clients, timely executions, and accuracy.

Standard IV(C) Duties to Employers: Responsibilities of Supervisors

Violations of Standard IV(C):

- The senior management at Preston Partners should have made reasonable efforts to identify and prevent violations of applicable laws, rules, and regulations. A compliance program should have been in place.
- Supervisors and managers have the responsibility of training, distributing a policies and procedures manual, and providing refresher courses.

Actions required to prevent these violations:

- Preston must have proper procedures established that would have prevented violations such as those that occurred.
- A compliance officer should be designated.

5. SUPER SELECTION CASE OUTLINE

The main facts of the Super Selection case are as follows:

- Patricia Cuff is the CFO and compliance officer for Super Selection Investment Advisors. Cuff is also a member of the CFA Institute. The CFA Institute's Standards of Practice have been incorporated into Super Selection's compliance manual.
- Karen Trader is a portfolio manager with Super Selection. She has recently purchased shares of Atlantis Medical Devices (AMD) for all of her clients' portfolios. AMD is a rapidly growing biotech firm.
- Trader's friend, Josey James, is president of AMD. James has been providing advice to Trader regarding the viability of certain biotech firms over the past few years. Trader has taken advantage of this advice for both her personal account and her clients' portfolios. In many cases, she has placed personal trades before trading for her clients. Trader's personal brokerage statements had not been submitted to Cuff until recently.
- Several years ago, James asked Trader to serve as an outside director for AMD. She was paid with AMD stock options that at the time had no value. AMD earnings and sales are up and AMD directors recently voted to take the firm public via an initial public offering. AMD also began paying directors $5,000 per year. Trader stands to gain considerably by exercising her stock options.
- By the time the offering was to go public, the initial public offering (IPO) market had soured considerably. James called Trader to ask if she could commit to the purchase of a block of AMD shares for her client accounts. Trader had previously determined that AMD shares were not a good investment for her clients—but she changed her mind on the recommendation of James and purchased a considerable amount of AMD stock for her clients.

CASE RESULTS

Several Code and Standard violations are evident relating to Trader's involvement with an outside firm. Although she is not a CFA charterholder or member, she is bound by the CFA Institute Code and Standards to the extent that they are a part of her own company's compliance procedures.

Standard IV(C) Duties to Employers: Responsibilities of Supervisors

The presumption is that Cuff is the "supervisor" and thus must comply with this standard. Cuff has the responsibility to take steps to prevent violations, and as compliance officer she should see that the firm's compliance procedures are adhered to by employees. Any violations must be addressed.

Actions required to prevent these violations:

- Cuff must take prompt action to correct violations by reporting the violations to the appropriate members of senior management.

- Cuff is a compliance officer and must monitor Trader's personal trades and impose sanctions when necessary.
- If the senior management does not back up Cuff, other options include disclosing the incident to the Board or the regulators, and even resigning from the firm.

Standard VI(A) Disclosure of Conflicts

Violations of Standard VI(A):

- Trader failed to disclose ownership of AMD stock options and the compensation she received as a director of AMD.

Actions required to prevent this violation:

- As a supervisor, Cuff must take action to ensure disclosure and, if necessary, limit behavior and impose sanctions.

Standard V(A) Diligence and Reasonable Basis

Violations of Standard V(A):

- Trader determined AMD was not a suitable security for her clients. Trader was pressured by James and reversed positions; thus, the AMD stock was purchased.

Actions required to prevent this violation:

- Trader should have conducted due diligence and thorough research before making an investment decision for clients' accounts. Any change in opinion must have a reasonable basis. Trader must also inform clients of any AMD conflicts such as directorship and stock options.
- The compliance officer, Cuff, should review investment actions taken for clients at least annually.

Standard III(A) Duties to Clients: Loyalty, Prudence, and Care

Violations of Standard III(A):

- The fiduciary duty to clients was violated. Remember that client interests always come first.

Actions required to prevent this violation:

- Trader should have taken any investment action for the sole benefit of her clients. Cuff must completely investigate Trader's activities to determine other fiduciary breaches. Following any fiduciary breaches, wrongdoers must have their activities limited.

Standard III(C) Duties to Clients: Suitability

Violations of Standard III(C):

- AMD stock was purchased for clients without considering client needs and circumstances.

Actions required to prevent this violation:

- Trader should have considered clients' needs and circumstances instead of taking actions that benefited her personally.
- The compliance officer should establish at least an annual review to compare suitability of investment actions with investment policy statements.

Standard VI(B) Priority of Transactions

Violations of Standard VI(B):

- Trader violated this Standard by trading personally before trading for clients.

Actions required to prevent this violation:

- By not reporting trades and brokerage accounts, Trader failed to follow her firm's procedures. The compliance officer needs to fully investigate Trader's transactions and recommend proper sanctions.

The following is a review of the Ethical and Professional Standards (2) principles designed to address the learning outcome statements set forth by CFA Institute. Cross-Reference to CFA Institute Assigned Reading #4.

READING 4

Trade Allocation: Fair Dealing and Disclosure

Study Session 2

EXAM FOCUS

This topic review provides a brief summary of trade allocation procedures recently updated by the CFA Institute. The CFA Institute Code and Standards speak directly to the issue of trade allocation procedures because allocating trades among clients is an example of taking investment action. Under CFA Institute Standard III(B) Duties to Clients: Fair Dealing, "Members and Candidates must deal fairly and objectively with all clients when providing investment analysis, making investment recommendations, taking investment action, or engaging in other professional activities."

MODULE 4.1: TRADE ALLOCATION

Video covering this content is available online.

LOS 4.a: Evaluate trade allocation practices and determine whether they comply with the CFA Institute Standards of Professional Conduct addressing fair dealing and client loyalty.

CFA® Program Curriculum, Volume 1, page 229

The allocation of client trades on an ad hoc basis lends itself to two fundamental fairness problems:

- The allocation of trades may be based on *compensation arrangements*.
- The allocation of trades may be based on *client relationships* with the firm.

As far as compensation arrangements are concerned, an ad hoc allocation procedure gives rise to the temptation to allocate a disproportionate share of profitable trades to performance-based fee accounts. In addition to violating Standard III(B) Duties to Clients: Fair Dealing, this is a clear violation of Standard

III(A) Duties to Clients: Loyalty, Prudence, and Care because this has the effect of increasing fees paid to the investment adviser at the expense of asset-based fee accounts.

As far as the client relationship with the firm is concerned, an ad hoc allocation procedure gives rise to the temptation to allocate a disproportionate share of profitable trades to favored clients. In addition to violating the fair dealing standard, this is again a clear violation of Standard III(A) Duties to Clients: Loyalty, Prudence, and Care, which states that members owe a duty of loyalty to clients and requires them to put clients' interests above their own. Conflicts of interest should be avoided. Giving certain clients special access to attractive IPOs with the intent to receive future investment banking business or more fees creates a conflict and breaches the duty to clients.

LOS 4.b: Describe appropriate actions to take in response to trade allocation practices that do not adequately respect client interests.

CFA® Program Curriculum, Volume 1, page 230

Appropriate responses to inadequate trade allocation practices include the following:

- Get advanced indication of client interest regarding any new issues.
- Distribute new issues by client, not by portfolio manager.
- Have in place a fair and objective method for trade allocation, such as pro rata or a similar system.
- Be fair to clients regarding both execution of trades and price.
- Execute orders in a timely and efficient manner.
- Keep records and periodically review them to ensure that all clients are being treated equitably.

The following is a review of the Ethical and Professional Standards (2) principles designed to address the learning outcome statements set forth by CFA Institute. Cross-Reference to CFA Institute Assigned Reading #5.

READING 5

Changing Investment Objectives

Study Session 2

EXAM FOCUS

This topic review provides a brief summary of CFA Institute Standard III(C) Duties to Clients: Suitability. When entering into an advisory relationship with a client, the investment manager must inquire about the client's investing experience and investment objectives and constraints before taking any investment actions or making any recommendations. The actions and recommendations must be suitable to the client's situation and must be judged in the context of the entire portfolio. If the investment manager is managing a portfolio according to a specific style or mandate, the recommendations and investment actions must be consistent with the stated objectives and constraints of the specific portfolio.

MODULE 5.1: CHANGING INVESTMENT OBJECTIVES

Video covering this content is available online.

LOS 5.a: Evaluate the disclosure of investment objectives and basic policies and determine whether they comply with the CFA Institute Standards of Professional Conduct.

CFA® Program Curriculum, Volume 1, page 233

In the case of pooled client funds such as mutual funds, it is particularly important that the portfolio manager's recommendations and investment actions be consistent with the stated objectives and constraints of the fund. The security selection and portfolio construction processes are typically described in the fund's prospectus. *These processes are the key elements upon which the determination of appropriateness and suitability may be determined.* A material deviation from these processes, in the absence of approval from clients, constitutes a violation of CFA Institute

Standard III(C) Duties to Clients: Suitability. *The investment must fit within the mandate or within the realm of investments that are allowed according to the fund's disclosures.*

LOS 5.b: Describe appropriate actions needed to ensure adequate disclosure of the investment process.

CFA® Program Curriculum, Volume 1, page 233

To remain compliant with CFA Institute Standards, a portfolio manager must:

- Determine the client's financial situation, investment objectives, and level of investing expertise.
- Adequately disclose the basic security selection and portfolio construction processes.
- Conduct regular internal checks for compliance with these processes.
- Stick to the stated investment strategy if managing to a specific mandate or strategy.
- Notify investors and potential investors of any potential change in the security selection and portfolio construction processes and secure documentation of authorization for proposed changes.

TOPIC ASSESSMENT: ETHICAL AND PROFESSIONAL STANDARDS

You have now finished the Ethics topic section. The following topic assessment will provide immediate feedback on how effective your study of this material has been. The test is best taken timed; allow 3 minutes per subquestion (18 minutes per item set). This topic assessment is more exam-like than a typical module quiz or QBank questions. A score less than 70% suggests that additional review of this topic is needed.

Use the following information to answer Questions 1 through 6.

Lewis Smithers, CFA, is the lead portfolio manager for Fundamental Investments Corp., a money manager serving several hundred wealthy individual investors. He spent his morning reading several articles on Phoenix-based Pineda Canyon Development in real estate industry publications. He concluded that, while Pineda is a majority owner of several developers with huge portfolios of mountainside real estate perfect for the development of ski resorts, the company lacks the cash to build the resorts.

While lunching at his club, Smithers ran into Judith Carson, an old college friend he hadn't seen in months. Carson is the managing partner of a land-speculation endeavor that owns thousands of acres of prime real estate. During the course of their conversation, Carson asked Smithers to invest in the partnership, which was about to buy a land developer and its acreage near Sassy River.

When Smithers returned to the office after lunch, he found an email from Liam O'Toole, his largest client, who is knowledgeable about and likes to invest in real estate. O'Toole, who in the past did business with money manager Big Ideas International, had read in Big Ideas' prospect newsletter that a large Arizona developer was close to a deal to sell property in the Sassy River Valley. The article did not identify the parties to the transaction but did reveal the acreage of the land and the proposed sale price. O'Toole wanted to know if Smithers had heard about this deal and if he could get O'Toole a piece of it in exchange for a week at O'Toole's condo in St. Thomas.

Smithers suspected Pineda was the seller and Carson's real estate partnership was the buyer. Seeking to verify this, Smithers called Carson and asked if the partnership's big deal involved Pineda Canyon Development. Carson responded by saying she could neither confirm nor deny that a transaction with Pineda or any other specific company was in the works. A couple of days later, however, Smithers observed Carson and two of her business partners having dinner with Pineda executives. Smithers checked public records and discovered that Pineda was the majority shareholder in the only major development company with significant land ownership in the Sassy River Valley. Smithers concluded that Carson's firm was about to purchase the Sassy River developer from Pineda.

That afternoon, Smithers prepared a purchase recommendation for Pineda stock. He cited the expected sale of Sassy River Valley land for enough cash to fund both the construction of several ski resorts and retire some high interest notes. Smithers worked up some revenue and profit numbers, detailed the location of the property, and submitted a report for approval by the company president.

1. In preparing his recommendation to purchase Pineda, Smithers violated:
   A. none of the standards.
   B. Standard III(A) Loyalty, Prudence, and Care with regard to Carson's information.
   C. Standard II(A) Material Nonpublic Information with regard to Carson's statements.

2. Immediately after submitting his purchase recommendation to his boss, Smithers takes three actions. Which of the following actions is *least likely* a violation of the Code and Standards?
   A. Immediately downgrading two ski equipment manufacturers based only on "trends in the industry."
   B. Advising a colleague in Fundamental's bond department of this new information regarding Pineda's debt.
   C. Giving Carson the names and summary financial information of O'Toole and two other clients as possible limited partners.

3. Fundamental's president, Dana Aaronson, is so impressed with Smithers's report that she sends it to the fulfillment department for printing and faxing five minutes after receiving it from Smithers's supervisor, who has read and approved the report. In her handling of the report, how many of the following standards has Aaronson violated?
   - I(B) Independence and Objectivity.
   - IV(C) Responsibilities of Supervisors.
   - V(A) Diligence and Reasonable Basis.
   - II(A) Material Nonpublic Information.

   A. One.
   B. Two.
   C. None.

4. With regard to his information-gathering activities and the creation of his report, did Smithers or anyone else violate Standard III(A) Loyalty, Prudence, and Care?
   A. No one violated the standard.
   B. O'Toole's disclosure of the Big Ideas newsletter to Smithers is a violation of the standard.
   C. Carson's discussion with Smithers about the partnership's plans is a violation of the standard.

5. Because O'Toole brought the information about the real estate deal to Smithers's attention, Smithers purchased Pineda stock for O'Toole immediately after submitting his report to management. The purchase was *most likely* to violate:
   A. Standard III(B) regarding fair dealing.
   B. Standard III(C) regarding suitability of investments.
   C. Standard IV(B) regarding additional compensation arrangements.

6. The Pineda report has been dispatched by email, fax, or mail to every client. The purchase will be announced in one day, not enough time to disseminate Smithers's research to clients with no email or fax capability. Fundamental's trading manager, Bill Johnson, is considering various directives regarding the trading of Pineda stock. Which of the following instructions for portfolio managers is *best*?
   A. Make no trades until the written reports are delivered to every client in 48 hours.
   B. Do not execute any pending sell order for Pineda stock until the client has been informed of the rating change.
   C. Purchase Pineda stock for all discretionary portfolios, then call nondiscretionary clients to seek permission to purchase the stock.

Use the following information to answer Questions 7 through 12.

Gerard Cutty, CFA, a technology-stock analyst and money manager at Unique Investments, has been hearing rumors for months that Simpson Semiconductor was near a breakthrough on a next-generation telecommunications microchip. Simpson is best known on the street for its expert design engineers, perennially shaky balance sheet, and extremely volatile stock.

One morning, as he is listening to a recorded Barron's interview with Simpson's CEO, who is also a CFA charterholder, he learns that Simpson has struck a licensing agreement with Simak Foundry, a privately held chip fabricator in Malaysia. Then he reads in *The Asian Wall Street Journal* that a Malaysian bank has loaned $500 million to Simak for construction of a new plant.

Cutty owns an apartment in Paris, which is leased to Gladys Catcher, CFA. The lease is about to expire and Cutty and Catcher are currently in the process of renegotiating the terms of the lease. Cutty has other potential tenants for the apartment who are willing to pay more than what Catcher is currently paying, so he would like to negotiate a significant increase in the monthly payments.

Catcher works for a Paris public relations firm that handles accounts for a lot of Asian technology companies. Cutty calls Catcher, and after learning that her firm handled the Simak account, he asks what she knows about the Simak loan. Catcher says Simak has inked a deal with a big U.S. firm to make a new kind of microchip. She refuses to identify the firm but does provide some impressive performance numbers for the new chip.

After conducting a detailed patent search using the chip performance figures as a guide, Cutty learns that a Simpson engineer has filed for a series of patents related to the new technology over the past 18 months and confirms Catcher's information on the performance of the new chip.

Cutty works up some revenue and market-share projections, then concludes that if the new technology works, it could triple the company's profits over the next three years. He writes up a research report on Simpson, detailing the licensing deal, specs on the new chip, and his opinion about the company's growth potential. Cutty then raises his rating on Simpson from neutral to high-risk buy.

Mary Wabb, lead portfolio manager for Unique Investments, calls Cutty into her office after reviewing the analyst's report. Wabb asks Cutty about his sources and methodology, and Cutty explains his thinking process. She then thanks Cutty for his good work and tells him he will receive Unique's World Series tickets this year. After Cutty leaves, Wabb makes minor edits to the report and sends it to the fulfillment department for inclusion in the daily email report and weekly printed report for clients and prospects. Then Wabb instructs the trading desk to purchase Simpson stock for all client accounts after the reports have been issued.

The day after Cutty's report is released, rival analyst Sue Ellen Slusher, CFA, publishes her own analysis of Simpson Semiconductor. She cites Cutty's report specifically, quoting him directly and rebutting his conclusions point by point with her own research, criticizing his lack of thoroughness and questioning his abilities as an analyst and his academic and professional credentials. Specifically, she says that she's a better analyst than he is because "he earned his charter way back in 1986, when the CFA Program exam was a lot easier to pass than it is today, but I earned my charter last year." Slusher writes that, after talking with executives at Werfel Wafers, she believes Simpson infringed on Werfel's patent and will never reap the profits from the new technology.

7. In the production of his research report, Cutty violated:
   A. Standard V(A) Diligence and Reasonable Basis.
   B. Standard II(A) Material Nonpublic Information.
   C. none of the standards.

8. Which of the following statements is *most accurate* regarding potential violations of Standard III(A) Loyalty, Prudence, and Care in this scenario?
   A. Neither Cutty, Catcher, nor Simpson violated the standard.
   B. Catcher violated the standard by revealing information about her client, Simak.
   C. Simpson's CEO violated the standard by discussing his company's licensing agreement.

9. Which of the following statements, if found in Cutty's report without clarification, would *most likely* violate Standard V(B) Communications With Clients and Prospective Clients?
   A. Simpson's sales have faltered in recent years, but I believe the new technology will bring back the days of 25% revenue growth.
   B. The new technology could boost Simpson's cash flows considerably and provide flexibility to clean up the balance sheet.
   C. After a few phone calls and an analysis of the relevant information from our internal database, I concluded that Simpson's new technology was more than just a rumor.

10. Which of Wabb's actions *most likely* violated the Code and Standards? Her:
    A. newsletter instructions violated Standard III(B) Fair Dealing.
    B. trading instructions violated Standard III(C) Suitability.
    C. awarding of World Series tickets to Cutty violated Standard IV(B) Additional Compensation Arrangements.

11. Which of the following actions could Cutty have taken while researching his report on Simpson *without* violating CFA Institute Standards of Professional Conduct?
    A. Not saving the results of the patent search.
    B. Ignoring a rival analyst's report on a Simpson competitor with a similar technology.
    C. Using statements from the Standard & Poor's report on Simpson without verifying them.

12. According to CFA Institute Standards of Professional Conduct, Slusher violated:
    A. Standard VII(B) Reference to CFA Institute, the CFA Designation, and the CFA Program because of her criticism of Cutty's credentials.
    B. Standard V(A) Diligence and Reasonable Basis because her conclusions differed from Cutty's.
    C. Standard I(B) Independence and Objectivity because of her criticism of Cutty's research report and conclusions.

Use the following information to answer Questions 13 through 18.

MH Securities is a subsidiary of MH Group, a large Korean conglomerate, and has recently established offices in the United States and Canada. MH plans to target Korean-Americans and Canadians for its services, which include selling the firm's research services as well as Korean equities, bonds, and won-denominated certificates of deposit (CD). Chan-Heung Lee, CFA, has been hired to develop, implement, and oversee MH's compliance activities. Because there are very few compliance procedures in place, Lee will have to build the entire compliance framework. His objective is to conform to the CFA Institute Code and Standards. As one of his first steps, Lee decides to interview several MH employees to determine what formal and informal policies and procedures currently exist at the firm. Lee calls meetings with Jamie Jin, Nadine Yu, and Mark Larson, each of whom is a CFA charterholder.

Jamie Jin has recently been hired as an investment officer by MH. Jin informs Lee during their meeting that her previous employer, Rearguard Funds, has agreed to pay her a 25-basis-point commission plus an annual bonus for all Rearguard Funds she sells to MH clients. Jin is unsure whether she will even use any Rearguard products with her new clients but agrees to the arrangement in case a client specifically requests a Rearguard product. Because the likelihood of actually receiving any compensation from Rearguard seems remote, Jamie has not previously disclosed the arrangement to MH.

In his meeting with Nadine Yu, an equity analyst at MH, Lee discovers that Yu has recently and abruptly changed her investment recommendation on Korean won-denominated bonds from buy to sell. She has prepared a research report to this effect and provides a copy to Lee in accordance with one of the firm's few existing compliance procedures. Her change of opinion is based upon nonpublic information provided to her in confidence by a friend on the monetary board at the Bank of Korea. While Lee is surprised at the abrupt change in the recommendation, he does not question the rationale and allows the report to be issued. Having received approval for her investment recommendation, Yu simultaneously releases the report to her individual and institutional research service subscribers as well as to MH's portfolio managers.

Lee's final meeting is with a new hire, Mark Larson, who has recently agreed to go to work for MH starting at the beginning of the next month. Lee is meeting with Larson to discuss new clients that Larson is expected to bring to MH. Larson, without providing details, assures Lee that he will have no problem increasing MH's client base. Before leaving his current employer, Affinity Advisors, Larson contacts 25 prospects by calling them, using public records and not Affinity's records, on Saturday mornings from his home. Of the prospects, 10 individuals had previously been rejected as being too small for Affinity, but they still meet MH standards. The other 15 individuals remained viable prospects for Affinity. After learning of their status with Affinity, Larson suggests that all 25 prospects consider directing their business to him and his new firm, MH.

Lee's meetings with Jin, Yu, and Larson help him formulate compliance procedures. Lee decides that he will develop a written compliance manual, which will be distributed to all of the firm's employees. The manual will delineate procedures for reporting violations and sanctions, describe the supervision hierarchy and each supervisor's duties, and outline the steps to monitor and evaluate the compliance program. Lee also designates Jin as the employee with ultimate responsibility for the compliance procedures and their enforcement.

13. Because there are currently no compliance procedures in place, Lee should:
    A. develop procedures that are in accordance with the CFA Institute Code and Standards as compliance situations arise.
    B. implement a comprehensive set of compliance procedures immediately and verify their conformance with the CFA Institute Code and Standards as circumstances dictate.
    C. determine what constitutes adequate compliance procedures under the CFA Institute Code and Standards and then implement such procedures immediately.

14. Before her meeting with Lee, did Jin's decision regarding the disclosure of the arrangement with Rearguard Funds violate any CFA Institute Standards of Professional Conduct?
    A. Yes.
    B. No, because she disclosed the arrangement with Rearguard to Lee in their meeting.
    C. No, because before the meeting with Lee, MH did not have any compliance procedures requiring such a disclosure.

15. With regard to Yu's recommendation that investors sell Korean bonds, did Lee and Yu violate any CFA Institute Standards of Professional Conduct?
    A. Neither Lee nor Yu is in violation.
    B. Both Lee and Yu are in violation.
    C. Only Yu is in violation.

16. With respect to the release of Yu's investment recommendation, did Yu violate any CFA Institute Standards of Professional Conduct?
    A. No.
    B. Yes. Yu should have released the recommendation to the individual clients first.
    C. Yes. Yu should have released the recommendation to the individual and institutional clients first.

17. In soliciting the list of 10 previously rejected prospects and the list of 15 viable prospects, did Larson violate any CFA Institute Standards of Professional Conduct?
    A. No, Larson did not violate a standard; he can solicit from either list.
    B. Yes, Larson violated a standard; he cannot solicit from either list.
    C. Yes, Larson violated a standard; he can only solicit from the previously rejected prospects list.

18. Does the compliance program developed by Lee after his meetings with MH employees comply with CFA Institute Standards of Professional Conduct?
    A. Yes.
    B. No. Authority to enforce the compliance program should rest with the compliance officer.
    C. No. Assigning supervisory duties takes away the responsibility of all supervisors to detect all violations of the compliance procedures.

TOPIC ASSESSMENT ANSWERS: ETHICAL AND PROFESSIONAL STANDARDS

1. **A** Smithers has assembled both material public and nonmaterial nonpublic information as the basis for his recommendation. By putting all of the information together, Smithers has utilized the mosaic theory to come to a conclusion of material nonpublic nature without actually using material nonpublic information. Therefore, he did not violate Standard II(A). Carson is not Smithers's client, and Smithers owes Carson no fiduciary responsibility under Standard III(A). Smithers had no reason to believe Carson would misrepresent anything about the situation. (Study Session 2, Module 2.4, LOS 2: III(A))

2. **B** Sharing information between the stock and bond divisions within a single company does not violate any fiduciary duties. It is possible that by not sharing the information, Smithers could violate a fiduciary duty to Fundamental's bond-investing clients. Immediately downgrading the ski equipment manufacturers implies the downgrades were issued solely because of a new deal for Pineda, an act that violates Standard V(A) Diligence and Reasonable Basis. Giving clients' financial information to a competitor would definitely violate Standard III(E) Preservation of Confidentiality. (Study Session 2, Module 2.4, LOS 2: III(A))

3. **C** Nothing in Aaronson's conduct implies any violation of the Independence and Objectivity Standard, nor the standard regarding the use of material nonpublic information. As president of the firm, Aaronson is not responsible for making sure that each analyst has a reasonable basis for every recommendation. Aaronson is entitled to rely on reasonable procedures to detect and prevent such violations. Therefore, she has not violated any of the four listed standards. (Study Session 2, Module 2.8, LOS 2: V(A))

4. **A** Standard III(A) Loyalty, Prudence, and Care requires members and candidates to act for the benefit of their clients and comply with applicable fiduciary duties. O'Toole has no fiduciary duty to Big Ideas and can share the information with anyone he wishes. As managing partner, Carson is presumably authorized to speak for the partnership and attempt to bring in new investors. She has a fiduciary duty to the limited partners, but revealing the purchase plans to Smithers did not violate that duty as the deal had already been struck, and the information would not affect the purchase price. No actions in the scenario reflect a breach of fiduciary duty. (Study Session 2, Module 2.4, LOS 2: III(A))

5. **A** O'Toole is an experienced real estate investor, and Pineda is probably a good fit for him. And because O'Toole is Smithers's biggest client, it can be assumed that Smithers has worked with O'Toole extensively and is familiar with his investment needs and preferences. As such, the purchase most likely satisfies Standard III(C) Suitability. Smithers did not violate Standard IV(B) Additional Compensation Arrangements because he did not accept O'Toole's offer, nor did he do what O'Toole asked in return

for the condo, which was to get O'Toole a piece of the deal. By favoring O'Toole over other clients, however, Smithers violates the fair dealing Standard and his fiduciary duty to other clients besides O'Toole. Smithers should not have purchased stock in Pineda for O'Toole until the report had been disseminated to all clients with an interest in the investment. (Study Session 2, Module 2.7, LOS 2: IV(B))

6. **B** The fair-dealing standard requires brokers to inform clients of any pending rating changes. If the clients still want to sell Pineda stock, then Fundamental must sell it for them. Purchasing Pineda stock for all discretionary portfolios violates Standard III(C) Suitability, as the stock may not be suitable for all account holders. Waiting to make buys until everyone has received a mailed report sounds fair, but it violates the firm's fiduciary duty to discretionary clients and those who can be reached by phone, fax, or email before the merger announcement is made. In addition, Standard III(B) Fair Dealing requires fair dissemination of recommendations, not "equal" dissemination, which is not always practical. (Study Session 2, Module 2.5, LOS 2: III(C))

7. **C** Cutty's use of someone with whom he does personal business as a source could be perceived by some as a conflict of interest. However, there seems to be no ill intent, and Cutty corroborated Catcher's information from an additional source (the patent search). The research reports Standard requires that the analyst use reasonable judgment and distinguish between fact and opinion—Cutty did that. Cutty's broad-based research also satisfies the requirements of the reasonable basis standard. None of the nonpublic information Cutty picked up was likely to be considered material by itself, and his conclusions about Simpson are an example of the mosaic theory. (Study Session 2, Module 2.8, LOS 2: V(A))

8. **A** Cutty owes no fiduciary duty to Catcher. Simpson's CEO did not reveal material information, but as CEO, he likely would not have been violating a fiduciary duty even if he had. Catcher is in public relations, and her job is to discuss her clients' business with third parties. As such, she is authorized to release information—Standard III(A). (Study Session 2, Module 2.4, LOS 2: III(A))

9. **C** While Cutty clearly states that his opinion is based on his own conclusions rather than verifiable facts, he violates Standard V(B) by not providing details about the evaluation process, which was quite complicated. Therefore, choice C is not an adequate description of the process and is a violation of the Standard. Cutty's use of "I believe" and "could" suggest the statements about sales and cash flows are his opinions. Therefore, choices A and B are not violations. (Study Session 2, Module 2.8, LOS 2: V(B))

10. **B** Because Simpson is a risky stock, it is probably not suitable for all clients, and a blanket purchase order violates Standard III(C) Suitability. Wabb's instructions for the fulfillment department meet the requirements of Standard III(B) Fair Dealing, as the Standard does not require that everyone be notified at the same time, only that the dissemination of

information is handled fairly. In this case, everyone with email will get the information at the same time, and those without email will get it later but at the same time as their low-tech peers. The additional compensation standard applies to compensation that doesn't come from the employer, and the World Series tickets did indeed come from the employer. (Study Session 2, Module 2.5, LOS 2: III(C))

11. **C** Members are in compliance with Standard V(A) Diligence and Reasonable Basis if they depend on the research of others they know to be competent and diligent. S&P qualifies as such a source. Standard V(C) Record Retention requires analysts to maintain records supporting their actions, so Cutty must save the results of the patent search. A rival's report about a competitor with similar technology could have a material effect on Cutty's financial model for Simpson and must be considered. (Study Session 2, Module 2.8, LOS 2: V(C))

12. **A** Slusher's claim that her credentials are superior to Cutty's because she earned her charter more recently is a violation of Standard VII(B) Reference to CFA Institute, the CFA Designation, and the CFA Program. Slusher did not plagiarize Cutty's work because she cited him as the author. Just because Slusher disagrees with, and criticizes, Cutty's well-researched opinion does not mean she lacks basis for her own analysis or has violated the independence and objectivity standard. (Study Session 2, Module 2.10, LOS 2: VII(B))

13. **C** In order to best conform to the CFA Institute Code and Standards, Lee should first define what constitutes adequate standards. According to Standard IV(C) Responsibilities of Supervisors, "'adequate' procedures are those designed to meet industry standards, regulatory requirements, the requirements of the Code and Standards, and the circumstances of the firm." Once this has been done, he should implement the procedures immediately. (Study Session 2, Module 2.7, LOS 2: IV(C))

14. **A** In order to be in compliance with Standard IV(B), Jin must disclose all additional compensation arrangements, in writing, to her employer. It does not matter whether Rearguard actually pays her a commission on the funds or whether the firm previously had such a policy. In addition, the relationship with Rearguard creates a potential conflict of interest between Jin and her clients because she may be tempted to increase her income by recommending Rearguard Funds that are inappropriate for her clients' needs. Standard VI(A) Disclosure of Conflicts requires disclosure of such conflicts to clients and prospects. There is no indication that Jin has made such a disclosure. (Study Session 2, Module 2.7, LOS 2: IV(B))

15. **B** Yu is in violation of Standard II(A) Material Nonpublic Information, as she has used material nonpublic information in her investment recommendations. She is forbidden to act upon such information. Lee, the firm's compliance officer, has violated Standard IV(C) Responsibilities of Supervisors, in the discharge of his responsibility as a supervisor. Given the abrupt change in the recommendation, Lee should have attempted to determine if there was a reasonable basis for the dramatic shift in opinion. (Study Session 2, Module 2.7, LOS 2: IV(C))

16. **A** According to Standard III(B) Fair Dealing, members and candidates must ensure that all clients are treated equitably with regard to investment recommendations and investment actions. Because MH has clients that subscribe to its research service but do not pay for portfolio management services and the firm has clients that pay for discretionary portfolio management, investment recommendations must be communicated to research subscribers and the firm's portfolio managers simultaneously in order to ensure that all clients have equal opportunity to trade on the firm's research without being disadvantaged because of the type of service the client receives. (Study Session 2, Module 2.5, LOS 2: III(B))

17. **C** According to Standard IV(A) Loyalty to Employer, Larson must not solicit current or prospective Affinity clients before he leaves. Larson is allowed to solicit prospects that have been rejected by Affinity as long as he does so on his own time, does not use Affinity's client lists, and his actions do not impair his performance at work. His solicitation of prospects who are still viable for Affinity is a clear violation of duty to his employer under Standard IV(A). (Study Session 2, Module 2.7, LOS 2: IV(A))

18. **B** According to Standard IV(C) Responsibilities of Supervisors, the responsibility to implement procedures and the authority to enforce the procedures should both reside with the compliance officer (in this case Lee, rather than Jin, who is an investment officer). (Study Session 2, Module 2.7, LOS 2: IV(C))

READING 6

Fintech in Investment Management

Study Session 3

EXAM FOCUS

This topic review is an introductory overview of technological developments affecting the financial services industry. Candidates are expected to be familiar with a variety of terminology introduced in this topic review.

MODULE 6.1: FINTECH IN INVESTMENT MANAGEMENT

Video covering this content is available online.

LOS 6.a: Describe "fintech."

CFA® Program Curriculum, Volume 1, page 240

The term **fintech** refers to developments in technology that can be applied to the financial services industry. Companies that are in the business of developing technologies for the finance industry are often referred to as fintech companies.

Some of the primary areas where fintech is developing include:

- Increasing functionality to handle large sets of data that may come from many sources and exist in a variety of forms.
- Tools and techniques for analyzing very large data sets, such as artificial intelligence.
- Automation of financial functions such as executing trades and providing investment advice.
- Emerging technologies for financial recordkeeping that may reduce the need for intermediaries.

LOS 6.b: Describe Big Data, artificial intelligence, and machine learning.

CFA® Program Curriculum, Volume 1, page 241

Big Data is a widely used expression that refers to all the potentially useful information that is generated in the economy. This includes not only data from traditional sources, such as financial markets, company financial reports, and government economic statistics, but also **alternative data** from nontraditional sources. Some of these nontraditional sources are:

- Individuals who generate usable data such as social media posts, online reviews, email, and website visits.
- Businesses that generate potentially useful information such as bank records and retail scanner data. These kinds of data are referred to as **corporate exhaust**.
- Sensors, such as radio frequency identification chips, that are embedded in numerous devices such as smart phones and smart buildings. The broad network of such devices is referred to as the **Internet of Things**.

Characteristics of Big Data include its volume, velocity, and variety.

The volume of data continues to grow by orders of magnitude. The units in which data can be measured have increased from megabytes and gigabytes to terabytes (1,000 gigabytes) and even petabytes (1,000 terabytes.)

Velocity refers to how quickly data are communicated. Real-time data such as stock market price feeds are said to have low latency. Data that are only communicated periodically or with a lag are said to have high latency.

The variety of data refers to the varying degrees of structure in which data may exist. These range from structured forms, such as spreadsheets and databases, to semistructured forms such as photos and web page code, to unstructured forms, such as video.

The field of **data science** concerns how we extract information from Big Data. Data science describes methods for processing and visualizing data. Processing methods include:

- *Capture*—collecting data and transforming it into usable forms.
- *Curation*—assuring data quality by adjusting for bad or missing data.
- *Storage*—archiving and accessing data.
- *Search*—examining stored data to find needed information.
- *Transfer*—moving data from their source or a storage medium to where they are needed.

Visualization techniques include the familiar charts and graphs that display structured data. To visualize less structured data requires other methods. Some examples of these are *word clouds* that illustrate the frequency words appear in a sample of text or *mind maps* that display logical relations among concepts.

Taking advantage of Big Data presents a number of challenges. Analysts must ensure that the data they use are of high quality, accounting for the possibilities of outliers, bad or missing data, or sampling biases. The volume of data collected must be sufficient and appropriate for its intended use.

The need to process and organize data before using it can be especially problematic with qualitative and unstructured data. This is a process to which **artificial intelligence**, or computer systems that can be programmed to simulate human cognition, may be applied usefully. **Neural networks** are an example of artificial intelligence in that they are programmed to process information in a way similar to the human brain.

An important development in the field of artificial intelligence is **machine learning** (ML). This refers to programming that gives a computer system the ability to improve its performance of a task over time. In ML, a computer algorithm is given inputs of source data and may be given outputs of target data. The algorithm is designed to learn how to model the output data based on the input data or to learn how to detect and recognize patterns in the input data. The machine learning process typically requires vast amounts of data.

In **supervised learning**, the input and output data are labelled, the machine learns to model the outputs from the inputs, and then the machine is given new data on which to use the model. In **unsupervised learning**, the input data are not labelled and the machine learns to describe the structure of the data. **Deep learning** is a technique that uses layers of neural networks to identify patterns, beginning with simple patterns and advancing to more complex ones. Deep learning may use supervised or unsupervised learning. Some of the applications of deep learning include image and speech recognition.

ML can produce models that overfit or underfit the data. **Overfitting** occurs when the machine learns the input and output data too exactly, treats noise as true parameters, and identifies spurious patterns and relationships. In effect, the machine creates a model that is too complex. **Underfitting** occurs when the machine fails to identify actual patterns and relationships, treating true parameters as noise. This means the model is not complex enough to describe the data. A further challenge with ML is that its results can be a "black box," producing outcomes based on relationships that are not readily explainable.

LOS 6.c: Describe fintech applications to investment management.

CFA® Program Curriculum, Volume 1, page 249

Applications of fintech that are relevant to investment management include text analytics, natural language processing, risk analysis, algorithmic trading, and robo-advisory services.

Text analytics refers to the analysis of unstructured data in text or voice forms. An example of text analytics is analyzing the frequency of words and phrases. In the finance industry, text analytics have the potential to partially automate specific tasks, such as evaluating company regulatory filings.

Natural language processing refers to the use of computers and artificial intelligence to interpret human language. Speech recognition and language translation are among the uses of natural language processing. Possible applications in finance could be to check for regulatory compliance by an examination of employee communications, or to evaluate large volumes of research reports to detect more subtle changes in sentiment than can be discerned from analysts' recommendations alone.

Risk governance requires an understanding of a firm's exposure to a wide variety of risks. Financial regulators require firms to perform risk assessments and stress testing. The simulations, scenario analysis, and other techniques used for risk analysis require large amounts of quantitative data along with a great deal of qualitative information. ML and other techniques related to Big Data can be useful in modeling and testing risk, particularly if firms use real-time data to monitor risk exposures.

Algorithmic trading refers to computerized securities trading based on a predetermined set of rules. For example, algorithms may be designed to enter the optimal execution instructions for any given trade based on real-time price and volume data. Algorithmic trading can also be useful for executing large orders by determining the best way to divide the orders across exchanges. Another application of algorithmic trading is **high-frequency trading** that identifies and takes advantage of intraday securities mispricings.

Robo-advisors are online platforms that provide automated investment advice based on a customer's answers to survey questions. The survey questions are designed to elicit an investor's financial position, return objectives, risk tolerance, and constraints, such as time horizon and liquidity needs. Robo-advisor services may be fully automated or assisted by a human investment advisor.

Robo-advisory services tend to offer passively managed investments with low fees, low minimum account sizes, traditional asset classes, and conservative recommendations. The primary advantage of robo-advisors is their low cost to customers, which may make advice more accessible to a larger number of investors.

A disadvantage of robo-advisors is that the reasoning behind their recommendations might not be apparent. Without a human investment advisor to explain the reasoning, customers may hesitate to trust the appropriateness of a robo-advisor's recommendations, particularly in crisis periods.

Regulation of robo-advisors is still emerging. However, in many countries robo-advisory services are subject to the same regulations and registration requirements as any other investment advisor.

LOS 6.d: Describe financial applications of distributed ledger technology.

CFA® Program Curriculum, Volume 1, page 253

A **distributed ledger** is a database that is shared on a network so that each participant has an identical copy. A distributed ledger must have a consensus mechanism to validate new entries into the ledger. Distributed ledger technology uses cryptography to ensure only authorized network participants can use the data.

A **blockchain** is a distributed ledger that records transactions sequentially in blocks and links these blocks in a chain. Each block has a cryptographically secured "hash" that links it to the previous block. The consensus mechanism in a blockchain requires some of the computers on the network to solve a cryptographic problem. These computers are referred to as **miners**. Mining requires vast resources of computing power and electricity. This imposes substantial costs on any attempt to manipulate a blockchain's historical record. To do so would also require one party to control a majority of the network. For this reason, a blockchain is more likely to succeed with a large number of participants in its network.

Distributed ledgers can take the form of permissionless or permissioned networks. In **permissionless networks**, all network participants can view all transactions. These networks have no central authority, which gives them the advantage of having no single point of failure. The ledger becomes a permanent record visible to all, and its history cannot be altered (short of the manipulation described previously). This removes the need for trust between the parties to a transaction.

In **permissioned networks**, users have different levels of access. For example, a permissioned network might allow network participants to enter transactions while giving government regulators permission to view the transaction history. A distributed ledger that allowed regulators to view records that firms are required to make available would increase transparency and decrease compliance costs.

Financial applications of distributed ledger technology

Cryptocurrencies are a current example of distributed ledger technology in finance. A cryptocurrency is an electronic medium of exchange that allows participants to engage in real-time transactions without a financial intermediary. Cryptocurrencies typically reside on permissionless networks.

Demonstrating the impact cryptocurrencies are already having in finance, companies have raised capital through **initial coin offerings**, in which they sell cryptocurrency for money or another cryptocurrency. This reduces the cost and time frame compared to carrying out a regulated IPO, and initial coin offerings typically do not come with voting rights. Investors should note that fraud has occurred with initial coin offerings and they may become subject to securities regulations.

Post-trade clearing and settlement is an area of finance to which distributed ledger technology might be productively applied. Distributed ledgers could automate many of the processes currently carried out by custodians and other third parties. The technology has the potential to bring about real-time trade verification and settlement, which currently takes one or more days for many securities. This would reduce trading costs and counterparty risk. On the other hand, the inability to alter past transactions on a distributed ledger is problematic when canceling a trade is required.

Other potential applications of distributed ledger technology in finance include smart contracts and tokenization. **Smart contracts** are electronic contracts that could be programmed to self-execute based on terms agreed to by the counterparties. For example, an options contract could be set up to be exercised automatically if certain defined conditions exist in the market. **Tokenization** refers to electronic proof of ownership of physical assets, which could be maintained on a distributed ledger. For example, such a ledger could potentially replace the paper real estate deeds currently filed at government offices.

MODULE QUIZ 6.1

To best evaluate your performance, enter your quiz answers online.

1. Fintech is *most accurately* described as:
   A. the application of technology to the financial services industry.
   B. the replacement of government-issued money with electronic currencies.
   C. the clearing and settling securities trades through distributed ledger technology.
2. Which of the following technological developments is *most likely* to be useful for analyzing Big Data?
   A. Machine learning (ML).
   B. High-latency capture.
   C. The Internet of Things.
3. A key criticism of robo-advisory services is that:
   A. they are costly for investors to use.
   B. the reasoning behind their recommendations can be unclear.
   C. they tend to produce overly aggressive investment recommendations.
4. Which of the following statements about distributed ledger technology is *most accurate?*
   A. A disadvantage of blockchain is that past records are vulnerable to manipulation.
   B. Tokenization can potentially streamline transactions involving high-value physical assets.
   C. Only parties who trust each other should carry out transactions on a permissionless network.

KEY CONCEPTS

LOS 6.a

Fintech refers to developments in technology that can be applied to the financial services industry. Companies that develop technologies for the finance industry are referred to as fintech companies.

LOS 6.b

Big Data refers to the potentially useful information that is generated in the economy, including data from traditional and nontraditional sources. Characteristics of Big Data include its volume, velocity, and variety.

Artificial intelligence refers to computer systems that can be programmed to simulate human cognition. Neural networks are an example of artificial intelligence.

Machine learning (ML) is programming that gives a computer system the ability to improve its performance of a task over time and is often used to detect patterns in large sets of data.

LOS 6.c

Applications of fintech to investment management include text analytics, natural language processing, risk analysis, algorithmic trading, and robo-advisory services.

Text analytics refers to analyzing unstructured data in text or voice forms. Natural language processing is the use of computers and artificial intelligence to interpret human language. Algorithmic trading refers to computerized securities trading based on predetermined rules.

Robo-advisors are online platforms that provide automated investment advice based on a customer's answers to survey questions. The primary advantage of robo-advisors is their low cost to customers. A disadvantage is that the reasoning behind their recommendations might not be apparent.

LOS 6.d

A distributed ledger is a database that is shared on a network, with a consensus mechanism so that each participant has an identical copy of the ledger.

A cryptocurrency is an electronic medium of exchange that allows network participants in a distributed ledger to engage in real-time transactions without a financial intermediary.

Potential financial applications of distributed ledger technology include smart contracts, tokenization, and more efficient post-trade clearing and settlement.

ANSWER KEY FOR MODULE QUIZ

Module Quiz 6.1

1. **A** Fintech refers to the application of technology to the financial services industry, and to companies that are involved in developing and applying technology for financial services. Cryptocurrencies and distributed ledger technology are examples of fintech-related developments. (LOS 6.a)

2. **A** ML is a computer programming technique useful for identifying and modeling patterns in large volumes of data. The Internet of Things refers to the network of devices that is one of the sources of Big Data. Capture is one aspect of processing data. Latency refers to the lag between when data is generated and when it is needed. (LOS 6.b)

3. **B** One criticism of robo-advisory services is that the reasoning behind their recommendations might not be readily apparent to customers. Recommendations from robo-advisors tend to be conservative rather than aggressive. Low cost is a primary advantage of robo-advisors. (LOS 6.c)

4. **B** By enabling electronic proof of ownership, tokenization has the potential to streamline transfers of physical assets, such as real estate. The high cost and difficulty of manipulating past records is a strength of blockchain technology. Permissionless networks do not require trust between the parties to a transaction because the record of a transaction is unchangeable and visible to all network participants. (LOS 6.d)

The following is a review of the Quantitative Methods principles designed to address the learning outcome statements set forth by CFA Institute. Cross-Reference to CFA Institute Assigned Reading #7.

READING 7

Correlation and Regression

Study Session 3

EXAM FOCUS

This introduction to regression analysis begins with the calculation of sample covariance and sample correlation. You should be able to calculate both of these measures and to test the significance of an estimated correlation coefficient. A simple linear regression involves two random variables, an independent and a dependent variable. Candidates should be able to construct a simple regression model (equation), state the assumptions under which such a (linear) model is valid, and discuss the limitations of a simple regression model. Given the estimated model parameters (coefficients), you should be able to use the model to predict the dependent variable using an assumed value of the independent variable. Finally, you may be required to interpret an ANOVA table and test the significance of estimated regression coefficients. Note that an *F*-test, in the context of a simple regression, is equivalent to a *t*-test of the significance of the estimated slope coefficient.

PROFESSOR'S NOTE

For more details on hypothesis testing and simple linear regression, please see the Schweser Resource Library videos.

MODULE 7.1: COVARIANCE AND CORRELATION

Video covering this content is available online.

LOS 7.a: Calculate and interpret a sample covariance and a sample correlation coefficient and interpret a scatter plot.

CFA® Program Curriculum, Volume 1, page 268

The **covariance** between two random variables is a statistical measure of the degree to which the two variables move together. The covariance captures the linear relationship between two variables. A positive covariance indicates that the variables tend to move together; a negative covariance indicates that the variables tend to move in opposite directions.

The **sample covariance** is calculated as:

$$cov_{XY} = \frac{\sum_{i=1}^{n}(X_i - \overline{X})(Y_i - \overline{Y})}{n-1}$$

where:
n = sample size
X_i = *i*th observation on variable X
$\overline{X}$ = mean of the variable X observations
Y_i = *i*th observation on variable Y
$\overline{Y}$ = mean of the variable Y observations

The actual value of the covariance is not very meaningful because its measurement is extremely sensitive to the scale of the two variables. Also, the covariance may range from negative to positive infinity, and it is presented in terms of squared units (e.g., percent squared when data are in percent). For these reasons, we take the additional step of calculating the correlation coefficient, which converts the covariance into a standardized measure that is easier to interpret.

SAMPLE CORRELATION COEFFICIENT

The **correlation coefficient**, *r*, is a measure of the strength of the linear relationship (correlation) between two variables. The correlation coefficient has no unit of measurement; it is a "pure" measure of the tendency of two variables to move together.

The **sample correlation coefficient** for two variables, *X* and *Y*, is calculated as:

$$r_{XY} = \frac{\text{covariance of X and Y}}{(\text{sample standard deviation of X})(\text{sample standard deviation of Y})} = \frac{cov_{XY}}{(s_X)(s_Y)}$$

The correlation coefficient is bounded by positive and negative one (i.e., $-1 \leq r \leq +1$), where a correlation coefficient of +1 indicates that changes in the variables are perfectly positively correlated (i.e., they go up and down together, in lock-step). In contrast, if the correlation coefficient is –1, the changes in the variables are perfectly negatively correlated.

Figure 7.1 provides the data for two variables, *X* and *Y*, and shows the calculation of the correlation between *X* and *Y*.

Figure 7.1: Procedure for Computing Correlation

Obs.	X	Y	$X-\overline{X}$	$(X-\overline{X})^2$	$Y-\overline{Y}$	$(Y-\overline{Y})^2$	$(X-\overline{X})(Y-\overline{Y})$
1	12	50	–1.50	2.25	8.40	70.56	–12.60
2	13	54	–0.50	0.25	12.40	153.76	–6.20
3	10	48	–3.50	12.25	6.40	40.96	–22.40
4	9	47	–4.50	20.25	5.40	29.16	–24.30
5	20	70	6.50	42.25	28.40	806.56	184.60
6	7	20	–6.50	42.25	–21.60	466.56	140.40
7	4	15	–9.50	90.25	–26.60	707.56	252.70
8	22	40	8.50	72.25	–1.60	2.56	–13.60
9	15	35	1.50	2.25	–6.60	43.56	–9.90
10	23	37	9.50	90.25	–4.60	21.16	–43.70
Sum	135	416	0.00	374.50	0.00	2,342.40	445.00

$\overline{X} = 135 / 10 = 13.5$ $\quad s_X^2 = 374.5 / 9 = 41.611$

$\overline{Y} = 416 / 10 = 41.6$ $\quad s_Y^2 = 2{,}342.4 / 9 = 260.267$

Using the information in Figure 7.1, the sample correlation coefficient for variables *X* and *Y* may be calculated as:

$$r_{XY} = \frac{\frac{445}{9}}{\sqrt{41.611}\sqrt{260.267}} = \frac{49.444}{(6.451)(16.133)} = 0.475$$

The interpretation of the possible correlation values is summarized in Figure 7.2.

Figure 7.2: Interpretation of Correlation Coefficients

Correlation Coefficient (r)	Interpretation
$r = +1$	perfect positive correlation
$0 < r < +1$	positive linear relationship
$r = 0$	no linear relationship
$-1 < r < 0$	negative linear relationship
$r = -1$	perfect negative correlation

Study Session 3

INTERPRETING A SCATTER PLOT

A **scatter plot** is a collection of points on a graph where each point represents the values of two variables (i.e., an X/Y pair). Figure 7.3 shows several scatter plots for the two random variables X and Y and the corresponding interpretation of correlation. As shown, an upward-sweeping scatter plot indicates a positive correlation between the two variables, while a downward sweeping plot implies a negative correlation. Also illustrated in Figure 7.3 is that as we move from left to right in the rows of scatter plots, the extent of the linear relationship between the two variables deteriorates, and the correlation gets closer to zero. Note that for $r = 1$ and $r = -1$ the data points lie exactly on a line, but the slope of that line is not necessarily +1 or –1.

Figure 7.3: Interpretations of Correlation

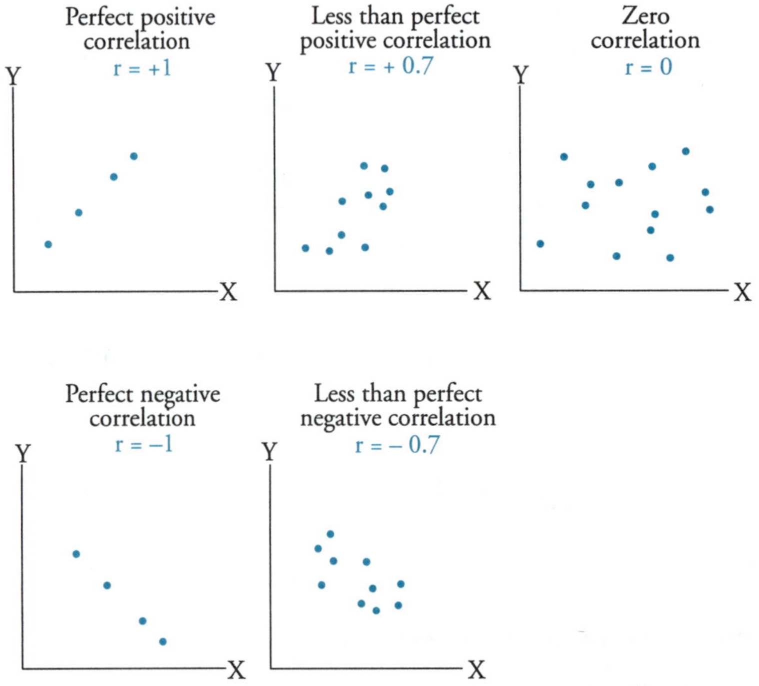

Suppose we wish to graphically represent the data for the returns on Stock A and returns on a market index over the last six months, shown in Figure 7.4. Figure 7.5 shows the data graphically with the returns on Stock A on the Y-axis and the returns on the market index on the X-axis. Each point of the scatter plot in Figure 7.5 represents one month of the six in our sample. The rightmost point in the scatter plot is for the month of March, a 2.0% return on the market index and a 1.8% return on Stock A.

Figure 7.4: Monthly Returns Data

Month	Return on Stock A	Return on Market Index
Jan	+0.8%	+1.2%
Feb	+0.6%	+0.5%
Mar	+1.8%	+2.0%
Apr	–0.7%	–0.9%
May	+0.3%	+0.2%
June	–0.1%	–0.5%

Figure 7.5: Scatter Plot of Returns

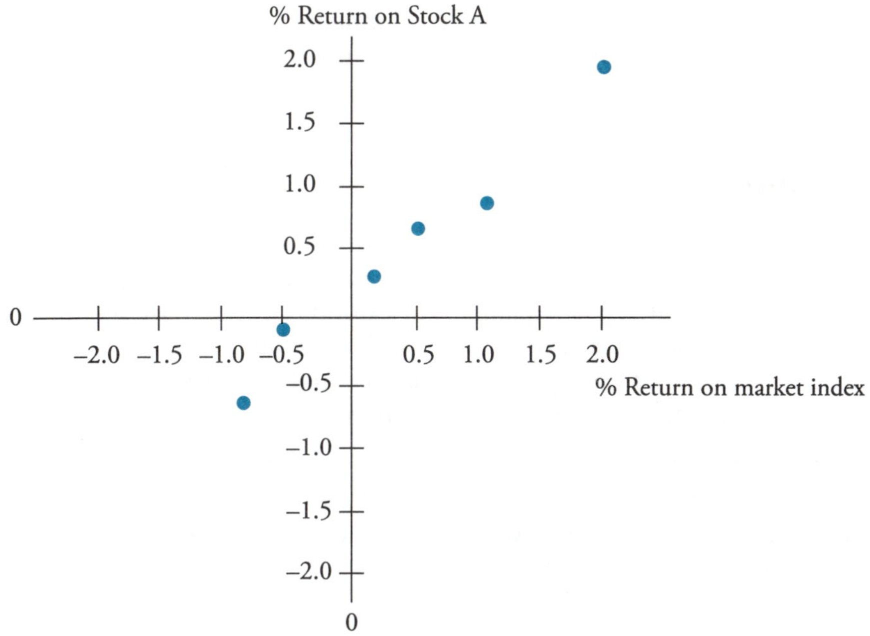

Notice that returns on Stock A appear to be positively correlated with the market index returns.

LOS 7.b: Describe limitations to correlation analysis.

CFA® Program Curriculum, Volume 1, page 270

Limitations to correlation analysis include the impact of outliers, the potential for spurious correlation, and nonlinear relationships.

Outliers

Computed correlation coefficients, as well as other sample statistics, may be affected by outliers. Outliers represent a few extreme values for sample observations. Relative to the rest of the sample data, the value of an outlier may be extraordinarily large or small. Outliers can result in apparent statistical evidence that a significant relationship exists when, in fact, there is none, or that there is no relationship when, in fact, there is a relationship.

Spurious Correlation

Spurious correlation refers to the appearance of a causal linear relationship when, in fact, there is no relation. Certain data items may be highly correlated purely by chance. For example, suppose that you compute the correlation coefficient for historical stock prices and snowfall totals in Minnesota and get a statistically significant relationship—especially for the month of January. Obviously there is no economic explanation for this relationship, so this would be considered a spurious correlation.

Nonlinear Relationships

Correlation measures the *linear* relationship between two variables. That's why in the first panel of Figure 7.3 the data points lie perfectly on a straight line when the two variables are perfectly positively correlated. For example, $Y = 6 - 3X$ is a linear relationship. However, two variables could have a *nonlinear* relationship yet a zero correlation. Therefore, another limitation of correlation analysis is that it does not capture strong nonlinear relationships between variables.

LOS 7.c: Formulate a test of the hypothesis that the population correlation coefficient equals zero and determine whether the hypothesis is rejected at a given level of significance.

CFA® Program Curriculum, Volume 1, page 282

As indicated earlier, the closer the correlation coefficient is to plus or minus one, the stronger the correlation. With the exception of these extremes (i.e., $r = \pm 1.0$), we cannot really speak of the strength of the relationship indicated by the correlation coefficient without a statistical test of significance.

For our purposes, we want *to test whether the correlation between the population of two variables is equal to zero*. Using the lower case Greek letter rho (ρ) to represent the population parameter, the appropriate null and alternative hypotheses can be structured as a two-tailed test as follows:

$$H_0: \rho = 0 \text{ versus } H_a: \rho \neq 0$$

Assuming that the two populations are normally distributed, we can use a *t*-test to determine whether the null hypothesis should be rejected. The test statistic is computed using the sample correlation, *r*, with n − 2 degrees of freedom (*df*):

$$t = \frac{r\sqrt{n-2}}{\sqrt{1-r^2}}$$

To make a decision, the calculated test statistic is compared with the critical *t*-value for the appropriate degrees of freedom and level of significance. Bearing in mind that we are conducting a two-tailed test, the decision rule can be stated as:

Reject H_0 if $+t_{critical} < t$, or $t < -t_{critical}$

EXAMPLE: Test of significance for the correlation coefficient

Using the information from the table in Figure 7.1, determine if the sample correlation is significant at the 5% level of significance.

Answer:

The hypotheses are structured as $H_0 : \rho = 0$ versus $H_a : \rho \neq 0$.

For the sample data in Figure 7.1, n = 10 and r = 0.475. Using this information, the test statistic can be computed as:

$$t = \frac{0.475\sqrt{8}}{\sqrt{1-0.475^2}} = \frac{1.3435}{0.88} = 1.527$$

The two-tailed critical *t*-values at a 5% level of significance with df = 10 − 2 = 8 are found in the *t*-table to be ±2.306. (Look in the df = 8 row and match that with the p = 0.05 two-tailed level of significance column.)

Because $-2.306 \leq 1.5267 \leq 2.306$ (i.e., $-t_{critical} \leq t \leq +t_{critical}$), the null cannot be rejected. We conclude that the correlation between variables *X* and *Y* is not significantly different from zero at a 5% significance level.

MODULE QUIZ 7.1

To best evaluate your performance, enter your quiz answers online.

1. What is the appropriate alternative hypothesis to test the statistical significance of the intercept term in the following regression?

   $Y = a_1 + a_2(X) + \varepsilon$

   A. $H_A: a_1 \neq 0$.
   B. $H_A: a_1 > 0$.
   C. $H_A: a_2 \neq 0$.

2. Which of the following statements *least accurately* describes a limitation of correlation analysis?
   A. Outliers may influence the results of regression.
   B. Serial correlation means that there may appear to be a relationship between two or more variables when, in fact, there is none.
   C. Correlation only measures linear relationships, but not nonlinear ones.

Study Session 3

3. Carla Preusser finds that the total assets under management by a popular hedge fund manager, and the number of lizards lying out in the sun in a nearby park, can be modeled as functions of time: $f(t) = t^{1.8}$ and $f(t) = t + 5$, respectively. The correlation between the two models is 0.98. Two potential problems with using the lizards to predict total assets include:
   A. spurious correlation and the non-linear relationship in the total assets function.
   B. spurious correlation and the non-geometric relationship in the lizard function.
   C. outliers and non-linear relationship in the total assets function.

Video covering this content is available online.

MODULE 7.2: LINEAR REGRESSION: INTRODUCTION

LOS 7.d: Distinguish between the dependent and independent variables in a linear regression.

CFA® Program Curriculum, Volume 1, page 285

The purpose of **simple linear regression** is to explain the variation in a dependent variable in terms of the variation in a single independent variable. Here, the term "variation" is interpreted as the degree to which a variable differs from its mean value. Don't confuse variation with variance—they are related but are not the same.

- The **dependent variable** is the variable whose variation is explained by the independent variable. We are interested in answering the question, "What explains fluctuations in the dependent variable?" The dependent variable is also referred to as the *explained variable*, the *endogenous variable*, or the *predicted variable*.
- The **independent variable** is the variable used to explain the variation of the dependent variable. The independent variable is also referred to as the *explanatory variable*, the *exogenous variable*, or the *predicting variable*.

EXAMPLE: Dependent vs. independent variables

Suppose that you want to predict stock returns with GDP growth. Which variable is the independent variable?

Answer:

Because GDP is going to be used as a predictor of stock returns, stock returns are being *explained* by GDP. Hence, stock returns are the dependent (explained) variable, and GDP is the independent (explanatory) variable.

Suppose we want to use excess returns on the S&P 500 (the independent variable) to explain the variation in excess returns on ABC Inc. (ABC) common stock (the dependent variable). Excess return is defined as the difference between the actual return and the return on 1-month Treasury bills.

We would start by creating a scatter plot with ABC excess returns on the vertical axis and S&P 500 excess returns on the horizontal axis. Monthly excess returns for both variables from June 2012 to May 2015 are plotted in Figure 7.6. For example, look at the point labeled May 2014. In that month the excess return on the S&P 500 was –7.8% and the excess return on ABC was 1.1%.

Figure 7.6: Scatter Plot of ABC Excess Returns vs. S&P 500 Index Excess Returns

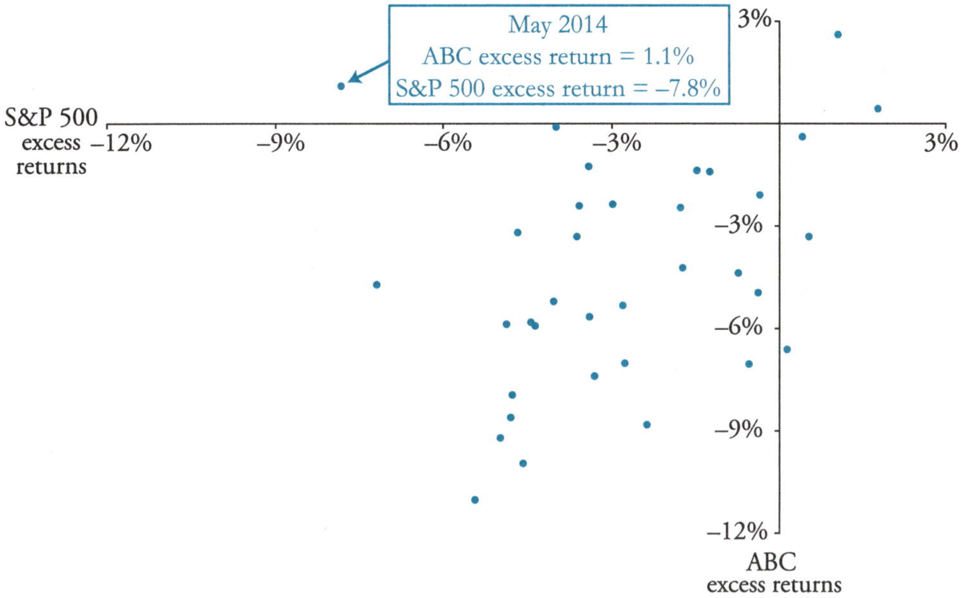

Notice that it appears that the two variables are positively correlated: excess ABC returns tended to be positive (negative) in the same month that S&P 500 excess returns were positive (negative). Note that this is not the case for all the observations, however (including, for example, May 2014). In fact, the correlation between the two is approximately 0.40.

LOS 7.e: Explain the assumptions underlying linear regression and interpret regression coefficients.

CFA® Program Curriculum, Volume 1, page 289

Linear regression requires a number of assumptions. As indicated in the following list, most of the major assumptions pertain to the regression model's residual term (ε).

1. A linear relationship exists between the dependent and the independent variable.
2. The independent variable is uncorrelated with the residuals.
3. The expected value of the residual term is zero $[E(\varepsilon) = 0]$.
4. The variance of the residual term is constant for all observations $\left[E\left(\varepsilon_i^2\right) = \sigma_\varepsilon^2\right]$.
5. The residual term is independently distributed; that is, the residual for one observation is not correlated with that of another observation $\left[E\left(\varepsilon_i \varepsilon_j\right) = 0, j \neq i\right]$.
6. The residual term is normally distributed.

SIMPLE LINEAR REGRESSION MODEL

PROFESSOR'S NOTE

We'll first calculate the regression coefficients and then interpret them. Note that the LOS does not ask you to calculate regression coefficients; we included that step so you can better understand the interpretation of the coefficients.

The following linear regression model is used to describe the relationship between two variables, *X* and *Y*:

$$Y_i = b_0 + b_1 X_i + \varepsilon_i,\ i=1, \ldots, n$$

where:

Y_i = *i*th observation of the dependent variable, Y

X_i = *i*th observation of the independent variable, X

b_0 = regression intercept term

b_1 = regression slope coefficient

ε_i = residual for the *i*th observation (also referred to as the disturbance term or error term)

Based on the regression model stated previously, the regression process estimates an equation for a line through a scatter plot of the data that "best" explains the observed values for *Y* in terms of the observed values for *X*.

The linear equation, often called the line of best fit, or regression line, takes the following form:

$$\hat{Y}_i = \hat{b}_0 + \hat{b}_1 X_i,\ i=1, \ldots, n$$

where:

$\hat{Y}_i$ = estimated value of Y_i given X_i

$\hat{b}_0$ = estimated intercept term

$\hat{b}_1$ = estimated slope coefficient

PROFESSOR'S NOTE

The hat "^" above a variable or parameter indicates a predicted value.

The regression line is just one of the many possible lines that can be drawn through the scatter plot of *X* and *Y*. In fact, the criteria used to estimate this line forms the very essence of linear regression. The regression line is the line for which the estimates of $\hat{b}_0$ and $\hat{b}_1$ are such that the sum of the squared differences (vertical distances) between the *Y*-values predicted by the regression equation ($\hat{Y}_i = \hat{b}_0 + \hat{b}_1 X_i$) and actual *Y*-values, Y_i, is minimized. The sum of the squared vertical distances between the estimated and actual *Y*-values is referred to as the **sum of squared errors** (SSE).

Thus, the regression line is the line that minimizes the SSE. This explains why simple linear regression is frequently referred to as *ordinary least squares* (OLS) regression, and the values estimated by the estimated regression equation, $\hat{Y}_i$, are called least squares estimates.

The estimated **slope coefficient** ($\hat{b}_1$) for the regression line describes the change in *Y* for a one unit change in *X*. It can be positive, negative, or zero, depending on the relationship between the regression variables. The slope term is calculated as:

$$\hat{b}_1 = \frac{\text{cov}_{XY}}{\sigma_X^2}$$

PROFESSOR'S NOTE

For the exam, know that the slope equals covariance divided by variance.

The **intercept** term ($\hat{b}_0$) is the line's intersection with the *Y*-axis at X = 0. It can be positive, negative, or zero. A property of the least squares method is that the intercept term may be expressed as:

$$\hat{b}_0 = \overline{Y} - \hat{b}_1\overline{X}$$

where:
$\overline{Y}$ = mean of Y
$\overline{X}$ = mean of X

The intercept equation highlights the fact that the regression line passes through a point with coordinates equal to the mean of the independent and dependent variables (i.e., the point $\overline{X}$, $\overline{Y}$).

EXAMPLE: Computing the slope coefficient and intercept term

Compute the slope coefficient and intercept term for the ABC regression example using the following information:

cov(S&P 500, ABC)	= 0.000336	$\overline{\text{S\&P 500}}$	= –2.70%
var(S&P 500)	= 0.000522	$\overline{\text{ABC}}$	= –4.05%

Answer:

The slope coefficient is calculated as $\hat{b}_1$ = 0.000336 / 0.000522 = 0.64.

The intercept term is:

$$\hat{b}_0 = \overline{\text{ABC}} - \hat{b}_1\,\overline{\text{S\&P 500}} = -4.05\% - 0.64(-2.70\%) = -2.3\%$$

The estimated regression line that minimizes the SSE in our ABC stock return example is shown in Figure 7.7.

This regression line has an intercept of –2.3% and a slope of 0.64. The model predicts that if the S&P 500 excess return is –7.8% (what it was in May 2014), then the ABC excess return would be –2.3% + (0.64)(–7.8%) = –7.3%. The residual for May 2014 is 8.4%, which is the difference between the actual ABC excess return (1.1%) and the predicted return (–7.3%).

Figure 7.7: Estimated Regression Equation for ABC vs. S&P 500 Excess Returns

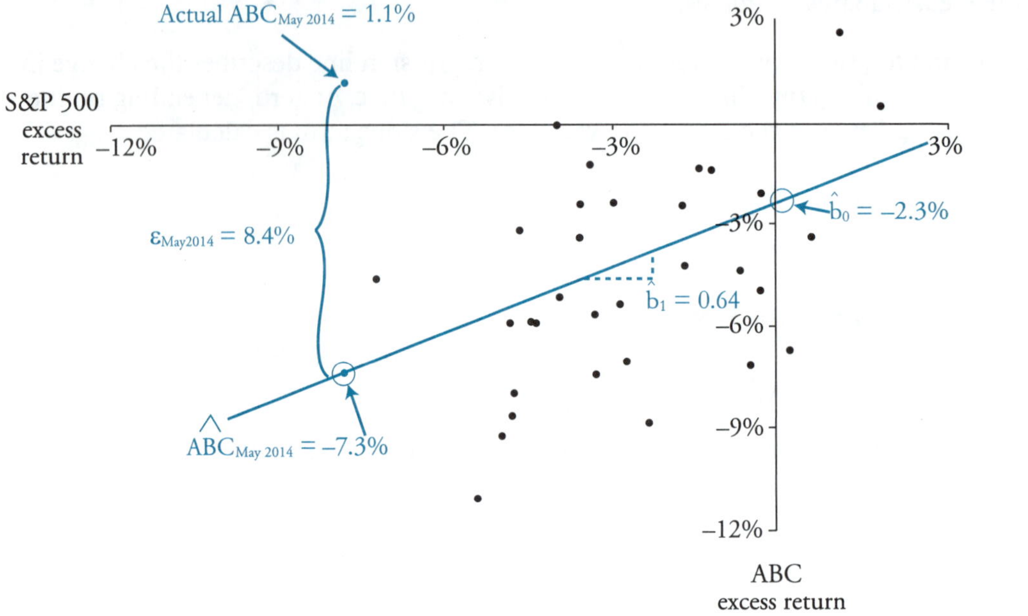

INTERPRETING A REGRESSION COEFFICIENT

The estimated intercept represents the value of the dependent variable at the point of intersection of the regression line and the axis of the dependent variable (usually the vertical axis). In other words, the intercept is an estimate of the dependent variable when the independent variable takes on a value of zero.

We also mentioned earlier that the estimated slope coefficient is interpreted as the change in the dependent variable for a 1-unit change in the independent variable. For example, an estimated slope coefficient of 2 would indicate that the dependent variable will change two units for every 1-unit change in the independent variable.

EXAMPLE: Interpreting regression coefficients

In the ABC regression example, the estimated slope coefficient was 0.64 and the estimated intercept term was –2.3%. Interpret each coefficient estimate.

Answer:

The slope coefficient of 0.64 can be interpreted to mean that when excess S&P 500 returns increase (decrease) by 1%, ABC excess returns increase (decrease) by 0.64%.

The intercept term of –2.3% can be interpreted to mean that when the excess return on the S&P 500 is zero, the return on ABC stock is –2.3%.

PROFESSOR'S NOTE

The slope coefficient in a regression like this is called the stock's beta, and it measures the relative amount of systematic risk in ABC's returns. Notice that ABC is less risky than average because its returns tend to increase or decrease by less than the change in the market returns. A stock with a beta of one would have an average level of systematic risk and a stock with a beta greater than one would have more than average systematic risk.

The intercept term in this regression is called the stock's ex-post alpha. It is a measure of excess risk-adjusted returns. A negative ex-post alpha means that ABC underperformed the S&P 500 on a risk-adjusted basis over the time period.

Keep in mind, however, that any conclusions regarding the importance of an independent variable in explaining a dependent variable require determining the statistical significance of the slope coefficient. Simply looking at the magnitude of the slope coefficient does not address the issue of the importance of the variable. A hypothesis test must be conducted, or a confidence interval must be formed, to assess the importance of the variable.

MODULE QUIZ 7.2

To best evaluate your performance, enter your quiz answers online.

1. Which of the following is not a necessary assumption of simple linear regression analysis?
   A. The residuals are normally distributed.
   B. There is a constant variance of the error term.
   C. The dependent variable is uncorrelated with the residuals.
2. Which of the following statements regarding simple linear regression is *most accurate*?
   A. If the units of the independent variable are tons instead of pounds, the estimated slope coefficient will be 2,000 times larger.
   B. If the slope of the regression line is +1, the variables are perfectly positively correlated.
   C. If a researcher knows the sum of squared errors, the number of observations, and the standard error of estimate, he can calculate the coefficient of determination for the regression.
3. What is the *most appropriate* interpretation of a slope coefficient estimate equal to 10.0?
   A. The predicted value of the dependent variable when the independent variable is zero is 10.0.
   B. For every one unit change in the independent variable, the model predicts that the dependent variable will change by 10 units.
   C. For every one unit change in the independent variable, the model predicts that the dependent variable will change by 0.1 units.

Study Session 3

Video covering this content is available online.

MODULE 7.3: HYPOTHESIS TESTS AND CONFIDENCE INTERVALS

LOS 7.f: Calculate and interpret the standard error of estimate, the coefficient of determination, and a confidence interval for a regression coefficient.

CFA® Program Curriculum, Volume 1, page 292

The **standard error of estimate** (SEE) measures the degree of variability of the actual *Y*-values relative to the estimated *Y*-values from a regression equation. The SEE gauges the "fit" of the regression line. *The smaller the standard error, the better the fit.*

The SEE is the standard deviation of the error terms in the regression. As such, SEE is also referred to as the standard error of the residual, or standard error of the regression.

PROFESSOR'S NOTE

There are multiple terms for SEE and you can expect to see any of these on the exam. Standard error, when used in the context of the whole regression (as opposed to for an individual coefficient), also refers to SEE.

In some regressions, the relationship between the independent and dependent variables is very strong (e.g., the relationship between 10-year Treasury bond yields and mortgage rates). In other cases, the relationship is much weaker (e.g., the relationship between stock returns and inflation). SEE will be low (relative to total variability) if the relationship is very strong and high if the relationship is weak.

COEFFICIENT OF DETERMINATION (R^2)

The **coefficient of determination** (R^2) is defined as the percentage of the total variation in the dependent variable explained by the independent variable. For example, an R^2 of 0.63 indicates that the variation of the independent variable explains 63% of the variation in the dependent variable.

PROFESSOR'S NOTE

For simple linear regression (i.e., one independent variable), the coefficient of determination, R^2, may be computed by simply squaring the correlation coefficient, r. In other words, $R^2 = r^2$ for a regression with one independent variable. This approach is not appropriate when more than one independent variable is used in the regression, as is the case with the multiple regression techniques presented in the next topic review.

We will show you how to calculate the SEE and the R^2 using an ANOVA table later in this topic review.

REGRESSION COEFFICIENT CONFIDENCE INTERVAL

Hypothesis testing for a regression coefficient may use the confidence interval for the coefficient being tested. For instance, a frequently asked question is whether an estimated slope coefficient is statistically different from zero. In other words, the null hypothesis is H_0: $b_1 = 0$ and the alternative hypothesis is H_a: $b_1 \neq 0$. If the confidence interval at the desired level of significance does not include zero, the null is rejected, and the coefficient is said to be statistically different from zero.

The confidence interval for the regression coefficient, b_1, is calculated as:

$$\hat{b}_1 \pm \left(t_c \times s_{\hat{b}_1}\right), \text{or} \left[\hat{b}_1 - \left(t_c \times s_{\hat{b}_1}\right) < b_1 < \hat{b}_1 + \left(t_c \times s_{\hat{b}_1}\right)\right]$$

In this expression, t_c is the critical two-tailed *t*-value for the selected confidence level with the appropriate number of degrees of freedom, which is equal to the number of sample observations minus 2 (i.e., n – 2).

The standard error of the regression coefficient is denoted as $s_{\hat{b}_1}$. It is a function of the SEE: as SEE rises $s_{\hat{b}_1}$, also increases, and the confidence interval widens. This makes sense because SEE measures the variability of the data about the regression line, and the more variable the data, the less confidence there is in the regression model to estimate a coefficient.

PROFESSOR'S NOTE

It is highly unlikely that you will have to calculate $s_{\hat{b}_1}$ on the exam.

It is included in the output of all statistical software packages and should be given to you if you need it.

Although the confidence interval for regression parameters looks slightly different than what you've seen at Level I, it is precisely the same concept. All confidence intervals take the predicted value, then add and subtract the critical test statistic multiplied by the variability of the parameter estimate.

EXAMPLE: Calculating the confidence interval for a regression coefficient

The estimated slope coefficient, b_1, from the ABC regression is 0.64 with a standard error equal to 0.26. Assuming that the sample had 36 observations, calculate the 95% confidence interval for b_1.

Answer:

The confidence interval for b_1 is:

$$\hat{b}_1 \pm \left(t_c \times s_{\hat{b}_1}\right), \text{or} \left[\hat{b}_1 - \left(t_c \times s_{\hat{b}_1}\right) < b_1 < \hat{b}_1 + \left(t_c \times s_{\hat{b}_1}\right)\right]$$

The critical two-tail *t*-values are ± 2.03 (from the *t*-table with n – 2 = 34 degrees of freedom). We can compute the 95% confidence interval as:

$$0.64 \pm (2.03)(0.26) = 0.64 \pm 0.53 = 0.11 \text{ to } 1.17$$

Because this confidence interval does not include zero, we can conclude that the slope coefficient is significantly different from zero.

LOS 7.g: Formulate a null and alternative hypothesis about a population value of a regression coefficient and determine the appropriate test statistic and whether the null hypothesis is rejected at a given level of significance.

CFA® Program Curriculum, Volume 1, page 297

A *t*-test may also be used to test the hypothesis that the true slope coefficient, b_1, is equal to some hypothesized value. Letting $\hat{b}_1$ be the point estimate for b_1, the appropriate test statistic with n – 2 degrees of freedom is:

$$t_{b_1} = \frac{\hat{b}_1 - b_1}{s_{\hat{b}_1}}$$

The decision rule for tests of significance for regression coefficients is:

Reject H_0 if $t > +t_{critical}$ or $t < -t_{critical}$

Rejection of the null means that the slope coefficient is *different* from the hypothesized value of b_1.

To test whether an independent variable explains the variation in the dependent variable (i.e., it is statistically significant), the hypothesis that is tested is whether the true slope is zero ($b_1 = 0$). The appropriate test structure for the null and alternative hypotheses is:

H_0: $b_1 = 0$ versus H_a: $b_1 \neq 0$

EXAMPLE: Hypothesis test for significance of regression coefficients

The estimated slope coefficient from the ABC example is 0.64 with a standard error equal to 0.26. Assuming that the sample has 36 observations, determine if the estimated slope coefficient is significantly different than zero at a 5% level of significance.

Answer:

The calculated test statistic is $t = \frac{\hat{b}_1 - b_1}{s_{\hat{b}_1}} = \frac{0.64 - 0}{0.26} = 2.46.$

The critical two-tailed *t*-values are ± 2.03 (from the *t*-table with df = 36 – 2 = 34). Because $t > t_{critical}$ (i.e., 2.46 > 2.03), we reject the null hypothesis and conclude that the slope is different from zero. Note that the *t*-test and the confidence interval lead to the same conclusion to reject the null hypothesis and conclude that the slope coefficient is statistically significant.

MODULE QUIZ 7.3

To best evaluate your performance, enter your quiz answers online.

Use the following data to answer Questions 1 through 3.

An analyst is interested in predicting annual sales for XYZ Company, a maker of paper products. The following table reports a regression of the annual sales for XYZ against paper product industry sales.

Regression Output

Parameters	Coefficient	Standard Error of the Coefficient
Intercept	–94.88	32.97
Slope (industry sales)	0.2796	0.0363

The correlation between company and industry sales is 0.9757. The regression was based on five observations.

1. Which of the following is *closest* to the value and reports the *most likely* interpretation of the R^2 for this regression? The R^2 is:
   A. 0.048, indicating that the variability of industry sales explains about 4.8% of the variability of company sales.
   B. 0.952, indicating that the variability of industry sales explains about 95.2% of the variability of company sales.
   C. 0.952, indicating that the variability of company sales explains about 95.2% of the variability of industry sales.
2. Based on the regression results, XYZ Company's market share of any increase in industry sales is expected to be *closest* to:
   A. 4%.
   B. 28%.
   C. 45%.
3. The analyst determines that the *t*-statistic is 7.72 and that the correlation coefficient is not significant (using 95% confidence). Is the analyst correct?
   A. Yes.
   B. No, because the test statistic is 60.93.
   C. No, because the correlation coefficient is significantly different from zero (using 95% confidence).

Study Session 3

Use the following information to answer Questions 4 and 5.

A study was conducted by the British Department of Transportation to estimate urban travel time between locations in London, England. Data was collected for motorcycles and passenger cars. Simple linear regression was conducted using data sets for both types of vehicles, where Y = urban travel time in minutes and X = distance between locations in kilometers. The following results were obtained:

Regression Results for Travel Times Between Distances in London		
Passenger cars:	$\hat{Y} = 1.85 + 3.86X$	$R^2 = 0.758$
Motorcycles:	$\hat{Y} = 2.50 + 1.93X$	$R^2 = 0.676$

4. The estimated increase in travel time for a motorcycle commuter planning to move 8 km farther from his workplace in London is *closest* to:
   A. 31 minutes.
   B. 15 minutes.
   C. 0.154 hours.
5. Based on the regression results, which model is more reliable?
   A. The passenger car model because 3.86 > 1.93.
   B. The motorcycle model because 1.93 < 3.86.
   C. The passenger car model because 0.758 > 0.676.
6. Consider the following statement: In a simple linear regression, the appropriate degrees of freedom for the critical *t*-value used to calculate a confidence interval around both a parameter estimate and a predicted Y-value is the same as the number of observations minus two. The statement is:
   A. justified.
   B. not justified, because the appropriate of degrees of freedom used to calculate a confidence interval around a parameter estimate is the number of observations.
   C. not justified, because the appropriate of degrees of freedom used to calculate a confidence interval around a predicted Y-value is the number of observations.

Video covering this content is available online.

MODULE 7.4: PREDICTING DEPENDENT VARIABLES AND CONFIDENCE INTERVALS

LOS 7.h: Calculate the predicted value for the dependent variable, given an estimated regression model and a value for the independent variable.

CFA® Program Curriculum, Volume 1, page 297

Predicted values are values of the dependent variable based on the estimated regression coefficients and a prediction about the value of the independent variable. They are the values that are *predicted* by the regression equation, given an estimate of the independent variable.

For a simple regression, the predicted (or forecast) value of *Y* is:

$$\hat{Y} = \hat{b}_0 + \hat{b}_1 X_p$$

where:
$\hat{Y}$ = predicted value of the dependent variable
X_p = forecasted value of the independent variable

EXAMPLE: Predicting the dependent variable

Given the ABC regression equation:

$$\widehat{ABC} = -2.3\% + (0.64)\ (\widehat{S\&P\ 500})$$

Calculate the predicted value of ABC excess returns if forecasted S&P 500 excess returns are 10%.

Answer:

The predicted value for ABC excess returns is determined as follows:

$$\widehat{ABC} = -2.3\% + (0.64)(10\%) = 4.1\%$$

LOS 7.i: Calculate and interpret a confidence interval for the predicted value of the dependent variable.

CFA® Program Curriculum, Volume 1, page 297

CONFIDENCE INTERVALS FOR PREDICTED VALUES

Confidence intervals for the predicted value of a dependent variable are calculated in a manner similar to the confidence interval for the regression coefficients. The equation for the confidence interval for a predicted value of *Y* is:

$$\hat{Y} \pm (t_c \times s_f) \Rightarrow \left[\hat{Y} - (t_c \times s_f) < Y < \hat{Y} + (t_c \times s_f)\right]$$

where:
t_c = two-tailed critical *t*-value at the desired level of significance with df = n – 2
s_f = standard error of the forecast

The challenge with computing a confidence interval for a predicted value is calculating s_f. It's highly unlikely that you will have to calculate the standard error of the forecast (it will probably be provided if you need to compute a confidence interval for the dependent variable). However, if you do need to calculate s_f, it can be done with the following formula for the variance of the forecast:

$$s_f^2 = SEE^2\left[1 + \frac{1}{n} + \frac{(X - \overline{X})^2}{(n-1)s_x^2}\right]$$

where:
SEE^2 = variance of the residuals = the square of the standard error of estimate
s_x^2 = variance of the independent variable
X = value of the independent variable for which the forecast was made

EXAMPLE: Confidence interval for a predicted value

Calculate a 95% prediction interval on the predicted value of ABC excess returns from the previous example. Suppose the standard error of the forecast is 3.67, and the forecasted value of S&P 500 excess returns is 10%.

Answer:

The predicted value for ABC excess returns is:

$$\widehat{ABC} = -2.3\% + (0.64)(10\%) = 4.1\%$$

The 5% two-tailed critical *t*-value with 34 degrees of freedom is 2.03. The prediction interval at the 95% confidence level is:

$$\widehat{ABC} \pm (t_c \times s_f) \Rightarrow [4.1\% \pm (2.03 \times 3.67\%)] = 4.1\% \pm 7.5\%$$

or

–3.4% to 11.6%

This range can be interpreted as, given a forecasted value for S&P 500 excess returns of 10%, we can be 95% confident that the ABC excess returns will be between –3.4% and 11.6%.

Video covering this content is available online.

MODULE 7.5: ANOVA TABLES, R², AND SEE

LOS 7.j: Describe the use of analysis of variance (ANOVA) in regression analysis, interpret ANOVA results, and calculate and interpret the *F*-statistic.

CFA® Program Curriculum, Volume 1, page 305

Analysis of variance (ANOVA) is a statistical procedure for analyzing the total variability of the dependent variable. Let's define some terms before we move on to ANOVA tables.

- **Total sum of squares** (SST) *measures the total variation* in the dependent variable. SST is equal to the sum of the squared differences between the actual *Y*-values and the mean of *Y*:

$$SST = \sum_{i=1}^{n} (Y_i - \overline{Y})^2$$

PROFESSOR'S NOTE

This is not the same as variance. Variance (of the dependent variable) = SST / (n – 1).

- **Regression sum of squares** (RSS) *measures the variation in the dependent variable that is explained by the independent variable.* RSS is the sum of the squared distances between the predicted *Y*-values and the mean of *Y*.

$$RSS = \sum_{i=1}^{n} (\hat{Y}_i - \overline{Y})^2$$

- **Sum of squared errors** (SSE) *measures the unexplained variation* in the dependent variable. It's also known as the sum of squared residuals or the residual sum of squares. SSE is the sum of the squared vertical distances between the actual *Y*-values and the predicted *Y*-values on the regression line.

$$SSE = \sum_{i=1}^{n} (Y_i - \hat{Y})^2$$

PROFESSOR'S NOTE

You don't have to memorize the formulas for the sums of squares. You do need to know what they measure and how you use them to construct an ANOVA table.

Thus, total variation = explained variation + unexplained variation, or:

SST = RSS + SSE

Figure 7.8 illustrates how the total variation in the dependent variable (SST) is composed of RSS and SSE.

Figure 7.8: Components of the Total Variation

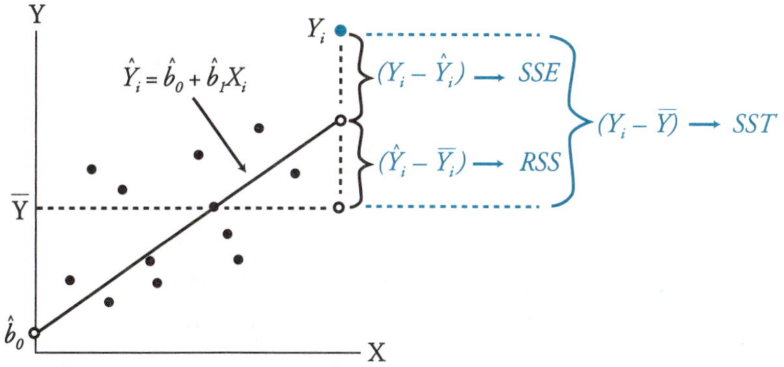

The output of the ANOVA procedure is an ANOVA table, which is a summary of the variation in the dependent variable. ANOVA tables are included in the regression output of many statistical software packages. You can think of the ANOVA table as the source of the data for the computation of many of the regression concepts discussed in this topic review. A generic ANOVA table for a simple linear regression (one independent variable) is presented in Figure 7.9.

Study Session 3

Figure 7.9: ANOVA Table

Source of Variation	Degrees of Freedom	Sum of Squares	Mean Sum of Squares
Regression (explained)	1	RSS	$MSR = \frac{RSS}{k} = \frac{RSS}{1} = RSS$
Error (unexplained)	n – 2	SSE	$MSE = \frac{SSE}{n-2}$
Total	n – 1	SST	

PROFESSOR'S NOTE

k is the number of slope parameters estimated and *n* is the number of observations. In general, the regression df = k and the error df = (n – k – 1). Because we are limited to simple linear regressions in this topic review (one independent variable), we use k = 1 for the regression df and n – 1 – 1 = n – 2 for the error df.

The mean regression sum of squares (MSR) and mean squared error (MSE) are simply calculated as the appropriate sum of squares divided by its degrees of freedom.

Calculating R^2 and SEE

The R^2 and the standard error of estimate (SEE) can also be calculated directly from the ANOVA table as mentioned earlier. The R^2 is the percentage of the total variation in the dependent variable explained by the independent variable:

$$R^2 = \frac{\text{total variation (SST)} - \text{unexplained variation (SSE)}}{\text{total variation (SST)}}$$

$$= \frac{\text{explained variation (RSS)}}{\text{total variation (SST)}}$$

The SEE is the standard deviation of the regression error terms and is equal to the square root of the mean squared error (MSE):

$$SEE = \sqrt{MSE} = \sqrt{\frac{SSE}{n-2}}$$

PROFESSOR'S NOTE

Make sure you recognize the distinction between the sum of squared errors (SSE) and the standard error of estimate (SEE). SSE is the sum of the squared residuals, while SEE is the standard deviation of the residuals.

EXAMPLE: Using the ANOVA table

Complete the ANOVA table for the ABC regression example and calculate the R^2 and the standard error of estimate (SEE).

Partial ANOVA Table for ABC Regression Example

Source of Variation	Degrees of Freedom	Sum of Squares	Mean Sum of Squares
Regression (explained)	?	0.00756	?
Error (unexplained)	?	0.04064	?
Total	?	?	

Answer:

Recall that the data included three years of monthly return observations, so the total number of observations (*n*) is 36.

Completed ANOVA Table for ABC Regression Example

Source of Variation	Degrees of Freedom	Sum of Squares	Mean Sum of Squares
Regression (explained)	**1**	0.0076	**0.0076**
Error (unexplained)	**34**	0.0406	**0.0012**
Total	**35**	**0.0482**	

$$R^2 = \frac{\text{explained variation (RSS)}}{\text{total variation (SST)}} = \frac{0.0076}{0.0482} = \mathbf{0.158}$$

$$\text{SEE} = \sqrt{\text{MSE}} = \sqrt{0.0012} = \mathbf{0.035}$$

THE *F*-STATISTIC

An *F*-test assesses how well a set of independent variables, as a group, explains the variation in the dependent variable. In multiple regression, the *F*-statistic is used to test whether *at least one* independent variable in a set of independent variables explains a significant portion of the variation of the dependent variable. We will discuss the use of the *F*-test in multiple regression with more than one independent variable in the next topic review.

The *F*-statistic is calculated as:

$$F = \frac{\text{MSR}}{\text{MSE}} = \frac{\text{RSS}/k}{\text{SSE}/(n-k-1)}$$

where:
MSR = mean regression sum of squares
MSE = mean squared error

Important: This is always a one-tailed test!

In multiple regression, the *F*-statistic tests *all* independent variables as a group.

The *F*-Statistic With One Independent Variable

For simple linear regression, there is only one independent variable, so the *F*-test tests the same hypothesis as the *t*-test for statistical significance of the slope coefficient:

$$H_0 : b_1 = 0 \text{ versus } H_a : b_1 \neq 0$$

To determine whether b_1 is statistically significant using the *F*-test, the calculated *F*-statistic is compared with the critical *F*-value, F_c, at the appropriate level of significance. The degrees of freedom for the numerator and denominator with one independent variable are:

$$df_{numerator} = k = 1$$
$$df_{denominator} = n - k - 1 = n - 2$$

where:
n = number of observations

The decision rule for the *F*-test is:

Decision rule: reject H_0 if $F > F_c$

Rejection of the null hypothesis at a stated level of significance indicates that the independent variable is significantly different than zero, which is interpreted to mean that it makes a significant contribution to the explanation of the dependent variable. In simple linear regression, it tells us the same thing as the *t*-test of the slope coefficient $\left(t_{b_1}\right)$. In fact, in simple linear regression with one independent variable, $F = t_{b_1}^2$.

EXAMPLE: Calculating and interpreting the *F*-statistic

Use the completed ANOVA table from the previous example to calculate and interpret the *F*-statistic. Test the null hypothesis at the 5% significance level that the slope coefficient is equal to 0.

Answer:

$$F = \frac{MSR}{MSE} = \frac{0.0076}{0.0012} = 6.33$$
$$df_{numerator} = k = 1$$
$$df_{denominator} = n - k - 1 = 36 - 1 - 1 = 34$$

The null and alternative hypotheses are: H_0: $b_1 = 0$ versus H_a: $b_1 \neq 0$. The critical *F*-value for 1 and 34 degrees of freedom at a 5% significance level is approximately 4.1. Remember, it's a one-tail test, so we use the 5% *F*-table! Therefore, we can reject the null hypothesis and conclude that the slope coefficient is significantly different than zero. Recall from the earlier examples that we also rejected the null hypothesis using the *t*-statistic and that the 95% confidence interval did not include 0. Note that here, $t^2 = 2.46^2 \approx F = 6.33$. The difference is due to rounding of the *t*-statistic to two decimal places.

PROFESSOR'S NOTE

The bottom line is that the *F*-test is not as useful when we only have one independent variable because it tells us the same thing as the *t*-test of the slope coefficient. Make sure you know that fact for the exam, and then concentrate on the application of the *F*-test in multiple regression.

LOS 7.k: Describe limitations of regression analysis.

CFA® Program Curriculum, Volume 1, page 311

Limitations of regression analysis include the following:

- Linear relationships can change over time. This means that the estimation equation based on data from a specific time period may not be relevant for forecasts or predictions in another time period. This is referred to as *parameter instability*.
- Even if the regression model accurately reflects the historical relationship between the two variables, its usefulness in investment analysis will be limited if other market participants are also aware of and act on this evidence.
- If the assumptions underlying regression analysis do not hold, the interpretation and tests of hypotheses may not be valid. For example, if the data is *heteroskedastic* (non-constant variance of the error terms) or exhibits *autocorrelation* (error terms are not independent), regression results may be invalid. We will discuss these issues in more detail in the next topic review.

MODULE QUIZ 7.4, 7.5

To best evaluate your performance, enter your quiz answers online.

1. The variation in the dependent variable explained by the independent variable is measured by the:
   A. mean squared error.
   B. sum of squared errors.
   C. regression sum of squares.

Use the following information for Questions 2 through 7.

Bill Coldplay, CFA, is analyzing the performance of the Vigorous Growth Index Fund (VIGRX) over the past three years. The fund employs a passive management investment approach designed to track the performance of the MSCI US Prime Market Growth index, a broadly diversified index of growth stocks of large U.S. companies.

Coldplay estimates a regression using excess monthly returns on VIGRX (exVIGRX) as the dependent variable and excess monthly returns on the S&P 500 Index (exS&P500) as the independent variable. The data are expressed in decimal terms (e.g., 0.03, not 3%).

$$exVIGRX_t = b_0 + b_1(exS\&P500_t) + \varepsilon_t$$

A scatter plot of excess returns for both return series from June 2014 to May 2017 are shown in the following figure.

Analysis of Large-Cap Growth Fund

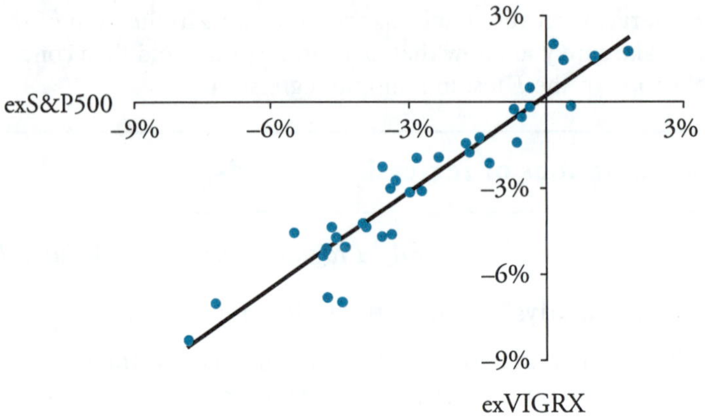

Results from that analysis are presented in the following figures.

Estimated Coefficients

Coefficient	Coefficient Estimate	Standard Error
b_0	0.0023	0.0022
b_1	1.1163	0.0624

Partial ANOVA Table

Source of Variation	Sum of Squares
Regression (explained)	0.0228
Error (unexplained)	0.0024

2. The 90% confidence interval for b_0 is *closest* to:
   A. –0.0014 to +0.0060.
   B. –0.0006 to +0.0052.
   C. +0.0001 to +0.0045.

3. Are the intercept term and the slope coefficient statistically significantly different from zero at the 5% significance level?

	Intercept term significant?	Slope coefficient significant?
A.	Yes	Yes
B.	Yes	No
C.	No	Yes

4. Coldplay would like to test the following hypothesis: H_0: $b_1 \leq 1$ versus H_1: $b_1 > 1$ at the 1% significance level. The calculated *t*-statistic and the appropriate conclusion are:

	Calculated *t*-statistic	Appropriate conclusion
A.	1.86	Reject H_0
B.	1.86	Fail to reject H_0
C.	2.44	Reject H_0

5. Coldplay forecasts the excess return on the S&P 500 for June 2017 to be 5% and the 95% confidence interval for the predicted value of the excess return on VIGRX for June 2017 to be 3.9% to 7.7%. The standard error of the forecast is *closest* to:
   A. 0.0080.
   B. 0.0093.
   C. 0.0111.

6. The R^2 from the regression is *closest* to:
   A. 0.095.
   B. 0.295.
   C. 0.905.

7. The standard error of estimate (SEE) is *closest* to:
   A. 0.008.
   B. 0.014.
   C. 0.049.

8. Regression analysis is *least likely* to be limited by:
   A. parameter instability.
   B. insufficient data.
   C. violations of the assumptions underlying regression analysis.

Study Session 3

KEY CONCEPTS

LOS 7.a

A scatter plot is a collection of points on a graph where each point represents the values of two variables (i.e., an X/Y pair).

The sample covariance, cov_{XY}, measures the linear relationship between two random variables and is calculated as $\dfrac{\sum_{i=1}^{n}(X_i-\overline{X})(Y_i-\overline{Y})}{n-1}$.

Sample correlation is a measure of the relationship between two variables:

$$r_{XY} = \frac{cov_{XY}}{(s_X)(s_Y)}, \text{ which takes on values from } -1.0 \text{ to } +1.0$$

LOS 7.b

There are three limitations of correlation analysis.

- Outliers, or values that are unusually large or small, may influence the results of regression and the estimate of the correlation coefficient.
- Spurious correlation means that there may appear to be a relationship between two variables when, in fact, there is none.
- Correlation only measures linear relationships, but not nonlinear ones.

LOS 7.c

A *t*-test is used to determine if a correlation coefficient, *r*, is statistically significant:

$$t = \frac{r\sqrt{n-2}}{\sqrt{1-r^2}}$$

Significance is supported if the test statistic is less than $-t_{critical}$ or greater than $t_{critical}$ with n – 2 degrees of freedom.

LOS 7.d

Linear regression provides an estimate of the linear relationship between an independent variable (the explanatory variable) and a dependent variable (the predicted variable).

The general form of a simple linear regression model is $Y_i = b_0 + b_1X_i + \varepsilon_i$.

- Y_i and X_i are the *i*th observations of the dependent and independent variable, respectively.
- b_0 = intercept.
- b_1 = slope coefficient.
- ε_i = residual error for the *i*th observation.

LOS 7.e

Assumptions made with simple linear regression include:

1. A linear relationship exists between the dependent and the independent variable.
2. The independent variable is uncorrelated with the residuals.
3. The expected value of the residual term is zero $[E(\varepsilon) = 0]$.
4. The variance of the residual term is constant for all observations $\left[E\left(\varepsilon_i^2\right) = \sigma_\varepsilon^2\right]$.
5. The residual term is independently distributed; that is, the residual for one observation is not correlated with that of another observation $\left[E\left(\varepsilon_i \varepsilon_j\right) = 0, j \neq i\right]$.
6. The residual term is normally distributed.

The estimated intercept, $\hat{b}_0$, represents the value of the dependent variable at the point of intersection of the regression line and the axis of the dependent variable (usually the vertical axis). The estimated slope coefficient, $\hat{b}_1$, is interpreted as the change in the dependent variable for a 1-unit change in the independent variable.

LOS 7.f

The confidence interval for the regression coefficient, b_1, is calculated as:

$$\hat{b}_1 \pm \left(t_c \times s_{\hat{b}_1}\right), \text{or } \left[\hat{b}_1 - \left(t_c \times s_{\hat{b}_1}\right) < b_1 < \hat{b}_1 + \left(t_c \times s_{\hat{b}_1}\right)\right]$$

LOS 7.g

A *t*-test with n – 2 degrees of freedom is used to conduct hypothesis tests of the estimated regression parameters:

$$t = \frac{\hat{b}_1 - b_1}{s_{\hat{b}_1}}$$

LOS 7.h

A predicted value of the dependent variable, $\hat{Y}$, is determined by inserting the predicted value of the independent variable, X_p, in the regression equation and calculating $\hat{Y}_p = \hat{b}_0 + \hat{b}_1 X_p$.

LOS 7.i

The confidence interval for a predicted *Y*-value is $\left[\hat{Y} - \left(t_c \times s_f\right) < Y < \hat{Y} + \left(t_c \times s_f\right)\right]$, where s_f is the standard error of the forecast.

Study Session 3

LOS 7.j

ANOVA Table for Simple Linear Regression (k = 1)

Source of Variation	Degrees of Freedom	Sum of Squares	Mean Sum of Squares
Regression (explained)	1	RSS	$MSR = \frac{RSS}{k} = \frac{RSS}{1} = RSS$
Error (unexplained)	n – 2	SSE	$MSE = \frac{SSE}{n-2}$
Total	n – 1	SST	

The standard error of the estimate in a simple linear regression is calculated as:

$$SEE = \sqrt{\frac{SSE}{n-2}}$$

The coefficient of determination, R^2, is the proportion of the total variation of the dependent variable explained by the regression:

$$R^2 = \frac{RSS}{SST} = \frac{SST - SSE}{SST}$$

In multiple regression (next topic review) the *F*-test tests the statistical significance of all of the independent variables.

In simple linear regression, because there is only one independent variable (k = 1), the *F*-test tests the same null hypothesis as testing the statistical significance of b_1, using the *t*-test: H_0: $b_1 = 0$ versus H_a: $b_1 \neq 0$. With only one independent variable, *F* is calculated as:

$$F\text{-stat} = \frac{MSR}{MSE} \text{ with 1 and } n - 2 \text{ degrees of freedom}$$

In fact, in simple linear regression, $F = t_{b_1}^2$.

LOS 7.k

The limitations of regression analysis include the following:

- Parameter instability (especially when dealing with economic and financial variables).
- The limited usefulness of regression models in identifying profitable investment strategies based on publicly available information.
- The possibility of violating the assumptions underlying regression analysis (heteroskedasticity and autocorrelation).

ANSWER KEY FOR MODULE QUIZZES

Module Quiz 7.1

1. **A** In this regression, a_1 is the intercept term. To test the statistical significance means to test the null hypothesis that a_1 is equal to zero versus the alternative that it is not equal to zero. (LOS 7.c)

2. **B** The appearance of a relationship between two variables when there is none is spurious correlation. Outliers may influence the results of regression and the estimate of the correlation coefficient. Correlation only measures linear relationships properly. (LOS 7.b)

3. **A** There is little to no chance that the relationship between total assets under management and lizards in a park is other than a coincidence. The correlation is spurious. The non-linear relationship in the total assets function makes correlation a poor choice of measure. (LOS 7.b)

Module Quiz 7.2

1. **C** The model does not assume that the dependent variable is uncorrelated with the residuals. It does assume that the independent variable is uncorrelated with the residuals. (LOS 7.e)

2. **A** If the independent variable is in pounds, the interpretation of the slope coefficient is the change in the dependent variable for a one pound change in the independent variable. If the independent variable is measured in tons (2,000 pounds) the slope coefficient is interpreted as the change in the dependent variable for a 2,000 pound change in the independent variable, which will be 2,000 times larger. The slope of the regression line is not a function of the correlation between the two variables. The researcher would need to know either the regression sum of squares or the total sum of squares, along with the sum of squared errors, in order to calculate the coefficient of determination. (LOS 7.e)

3. **B** The slope coefficient is best interpreted as the predicted change in the dependent variable for a 1-unit change in the independent variable. If the slope coefficient estimate is 10.0 and the independent variable changes by one unit, the dependent variable will change by 10 units. The intercept term is best interpreted as the value of the dependent variable when the independent variable is equal to zero. (LOS 7.e)

Module Quiz 7.3

1. **B** The R^2 is computed as the correlation squared: $(0.9757)^2 = 0.952$.

   The interpretation of this R^2 is that 95.2% of the variation in Company XYZ's sales is explained by the variation in industry sales. Answer C is incorrect because it is the independent variable (industry sales) that explains the variation in the dependent variable (company sales). This interpretation is based on the economic reasoning used in constructing the regression model. (Module 7.3, LOS 7.f)

2. **B** The slope coefficient of 0.2796 indicates that a $1 million increase in industry sales will result in an increase in firm sales of approximately 28% ($279,600) of that amount. (Module 7.1, LOS 7.a)

3. **C** The test of significance for the correlation coefficient is evaluated using the following *t*-statistic:

$$t = \frac{r\sqrt{n-2}}{\sqrt{1-r^2}} = \frac{0.9757\sqrt{3}}{\sqrt{1-0.952}} = \frac{1.69}{0.219} = 7.72$$

   From the *t*-table, we find that with df = 3 and 95% significance, the two-tailed critical *t*-values are ±3.182 (recall that for the *t*-test the degrees of freedom = n − 2). Because the computed *t* is greater than +3.182, the correlation coefficient is significantly different from zero. (Module 7.1, LOS 7.a)

4. **B** The slope coefficient is 1.93, indicating that each additional kilometer increases travel time by 1.93 minutes:

   $1.93 \times 8 = 15.44$

   (Module 7.1, LOS 7.a)

5. **C** The higher R^2 for the passenger car model indicates that regression results are more reliable. Distance is a better predictor of travel time for cars. Perhaps the aggressiveness of the driver is a bigger factor in travel time for motorcycles than it is for autos. (Module 7.3, LOS 7.f)

6. **A** In simple linear regression, the appropriate degrees of freedom for both confidence intervals is the number of observations in the sample (*n*) minus two. (Module 7.3, LOS 7.g)

Module Quiz 7.4, 7.5

1. **C** The regression sum of squares measures the variation in the dependent variable explained by the independent variable (i.e., the explained variation). The sum of squared errors measures the variation in the dependent variable NOT explained by the independent variable. The mean squared error is equal to the sum of squared errors divided by its degrees of freedom. (Module 7.5, LOS 7.j)

2. **A** Note that there are 36 monthly observations from June 2014 to May 2017, so n = 36. The critical two-tailed 10% *t*-value with 34 (n – 2 = 36 – 2 = 34) degrees of freedom is approximately 1.69. Therefore, the 90% confidence interval for b_0 (the intercept term) is 0.0023 +/– (0.0022)(1.69), or –0.0014 to +0.0060. (Module 7.3, LOS 7.f)

3. **C** The critical two-tailed 5% *t*-value with 34 degrees of freedom is approximately 2.03. The calculated *t*-statistics for the intercept term and slope coefficient are, respectively, 0.0023 / 0.0022 = 1.05 and 1.1163 / 0.0624 = 17.9. Therefore, the intercept term is not statistically different from zero at the 5% significance level, while the slope coefficient is. (Module 7.3, LOS 7.g)

4. **B** Notice that this is a one-tailed test. The critical one-tailed 1% *t*-value with 34 degrees of freedom is approximately 2.44. The calculated *t*-statistic for the slope coefficient is (1.1163 – 1) / 0.0624 = 1.86. Therefore, the slope coefficient is not statistically different from one at the 1% significance level and Coldplay should fail to reject the null hypothesis. (Module 7.3, LOS 7.g)

5. **B** This is a tricky question because you are given the confidence interval and its midpoint and asked to solve for the standard error of the forecast (s_f). Remember to also convert the percentages to decimals. The critical two-tailed 5% *t*-value with 34 degrees of freedom is approximately 2.03. The midpoint, or predicted value is 0.0023 + 1.1163 × 0.05 = 0.058. Therefore, 0.058 +/– (2.03)(s_f) is equivalent to 0.039 to 0.077 and solving for s_f yields s_f = 0.0093. (Module 7.5, LOS 7.j)

6. **C** SST is equal to the sum of RSS and SSE: 0.0228 + 0.0024 = 0.0252. R^2 = RSS / SST = 0.0228 / 0.0252 = 0.905. (Module 7.5, LOS 7.j)

7. **A** Because n = 36, and the degrees of freedom for the sum of squared errors (SSE) is n – 2 in simple linear regression, the degrees of freedom for SSE is 34, and the mean squared error is SSE / 34. The standard error of estimate (SEE) is equal to the square root of the mean squared error:

$$\text{SEE} = \sqrt{\frac{0.0024}{34}} = 0.008$$

(Module 7.5, LOS 7.j)

8. **B** The insufficient availability of data is not likely to be much of a limitation for most financial and economic models; usually an abundance of data is available. The other choices are limitations of regression analysis. (Module 7.5, LOS 7.k)

The following is a review of the Quantitative Methods principles designed to address the learning outcome statements set forth by CFA Institute. Cross-Reference to CFA Institute Assigned Reading #8.

READING 8

Multiple Regression and Issues in Regression Analysis

Study Session 3

EXAM FOCUS

Multiple regression is the centerpiece of the quantitative methods topic at Level II. It is a useful analysis tool that closely relates to the multifactor models that appear later in the Level II curriculum, in the Equity and Portfolio Management Study Sessions. Know this material well.

You should know how to use a t-test to assess the significance of the individual regression parameters and an *F*-test to assess the effectiveness of the model as a whole in explaining the dependent variable. You should understand the effect that heteroskedasticity, serial correlation, and multicollinearity have on regression results. Also be able to identify the common model misspecifications.

Focus on interpretation of the regression equation and the test statistics. Remember that most of the test and descriptive statistics discussed (e.g., *t*-stat, *F*-stat, and R^2) are provided in the output of statistical software. Hence, application and interpretation of these measurements are more likely than actual computations on the exam.

WARM-UP: MULTIPLE REGRESSION BASICS

Multiple regression is regression analysis with more than one independent variable. It is used to quantify the influence of two or more independent variables on a dependent variable. For instance, simple (or univariate) linear regression explains the variation in stock returns in terms of the variation in systematic risk as measured by beta. With multiple regression, stock returns can be regressed against beta and against additional variables, such as firm size, equity, and industry classification, that might influence returns.

The general multiple linear regression model is:

$$Y_i = b_0 + b_1X_{1i} + b_2X_{2i} + \ldots + b_kX_{ki} + \varepsilon_i$$

where:

Y_i = ith observation of the dependent variable Y, i = 1, 2, ..., n
X_j = independent variables, j = 1, 2, ..., k
X_{ji} = ith observation of the jth independent variable
b_0 = intercept term
b_j = slope coefficient for each of the independent variables
ε_i = error term for the ith observation
n = number of observations
k = number of independent variables

The multiple regression methodology estimates the intercept and slope coefficients such that the sum of the squared error terms, $\sum_{i=1}^{n} \varepsilon_i^2$, is minimized. The result of this procedure is the following regression equation:

$$\hat{Y}_i = \hat{b}_0 + \hat{b}_1X_{1i} + \hat{b}_2X_{2i} + \ldots + \hat{b}_kX_{ki}$$

where the "^" indicates an estimate for the corresponding regression coefficient

The residual, $\hat{\varepsilon}_i$, is the difference between the observed value, Y_i, and the predicted value from the regression, $\hat{Y}_i$:

$$\hat{\varepsilon}_i = Y_i - \hat{Y}_i = Y_i - \left(\hat{b}_0 + \hat{b}_1X_{1i} + \hat{b}_2X_{2i} + \ldots + \hat{b}_kX_{ki}\right)$$

MODULE 8.1: MULTIPLE REGRESSION: INTRODUCTION

Video covering this content is available online.

LOS 8.a: Formulate a multiple regression equation to describe the relation between a dependent variable and several independent variables and determine the statistical significance of each independent variable.

CFA® Program Curriculum, Volume 1, page 328

PROFESSOR'S NOTE

Testing the statistical significance of the regression coefficients means conducting a *t*-test with a null hypothesis that the regression coefficient is equal to zero. Rather than cover that concept here, even though it is mentioned in this LOS, we will cover it in detail in a later LOS as part of our general discussion of hypothesis testing.

Let's illustrate multiple regression using research by Arnott and Asness (2003).[1] As part of their research, the authors test the hypothesis that future 10-year real earnings growth in the S&P 500 (EG10) can be explained by the trailing dividend

1. Arnott, Robert D., and Clifford S. Asness. 2003. "Surprise! Higher Dividends = Higher Earnings Growth." *Financial Analysts Journal*, vol. 59, no. 1 (January/February): 70–87.

payout ratio of the stocks in the index (PR) and the yield curve slope (YCS). YCS is calculated as the difference between the 10-year T-bond yield and the 3-month T-bill yield at the start of the period. All three variables are measured in percent.

Formulating the Multiple Regression Equation

The authors formulate the following regression equation using annual data (46 observations):

$$EG10 = b_0 + b_1PR + b_2YCS + \varepsilon$$

The results of this regression are shown in Figure 8.1.

Figure 8.1: Coefficient and Standard Error Estimates for Regression of EG10 on PR and YCS

	Coefficient	Standard Error
Intercept	–11.6%	1.657%
PR	0.25	0.032
YCS	0.14	0.280

LOS 8.b: Interpret estimated regression coefficients and their *p*-values.

CFA® Program Curriculum, Volume 1, page 333

PROFESSOR'S NOTE

We will defer a discussion of *p*-values to a later LOS.

Interpreting the Multiple Regression Results

The interpretation of the estimated regression coefficients from a multiple regression is the same as in simple linear regression for the intercept term but significantly different for the slope coefficients:

- The **intercept term** is the value of the dependent variable when the independent variables are all equal to zero.
- Each slope coefficient is the estimated change in the dependent variable for a one-unit change in that independent variable, *holding the other independent variables constant.* That's why the slope coefficients in a multiple regression are sometimes called **partial slope coefficients**.

For example, in the real earnings growth example, we can make these interpretations:

- *Intercept term*: If the dividend payout ratio is zero and the slope of the yield curve is zero, we would expect the subsequent 10-year real earnings growth rate to be –11.6%.

- *PR coefficient*: If the payout ratio increases by 1%, we would expect the subsequent 10-year earnings growth rate to increase by 0.25%, *holding YCS constant.*
- *YCS coefficient*: If the yield curve slope increases by 1%, we would expect the subsequent 10-year earnings growth rate to increase by 0.14%, *holding PR constant.*

Let's discuss the interpretation of the multiple regression slope coefficients in more detail. Suppose we run a regression of the dependent variable *Y* on a single independent variable *X1* and get the following result:

$$Y = 2.0 + 4.5X1$$

The appropriate interpretation of the estimated slope coefficient is that if *X1* increases by 1 unit, we would expect *Y* to increase by 4.5 units.

Now suppose we add a second independent variable *X2* to the regression and get the following result:

$$Y = 1.0 + 2.5X1 + 6.0X2$$

Notice that the estimated slope coefficient for *X1* changed from 4.5 to 2.5 when we added *X2* to the regression. We would expect this to happen most of the time when a second variable is added to the regression, unless *X2* is uncorrelated with *X1*, because if *X1* increases by 1 unit, then we would expect *X2* to change as well. The multiple regression equation captures this relationship between *X1* and *X2* when predicting *Y*.

Now the interpretation of the estimated slope coefficient for *X1* is that if *X1* increases by 1 unit, we would expect *Y* to increase by 2.5 units, *holding* X2 *constant*.

Video covering this content is available online.

MODULE 8.2: HYPOTHESIS TESTS AND CONFIDENCE INTERVALS

LOS 8.c: Formulate a null and an alternative hypothesis about the population value of a regression coefficient, calculate the value of the test statistic, and determine whether to reject the null hypothesis at a given level of significance.

LOS 8.d: Interpret the results of hypothesis tests of regression coefficients.

CFA® Program Curriculum, Volume 1, page 330 and 337

Hypothesis Testing of Regression Coefficients

As with simple linear regression, the magnitude of the coefficients in a multiple regression tells us nothing about the importance of the independent variable in explaining the dependent variable. Thus, we must conduct hypothesis testing on the estimated slope coefficients to determine if the independent variables make a significant contribution to explaining the variation in the dependent variable.

The *t*-statistic used to test the significance of the individual coefficients in a multiple regression is calculated using the same formula that is used with simple linear regression:

$$t = \frac{\hat{b}_j - b_j}{s_{\hat{b}_j}} = \frac{\text{estimated regression coefficient} - \text{hypothesized value}}{\text{coefficient standard error of } b_j}$$

The *t*-statistic has n − k − 1 degrees of freedom.

PROFESSOR'S NOTE

An easy way to remember the number of degrees of freedom for this test is to recognize that "k" is the number of regression coefficients in the regression, and the "1" is for the intercept term. Therefore, the degrees of freedom is the number of observations minus k minus 1.

Determining Statistical Significance

The most common hypothesis test done on the regression coefficients is to test statistical significance, which means testing the null hypothesis that the coefficient is zero versus the alternative that it is not:

"testing statistical significance" ⇒ H_0: $b_j = 0$ versus H_a : $b_j \neq 0$

EXAMPLE: Testing the statistical significance of a regression coefficient

Test the statistical significance of the independent variable PR in the real earnings growth example at the 10% significance level. The results of that regression are reproduced in the following figure.

Coefficient and Standard Error Estimates for Regression of EG10 on PR and YCS

	Coefficient	Standard Error
Intercept	–11.6%	1.657%
PR	0.25	0.032
YCS	0.14	0.280

Answer:

We are testing the following hypothesis:

H_0: PR = 0 versus H_a: PR ≠ 0

The 10% two-tailed critical *t*-value with 46 − 2 − 1 = 43 degrees of freedom is approximately 1.68. We should reject the null hypothesis if the *t*-statistic is greater than 1.68 or less than –1.68.

The *t*-statistic is:

$$t = \frac{0.25}{0.032} = 7.8$$

Therefore, because the *t*-statistic of 7.8 is greater than the upper critical *t*-value of 1.68, we can reject the null hypothesis and conclude that the PR regression coefficient is statistically significantly different from zero at the 10% significance level.

Interpreting *p*-Values

The *p*-value is the smallest level of significance for which the null hypothesis can be rejected. An alternative method of doing hypothesis testing of the coefficients is to compare the *p*-value to the significance level:

- If the *p*-value is less than significance level, the null hypothesis can be rejected.
- If the *p*-value is greater than the significance level, the null hypothesis cannot be rejected.

EXAMPLE: Interpreting *p*-values

Given the following regression results, determine which regression parameters for the independent variables are statistically significantly different from zero at the 1% significance level, assuming the sample size is 60.

Variable	Coefficient	Standard Error	*t*-Statistic	*p*-Value
Intercept	0.40	0.40	1.0	0.3215
X1	8.20	2.05	4.0	0.0002
X2	0.40	0.18	2.2	0.0319
X3	–1.80	0.56	-3.2	0.0022

Answer:

The independent variable is statistically significant if the *p*-value is less than 1%, or 0.01. Therefore *X*1 and *X*3 are statistically significantly different from zero.

Figure 8.2 shows the results of the *t*-tests for each of the regression coefficients of our 10-year earnings growth example, including the *p*-values.

Figure 8.2: Regression Results for Regression of EG10 on PR and YCS

	Coefficient	Standard Error	*t*-statistic	*p*-value
Intercept	–11.6%	1.657%	–7.0	< 0.0001
PR	0.25	0.032	7.8	< 0.0001
YCS	0.14	0.280	0.5	0.62

As we determined in a previous example, we can reject the null hypothesis and conclude that PR is statistically significant. We can also draw the same conclusion for the intercept term because –7.0 is less than the lower critical value of –1.68 (because it is a two-tailed test). However, we fail to reject the null hypothesis for YCS, so we cannot conclude that YCS has a statistically significant effect on the dependent variable, EG10, when PR is also included in the model. The *p*-values tell us exactly the same thing (as they always will): the intercept term and PR are statistically significant at the 10% level because their *p*-values are less than 0.10, while YCS is not statistically significant because its *p*-value is greater than 0.10.

Other Tests of the Regression Coefficients

You should also be prepared to formulate one- and two-tailed tests in which the null hypothesis is that the coefficient is equal to some value other than zero, or that it is greater than or less than some value.

EXAMPLE: Testing regression coefficients (two-tail test)

Using the data from Figure 8.2, test the null hypothesis that PR is equal to 0.20 versus the alternative that it is not equal to 0.20 using a 5% significance level.

Answer:

We are testing the following hypothesis:

H_0: PR = 0.20 versus H_a: PR ≠ 0.20

The 5% two-tailed critical *t*-value with 46 – 2 – 1 = 43 degrees of freedom is approximately 2.02. We should reject the null hypothesis if the *t*-statistic is greater than 2.02 or less than –2.02.

The *t*-statistic is:

$$t = \frac{0.25 - 0.20}{0.032} = 1.56$$

Therefore, because the *t*-statistic of 1.56 is between the upper and lower critical *t*-values of –2.02 and 2.02, we cannot reject the null hypothesis and must conclude that the PR regression coefficient is not statistically significantly different from 0.20 at the 5% significance level.

EXAMPLE: Testing regression coefficients (one-tail test)

Using the data from Figure 8.2, test the null hypothesis that the intercept term is greater than or equal to –10.0% versus the alternative that it is less than –10.0% using a 1% significance level.

Answer:

We are testing the following hypothesis:

H_0: Intercept ≥ –10.0% versus H_a: Intercept < –10.0%

The 1% **one**-tailed critical *t*-value with 46 – 2 – 1 = 43 degrees of freedom is approximately 2.42. We should reject the null hypothesis if the *t*-statistic is less than –2.42.

The *t*-statistic is:

$$t = \frac{-11.6\% - (-10.0\%)}{1.657\%} = -0.96$$

Therefore, because the *t*-statistic of –0.96 is not less than –2.42, we cannot reject the null hypothesis.

LOS 8.e: Calculate and interpret 1) a confidence interval for the population value of a regression coefficient and 2) a predicted value for the dependent variable, given an estimated regression model and assumed values for the independent variables.

CFA® Program Curriculum, Volume 1, page 339

Confidence Intervals for a Regression Coefficient

The confidence interval for a regression coefficient in multiple regression is calculated and interpreted the same way as it is in simple linear regression. For example, a 95% confidence interval is constructed as follows:

$$\hat{b}_j \pm (t_c \times s_{\hat{b}_j})$$

or

estimated regression coefficient ± (critical *t*-value)(coefficient standard error)

The critical *t*-value is a two-tailed value with n − k − 1 degrees of freedom and a 5% significance level, where *n* is the number of observations and *k* is the number of independent variables.

EXAMPLE: Calculating a confidence interval for a regression coefficient

Calculate the 90% confidence interval for the estimated coefficient for the independent variable PR in the real earnings growth example.

Answer:

The critical *t*-value is 1.68, the same as we used in testing the statistical significance at the 10% significance level (which is the same thing as a 90% confidence level). The estimated slope coefficient is 0.25 and the standard error is 0.032. The 90% confidence interval is:

$$0.25 \pm (1.68)(0.032) = 0.25 \pm 0.054 = 0.196 \text{ to } 0.304$$

PROFESSOR'S NOTE

Notice that because zero is not contained in the 90% confidence interval, we can conclude that the PR coefficient is statistically significant at the 10% level—the same conclusion we made when using the t-test earlier in this topic review. Constructing a confidence interval and conducting a t-test with a null hypothesis of "equal to zero" will always result in the same conclusion regarding the statistical significance of the regression coefficient.

PREDICTING THE DEPENDENT VARIABLE

We can use the regression equation to make predictions about the dependent variable *based on forecasted values of the independent variables*. The process is similar to forecasting with simple linear regression, only now we need predicted values for more than one independent variable. The predicted value of dependent variable *Y* is:

$$\hat{Y}_i = \hat{b}_0 + \hat{b}_1 \hat{X}_{1i} + \hat{b}_2 \hat{X}_{2i} + \ldots + \hat{b}_k \hat{X}_{ki}$$

where:

$\hat{Y}_i$ = the predicted value of the dependent variable

$\hat{b}_j$ = the estimated slope coefficient for the *j*th independent variable

$\hat{X}_{ji}$ = the forecast of the *j*th independent variable, $j = 1, 2, \ldots, k$

PROFESSOR'S NOTE

The prediction of the dependent variable uses the estimated intercept and all of the estimated slope coefficients, regardless of whether the estimated coefficients are statistically significantly different from zero. For example, suppose you estimate the following regression equation: $\hat{Y} = 6 + 2X_1 + 4X_2$, and you determine that only the first independent variable (X_1) is statistically significant (i.e., you rejected the null that $b_1 = 0$). To predict Y given forecasts of $X_1 = 0.6$ and $X_2 = 0.8$, you would use the complete model: $\hat{Y} = 6 + (2 \times 0.6) + (4 \times 0.8) = 10.4$. Alternatively, you could drop X_2 and reestimate the model using just X_1, but remember that the coefficient on X_1 will probably change.

EXAMPLE: Calculating a predicted value for the dependent variable

An analyst would like to use the estimated regression equation from the previous example to calculate the predicted 10-year real earnings growth for the S&P 500, assuming the payout ratio of the index is 50%. He observes that the slope of the yield curve is currently 4%.

Answer:

$$\widehat{EG10} = -11.6\% + 0.25(50\%) + 0.14(4\%) = 1.46\%$$

The model predicts a 1.46% real earnings growth rate for the S&P 500, assuming a 50% payout ratio, when the slope of the yield curve is 4%.

MODULE 8.3: ANOVA AND THE *F*-TEST

Video covering this content is available online.

LOS 8.g: Calculate and interpret the *F*-statistic, and describe how it is used in regression analysis.

CFA® Program Curriculum, Volume 1, page 341

THE *F*-STATISTIC

An *F*-test assesses how well the set of independent variables, as a group, explains the variation in the dependent variable. That is, the *F*-statistic is used to test whether *at least one* of the independent variables explains a significant portion of the variation of the dependent variable.

For example, if there are four independent variables in the model, the hypotheses are structured as:

$$H_0: b_1 = b_2 = b_3 = b_4 = 0 \text{ versus } H_a: \text{at least one } b_j \neq 0$$

The *F*-statistic, *which is always a one-tailed test*, is calculated as:

$$F = \frac{MSR}{MSE} = \frac{RSS/k}{SSE/(n-k-1)}$$

where:
RSS = regression sum of squares
SSE = sum of squared errors
MSR = mean regression sum of squares
MSE = mean squared error

PROFESSOR'S NOTE

Recall from the previous topic review that the regression sum of squares and the sum of squared errors are found in an ANOVA table. We analyze an ANOVA table from a multiple regression later in this topic review.

To determine whether at least one of the coefficients is statistically significant, the calculated *F*-statistic is compared with the **one-tailed** critical *F*-value, F_c, at the appropriate level of significance. The degrees of freedom for the numerator and denominator are:

$$df_{numerator} = k$$
$$df_{denominator} = n - k - 1$$

where:
n = number of observations
k = number of independent variables

The decision rule for the *F*-test is:

Decision rule: reject H_0 if F (test-statistic) > F_c (critical value)

Rejection of the null hypothesis at a stated level of significance indicates that at least one of the coefficients is significantly different than zero, which is interpreted to mean that at least one of the independent variables in the regression model makes a significant contribution to the explanation of the dependent variable.

PROFESSOR'S NOTE

It may have occurred to you that an easier way to test all of the coefficients simultaneously is to just conduct all of the individual t-tests and see how many of them you can reject. This is the wrong approach, however, because if you set the significance level for each t-test at 5%, for example, the significance level from testing them all simultaneously is NOT 5%, but rather some higher percentage. Just remember to use the F-test on the exam if you are asked to test all of the coefficients simultaneously.

EXAMPLE: Calculating and interpreting the *F*-statistic

An analyst runs a regression of monthly value-stock returns on five independent variables over 60 months. The total sum of squares is 460, and the sum of squared errors is 170. Test the null hypothesis at the 5% significance level that all five of the independent variables are equal to zero.

Answer:

The null and alternative hypotheses are:

H_0: $b_1 = b_2 = b_3 = b_4 = b_5 = 0$ versus H_a: at least one $b_j \neq 0$

$RSS = SST - SSE = 460 - 170 = 290$

$$MSR = \frac{290}{5} = 58.0$$

$$MSE = \frac{170}{60 - 5 - 1} = 3.15$$

$$F = \frac{58.0}{3.15} = 18.41$$

The critical *F*-value for 5 and 54 degrees of freedom at a 5% significance level is approximately 2.40. Remember, it's a **one-tailed** test, so we use the 5% *F*-table! Therefore, we can reject the null hypothesis and conclude that at least one of the five independent variables is significantly different than zero.

PROFESSOR'S NOTE

When testing the hypothesis that all the regression coefficients are simultaneously equal to zero, the F-test is always a one-tailed test, despite the fact that it looks like it should be a two-tailed test because there is an equal sign in the null hypothesis. This is a common source of confusion among Level II candidates; make sure you don't make that mistake on the exam.

LOS 8.i: Evaluate how well a regression model explains the dependent variable by analyzing the output of the regression equation and an ANOVA table.

CFA® Program Curriculum, Volume 1, page 341

ANOVA TABLES

Analysis of variance (ANOVA) is a statistical procedure that provides information on the explanatory power of a regression. We first discussed the use of ANOVA tables in the previous topic review of simple linear regression. Once again, the interpretation is the same in multiple regression.

The results of the ANOVA procedure are presented in an ANOVA table, which accompanies the multiple regression results from a statistical analysis or spreadsheet software program. An example of a generic ANOVA table is presented in Figure 8.3.

Study Session 3

Figure 8.3: ANOVA Table

Source	df (Degrees of Freedom)	SS (Sum of Squares)	MS (Mean Square= SS/df)
Regression	k	RSS	MSR
Error	n – k – 1	SSE	MSE
Total	n – 1	SST	

The information in an ANOVA table is used to attribute the total variation of the dependent variable to one of two sources: the regression model or the residuals. This is indicated in the first column in the table, where the "source" of the variation is listed.

The information in an ANOVA table can be used to calculate R^2, the *F*-statistic, and the standard error of estimate (SEE). That is:

$$R^2 = \frac{RSS}{SST}$$

$$F = \frac{MSR}{MSE} \text{ with k and n} - \text{k} - 1 \text{ degrees of freedom}$$

$$SEE = \sqrt{MSE}$$

PROFESSOR'S NOTE

R^2, F, and SEE are provided along with the standard ANOVA table produced by most statistical software packages. On the exam, be prepared to fill in "missing data" from an ANOVA output.

Let's look at an example to tie all of this together.

EXAMPLE: Using an ANOVA table with regression output

In an attempt to estimate a regression equation that can be used to forecast BuildCo's future sales, 22 years of BuildCo's annual sales were regressed against two independent variables:

GDP = the level of gross domestic product

ΔI = changes in 30-year mortgage interest rates (expressed in percentage terms)

The output from a common statistical software package is contained in the following table.

Regression Results for BuildCo Sales Data

	Coefficient	Standard Error	*t*-Statistic	*p*-Value
Intercept	6.000	4.520	1.327	0.20
Level of gross domestic product (GDP)	0.004	0.003	?	0.20
Changes in 30-year mortgage rates (ΔI)	–20.500	3.560	?	< 0.001

ANOVA	*df*	*SS*	*MS*	*F*	*Significance F*
Regression	?	236.30	?	?	p < 0.005
Error	?	116.11	?		
Total	?	?			
R^2	?				
R^2_a	?				

Based on the output in the table, the regression equation can be stated as:

$\widehat{\text{BuildCo Sales}} = 6.000 + 0.004(\text{GDP}) - 20.500(\Delta\text{I})$

Fill in the missing data and interpret the results of the regression at a 5% level of significance with respect to:

- The significance of the individual independent variables.
- The utility of the model as a whole.

Answer:

Step 1: Fill in the missing data.

The computed test statistics for the regression coefficients are:

$$t_{GDP} = \frac{0.004}{0.003} = 1.333$$

$$t_{\Delta I} = \frac{-20.500}{3.560} = -5.758$$

Degrees of freedom are:

$$df_{regression} = k = 2$$
$$df_{error} = n - k - 1 = 22 - 2 - 1 = 19$$
$$df_{total} = n - 1 = 22 - 1 = 21$$

Other calculations:

$$SST = RSS + SSE = 236.30 + 116.11 = \mathbf{352.41}$$

$$MSR = \frac{RSS}{k} = \frac{236.30}{2} = \mathbf{118.15}$$

$$MSE = \frac{SSE}{n-k-1} = \frac{116.11}{19} = \mathbf{6.11}$$

$$F = \frac{MSR}{MSE} = \frac{118.15}{6.11} = \mathbf{19.34}$$

$$R^2 = \frac{RSS}{SST} = \frac{236.30}{352.41} = \mathbf{67.05\%}$$

$$R_a^2 = 1 - \left(\frac{n-1}{n-k-1}\right)(1-R^2) = 1 - \left(\frac{21}{19}\right)(1-0.6705) = \mathbf{63.58\%}$$

The following table shows what the complete ANOVA table looks like.

Regression Results for BuildCo Sales Data

	Coefficient	Standard Error	*t*-Statistic	*p*-Value
Intercept	6.000	4.520	1.327	0.20
Level of gross domestic product (GDP)	0.004	0.003	**1.333**	0.20
Changes in 30-year mortgage rates (ΔI)	–20.500	3.560	**–5.758**	< 0.001

ANOVA	*df*	*SS*	*MS*	*F*	*Significance F*
Regression	**2**	236.30	**118.15**	**19.34**	p < 0.005
Error	**19**	116.11	**6.11**		
Total	**21**	**352.41**			
R^2	**67.05%**				
R_a^2	**63.58%**				

Step 2: Determine the significance of the individual independent variables.

The contribution of the individual variables, as indicated by the significance of their slope coefficients, can be tested using *t*-tests. However, since the *p*-values are included with the regression output, as is usually the case, the level of significance can be observed directly. Just for practice, let's test for significance of the individual coefficients using *t*-tests *and p*-values.

- Using *p*-values. Only the *p*-value of the coefficient for ΔI is less than the 5% level of significance, so we conclude that only ΔI contributes significantly to the level of BuildCo's annual sales.
- Using *t*-statistics. The hypothesis test structure is:

  $H_0 : b_j = 0$ versus $H_a : b \neq 0$

  The critical two-tailed *t*-values with df = 19 are ±2.093.

  The decision rule is reject H_0 if is greater than 2.093 or less than –2.093.

Since t_{GDP} = 1.33 does not fall in the rejection region, we cannot reject the null for GDP, and we conclude that the level of GDP does not make a statistically significant contribution to the variation in sales at the 5% level.

Since ($t_{\Delta I}$ = –5.758) < (t_c = –2.093), we conclude that changes in mortgage rates make a significant contribution to the variation in sales at the 5% level.

PROFESSOR'S NOTE

The use of *p*-values or *t*-tests will always result in the same conclusions about the statistical significance of the slope estimate (i.e., coefficients on the independent variables). On the exam, use the *p*-value if it is provided!

Step 3: Determine the utility of the model as a whole.

The overall utility of the model can be generally assessed with the coefficient of determination, R^2. The R^2 value indicates that GDP and ΔI explain 67.05% of the variation in BuildCo's annual sales.

Tests of significance for the set of independent variables should be performed using the *F*-test. The hypotheses for the one-sided *F*-test can be structured as:

H_0: $b_{\Delta I} = b_{GDP} = 0$ versus H_a: $b_{\Delta I} \neq 0$, or $b_{GDP} \neq 0$

F_c at the 5% significance level with $df_{numerator}$ = 2 and $df_{denominator}$ = 19 is 3.52. Remember, this is a one-tailed test.

The decision rule is reject H_0 if F is greater than 3.52.

Since F > 3.52, the null hypothesis can be rejected and we can conclude that at least one of the independent variables significantly contributes to the dependent variable. That is, changes in mortgage rates *and* the level of GDP together explain a significant amount of the variation in BuildCo's annual sales at the 5% significance level. Notice that we could have reached this conclusion by observing that the ANOVA table reports that *F* is significant at a level less than 0.5%.

MODULE QUIZ 8.1, 8.2, 8.3

To best evaluate your performance, enter your quiz answers online.

Use the following information to answer Questions 1 and 2.

An analyst evaluates the sum of squared error and total sum of squares from a multiple regression with four independent variables to be 4,320 and 9,105 respectively. There are 65 observations in the sample.

1. The *F*-statistic is *closest* to:
   A. 13.54.
   B. 13.77.
   C. 16.61.

2. The critical *F*-value for testing $H_0 = b_1 = b_2 = b_3 = b_4 = 0$ vs. H_a: at least one $b_j \neq 0$ at the 5% significance level is *closest* to:
   A. 2.37.
   B. 2.53.
   C. 2.76.

Study Session 3

Video covering this content is available online.

MODULE 8.4: COEFFICIENT OF DETERMINATION AND ADJUSTED R-SQUARED

LOS 8.h: Distinguish between and interpret the R^2 and adjusted R^2 in multiple regression.

CFA® Program Curriculum, Volume 1, page 343

COEFFICIENT OF DETERMINATION, R^2

In addition to an *F*-test, the multiple coefficient of determination, R^2, can be used to test the overall effectiveness of the entire set of independent variables in explaining the dependent variable. Its interpretation is similar to that for simple linear regression: the percentage of variation in the dependent variable that is *collectively* explained by all of the independent variables. For example, an R^2 of 0.63 indicates that the model, as a whole, explains 63% of the variation in the dependent variable.

R^2 is also calculated the same way as in simple linear regression.

$$R^2 = \frac{\text{total variation} - \text{unexplained variation}}{\text{total variation}} =$$

$$\frac{\text{SST} - \text{SSE}}{\text{SST}} = \frac{\text{explained variation}}{\text{total variation}} = \frac{\text{RSS}}{\text{SST}}$$

PROFESSOR'S NOTE

Regression output often includes multiple R, which is the correlation between actual values of y and forecasted values of y. Multiple R is the square root of R^2. For a regression with one independent variable, the correlation between the independent variable and dependent variable is the same as multiple R (with the same sign as the sign of the slope coefficient).

Adjusted R^2

Unfortunately, R^2 by itself *may not be a reliable measure of the explanatory power of the multiple regression model*. This is because R^2 almost always increases as variables are added to the model, even if the marginal contribution of the new variables is not statistically significant. Consequently, a relatively high R^2 may reflect the impact of a large set of independent variables rather than how well the set explains the dependent variable. This problem is often referred to as overestimating the regression.

To overcome the problem of overestimating the impact of additional variables on the explanatory power of a regression model, many researchers recommend adjusting R^2 for the number of independent variables. The *adjusted* R^2 value is expressed as:

$$R_a^2 = 1 - \left[\left(\frac{n-1}{n-k-1}\right) \times (1 - R^2)\right]$$

where:
n = number of observations
k = number of independent variables
R_a^2 = adjusted R^2

R_a^2 is less than or equal to R^2. So while adding a new independent variable to the model will increase R^2, it may either *increase or decrease* the R_a^2. If the new variable has only a small effect on R^2, the value of R_a^2 may decrease. In addition, R_a^2 may be less than zero if the R^2 is low enough.

EXAMPLE: Calculating R^2 and adjusted R^2

An analyst runs a regression of monthly value-stock returns on five independent variables over 60 months. The total sum of squares for the regression is 460, and the sum of squared errors is 170. Calculate the R^2 and adjusted R^2.

Answer:

$$R^2 = \frac{460 - 170}{460} = 0.630 = 63.0\%$$

$$R_a^2 = 1 - \left[\left(\frac{60-1}{60-5-1}\right) \times (1 - 0.63)\right] = 0.596 = 59.6\%$$

The R^2 of 63% suggests that the five independent variables together explain 63% of the variation in monthly value-stock returns.

EXAMPLE: Interpreting adjusted R^2

Suppose the analyst now adds four more independent variables to the regression, and the R^2 increases to 65.0%. Identify which model the analyst would most likely prefer.

Answer:

With nine independent variables, even though the R^2 has increased from 63% to 65%, the adjusted R^2 has decreased from 59.6% to 58.7%:

$$R_a^2 = 1 - \left[\left(\frac{60-1}{60-9-1}\right) \times (1 - 0.65)\right] = 0.587 = 58.7\%$$

The analyst would prefer the first model because the adjusted R^2 is higher and the model has five independent variables as opposed to nine.

Study Session 3

MODULE QUIZ 8.4

To best evaluate your performance, enter your quiz answers online.

Use the following ANOVA table for Questions 1 through 4.

Source	Sum of Squares (SS)	Degrees of Freedom
Regression	1,025	5
Error	925	25

1. The number of sample observations in the regression estimation is *closest* to:
   A. 29.
   B. 30.
   C. 31.
2. The mean squared error (MSE) is *closest* to:
   A. 37.
   B. 82.
   C. 205.
3. The R^2 statistic is *closest* to:
   A. 53%.
   B. 50%.
   C. 47%.
4. The *F*-statistic is *closest* to:
   A. 1.1.
   B. 3.3.
   C. 5.5.
5. Which of the following situations is *least likely* the result of a multiple regression analysis with more than 50 observations?

	R^2	Adjusted R^2
A.	71%	69%
B.	83%	86%
C.	10%	–2%

MODULE 8.5: DUMMY VARIABLES

Video covering this content is available online.

LOS 8.j: Formulate a multiple regression equation by using dummy variables to represent qualitative factors and interpret the coefficients and regression results.

CFA® Program Curriculum, Volume 1, page 344

Observations for most independent variables (e.g., firm size, level of GDP, and interest rates) can take on a wide range of values. However, there are occasions when the independent variable is binary in nature—it is either "on" or "off." Independent variables that fall into this category are called *dummy variables* and are often used to quantify the impact of qualitative events.

Dummy variables are assigned a value of "0" or "1." For example, in a time series regression of monthly stock returns, you could employ a "January" dummy variable that would take on the value of "1" if a stock return occurred in January and "0" if it occurred in any other month. The purpose of including the January dummy variable would be to see if stock returns in January were significantly different than stock returns in all other months of the year. Many "January Effect" anomaly studies employ this type of regression methodology.

The estimated regression coefficient for dummy variables indicates the difference in the dependent variable for the category represented by the dummy variable and the average value of the dependent variable for all classes except the dummy variable class. For example, testing the slope coefficient for the January dummy variable would indicate whether, and by how much, security returns are different in January as compared to the other months.

An *important consideration* when performing multiple regression with dummy variables is the choice of the number of dummy variables to include in the model. Whenever we want to distinguish between *n* classes, we must use n – 1 dummy variables. Otherwise, the regression assumption of no exact linear relationship between independent variables would be violated.

Interpreting the Coefficients in a Dummy Variable Regression

Consider the following regression equation for explaining quarterly EPS in terms of the quarter of their occurrence:

$$EPS_t = b_0 + b_1Q_{1t} + b_2Q_{2t} + b_3Q_{3t} + \varepsilon_t$$

where:
EPS_t = a quarterly observation of earnings per share
Q_{1t} = 1 if period *t* is the first quarter, Q_{1t} = 0 otherwise
Q_{2t} = 1 if period *t* is the second quarter, Q_{2t} = 0 otherwise
Q_{3t} = 1 if period *t* is the third quarter, Q_{3t} = 0 otherwise

The intercept term, b_0, represents the average value of *EPS* for the fourth quarter. The slope coefficient on each dummy variable estimates the *difference* in earnings per share (on average) between the respective quarter (i.e., quarter 1, 2, or 3) and the omitted quarter (the fourth quarter in this case). *Think of the omitted class as the reference point.*

For example, suppose we estimate the quarterly EPS regression model with 10 years of data (40 quarterly observations) and find that $b_0 = 1.25$, $b_1 = 0.75$, $b_2 = -0.20$, and $b_3 = 0.10$:

$$\widehat{EPS}_t = 1.25 + 0.75Q_{1t} - 0.20Q_{2t} + 0.10Q_{3t}$$

We can use the equation to determine the average EPS in each quarter over the past 10 years:

average fourth quarter EPS	= 1.25
average first quarter EPS	= 1.25 + 0.75 = 2.00
average second quarter EPS	= 1.25 – 0.20 = 1.05
average third quarter EPS	= 1.25 + 0.10 = 1.35

These are also the model's predictions of future EPS in each quarter of the following year. For example, to use the model to predict EPS in the first quarter of the next year, set $\widehat{Q}_1 = 1$, $\widehat{Q}_2 = 0$, and $\widehat{Q}_3 = 0$. Then $\widehat{EPS}_{2010} = 1.25 + 0.75(1) - 0.20(0) + 0.10(0) = 2.00$. This simple model uses average EPS for any specific quarter over the past 10 years as the forecast of EPS in its respective quarter of the following year.

As with all multiple regression results, the *F*-statistic for the set of coefficients and the R^2 should be evaluated to determine if the quarters, individually or collectively, contribute to the explanation of quarterly EPS.

We can also test whether the average EPS in each of the first three quarters is equal to the fourth quarter EPS (the omitted quarter) by testing the individual slope coefficients using the following null hypotheses:

H_0: $b_1 = 0$ tests whether fourth quarter EPS = first quarter EPS
H_0: $b_2 = 0$ tests whether fourth quarter EPS = second quarter EPS
H_0: $b_3 = 0$ tests whether fourth quarter EPS = third quarter EPS

As before, the *t*-statistic for each test is equal to the coefficient divided by its standard error, and the critical *t*-value is a two-tailed value with $n - k - 1 = 40 - 3 - 1 = 36$ degrees of freedom.

EXAMPLE: Hypothesis testing with dummy variables

The standard error of the coefficient b_1 is equal to 0.15 from the EPS regression model. Test whether first quarter EPS is equal to fourth quarter EPS at the 5% significance level.

Answer:

We are testing the following hypothesis:

H_0: $b_1 = 0$ vs. H_A: $b_1 \neq 0$

The *t*-statistic is $0.75 / 0.15 = 5.0$ and the two-tail 5% critical value with 36 degrees of freedom is approximately 2.03. Therefore, we should reject the null and conclude that first quarter EPS is statistically significantly different than fourth quarter EPS at the 5% significance level.

Example of Regression Application with Dummy Variables

Mazumdar and Sengupta (2005)[2] provide a more complex example of an investment application of multiple regression using dummy variables. They determine that loan spreads relative to LIBOR on private debt contracts are negatively associated with measures of the quality of the company's financial disclosures.

The dependent variable (SPREAD) is the quoted spread in basis points over LIBOR on the first year of the loan. The independent variables include a number of quantitative variables, including, for example, average total disclosure score (DISC), standard deviation of daily stock returns (STDRETN), current ratio (CRATIO), and

2. Mazumdar, S. and P. Sengupta. 2005. "Disclosure of the Loan Spread on Private Debt." *Financial Analysts Journal*, vol. 61, no. 3 (May/June): 83–95.

market to book ratio (MKBK). The authors also include three dummy variables in the regression:

- SECURE, which is equal to one if the loan is collateralized, and equal to zero otherwise.
- BID, which is equal to one if the loan contained the option to price the loan relative to a different index, and equal to zero otherwise.
- RESTRUC, which is equal to one if the loan was a result of corporate restructuring, and equal to zero otherwise.

In the model both SECURE and RESTRUC are positive and statistically significantly different from zero, while BID is not. The proper interpretation is that the loan spreads on private debt contracts are higher for collateralized loans than for uncollateralized loans, and higher for loans used for corporate restructuring than for loans used for other purposes, *after controlling for the other independent variables in the model.*

WARM-UP: WHY MULTIPLE REGRESSION ISN'T AS EASY AS IT LOOKS

Regression analysis relies on the assumptions listed earlier in this topic review. When these assumptions are violated, the inferences drawn from the model are questionable. There are three primary assumption violations that you will encounter: (1) heteroskedasticity, (2) serial correlation (i.e., autocorrelation), and (3) multicollinearity.

On exam day, you must be able to answer the following four questions about each of the three assumption violations:

- What is it?
- What is its effect on regression analysis?
- How do we detect it?
- How do we correct for it?

Recall that the calculated test statistic for the estimated regression coefficient on the *j*th independent variable is:

$$t = \frac{\hat{b}_j - b_j}{s_{\hat{b}_j}}$$

Note that the denominator in the test statistic equation above, $s_{\hat{b}_j}$, is the standard error for coefficient *j*. Without getting into the math, suffice it to say that the coefficient standard error is calculated using the standard error of estimate (SEE), which is the standard deviation of the error term. Any violation of an assumption that affects the error term will ultimately affect the coefficient standard error. Consequently, this will affect the *t*-statistic and *F*-statistic and any conclusions drawn from hypothesis tests involving these statistics.

MODULE QUIZ 8.5

To best evaluate your performance, enter your quiz answers online.

Use the following information for Questions 1 and 2.

Phil Ohlmer estimates a cross sectional regression in order to predict price to earnings ratios (P/E) with fundamental variables that are related to P/E, including dividend payout ratio (DPO), growth rate (G), and beta (B). In addition, all 50 stocks in the sample come from two industries, electric utilities or biotechnology. He defines the following dummy variable:

IND = 0 if the stock is in the electric utilities industry, or
= 1 if the stock is in the biotechnology industry

The results of his regression are shown in the following table.

Variable	Coefficient	*t*-Statistic
Intercept	6.75	3.89*
IND	8.00	4.50*
DPO	4.00	1.86
G	12.35	2.43*
B	–0.50	1.46

*significant at the 5% level

1. Based on these results, it would be *most appropriate* to conclude that:
   A. biotechnology industry PEs are statistically significantly larger than electric utilities industry PEs.
   B. electric utilities PEs are statistically significantly larger than biotechnology industry PEs, holding DPO, G, and B constant.
   C. biotechnology industry PEs are statistically significantly larger than electric utilities industry PEs, holding DPO, G, and B constant.
2. Ohlmer is valuing a biotechnology stock with a dividend payout ratio of 0.00, a beta of 1.50, and an expected earnings growth rate of 0.14. The predicted P/E on the basis of the values of the explanatory variables for the company is *closest* to:
   A. 7.7.
   B. 15.7.
   C. 17.2.

MODULE 8.6: ASSUMPTIONS: HETEROSKEDASTICITY

Video covering this content is available online.

LOS 8.f: Explain the assumptions of a multiple regression model.

CFA® Program Curriculum, Volume 1, page 335

As with simple linear regression, most of the assumptions made with the multiple regression pertain to ε, the model's error term:

- A linear relationship exists between the dependent and independent variables. In other words, the model on the first page of this topic review correctly describes the relationship.
- The independent variables are not random, and there is no exact linear relation between any two or more independent variables.
- The expected value of the error term, conditional on the independent variable, is zero [i.e., $E(\varepsilon | X_1, X_2, \ldots X_k) = 0$].
- The variance of the error terms is constant for all observations [i.e., $E(\varepsilon_i^2) = \sigma_\varepsilon^2$].
- The error term for one observation is not correlated with that of another observation [i.e., $E(\varepsilon_i \varepsilon_j) = 0, j \neq i$].
- The error term is normally distributed.

LOS 8.k: Explain the types of heteroskedasticity and how heteroskedasticity and serial correlation affect statistical inference.

CFA® Program Curriculum, Volume 1, page 348

WHAT IS HETEROSKEDASTICITY?

Recall that one of the assumptions of multiple regression is that the variance of the residuals is constant across observations. **Heteroskedasticity** occurs when the variance of the residuals is not the same across all observations in the sample. This happens when there are subsamples that are more spread out than the rest of the sample.

Unconditional heteroskedasticity occurs when the heteroskedasticity is not related to the level of the independent variables, which means that it doesn't systematically increase or decrease with changes in the value of the independent variable(s). While this is a violation of the equal variance assumption, *it usually causes no major problems with the regression.*

Conditional heteroskedasticity is heteroskedasticity that is related to the level of (i.e., conditional on) the independent variables. For example, conditional heteroskedasticity exists if the variance of the residual term increases as the value of the independent variable increases, as shown in Figure 8.4. Notice in this figure that the residual variance associated with the larger values of the independent variable, *X*, is larger than the residual variance associated with the smaller values of *X*. Conditional heteroskedasticity *does create significant problems for statistical inference.*

Figure 8.4: Conditional Heteroskedasticity

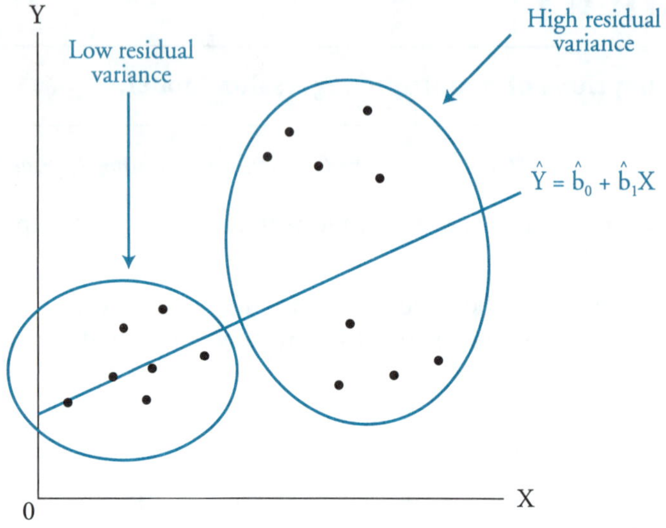

Effect of Heteroskedasticity on Regression Analysis

There are four effects of heteroskedasticity you need to be aware of:

- The standard errors are usually unreliable estimates.
- The coefficient estimates (the $\hat{b}_j$) aren't affected.
- If the standard errors are too small, but the coefficient estimates themselves are not affected, the *t*-statistics will be too large and the null hypothesis of no statistical significance is rejected too often. The opposite will be true if the standard errors are too large.
- The *F*-test is also unreliable.

Detecting Heteroskedasticity

There are two methods to detect heteroskedasticity: examining scatter plots of the residuals and using the Breusch-Pagan chi-square (χ^2) test. A scatter plot of the residuals versus one or more of the independent variables can reveal patterns among observations.

EXAMPLE: Detecting heteroskedasticity with a residual plot

You have been studying the monthly returns of a mutual fund over the past five years, hoping to draw conclusions about the fund's average performance. You calculate the mean return, the standard deviation, and the portfolio's beta by regressing the fund's returns on S&P 500 index returns (the independent variable). The standard deviation of returns and the fund's beta don't seem to fit the firm's stated risk profile. For your analysis, you have prepared a scatter plot of the error terms (actual return – predicted return) for the regression using five years of returns, as shown in the following figure. Determine whether the residual plot indicates that there may be a problem with the data.

Residual Plot

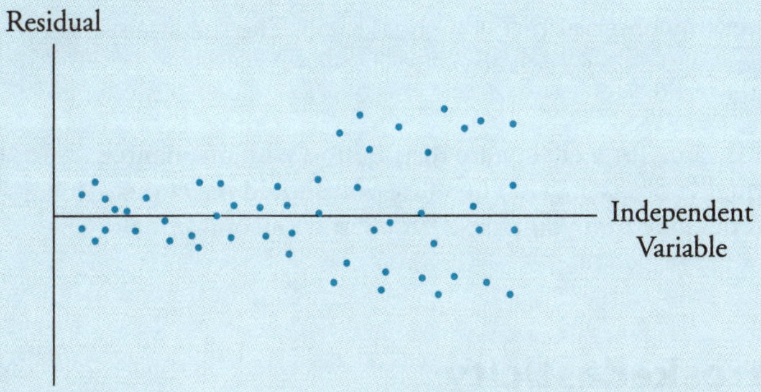

Answer:

The residual plot in the previous figure indicates the presence of conditional heteroskedasticity. Notice how the variation in the regression residuals increases as the independent variable increases. This indicates that the variance of the fund's returns about the mean is related to the level of the independent variable.

The more common way to detect conditional heteroskedasticity is the *Breusch-Pagan test*, which calls for the regression of the squared residuals on the independent variables. If conditional heteroskedasticity is present, the independent variables will significantly contribute to the explanation of the squared residuals. The test statistic for the Breusch-Pagan test, which has a chi-square (χ^2) distribution, is calculated as:

$$\text{BP chi-square test} = n \times R^2_{resid} \text{ with k degrees of freedom}$$

where:
n = the number of observations
R^2_{resid} = R^2 from a second regression of the squared residuals from the first regression on the independent variables
k = the number of independent variables

PROFESSOR'S NOTE

The R^2 used in the BP test is the R^2 from a second regression, NOT the original regression.

This is a one-tailed test because heteroskedasticity is only a problem if the R^2 and the BP test statistic are too large.

EXAMPLE: The Breusch-Pagan test

The residual plot of mutual fund returns over time shows evidence of heteroskedasticity. To confirm your suspicions, you regress the squared residuals from the original regression on the independent variable, S&P 500 index returns. The R^2 from that regression is 8%. Use the Breusch-Pagan test to determine whether heteroskedasticity is present at the 5% significance level.

Answer:

With five years of monthly observations, n is equal to 60. The test statistic is:

$$n \times R^2 = 60 \times 0.08 = 4.8$$

The one-tailed critical value for a chi-square distribution with one degree of freedom and α equal to 5% is 3.841. Therefore you should reject the null hypothesis and conclude that you have a problem with conditional heteroskedasticity.

Correcting Heteroskedasticity

The most common remedy and the one recommended in the CFA curriculum is to calculate *robust standard errors* (also called White-corrected standard errors or heteroskedasticity-consistent standard errors). These robust standard errors are then used to recalculate the *t*-statistics using the original regression coefficients. On the exam, use robust standard errors to calculate *t*-statistics if there is evidence of heteroskedasticity. A second method to correct for heteroskedasticy is the use of *generalized least squares*, which attempts to eliminate the hetereoskedasticity by modifying the original equation.

EXAMPLE: Using White-corrected standard errors

An analyst runs a regression of annualized Treasury bill rates (the dependent variable) on annual inflation rates (the independent variable) using monthly data for 10 years. The results of the regression are shown in the following table.

Regression of T-Bill Rates on Inflation Rates

Variable	Coefficient	Standard Error	*t*-Statistic	*p*-Value
Intercept	4.82	0.85	5.67	< 0.0001
Inflation	0.60	0.28	2.14	0.0340

He determines using the Breusch-Pagan test that heteroskedasticity is present, so he also estimates the White-corrected standard error for the coefficient on inflation to be 0.31. The critical two-tail 5% *t*-value for 118 degrees of freedom is 1.98. Is inflation statistically significant at the 5% level?

Answer:

The *t*-statistic should be recalculated using the White-corrected standard error as:

$$t = \frac{0.60}{0.31} = 1.94$$

This is less than the critical *t*-value of 1.98, which means after correcting for heteroskedasticity, the null hypothesis that the inflation coefficient is zero cannot be rejected. Therefore, inflation is not statistically significant. Notice that because the coefficient estimate of 0.60 was not affected by heteroskedasticity, but the original standard error of 0.28 was too low, the original *t*-statistic of 2.14 was too high. After using the higher White-corrected standard error of 0.31, the *t*-statistic fell to 1.94.

MODULE QUIZ 8.6

To best evaluate your performance, enter your quiz answers online.

1. Assumptions underlying a multiple regression are *most likely* to include:
   A. The expected value of the error term is 0.00 < i < 1.00.
   B. Linear and non-linear relationships exist between the dependent and independent variables.
   C. The error for one observation is not correlated with that of another observation.

MODULE 8.7: SERIAL CORRELATION

Video covering this content is available online.

WHAT IS SERIAL CORRELATION?

Serial correlation, also known as **autocorrelation**, refers to the situation in which the residual terms are correlated with one another. Serial correlation is a relatively common problem with time series data.

- *Positive serial correlation* exists when a positive regression error in one time period increases the probability of observing a positive regression error for the next time period.
- *Negative serial correlation* occurs when a positive error in one period increases the probability of observing a negative error in the next period.

Effect of Serial Correlation on Regression Analysis

Because of the tendency of the data to cluster together from observation to observation, positive serial correlation typically results in coefficient standard errors that are too small, even though the estimated coefficients are consistent. These small standard error terms will cause the computed *t*-statistics to be larger than they should be, which will cause too many Type I errors: the rejection of the null hypothesis when it is actually true. The *F*-test will also be unreliable because the MSE will be underestimated leading again to too many Type I errors.

PROFESSOR'S NOTE

Positive serial correlation is much more common in economic and financial data, so we focus our attention on its effects. Additionally, if one of the independent variables in the regression is a lagged value of the dependent variable, it may make the parameter estimates inconsistent. This is discussed in our topic review on Time Series Analysis.

Detecting Serial Correlation

There are two methods that are commonly used to detect the presence of serial correlation: residual plots and the Durbin-Watson statistic.

A scatter plot of residuals versus time, like those shown in Figure 8.5, can reveal the presence of serial correlation. Figure 8.5 illustrates examples of positive and negative serial correlation.

Figure 8.5: Residual Plots for Serial Correlation

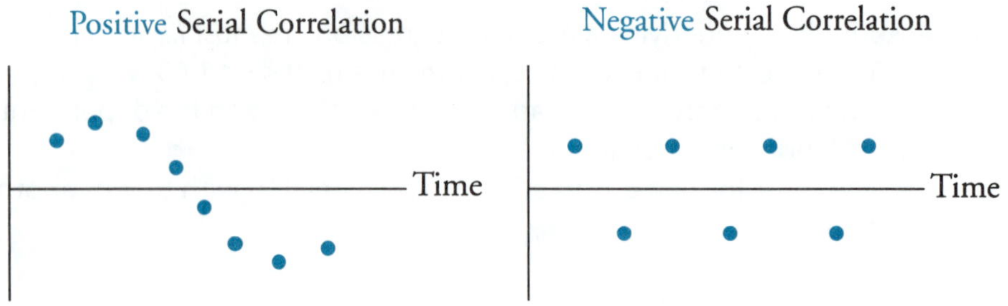

The more common method is to use the **Durbin-Watson statistic** (DW) to detect the presence of serial correlation. It is calculated as:

$$DW = \frac{\sum_{t=2}^{T}(\hat{\varepsilon}_t - \hat{\varepsilon}_{t-1})^2}{\sum_{t=1}^{T}\hat{\varepsilon}_t^2}$$

where:
$\hat{\varepsilon}_t$ = residual for period t

If the sample size is very large:

$DW \approx 2(1 - r)$

where:
r = correlation coefficient between residuals from one period and those from the previous period

You can see from the approximation that the Durbin-Watson test statistic is approximately equal to 2 if the error terms are homoskedastic and not serially correlated ($r = 0$). $DW < 2$ if the error terms are positively serially correlated ($r > 0$), and $DW > 2$ if the error terms are negatively serially correlated ($r < 0$). But how much below the magic number 2 is statistically significant enough to reject the null hypothesis of no positive serial correlation?

There are tables of DW statistics that provide upper and lower critical DW-values (d_u and d_l, respectively) for various sample sizes, levels of significance, and numbers of degrees of freedom against which the computed DW test statistic can be compared. The DW-test procedure for positive serial correlation is as follows:

H_0: the regression has *no* positive serial correlation

The decision rules are rather complicated because they allow for rejecting the null in favor of either positive or negative correlation. The test can also be inconclusive, which means we neither accept nor reject (See Figure 8.6).

- If $DW < d_l$, the error terms are *positively* serially correlated (i.e., reject the null hypothesis of no positive serial correlation).
- If $d_l < DW < d_u$, the test is inconclusive.
- If $DW > d_u$, there is *no* evidence that the error terms are positively correlated. (i.e., fail to reject the null of no positive serial correlation).

Figure 8.6: Durbin-Watson Decision Rule

(H_0: No positive serial correlation)

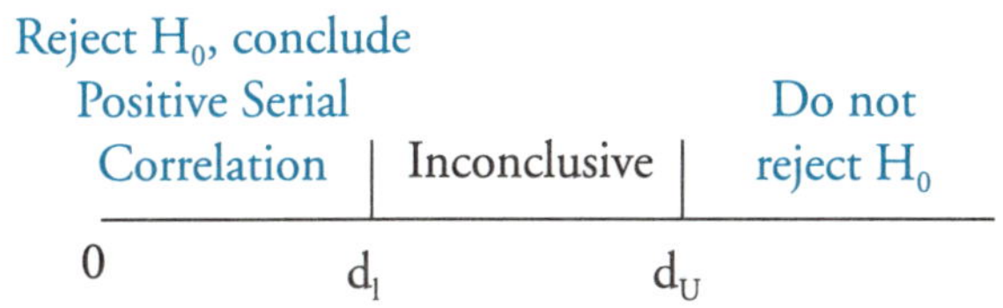

> **EXAMPLE: The Durbin-Watson test for serial correlation**
>
> Suppose you have a regression output which includes three independent variables that provide you with a DW statistic of 1.23. Also suppose that the sample size is 40. At a 5% significance level, determine if the error terms are serially correlated.
>
> **Answer:**
>
> From a 5% DW table with n = 40 and k = 3, the upper and lower critical DW values are found to be d_l = 1.34 and d_u = 1.66, respectively. Since DW < d_l (i.e., 1.23 < 1.34), you should reject the null hypothesis and conclude that the regression has positive serial correlation among the error terms.

Correcting Serial Correlation

Possible remedies for serial correlation include:

- *Adjust the coefficient standard errors*, which is the method recommended in the CFA curriculum, using the Hansen method. The Hansen method also corrects for conditional heteroskedasticity. These adjusted standard errors, which are sometimes called serial correlation consistent standard errors or Hansen-White standard errors, are then used in hypothesis testing of the regression coefficients. Only use the Hansen method if serial correlation is a problem. The White-corrected standard errors are preferred if only heteroskedasticity is a problem. If both conditions are present, use the Hansen method.
- *Improve the specification of the model*. The best way to do this is to explicitly incorporate the time-series nature of the data (e.g., include a seasonal term). This can be tricky.

MODULE QUIZ 8.7

To best evaluate your performance, enter your quiz answers online.

1. What condition is the Durbin-Watson statistic designed to detect in multiple regression, and what is the *most appropriate* remedy to correct for that condition?

	Condition	Remedy
A.	Serial correlation	Use the Hansen method
B.	Autocorrelation	Use generalized least squares
C.	Heteroskedasticity	Use generalized least squares

Video covering this content is available online.

MODULE 8.8: MULTICOLLINEARITY

LOS 8.1: Describe multicollinearity and explain its causes and effects in regression analysis.

CFA® Program Curriculum, Volume 1, page 359

Multicollinearity refers to the condition when two or more of the independent variables, or linear combinations of the independent variables, in a multiple regression are highly correlated with each other. This condition distorts the standard error of estimate and the coefficient standard errors, leading to problems when conducting *t*-tests for statistical significance of parameters.

Effect of Multicollinearity on Regression Analysis

Even though multicollinearity does not affect the consistency of slope coefficients, such coefficients themselves tend to be *unreliable*. Additionally, the standard errors of the slope coefficients are artificially inflated. Hence, there is a *greater probability that we will incorrectly conclude that a variable is not statistically significant* (i.e., a Type II error). Multicollinearity is likely to be present to some extent in most economic models. The issue is whether the multicollinearity has a significant effect on the regression results.

Detecting Multicollinearity

The most common way to detect multicollinearity is the situation where *t*-tests indicate that none of the individual coefficients is significantly different than zero, while the *F*-test is statistically significant and the R^2 is high. This suggests that the variables together explain much of the variation in the dependent variable, but the individual independent variables don't. The only way this can happen is when the independent variables are highly correlated with each other, so while their common source of variation is explaining the dependent variable, the high degree of correlation also "washes out" the individual effects.

High correlation among independent variables is sometimes suggested as a sign of multicollinearity. In fact, answers to some old CFA questions suggest the following general rule of thumb: If the absolute value of the sample correlation between any two independent variables in the regression is greater than 0.7, multicollinearity is a potential problem.

However, this only works if there are exactly two independent variables. If there are more than two independent variables, while individual variables may not be highly correlated, linear combinations might be, leading to multicollinearity. High correlation among the independent variables suggests the possibility of multicollinearity, but low correlation among the independent variables *does not necessarily* indicate multicollinearity is *not* present.

EXAMPLE: Detecting multicollinearity

Bob Watson, CFA, runs a regression of mutual fund returns on average P/B, average P/E, and average market capitalization, with the following results:

Variable	Coefficient	*p*-Value
Average P/B	3.52	0.15
Average P/E	2.78	0.21
Market Cap	4.03	0.11
F-test	34.6	< 0.001
R^2	89.6%	

Determine whether or not multicollinearity is a problem in this regression.

Answer:

The R^2 is high and the *F*-test is statistically significant, which suggest that the three variables as a group do an excellent job of explaining the variation in mutual fund returns. However, none of the independent variables individually is statistically significant to any reasonable degree, since the *p*-values are larger than 10%. This is a classic indication of multicollinearity.

Correcting Multicollinearity

The most common method to correct for multicollinearity is to omit one or more of the correlated independent variables. Unfortunately, it is not always an easy task to identify the variable(s) that are the source of the multicollinearity. There are statistical procedures that may help in this effort, like stepwise regression, which systematically remove variables from the regression until multicollinearity is minimized.

WARM-UP: MODEL SPECIFICATION

Regression model specification is the selection of the explanatory (independent) variables to be included in the regression and the transformations, if any, of those explanatory variables.

For example, suppose we're trying to predict a P/E ratio using a cross-sectional regression with fundamental variables that are related to P/E. Valuation theory tells us that the stock's dividend payout ratio (DPO), growth rate (G), and beta (B) are associated with P/E. One specification of the model would be:

Specification 1: $P/E = b_0 + b_1DPO + b_2G + b_3B + \varepsilon$

If we also decide that market capitalization (M) is related to P/E ratio, we would create a second specification of the model by including M as an independent variable:

Specification 2: $P/E = a_0 + a_1DPO + a_2G + a_3B + a_4M + \varepsilon$

Finally, suppose we conclude that market cap is not linearly related to P/E, but the natural log of market cap is linearly related to P/E. Then, we would transform M by taking its natural log and creating a new variable lnM. Thus, our third specification would be:

Specification 3: $P/E = c_0 + c_1DPO + c_2G + c_3B + c_4lnM + \varepsilon$

PROFESSOR'S NOTE

Notice that we used "a" instead of "b" in Specification 2 and "c" in Specification 3. We must do that to recognize that when we change the specifications of the model, the regression parameters change. For example, we wouldn't expect the intercept in Specification 1 (b_0) to be the same as in Specification 2 (a_0) or the same as in Specification 3 (c_0).

Video covering this content is available online.

MODULE 8.9: MODEL MISSPECIFICATION, AND QUALITATIVE DEPENDENT VARIABLES

LOS 8.m: Describe how model misspecification affects the results of a regression analysis and describe how to avoid common forms of misspecification.

CFA® Program Curriculum, Volume 1, page 363

There are three broad categories of *model misspecification*, or ways in which the regression model can be specified incorrectly, each with several subcategories:

1. The functional form can be misspecified.
   - Important variables are omitted.
   - Variables should be transformed.
   - Data is improperly pooled.
2. Explanatory variables are correlated with the error term in time series models.
   - A lagged dependent variable is used as an independent variable.
   - A function of the dependent variable is used as an independent variable ("forecasting the past").
   - Independent variables are measured with error.
3. Other time-series misspecifications that result in nonstationarity.

PROFESSOR'S NOTE

We'll focus on the first two categories because nonstationarity in time series regressions is covered in the next topic review.

The *effects of the model misspecification on the regression results*, as shown in Figure 8.7, are basically the same for all of the misspecifications we will discuss: regression coefficients are often biased and/or inconsistent, which means we can't have any confidence in our hypothesis tests of the coefficients or in the predictions of the model.

Figure 8.7: Effects of Model Misspecification

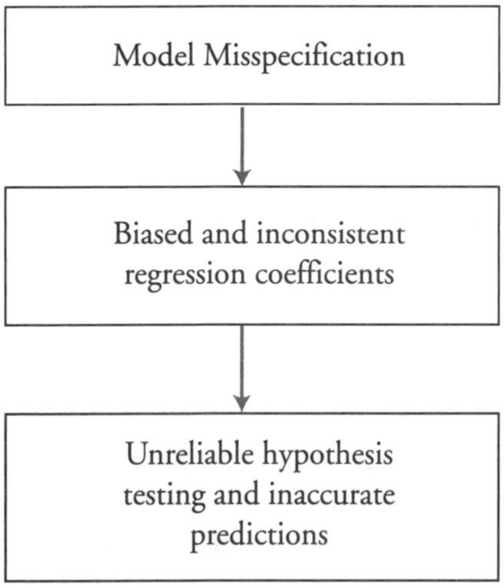

PROFESSOR'S NOTE

Recall the definitions of unbiased and consistent estimators from the Level I curriculum:

- An unbiased estimator is one for which the expected value of the estimator is equal to the parameter you are trying to estimate. For example, because the expected value of the sample mean is equal to the population mean, the sample mean is an unbiased estimator of the population mean.
- A consistent estimator is one for which the accuracy of the parameter estimate increases as the sample size increases. As the sample size increases, the standard error of the sample mean falls, and the sampling distribution bunches more closely around the population mean. In fact, as the sample size approaches infinity, the standard error approaches zero.

EXAMPLES OF MISSPECIFICATION OF FUNCTIONAL FORM

Let's start with a regression in which we're trying to predict monthly returns on portfolios of Chinese stocks (R) using four independent variables: portfolio beta (B), the natural log of market capitalization (lnM), the natural log of the price-to-book ratio ln(PB), and free float (FF). Free float is equal to the ratio of shares available to be traded by the investing public to total company shares. The regression is estimated with 72 monthly observations from July 1996 to June 2002. The *correct* specification of the model is as follows:

$$R = b_0 + b_1B + b_2\ln M + b_3\ln PB + b_4FF + \varepsilon$$

Suppose we determine in this specification that both lnM and FF are statistically significant at the 1% level.

PROFESSOR'S NOTE

The correct regression model specification is based on a study by Wang and Xu (2004).[3] The incorrect specifications that follow are designed to illustrate examples of common misspecifications, but they are not included in the Wang and Xu study.

Misspecification #1: Omitting a Variable

Suppose we do not include lnM in the regression model:

$$R = a_0 + a_1B + a_2\text{lnPB} + a_3FF + \varepsilon$$

If lnM is correlated with any of the remaining independent variables (B, lnPB, or FF), then the error term is also correlated with the same independent variables and the resulting regression coefficients (the estimates of a_0, a_1, and a_2) are biased and inconsistent. That means our hypothesis tests and predictions using the model are unreliable.

PROFESSOR'S NOTE

Omission of a variable in this context means that the variable should be included in the model but is not. Absence of a variable in the model does not necessarily imply omission.

Just because a variable is highly correlated with an independent variable does not mean it has to be included in the model to avoid omission error.

Misspecification #2: Variable Should Be Transformed

Regression assumes that the dependent variable is linearly related to each of the independent variables. Typically, however, market capitalization is not linearly related to portfolio returns, but rather the natural log of market cap is linearly related. If we include market cap in the regression without transforming it by taking the natural log—if we use M and not ln(M)—we've misspecified the model.

$$R = c_0 + c_1B + c_2M + c_3\text{lnPB} + c_4FF + \varepsilon$$

Other examples of transformations include squaring the variable or taking the square root of the variable. If financial statement data are included in the regression model, a common transformation is to standardize the variables by dividing by sales (for income statement or cash flow items) or total assets (for balance sheet items). You should recognize these as items from *common-size financial statements*.

Misspecification #3: Incorrectly Pooling Data

Suppose the relationship between returns and the independent variables during the first three years is actually different than relationship in the second 3-year period (i.e., the regression coefficients are different from one period to the next). By pooling the data and estimating one regression over the entire period, rather than estimating two separate regressions over each of the subperiods, we have

3. Fenghua Wang and Yexiao Xu. "What Determines Chinese Stock Returns." *Financial Analysts Journal* no. 6 (November/December 2004): 65–77.

misspecified the model and our hypothesis tests and predictions of portfolio returns will be misleading.

Misspecification #4: Using a Lagged Dependent Variable as an Independent Variable

A lagged variable in a time series regression is the value of a variable from a prior period. In our example, the dependent variable is portfolio return in month *t*, so a lagged dependent variable would be the portfolio return in the previous period, month t − 1 (which is denoted as R_{t-1}).

$$R = d_0 + d_1B + d_2\ln M + d_3\ln PB + d_4FF + d_5R_{t-1} + \varepsilon$$

If the error term in the regression model is serially correlated as a result of inclusion of the lagged dependent variable (which is common in time series regressions), then this model misspecification will result in biased and inconsistent regression estimates and unreliable hypothesis tests and return predictions.

PROFESSOR'S NOTE

In the reading on time series analysis, AR models are introduced which rely exclusively on lagged dependent variables. The difference relates to the data set: if lagged dependent variables help *explain (and NOT cause)* serial correlation in residuals, they are okay!

Misspecification #5: Forecasting the Past

The proper specification of the model is to measure the dependent variable as returns during a particular month (say July 1996), and the independent variable ln(M) as the natural log of market capitalization *at the beginning* of July. Remember that market cap is equal to shares outstanding times price per share. If we measure market cap *at the end* of July and use it in our regression, we're naturally going to conclude that stocks with higher market cap at the end of July had higher returns during July. In other words, our model is misspecified because it is forecasting the past: we're using variables measured at the *end* of July to predict a variable measured *during* July.

Misspecification #6: Measuring Independent Variables with Error

The free float (FF) independent variable is actually trying to capture the relationship between corporate governance quality and portfolio returns. However, because we can't actually measure "corporate governance quality," we have to use a proxy variable. Wang and Xu used free float to proxy for corporate governance quality. The presumption is that the higher the level of free float, the more influence the capital markets have on management's decision making process and the more effective the corporate governance structure. However, because we're using free float as a proxy, we're actually measuring the variable we want to include in our regression—corporate governance quality—with error. Once again our regression estimates will be biased and inconsistent and our hypothesis testing and predictions unreliable.

PROFESSOR'S NOTE

For more information on corporate governance and the valuation implications of effective corporate governance practices, see the topic review of corporate governance.

Another common example when an independent variable is measured with error is when we want to use *expected* inflation in our regression but use *actual* inflation as a proxy.

LOS 8.n: Describe models with qualitative dependent variables.

CFA® Program Curriculum, Volume 1, page 378

Financial analysis often calls for the use of a model that has a **qualitative dependent variable**, a dummy variable that takes on a value of either zero or one. An example of an application requiring the use of a qualitative dependent variable is a model that attempts to predict when a bond issuer will default. In this case, the dependent variable may take on a value of one in the event of default and zero in the event of no default. An ordinary regression model is not appropriate for situations that require a qualitative dependent variable. However, there are several different types of models that use a qualitative dependent variable.

- **Probit and logit models**. A probit model is based on the normal distribution, while a logit model is based on the logistic distribution. Application of these models results in estimates of the probability that the event occurs (e.g., probability of default). The maximum likelihood methodology is used to estimate coefficients for probit and logit models. These coefficients relate the independent variables to the likelihood of an event occurring, such as a merger, bankruptcy, or default.
- **Discriminant models**. Discriminant models are similar to probit and logit models but make different assumptions regarding the independent variables. Discriminant analysis results in a linear function similar to an ordinary regression, which generates an overall score, or ranking, for an observation. The scores can then be used to rank or classify observations. A popular application of a discriminant model makes use of financial ratios as the independent variables to predict the qualitative dependent variable bankruptcy. A linear relationship among the independent variables produces a value for the dependent variable that places a company in a bankrupt or not bankrupt class.

The analysis of regression models with qualitative dependent variables is the same as we have been discussing all through this topic review. Examine the individual coefficients using *t*-tests, determine the validity of the model with the *F*-test and the R^2, and look out for heteroskedasticity, serial correlation, and multicollinearity.

LOS 8.o: Evaluate and interpret a multiple regression model and its results.

CFA® Program Curriculum, Volume 1, page 336

The economic meaning of the results of a regression estimation focuses primarily on the slope coefficients. For example, suppose that we run a regression using a cross section of stock returns (in percent) as the dependent variable, and the stock betas (CAPM) and market capitalizations (in $ billions) as our independent variables. The slope coefficients indicate the expected change in the stock returns for a one unit change in beta or market capitalization. The estimated regression equation is:

$$\text{Return} = 5.0 + 4.2\ \text{Beta} - 0.05\ \text{Mkt.Cap.} + \varepsilon$$

Furthermore, assume that these coefficient estimates are significantly different from zero in a statistical sense. The economic meaning of these results is that, on average, a one unit increase in beta risk is associated with a 4.2% *increase* in return, while a $1 billion increase in market capitalization implies a 0.05% *decrease* in return.

As is always the case with statistical inferences, it is possible to identify a relationship that has statistical significance without having any economic significance. For instance, a study of dividend announcements may identify a statistically significant abnormal return following the announcement, but these returns may not be sufficient to cover transactions costs.

ASSESSING A MULTIPLE REGRESSION MODEL—PUTTING IT ALL TOGETHER

The flow chart in Figure 8.8 will help you evaluate a multiple regression model and grasp the "big picture" in preparation for the exam.

Figure 8.8: Assessment of a Multiple Regression Model

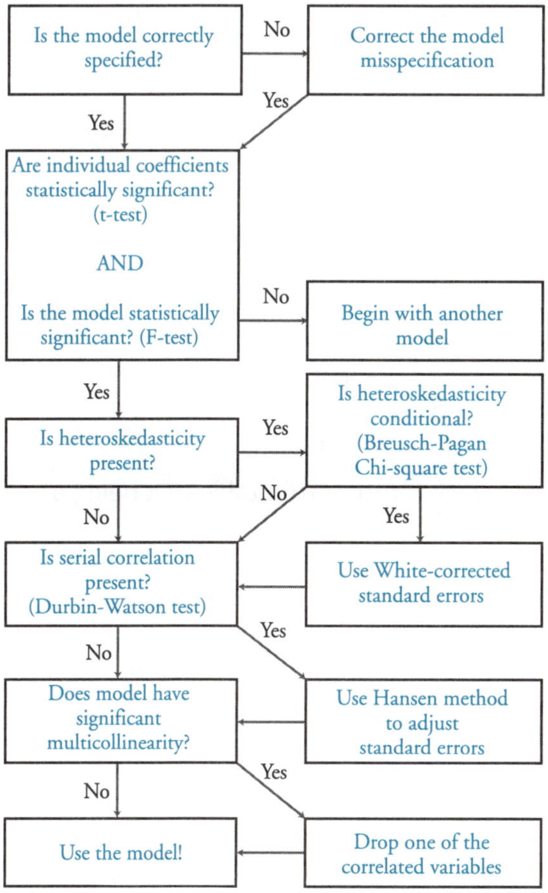

MODULE QUIZ 8.8, 8.9

To best evaluate your performance, enter your quiz answers online.

Use the following information to answer Questions 1 through 5.

Multiple regression was used to explain stock returns using the following variables:

Dependent variable:

RET = annual stock returns (%)

Independent variables:

MKT = Market capitalization = Market capitalization / $1.0 million

IND = Industry quartile ranking (IND = 4 is the highest ranking)

FORT = Fortune 500 firm, where {FORT = 1 if the stock is that of a Fortune 500 firm, FORT = 0 if not a Fortune 500 stock}

The regression results are presented in the tables below.

	Coefficient	Standard Error	*t*-Statistic	*p*-Value
Intercept	0.5220	1.2100	0.430	0.681
Market Capitalization	0.0460	0.0150	3.090	0.021
Industry Ranking	0.7102	0.2725	2.610	0.040
Fortune 500	0.9000	0.5281	1.700	0.139

ANOVA	df	SS	MSS	F	Significance F
Regression	3	20.5969	6.8656	12.100	0.006
Error	6	3.4031	0.5672		
Total	9	24.0000			

Test	Test-Statistic
Breusch-Pagan	17.7
Durbin-Watson	1.8

1. Based on the results in the table, which of the following *most accurately* represents the regression equation?
   A. 0.43 + 3.09(MKT) + 2.61(IND) + 1.70(FORT).
   B. 0.681 + 0.021(MKT) + 0.04(IND) + 0.139(FORT).
   C. 0.522 + 0.0460(MKT) + 0.7102(IND) + 0.9(FORT).

2. The expected amount of the stock return attributable to it being a Fortune 500 stock is *closest* to:
   A. 0.522.
   B. 0.139.
   C. 0.900.

3. The expected return on the stock of a firm that is not in the Fortune 500, has a market capitalization of $5 million, and is in an industry with a rank of 3 is *closest* to:
   A. 2.88%.
   B. 3.98%.
   C. 1.42%.

4. Does being a Fortune 500 stock contribute significantly to stock returns?
   A. Yes, at a 10% level of significance.
   B. Yes, at a 5% level of significance.
   C. No, not at a reasonable level of significance.
5. The *p*-value of the Breusch-Pagan test is 0.0005. The lower and upper limits for the Durbin-Watson test are 0.40 and 1.90, respectively. Based on this data and the information in the tables, there is evidence of:
   A. only serial correlation.
   B. serial correlation and heteroskedasticity.
   C. only heteroskedasticity.
6. Which of the following situations is *least likely* to result in the misspecification of a regression model with monthly returns as the dependent variable?
   A. Failing to include an independent variable that is related to monthly returns.
   B. Using leading P/E from the previous period as an independent variable.
   C. Using actual inflation as an independent variable to proxy for expected inflation.
7. The *least likely* result of regression model misspecification is:
   A. unreliable hypothesis tests of the regression coefficients.
   B. inconsistent regression coefficients.
   C. unbiased regression coefficients.
8. Phil Ohlmer is developing a regression model to predict returns on a hedge fund composite index using several different independent variables. Which of the following list of independent variables, if included in the model, is *most likely* to lead to biased and inconsistent regression coefficients and why?
   A. Small-cap index returns, high-yield bond index returns, and emerging market index returns; because small-cap returns and hedge fund index returns are likely to be correlated.
   B. Small-cap index returns, high-yield bond index returns, and emerging market index returns; because small-cap returns and emerging market index returns are likely to be correlated.
   C. Small-cap index returns, previous period hedge fund composite index returns, high-yield bond index returns, and emerging market index returns; because the regression model is likely to be misspecified.
9. Qualitative dependent variables should be verified using:
   A. a dummy variable based on the logistic distribution.
   B. a discriminant model using a linear function for ranked observations.
   C. tests for heteroskedasticity, serial correlation, and multicollinearity.

Video covering this content is available online.

MODULE 8.10: SUPERVISED AND UNSUPERVISED MACHINE LEARNING

WARM UP

Data collection as part of business intelligence often produces very large sets of data, both observations and attributes. Multiple regression and other tools are often inadequate to model the complex relationships in these data sets because the underlying relationships are often nonlinear and nondirect for linear models.

Big Data simply refers to these very large data sets which may include both structured (e.g., spreadsheet) data and unstructured (e.g., emails, text, or pictures) data. **Data analytics** uses computer-based algorithms to analyze Big Data and obtain meaningful information about patterns and relationships in the data.

Among other things, data analytics seeks to:

- Measure correlations between variables.
- Make predictions about some variable of interest.
- Make causal inferences [i.e., identify the mechanism by which one variable (the causal variable) affects another variable (the outcome variable)]. Causal relationships are stronger measures than correlations and predictions.
- Classify data into distinct categories.
- Sort data into clusters (**clustering**) whereby data about relatively homogenous observations (i.e., observations with some similarities in traits) are grouped into clusters.
- Reduce the dimension (or number of attributes) of data by discarding redundant and insignificant attributes of objects and entities.

Machine learning (ML) refers to computer programs that learn from their errors and refine predictive models to improve their predictive accuracy over time. ML is one method used to extract useful information from Big Data.

ML terms:

- **Target variable or tag variable** is the dependent variable (i.e., the y-variable). Target variables can be continuous, categorical, or ordinal.
- **Features** are the independent variables (i.e., the x-variables).
- **Feature engineering** is curating a dataset of features for ML processing.

Candidates are expected to have a high-level understanding of the terminology and techniques discussed here.

LOS 8.p: Distinguish between supervised and unsupervised machine learning.

CFA® Program Curriculum, Volume 1, page 381

Supervised learning uses labeled training data to guide the ML program in achieving superior forecasting accuracy. To forecast earnings manipulators, for example, a large collection of attributes could be provided for known manipulators and for known non-manipulators. A computer program could then be used to identify patterns that identify manipulators in another data set. Typical data analytics tasks for supervised learning include classification and prediction.

In **unsupervised learning,** the ML program is not given labeled training data. Instead, inputs are provided without any conclusions about those inputs. In the absence of any tagged data, the program seeks out structure or interrelationships in the data. Clustering is one example of the output of an unsupervised ML program.

MODULE QUIZ 8.10

To best evaluate your performance, enter your quiz answers online.

1. Which statement about tag variables is *most accurate*? Tag variables:
   A. can be continuous, ordinal, or categorical.
   B. are not specified for supervised learning.
   C. refer to independent variables.
2. Which statement *best* describes supervised learning? Supervised learning:
   A. uses labeled training data.
   B. needs periodic human intervention.
   C. is best suited for structured data.

MODULE 8.11: MACHINE LEARNING ALGORITHMS

Video covering this content is available online.

LOS 8.q: Describe machine learning algorithms used in prediction, classification, clustering, and dimension reduction.

CFA® Program Curriculum, Volume 1, page 383

SUPERVISED LEARNING ALGORITHMS

Supervised learning algorithms are used for prediction (i.e., regression) and classification. When the y-variable is continuous, the appropriate approach is that of regression (used in a broad, ML context). When the y-variable is categorical (i.e., belonging to a category or classification) or ordinal (i.e., ordered or ranked), a classification model is used.

Regression Models

Linear (previously discussed in our coverage of multiple regressions) and nonlinear regression models can be used to generate forecasts. A special case of **generalized linear model** (GLM) is **penalized regression**. Penalized regression models seek to minimize forecasting errors by reducing the problem of **overfitting**. Overfitting results when a large number of features (i.e., independent variables) are included in the data sample. The resulting model can use the "noise" in the dependent variables to improve the model fit. Overfitting the model in this way will decrease the accuracy of model forecasts on other (out-of-sample) data. To reduce the problem of overfitting, researchers may impose a penalty based on the number of features used by the model. Penalized regression models seek to minimize the sum of square errors (same as in multiple regression models) as well as a penalty value. This penalty value increases with the number of independent variables (features) used by the model. Imposing such a penalty can exclude features that are not meaningfully contributing to out-of-sample prediction accuracy (i.e., it makes the model more parsimonious). In summary, penalized regression models seek to reduce the number of features included in the model while retaining as much predictive information in the data as possible.

Classification and Regression Trees (CART)

Classification trees are appropriate when the target variable is categorical while regression trees are appropriate when the target is continuous. More typically, classification trees are used when the target is binary (e.g., IPO will be successful vs. not successful). Logit and probit models, discussed previously, are used when the target is binary but are ill-suited when there are significant nonlinear relationships among variables. In such cases, classification trees may be a viable alternative.

Classification trees assign observations to one of two possible classifications at each node. At the top of the tree, the top feature (the one most important in explaining the target) is selected and a cutoff value "c" is estimated. Observations with feature values greater than c are assigned to one classification and the remainder are assigned to the other classification. The resulting classes are then evaluated based on a second feature and again divided into one of two classes. Every successive classification should result in a lower estimation error than the nodes that preceded it. The tree stops when the error cannot be reduced further resulting in a terminal node as shown in Figure 8.9.

Figure 8.9: Classification Tree Example

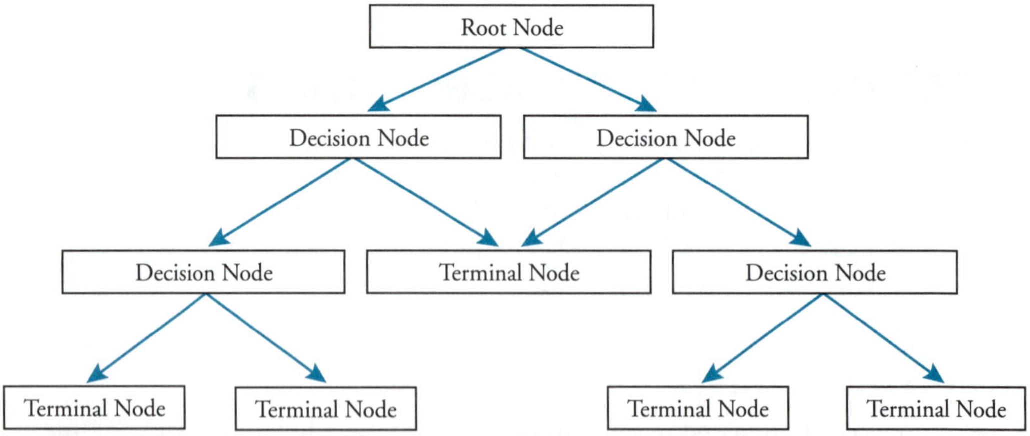

A variant of a classification tree is a **random forest**. A random forest is a collection of randomly generated classification trees from the same data set. A randomly selected subset of features is used in creating each tree and each tree is slightly different from the others. The process of using multiple classification trees uses crowdsourcing (majority wins) in determining the final classification. Because each tree only uses a subset of features, random forests can mitigate the problem of overfitting. Using random forests can increase the signal-to-noise ratio because errors across different trees tend to cancel each other out.

Neural Networks (Artificial Neural Networks)

Neural networks are constructed with nodes connected by links. The input layer is the nodes with values for the features (independent variables). These values may need to be scaled so that the information from multiple nodes is comparable and can be used to calculate a weighted average of the input values from the nodes in the input layer to a second set of nodes (the hidden layer). Typically, several inputs are connected to a particular hidden node, meaning that that node receives several input values via the links. Each node uses an **activation function**, typically a nonlinear function, to generate a value from the weighted average of the input values from those nodes linked as inputs to each hidden node. There may be multiple hidden layers with linked nodes. Again, each node in a hidden layer will use an activation function to the values from other nodes. There is typically a single node in the output layer that is the prediction of the model. Linking the information in the input layer to multiple nodes in the hidden layers, each with its own activation function, allows the neural network to model complex nonlinear functions to use the information in the input variables well.

The researcher must determine the structure of the network. For example, for a network with three inputs (features), we would have three nodes in the input layer. We might specify a single hidden layer with four nodes, in addition to an output layer with a single node. This structure, 3, 4, and 1, is set by the researcher and referred to as the **hyperparameters** of the neural network.

Additional layers can improve the predictive accuracy of neural networks. **Deep learning nets (DLNs)** are neural networks with many hidden layers (often more than 20).

UNSUPERVISED LEARNING ALGORITHMS

Recall that in case of unsupervised learning, there is no target variable; the task is to find a pattern in the features (independent or x-variables).

Clustering

Given a data set, clustering is the process of grouping observations into categories based on similarities in their attributes. For example, stocks can be assigned to different categories based on their past performances, rather than standard sector classifiers (e.g., finance, healthcare, technology, etc.). Clustering can be bottom-up or top-down. In the case of bottom-up clustering, we start with one observation as its own cluster and add other similar observations to that cluster, or form another non-overlapping cluster. Top-down clustering starts with one giant cluster and then partitions that cluster into smaller and smaller clusters.

Dimension Reduction

Problems associated with too much noise often arise when the number of features in a data set (its dimension) is excessive. Dimension reduction seeks to remove the noise (i.e., those attributes that do not contain much information). One method is principal component analysis (PCA) which summarizes the information in a large number of correlated factors into a much smaller set of uncorrelated factors. The first factor in PCA would be the most important factor in explaining the variation across observations. The second factor would be the second most important and so on, up to the number of uncorrelated factors specified by the researcher.

STEPS IN MODEL TRAINING

LOS 8.r: Describe the steps in model training.

CFA® Program Curriculum, Volume 1, page 390

Steps in model training:

1. Specify the algorithm.
2. Specify the hyperparameters (before the processing begins).
3. Divide data into training and validation samples. In the case of **cross validation**, the training and validation samples are randomly generated every learning cycle.
4. Evaluate the training using a performance parameter, P, in the validation sample.
5. Repeat the training until adequate level of performance is achieved. In choosing the number of times to repeat, the researcher must use caution to avoid overfitting the model.

MODULE QUIZ 8.11

To best evaluate your performance, enter your quiz answers online.

1. The *most appropriate* machine learning (ML) approach when the target variable is continuous is:
   A. structured regression models.
   B. structured categorical models.
   C. unstructured regression models.
2. A category of general linear regression models that focuses on reduction in the total number of features used is *best* described as:
   A. a clustering model.
   B. a dimension reduction model.
   C. a penalized regression model.
3. A decision tree-based clustering algorithm would *most likely* be described as:
   A. an unstructured dimension reduction.
   B. a CART.
   C. a deep learning network.

4. Neural networks are *best* suited for situations where:
   A. the underlying relationship between features is nonlinear.
   B. the relationship is similar to the links between human neurons.
   C. the features are all based on a common unit of measurement.
5. Cross validation occurs when:
   A. training and validation samples change over the learning cycle.
   B. prediction is tested in another heterogeneous sample.
   C. the performance parameter is set by another algorithm.
6. The *most appropriate* first step in model training is:
   A. determination of the model hyperparameters.
   B. separation of data into training and validation samples.
   C. specification of the algorithm.

KEY CONCEPTS

LOS 8.a

The multiple regression equation specifies a dependent variable as a linear function of two or more independent variables:

$$Y_i = b_0 + b_1X_{1i} + b_2X_{2i} + \ldots + b_kX_{ki} + \varepsilon_i$$

The intercept term is the value of the dependent variable when the independent variables are equal to zero. Each slope coefficient is the estimated change in the dependent variable for a one-unit change in that independent variable, holding the other independent variables constant.

LOS 8.b

The *p*-value is the smallest level of significance for which the null hypothesis can be rejected.

- If the *p*-value is less than the significance level, the null hypothesis can be rejected.
- If the *p*-value is greater than the significance level, the null hypothesis cannot be rejected.

LOS 8.c

A *t*-test is used for hypothesis testing of regression parameter estimates:

$$t_{bj} = \frac{\hat{b}_j - b_j}{s_{\hat{b}_j}} \text{ with } n - k - 1 \text{ degrees of freedom}$$

Testing for statistical significance means testing H_0: $b_j = 0$ vs. H_a: $b_j \neq 0$.

LOS 8.d

For a two-tailed test of a regression coefficient, if the *t*-statistic is between the upper and lower critical *t*-values, we cannot reject the null hypothesis. We cannot conclude that the regression coefficient is statistically significantly different from the null hypothesis value at the chosen significance level.

If the *t*-statistic is greater than the upper critical *t*-value or lower than the lower critical *t*-value, we can reject the null hypothesis and conclude that the regression coefficient is statistically significantly different from the null hypothesis value at the specified significance level.

LOS 8.e

The confidence interval for regression coefficient is:

estimated regression coefficient ± (critical *t*-value)(coefficient standard error)

The value of dependent variable Y is predicted as:

$$\hat{Y} = \hat{b}_0 + \hat{b}_1X_1 + \hat{b}_2X_2 + \ldots + \hat{b}_kX_k$$

LOS 8.f

Assumptions of multiple regression mostly pertain to the error term, ε_i.

- A linear relationship exists between the dependent and independent variables.
- The independent variables are not random, and there is no exact linear relation between any two or more independent variables.
- The expected value of the error term is zero.
- The variance of the error terms is constant.
- The error for one observation is not correlated with that of another observation.
- The error term is normally distributed.

LOS 8.g

The *F*-distributed test statistic can be used to test the significance of all (or any subset of) the independent variables (i.e., the overall fit of the model) using a one-tailed test:

$$F = \frac{MSR}{MSE} = \frac{RSS/k}{SSE/(n-k-1)} \text{ with k and n} - \text{k} - \text{1 degrees of freedom}$$

LOS 8.h

The coefficient of determination, R^2, is the percentage of the variation in Y that is explained by the set of independent variables.

- R^2 increases as the number of independent variables increases—this can be a problem.
- The adjusted R^2 adjusts the R^2 for the number of independent variables.
- $R_a^2 = 1 - \left[\left(\frac{n-1}{n-k-1}\right) \times \left(1 - R^2\right)\right]$

LOS 8.i

An ANOVA table is used to assess the usefulness of a regression model's independent variable(s) in explaining the dependent variable:

Source	**df (Degrees of Freedom)**	**SS (Sum of Squares)**	**MS Mean Square = (SS/df)**
Regression	k	RSS	MSR
Error	n – k –1	SSE	MSE
Total	n – 1	SST	

$$MSE = \frac{SSE}{n-k-1};\ MSR = \frac{RSS}{k};\ R^2 = \frac{RSS}{SST};\ F = \frac{MSR}{MSE};\ SEE = \sqrt{MSE}$$

LOS 8.j

Qualitative independent variables (dummy variables) capture the effect of a binary independent variable:

- Slope coefficient is interpreted as the change in the dependent variable for the case when the dummy variable is one.
- Use one less dummy variable than the number of categories.

LOS 8.k, 8.l

Summary of what you need to know regarding violations of the assumptions of multiple regression:

Violation	Conditional Heteroskedasticity	Serial Correlation	Multicollinearity
What is it?	Residual variance related to level of independent variables	Residuals are correlated	Two or more independent variables are correlated
Effect?	Coefficients are consistent. Standard errors are underestimated. Too many Type I errors.	Coefficients are consistent. Standard errors are underestimated. Too many Type I errors (positive correlation).	Coefficients are consistent (but unreliable). Standard errors are overestimated. Too many Type II errors.
Detection?	Breusch-Pagan chi-square test = $n \times R^2$	Durbin-Watson test ≈ $2(1 - r)$	Conflicting *t* and *F* statistics; correlations among independent variables if $k = 2$
Correction?	Use White-corrected standard errors	Use the Hansen method to adjust standard errors	Drop one of the correlated variables

LOS 8.m

There are six common misspecifications of the regression model that you should be aware of and able to recognize:

- Omitting a variable.
- Variable should be transformed.
- Incorrectly pooling data.
- Using lagged dependent variable as independent variable.
- Forecasting the past.
- Measuring independent variables with error.

The effects of the model misspecification on the regression results are basically the same for all of the misspecifications: regression coefficients are biased and inconsistent, which means we can't have any confidence in our hypothesis tests of the coefficients or in the predictions of the model.

LOS 8.n

Qualitative dependent variables (e.g., bankrupt versus non-bankrupt) require methods other than ordinary least squares (e.g., probit, logit, or discriminant analysis).

LOS 8.o

The values of the slope coefficients suggest the economic meaning of the relationship between the independent and dependent variables, but it is important for the analyst to keep in mind that a regression may have statistical significance even when there is no practical economic significance in the relationship.

LOS 8.p

Supervised learning: Inputs and outputs are identified for the computer, and the algorithm uses this labeled training data to model relationships.

Unsupervised learning: The computer is not given labeled data; rather, it is provided unlabeled data that the algorithm uses to determine the structure of the data.

LOS 8.q

Examples of Machine Learning (ML) Algorithms:

Supervised Learning:

- Prediction (e.g., penalized regression, neural networks)
- Classification (e.g., classification and regression trees, random forests)

Unsupervised Learning:

- Clustering algorithms (e.g., K-means algorithm)
- Dimension reduction (e.g., principal component analysis)

LOS 8.r

Steps in Model Training:

1. Select the ML algorithm or technique.
2. Before training begins, choose the required hyperparameters (e.g., the number of training cycles).
3. Divide data into samples for:
   - Training—use labeled targets to fit the algorithm.
   - Validation—test how well the model works out-of-sample.
4. Use performance measure P and the validation sample to evaluate the learning and then adjust the hyperparameters.
5. Repeat the training cycle until the required level of accuracy is obtained, or the predetermined number of cycles is reached.

ANSWER KEY FOR MODULE QUIZZES

Module Quiz 8.1, 8.2, 8.3

1. **C** RSS = 9,105 – 4,320 = 4,785

$$F = \frac{\frac{4,785}{4}}{\frac{4,320}{65-4-1}} = \frac{1,196.25}{72} = 16.61$$

(Module 8.3, LOS 8.g)

2. **B** This is a one-tailed test, so the critical *F*-value at the 5% significance level with 4 and 60 degrees of freedom is approximately 2.53. (Module 8.3, LOS 8.g)

Module Quiz 8.4

1. **C** k = 5 and n – 5 – 1 = 25, so n = 31 (Module 8.3, LOS 8.g)

2. **A** $MSE = \frac{SSE}{df_{error}} = \frac{925}{25} = 37$ (Module 8.3, LOS 8.g)

3. **A** $R^2 = \frac{RSS}{SST} = \frac{1,025}{1,950} = 53\%$ (Module 8.4, LOS 8.h)

4. **C** $F = \frac{MSR}{MSE} = \frac{\frac{RSS}{df_{regression}}}{\frac{SSE}{df_{error}}} = \frac{\frac{1,025}{5}}{\frac{925}{25}} = \frac{205}{37} = 5.5$ (Module 8.3, LOS 8.g)

5. **B** Adjusted R^2 must be less than or equal to R^2. However, if R^2 is low enough and the number of independent variables is large, adjusted R^2 may be negative. (Module 8.4, LOS 8.h)

Module Quiz 8.5

1. **C** The *t*-statistic tests the null that industry PEs are equal. The dummy variable is significant and positive, and the dummy variable is defined as being equal to one for biotechnology stocks, which means that biotechnology PEs are statistically significantly larger than electric utility PEs. Remember, however, this is only accurate if we hold the other independent variables in the model constant. (LOS 8.j)

2. **B** Note that IND = 1 because the stock is in the biotech industry. Predicted P/E = 6.75 + (8.00 × 1) + (4.00 × 0.00) + (12.35 × 0.14) – (0.50 × 1.5) = 15.7. (LOS 8.j)

Module Quiz 8.6

1. **C** Assumptions underlying a multiple regression include: the error for one observation is not correlated with that of another observation; the expected value of the error term is zero; a linear relationship exists between the dependent and independent variables; the variance of the error terms is constant. (LOS 8.f)

Module Quiz 8.7

1. **A** The Durbin-Watson statistic tests for serial correlation of the residuals. The appropriate remedy if serial correlation is detected is to use the Hansen method. (LOS 8.k)

Module Quiz 8.8, 8.9

1. **C** The coefficients column contains the regression parameters. The regression equation is thus RET = 0.522 + 0.0460(MKT) + 0.7102(IND) + 0.9(FORT). (Module 8.9, LOS 8.o)

2. **C** The coefficient on FORT is the amount of the return attributable to the stock of a Fortune 500 firm. Other things equal, the return on a Fortune 500 company is expected to exceed the return on a non-Fortune 500 company by 0.9% annually. (Module 8.2, LOS 8.d)

3. **A** The regression equation is 0.522 + 0.0460(MKT) + 0.7102(IND) + 0.9(FORT), so RET = 0.522 + 0.0460(5) + 0.7102(3) + 0.900(0) = 2.88%. (Module 8.1, LOS 8.b)

4. **C** The *p*-value = 0.139, or 13.9%, which is not a reasonable level of significance. (Module 8.2, LOS 8.d)

5. **C** The Breusch-Pagan test is statistically significant at any reasonable level of significance, which indicates heteroskedasticity. The Durbin-Watson statistic is greater than the lower limit, but less than the upper limit, which places it in the "inconclusive" area. Thus, we are unable to reject the null hypothesis that there is no serial correlation present. (Module 8.7, LOS 8.k)

6. **B** Using leading P/E from a prior period as an independent variable in the regression is unlikely to result in misspecification because it is not related to any of the six types of misspecifications previously discussed. We're not forecasting the past because leading P/E is calculated using beginning-of-period stock price and a forecast of earnings for the next period. Also, because the dependent variable is monthly returns and not leading P/E, there is no concern about inclusion of a lagged dependent variable in the model. Omitting a relevant independent variable from the regression and using actual instead of expected inflation (measuring the independent variable in error) are likely to result in model misspecification. (Module 8.9, LOS 8.m)

7. **C** The effects of the model misspecification on the regression results are basically the same for all of the misspecifications: regression coefficients are biased and inconsistent, which means we can't have any confidence in our hypothesis tests of the coefficients or in the predictions of the model. Notice that choice C states that model misspecification will result in "unbiased" regression coefficients, while in fact model misspecification is most likely to result in "biased" regression coefficients. (Module 8.9, LOS 8.m)

8. **C** Including a lagged dependent variable (previous period hedge fund composite index returns) in the list of independent variables is likely to lead to model misspecification and biased and inconsistent regression coefficients.

   The fact that an independent variable (small-cap returns) and the dependent variable (hedge fund index returns) are correlated is not a problem for the regression model; we would expect that if the model has predictive power, the dependent variable would be correlated with the independent variables. The fact that two independent variables (small-cap returns and emerging market index returns) are correlated is not a problem of model misspecification, but potentially one of multicollinearity. Without additional information, we can't draw any conclusions concerning whether multicollinearity is a problem (remember "most likely"). (Module 8.9, LOS 8.m)

9. **C** All qualitative dependent variable models must be tested for heteroskedasticity, serial correlation, and multicollinearity. Each of the alternatives are potential examples of a qualitative dependent variable model, but none are universal elements of all qualitative dependent variable models. (Module 8.9, LOS 8.n)

Module Quiz 8.10

1. **A** A tag variable (or dependent variable) can be continuous, ordinal, or categorical. Tag variables are not specified for unsupervised learning. (LOS 8.p)

2. **A** Supervised learning uses labeled training data, does not need human intervention, and can be used for nonstructured data. (LOS 8.p)

Module Quiz 8.11

1. **A** When a target variable is specified, the problem is structured. When the target is continuous, structured regression models are appropriate. (LOS 8.q)

2. **C** Clustering does not seek to reduce the number of features. While dimension reduction models seek to reduce the number of relatively unimportant features, it is not a linear model. Penalized regressions are a category of generalized linear models (GLMs) that focus on reduction in the number of features. (LOS 8.q)

3. **B** Unstructured dimension reduction is not a decision tree algorithm. Deep learning nets (DLMs) are neural networks and are not decision trees. Classification and Regression Trees (CART) (or more specifically classification trees) are used for classifying data into categories. (LOS 8.q)

4. **A** Neural networks are suitable when the underlying relationship between the features is nonlinear. It does not mimic human neurons. Also, the features need not have a common unit of measurement, although the input values are usually standardized before being used as a node input value. (LOS 8.q)

5. **A** In the case of **cross validation**, the training and validation samples are randomly generated every learning cycle. (LOS 8.r)

6. **C** The first step in model training is specification of the algorithm. (LOS 8.r)

The following is a review of the Quantitative Methods principles designed to address the learning outcome statements set forth by CFA Institute. Cross-Reference to CFA Institute Assigned Reading #9.

READING 9

Time-Series Analysis

Study Session 3

EXAM FOCUS

A time series is a set of observations of a random variable spaced evenly through time (e.g., quarterly sales revenue for a company over the past 60 quarters). For the exam, given a regression output, identifying violations such as heteroskedasticity, nonstationarity, serial correlation, etc., will be important, as well as being able to calculate a predicted value given a time-series model. Know why a log-linear model is sometimes used; understand the implications of seasonality and how to detect and correct it, as well as the root mean squared error (RMSE) criterion.

MODULE 9.1: LINEAR AND LOG-LINEAR TREND MODELS

Video covering this content is available online.

LOS 9.a: Calculate and evaluate the predicted trend value for a time series, modeled as either a linear trend or a log-linear trend, given the estimated trend coefficients.

CFA® Program Curriculum, Volume 1, page 437

A **time series** is a set of observations for a variable over successive periods of time (e.g., monthly stock market returns for the past ten years). The series has a **trend** if a consistent pattern can be seen by plotting the data (i.e., the individual observations) on a graph. For example, a seasonal trend in sales data is easily detected by plotting the data and noting the significant jump in sales during the same month(s) each year.

Linear Trend Model

A **linear trend** is a time series pattern that can be graphed using a straight line. A downward sloping line indicates a negative trend, while an upward-sloping line indicates a positive trend.

The simplest form of a linear trend is represented by the following linear trend model:

$$y_t = b_0 + b_1(t) + \varepsilon_t$$

where:
y_t = the value of the time series (the dependent variable) at time t
b_0 = intercept at the vertical axis (y-axis)
b_1 = slope coefficient (or trend coefficient)
ε_t = error term (or residual term or disturbance term)
t = time (the independent variable); t = 1, 2, 3...T

Ordinary least squares (OLS) regression is used to estimate the coefficient in the trend line, which provides the following prediction equation:

$$\hat{y}_t = \hat{b}_0 + \hat{b}_1(t)$$

where:
$\hat{y}_t$ = the predicted value of y (the dependent variable) at time t
$\hat{b}_0$ = the estimated value of the intercept term
$\hat{b}_1$ = the estimated value of the slope coefficient

Don't let this model confuse you. It's very similar to the simple linear regression model we covered previously; only here, (t) takes on the value of the time period. For example, in period 2, the equation becomes:

$$\hat{y}_2 = \hat{b}_0 + \hat{b}_1(2)$$

And, likewise, in period 3:

$$\hat{y}_3 = \hat{b}_0 + \hat{b}_1(3)$$

This means $\hat{y}$ increases by the value of $\hat{b}_1$ each period.

EXAMPLE: Using a linear trend model

Suppose you are given a linear trend model with $\hat{b}_0 = 1.70$ and $\hat{b}_1 = 3.0$.

Calculate $\hat{y}_t$ for t = 1 and t = 2.

Answer:

When t = 1, $\hat{y}_1 = 1.70 + 3.0(1) = 4.70$

When t = 2, $\hat{y}_2 = 1.70 + 3.0(2) = 7.70$

Note that the difference between $\hat{y}_1$ and $\hat{y}_2$ is 3.0, or the value of the trend coefficient b_1.

EXAMPLE: Trend analysis

Consider hypothetical time series data for manufacturing capacity utilization.

Manufacturing Capacity Utilization

Quarter	Time (t)	Manufacturing Capacity Utilization (in %)	Quarter	Time (t)	Manufacturing Capacity Utilization (in %)
2013.1	1	82.4	2014.4	8	80.9
2013.2	2	81.5	2015.1	9	81.3
2013.3	3	80.8	2015.2	10	81.9
2013.4	4	80.5	2015.3	11	81.7
2014.1	5	80.2	2015.4	12	80.3
2014.2	6	80.2	2016.1	13	77.9
2014.3	7	80.5	2016.2	14	76.4

Applying the OLS methodology to fit the linear trend model to the data produces the results shown below.

Time Series Regression Results for Manufacturing Capacity Utilization

Regression model: $y_t = b_0 + b_1 t + \varepsilon_t$			
R square	0.346		
Adjusted R square	0.292		
Standard error	1.334		
Observations	14		
	Coefficients	*Standard Error*	*t-Statistic*
Intercept	82.137	0.753	109.066
Manufacturing utilization	–0.223	0.088	–2.534

Based on this information, predict the projected capacity utilization for the time period involved in the study (i.e., in-sample estimates).

Answer:

As shown in the regression output, the estimated intercept and slope parameters for our manufacturing capacity utilization model are $\hat{b}_0 = 82.137$ and $\hat{b}_1 = -0.223$, respectively. This means that the prediction equation for capacity utilization can be expressed as:

$$\hat{y}_t = 82.137 - 0.223t$$

With this equation, we can generate estimated values for capacity utilization, $\hat{y}_t$, for each of the 14 quarters in the time series. For example, using the model capacity utilization for the first quarter of 2013 is estimated at 81.914:

$$\hat{y}_t = 82.137 - 0.223(1) = 82.137 - 0.223 = 81.914$$

Note that the estimated value of capacity utilization in that quarter (using the model) is not exactly the same as the actual, measured capacity utilization for that quarter (82.4). The difference between the two is the error or residual term associated with that observation:

Residual (error) = actual value – predicted value ≈ 82.4 – 81.914 = 0.486

Note that since the actual, measured value is greater than the predicted value of y for 2013.1, the error term is positive. Had the actual, measured value been less than the predicted value, the error term would have been negative.

The projections (i.e., values generated by the model) for all quarters are compared to the actual values below.

Projected Versus Actual Capacity Utilization

Quarter	Time	$\hat{y}_t$	y_t	Quarter	Time	$\hat{y}_t$	y_t
2013.1	1	81.914	82.4	2014.4	8	80.353	80.9
2013.2	2	81.691	81.5	2015.1	9	80.130	81.3
2013.3	3	81.468	80.8	2015.2	10	79.907	81.9
2013.4	4	81.245	80.5	2015.3	11	79.684	81.7
2014.1	5	81.022	80.2	2015.4	12	79.460	80.3
2014.2	6	80.799	80.2	2016.1	13	79.237	77.9
2014.3	7	80.576	80.5	2016.2	14	79.014	76.4

The following graph shows visually how the predicted values compare to the actual values, which were used to generate the regression equation. The **residuals**, or **error terms**, are represented by the distance between the predicted (straight) regression line and the actual data plotted in blue. For example, the residual for t = 10 is 81.9 – 79.907 = 1.993

Predicted vs. Actual Capacity Utilization

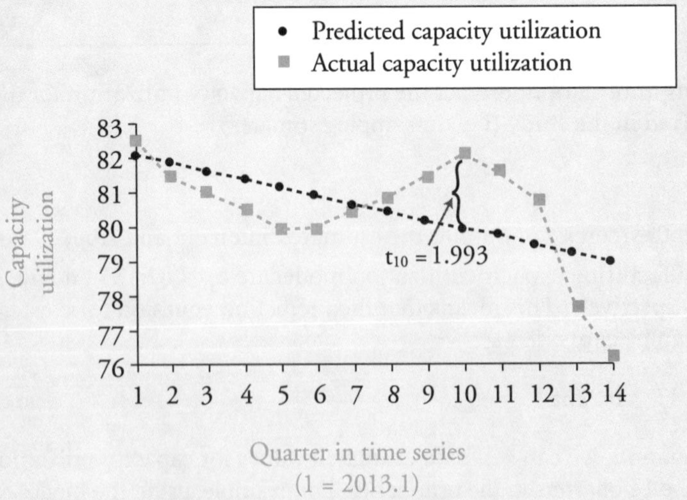

Since we utilized a linear regression model, the predicted values will by definition fall on a straight line. Since the raw data does not display a linear relationship, the model will probably not do a good job of predicting future values.

Log-Linear Trend Models

Time series data, particularly financial time series, often display *exponential growth* (growth with continuous compounding). Positive exponential growth means that the random variable (i.e., the time series) tends to increase at some constant rate of growth. If we plot the data, the observations will form a convex curve. Negative exponential growth means that the data tends to decrease at some constant rate of decay, and the plotted time series will be a concave curve.

When a series exhibits exponential growth, it can be modeled as:

$$y_t = e^{b_0 + b_1(t)}$$

where:
y_t = the value of the dependent variable at time t
b_0 = the intercept term
b_1 = the constant rate of growth
e = the base of the natural logarithm
t = time = 1, 2, 3...T

This model defines *y*, the dependent variable, as an *exponential* function of time, the independent variable. Rather than try to fit the nonlinear data with a linear (straight line) regression, we take the natural log of both sides of the equation and arrive at the *log-linear* model. This is frequently used when time series data exhibit exponential growth.

$$\ln(y_t) = \ln(e^{b_0 + b_1(t)}) \Rightarrow \ln(y_t) = b_0 + b_1(t)$$

Now that the equation has been transformed from an exponential to a linear function, we can use a linear regression technique to model the series. The use of the transformed data produces a *linear* trend line with a better fit for the data and increases the predictive ability of the model.

EXAMPLE: Log-linear trend model

An analyst estimates a log-linear trend model using quarterly revenue data (in millions of $) from the first quarter of 2005 to the fourth quarter of 2016 for JP Northfield, Inc.:

$$\ln \text{revenue}_t = b_0 + b_1(t) + \varepsilon_t$$

$$t = 1, 2, \ldots 48$$

The results are shown in the following table.

	Coefficient	Standard Error	*t*-statistic
Intercept	4.00	0.05	80.0
Trend	0.09	0.01	9.0

Calculate JP Northfield's predicted revenues in the first quarter of 2017.

Answer:

In the first quarter of 2017, *t* is equal to 49 because the sample has 48 observations.

$$\ln \text{revenue}_{49} = 4.00 + 0.09(49) = 8.41$$

$$\text{revenue}_{49} = e^{\ln \text{revenue}_{49}} = e^{8.41} = \$4{,}492 \text{ million}$$

The first answer you get in this calculation is the natural log of the revenue forecast. In order to turn the natural log into a revenue figure, you use the 2nd function of the LN key (e^x) on your BA II Plus: enter 8.41 and press [2nd] e^x = 4,492 million.

LOS 9.b: Describe factors that determine whether a linear or a log-linear trend should be used with a particular time series and evaluate limitations of trend models.

CFA® Program Curriculum, Volume 1, page 440

FACTORS THAT DETERMINE WHICH MODEL IS BEST

To determine if a linear or log-linear trend model should be used, the analyst should plot the data. A *linear trend model* may be appropriate if the data points appear to be equally distributed above and below the regression line. Inflation rate data can often be modeled with a linear trend model.

If, on the other hand, the data plots with a non-linear (curved) shape, then the residuals from a linear trend model will be persistently positive or negative for a period of time. In this case, the *log-linear model* may be more suitable. In other words, when the residuals from a linear trend model are serially correlated, a log-linear trend model may be more appropriate. By taking the log of the *y* variable, a regression line can better fit the data. Financial data (e.g., stock indices and stock prices) and company sales data are often best modeled with log-linear models.

Figure 9.1 shows a time series that is best modeled with a log-linear trend model rather than a linear trend model.

Figure 9.1: Linear vs. Log-Linear Trend Models

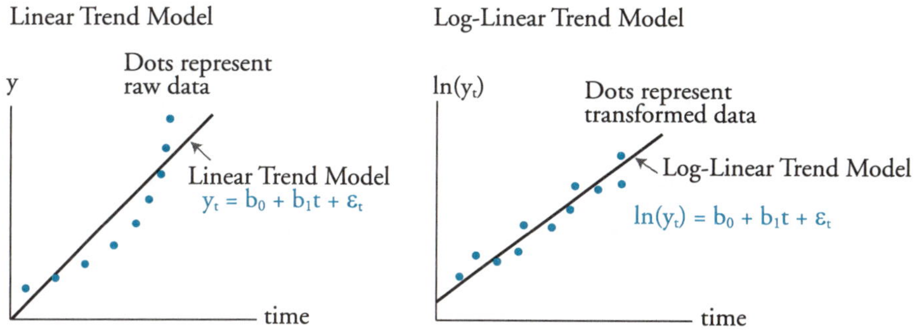

The left panel is a plot of data that exhibits exponential growth along with a linear trend line. The panel on the right is a plot of the natural logs of the original data and a representative log-linear trend line. The log-linear model fits the transformed data better than the linear trend model and, therefore, yields more accurate forecasts.

The bottom line is that when a variable grows at a constant *rate*, a log-linear model is most appropriate. When the variable increases over time by a constant *amount*, a linear trend model is most appropriate.

LIMITATIONS OF TREND MODELS

Recall from the previous two topic reviews that one of the assumptions underlying linear regression is that the residuals are uncorrelated with each other. A violation of this assumption is referred to as autocorrelation. In this case, the residuals are persistently positive or negative for periods of time and it is said that the data exhibit serial correlation. This is a significant limitation, as it means that the model is not appropriate for the time series and that we should not use it to predict future values.

In the preceding discussion, we suggested that a log-linear trend model would be better than a linear trend model when the variable exhibits a constant growth rate. However, it may be the case that even a log-linear model is not appropriate in the presence of serial correlation. In this case, we will want to turn to an autoregressive model.

Recall from the previous topic review that the Durbin Watson statistic (DW) is used to detect autocorrelation. For a time series model without serial correlation DW should be approximately equal to 2.0. A DW significantly different from 2.0 suggests that the residual terms are correlated.

MODULE QUIZ 9.1

To best evaluate your performance, enter your quiz answers online.

Use the following data to answer Questions 1 through 5.

Consider the results of the regression of monthly real estate loans (RE) in billions of dollars by commercial banks over the period January 2013 through September 2016 in the following table:

Time Series Regression Results for Real Estate Loans

Model: $RE_t = b_0 + b_1t + \varepsilon_t$	$t = 1, 2, ..., 45$
R^2	0.967908
Adjusted R^2	0.9671617
Standard error	29.587649
Observations	45
Durbin-Watson	0.601

	Coefficients	Standard Error
Intercept	1195.6241	8.9704362
b_1	12.230448	0.3396171

1. The regression of real estate loans against time is a(an):
   A. trend model.
   B. AR model.
   C. ARCH model.
2. The results of the estimation indicate a(an):
   A. upward trend.
   B. AR(2) model.
   C. ARCH system.
3. Are the intercept and slope coefficient significantly different from zero at the 5% level of significance?
   A. Both are statistically significant.
   B. One is, but the other is not.
   C. Neither of them is statistically significant.
4. The forecasted value of real estate loans for October 2016 is *closest* to:
   A. $1,733.764 billion.
   B. $1,745.990 billion.
   C. $1,758.225 billion.
5. Based on the time series regression results, is there evidence of serial correlation of the residuals?
   A. Yes, there is evidence of presence of serial correlation.
   B. No, serial correlation is not present.
   C. The test for serial correlation is inconclusive.
6. An analyst has determined that monthly sport utility vehicle (SUV) sales in the United States have been increasing over the last ten years, but the growth rate over that period has been relatively constant. Which model is *most appropriate* to predict future SUV sales?
   A. $SUVsales_t = b_0 + b_1(t) + e_t$.
   B. $lnSUVsales_t = b_0 + b_1(t) + e_t$.
   C. $lnSUVsales_t = b_0 + b_1(SUVsales_{t-1}) + e_t$.

MODULE 9.2: AUTOREGRESSIVE (AR) MODELS

Video covering this content is available online.

LOS 9.c: Explain the requirement for a time series to be covariance stationary and describe the significance of a series that is not stationary.

CFA® Program Curriculum, Volume 1, page 447

When the dependent variable is regressed against one or more lagged values of itself, the resultant model is called as an **autoregressive model** (AR). For example, the sales for a firm could be regressed against the sales for the firm in the previous month.

Consider:

$$x_t = b_0 + b_1 x_{t-1} + \varepsilon_t$$

where:
x_t = value of time series at time t
b_0 = intercept at the vertical axis (y-axis)
b_1 = slope coefficient
x_{t-1} = value of time series at time $t - 1$
ε_t = error term (or residual term or disturbance term)
t = time; $t = 1, 2, 3 \ldots T$

In an autoregressive time series, past values of a variable are used to predict the current (and hence future) value of the variable.

Statistical inferences based on ordinary least squares (OLS) estimates for an AR time series model may be invalid unless the time series being modeled is **covariance stationary.**

A time series is covariance stationary if it satisfies the following three conditions:

1. *Constant and finite expected value.* The expected value of the time series is constant over time. (Later, we will refer to this value as the mean-reverting level.)
2. *Constant and finite variance.* The time series' volatility around its mean (i.e., the distribution of the individual observations around the mean) does not change over time.
3. *Constant and finite covariance between values at any given lag.* The covariance of the time series with leading or lagged values of itself is constant.

LOS 9.d: Describe the structure of an autoregressive (AR) model of order *p* and calculate one- and two-period-ahead forecasts given the estimated coefficients.

CFA® Program Curriculum, Volume 1, page 447

The following model illustrates how variable *x* would be regressed on itself with a lag of one and two periods:

$$x_t = b_0 + b_1 x_{t-1} + b_2 x_{t-2} + \varepsilon_t$$

Study Session 3

Such a model is referred to as a *second-order* autoregressive model, or an AR(2) model. In general, an AR model of order *p*, AR(*p*), is expressed as:

$$x_t = b_0 + b_1x_{t-1} + b_2x_{t-2} + \ldots + b_px_{t-p} + \varepsilon_t$$

where *p* indicates the number of lagged values that the autoregressive model will include as independent variables.

Forecasting With an Autoregressive Model

Autoregressive time series model forecasts are calculated in the same manner as those for other regression models, but since the independent variable is a lagged value of the dependent variable, it is necessary to calculate a one-step-ahead forecast before a two-step-ahead forecast can be calculated. The calculation of successive forecasts in this manner is referred to as the **chain rule of forecasting**.

A one-period-ahead forecast for an AR(1) model is determined in the following manner:

$$\hat{x}_{t+1} = \hat{b}_0 + \hat{b}_1 x_t$$

Likewise, a two-step-ahead forecast for an AR(1) model is calculated as:

$$\hat{x}_{t+2} = \hat{b}_0 + \hat{b}_1 \hat{x}_{t+1}$$

Note that the ^ symbol above the variables in the equations indicates that the inputs used in multi-period forecasts are actually forecasts (estimates) themselves. This implies that multi-period forecasts are more uncertain than single-period forecasts. For example, for a two-step-ahead forecast, there is the usual uncertainty associated with forecasting x_{t+1} using x_t, plus the additional uncertainty of forecasting x_{t+2} using the forecasted value for x_{t+1}.

EXAMPLE: Forecasting

Suppose that an AR(1) model has been estimated and has produced the following prediction equation: $x_t = 1.2 + 0.45x_{t-1}$. Calculate a two-step-ahead forecast if the current value of *x* is 5.0.

Answer:

One-step-ahead forecast: If $x_t = 5$, then $\hat{x}_t + 1 = 1.2 + 0.45(5) = 3.45$.

Two-step-ahead forecast: If $\hat{x}_{t+1} = 3.45$, then $\hat{x}_{t+2} = 1.2 + 0.45(3.45) = 2.75$.

LOS 9.e: Explain how autocorrelations of the residuals can be used to test whether the autoregressive model fits the time series.

CFA® Program Curriculum, Volume 1, page 449

Autocorrelation & Model Fit

When an AR model is correctly specified, the residual terms will not exhibit *serial correlation*. Serial correlation (or autocorrelation) means the error terms are positively or negatively correlated. When the error terms are correlated, standard errors are unreliable and *t*-tests of individual coefficients can incorrectly show statistical significance or insignificance.

If the residuals have significant autocorrelation, the AR model that produced the residuals is not the best model for the time series being analyzed. The procedure to test whether an AR time series model is correctly specified involves three steps:

Step 1: **Estimate** the AR model being evaluated using linear regression:
Start with a first-order AR model [i.e., AR(1)] using $x_t = b_0 + b_1x_{t-1} + \varepsilon_t$.

Step 2: **Calculate** the autocorrelations of the model's residuals (i.e., the level of correlation between the forecast errors from one period to the next).

Step 3: **Test** whether the autocorrelations are significantly different from zero:
If the model is correctly specified, none of the autocorrelations will be statistically significant. To test for significance, a *t*-test is used to test the hypothesis that the correlations of the residuals are zero. The *t*-statistic is the estimated autocorrelation divided by the standard error. The standard error is $1 / \sqrt{T}$, where *T* is the number of observations, so the test statistic for each autocorrelation is $t = \dfrac{\rho_{\varepsilon_t, \varepsilon_{t-k}}}{1/\sqrt{T}}$ with (T – 2) degrees of freedom and $\rho_{\varepsilon_t, \varepsilon_{t-k}}$ is the correlation of error term *t* with the *k*th lagged error term.

PROFESSOR'S NOTE

The Durbin-Watson test that we used with trend models is not appropriate for testing for serial correlation of the error terms in an autoregressive model. Use this t-test instead.

EXAMPLE: Testing an AR model for proper specification

The correlations of the error terms from the estimation of an AR(1) model using a sample with 102 observations are presented in the following figure. Determine whether the model is correctly specified.

Autocorrelation Analysis

Model: $y_t = b_0 + b_1y_{t-1} + \varepsilon_t$

Lag	Autocorrelation	*t*-Statistic	Lag	Autocorrelation	*t*-Statistic
1	0.0616114	0.622245	7	–0.010146	–0.102470
2	0.0843368	0.851760	8	0.0211711	0.213818
3	0.0258823	0.261398	9	–0.0959502	–0.969050
4	0.0188928	0.190808	10	0.0389730	0.393608
5	0.1001404	1.011368	11	–0.0677132	–0.683870
6	–0.0638219	–0.644570	12	–0.0122798	–0.124020

Answer:

In this example, the standard error is $1/\sqrt{102}$ or 0.099. The *t*-statistic for Lag 2 is then computed as 0.0843368 / 0.099 = 0.8518.

The critical two-tail *t*-value at the 5% significance level and 100 degrees of freedom is 1.98. The *t*-statistics indicate that none of the autocorrelations of the residuals in the previous figure is statistically different from zero because their absolute values are less than 1.98. Thus, there is sufficient reason to believe that the error terms from the AR(1) model are not serially correlated.

If the t-tests indicate that any of the correlations computed in Step 2 are statistically significant (i.e., $t \geq 1.98$), the AR model is not specified correctly. Additional lags are included in the model and the correlations of the residuals (error terms) are checked again. This procedure will be followed until all autocorrelations are insignificant.

LOS 9.f: Explain mean reversion and calculate a mean-reverting level.

CFA® Program Curriculum, Volume 1, page 452

A time series exhibits **mean reversion** if it has a tendency to move toward its mean. In other words, the time series has a tendency to decline when the current value is above the mean and rise when the current value is below the mean. If a time series is at its mean-reverting level, the model predicts that the next value of the time series will be the same as its current value (i.e., $\hat{x}_t = x_{t-1}$ when a time series is at its mean-reverting level).

For an AR(1) model, $x_t = b_0 + b_1x_{t-1}$, the above equality implies that $x_t = b_0 + b_1x_t$. Solving for x_t, the mean-reverting level is expressed as $x_t = \dfrac{b_0}{(1 - b_1)}$.

So, if $x_t > \dfrac{b_0}{(1 - b_1)}$, the AR(1) model predicts that x_{t+1} will be lower than x_t, and if $x_t < \dfrac{b_0}{1 - b_1}$, the model predicts that x_{t+1} will be higher than x_t.

EXAMPLE: Mean-reverting time series

Calculate the mean-reverting level for the manufacturing capacity utilization time series using the following regression results:

Time Series Regression Results for Manufacturing Capacity Utilization

Regression model: $x_t = b_0 + b_1x_{t-1}$				
R square	0.346508			
Adjusted R square	0.29205			
Standard error	1.333885			
Observations	14			
		Coefficients	*Standard Error*	*t-Statistic*
Intercept		82.137	0.753	109.080
Manufacturing utilization		–0.223	0.0884	–2.522

Answer:

$b_0 = 82.137$ and $b_1 = -0.223$, so the mean-reverting level, $b_0 / (1 - b_1)$, is computed as: mean-reverting level $= \dfrac{82.137}{[1 - (-0.223)]} = 67.16$

This means that if the current level of manufacturing capacity utilization is above 67.16, it is expected to fall in the next period, and if manufacturing capacity utilization is below 67.16 in the current period, it is expected to rise in the next period.

All covariance stationary time series have a finite mean-reverting level. An AR(1) time series will have a finite mean-reverting level when the absolute value of the lag coefficient is less than 1 (i.e., $|b_1| < 1$).

LOS 9.g: Contrast in-sample and out-of-sample forecasts and compare the forecasting accuracy of different time-series models based on the root mean squared error criterion.

CFA® Program Curriculum, Volume 1, page 456

In-sample forecasts $(\hat{y}_t)$ are *within* the range of data (i.e., time period) used to estimate the model, which for a time series is known as the sample or test period. In-sample forecast errors are $(y_t - \hat{y}_t)$, where *t* is an observation within the sample period. In other words, we are comparing how accurate our model is in forecasting the actual data we used to develop the model. The Predicted vs. Actual Capacity Utilization figure in our Trend Analysis example shows an example of values predicted by the model compared to the values used to generate the model.

Out-of-sample forecasts are made *outside* of the sample period. In other words, we compare how accurate a model is in forecasting the *y* variable value for a time period outside the period used to develop the model. Out-of-sample forecasts are important because they provide a test of whether the model adequately describes the time series and whether it has relevance (i.e., predictive power) in the real world. Nonetheless, an analyst should be aware that most published research employs in-sample forecasts only.

The **root mean squared error** criterion (RMSE) is used to compare the accuracy of autoregressive models in forecasting out-of-sample values. For example, a researcher may have two autoregressive (AR) models: an AR(1) model and an AR(2) model. To determine which model will more accurately forecast future values, we calculate the RMSE (the square root of the average of the squared errors) for the out-of-sample data. Note that the model with the lowest RMSE for in-sample data may not be the model with the lowest RMSE for out-of-sample data.

For example, imagine that we have 60 months of historical unemployment data. We estimate both models over the first 36 of 60 months. To determine which model will produce better (i.e., more accurate) forecasts, we then forecast the values for the last 24 of 60 months of historical data. Using the actual values for the last 24 months as well as the values predicted by the models, we can calculate the RMSE for each model.

The model with the lower RMSE for the out-of-sample data will have lower forecast error and will be expected to have better predictive power in the future.

In addition to examining the RMSE criteria for a model, we will also want to examine the stability of regression coefficients, which we discuss in the following.

LOS 9.h: Explain the instability of coefficients of time-series models.

CFA® Program Curriculum, Volume 1, page 458

Financial and economic time series inherently exhibit some form of *instability* or *nonstationarity*. This is because financial and economic conditions are dynamic, and the estimated regression coefficients in one period may be quite different from those estimated during another period.

Models estimated with shorter time series are usually more stable than those with longer time series because a longer sample period increases the chance that the underlying economic process has changed. Thus, there is a tradeoff between the increased statistical reliability when using longer time periods and the increased stability of the estimates when using shorter periods.

The primary concern when selecting a time series sample period is the underlying economic processes. Have there been regulatory changes? Has there been a dramatic change in the underlying economic environment?

If the answer is yes, then the historical data may not provide a reliable model. Merely examining the significance of the autocorrelation of the residuals will not indicate whether the model is valid. We must also examine whether the data is covariance stationary.

MODULE QUIZ 9.2

To best evaluate your performance, enter your quiz answers online.

1. Is the time series shown in the following figure likely to be covariance stationary?

Time Series X:
Annual Data

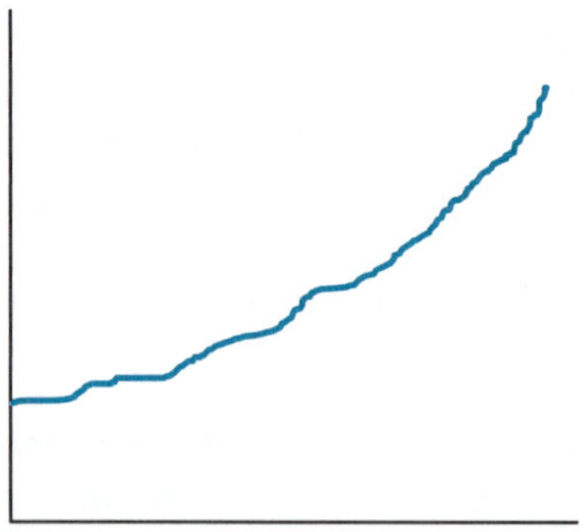

A. X is not covariance stationary due to homoskedasticity.
B. X is not covariance stationary due to non-constant mean.
C. X is covariance stationary.

2. Given the prediction equation: $\hat{x}_t = 5 + 1.75x_{t-1}$, what is the forecast value of x_{t+2} if x_{t-1} is 16.5?
A. 64.28.
B. 117.49.
C. 210.61.

3. Which of the following AR models is *most appropriate* for a time series with annual seasonality using quarterly observations?
   A. $b_1x_{t-1} + b_2x_{t-12} + \varepsilon_t$.
   B. $b_0 + b_1x_{t-1} + b_2x_{t-4} + \varepsilon_t$.
   C. $b_0 + b_1x_{t-4} + b_2x_{t-12} + \varepsilon_t$.
4. When evaluating a time series model's real-world ability to forecast, we would have the most confidence in a model with small:
   A. in-sample forecast error.
   B. out-of-sample forecast error.
   C. residuals.

MODULE 9.3: RANDOM WALKS AND UNIT ROOTS

Video covering this content is available online.

LOS 9.i: Describe characteristics of random walk processes and contrast them to covariance stationary processes.

CFA® Program Curriculum, Volume 1, page 461

Random walk. If a time series follows a random walk process, the predicted value of the series (i.e., the value of the dependent variable) in one period is equal to the value of the series in the previous period plus a random error term.

A time series that follows a simple random walk process is described in equation form as $x_t = x_{t-1} + \varepsilon_t$, where the best forecast of x_t is x_{t-1} and:

1. $E(\varepsilon_t) = 0$: The expected value of each error term is zero.
2. $E(\varepsilon_t^2) = \sigma^2$: The variance of the error terms is constant.
3. $E(\varepsilon_i\varepsilon_j) = 0$; if $i \neq j$: There is no serial correlation in the error terms.

Random Walk with a Drift. If a time series follows a random walk *with a drift*, the intercept term is not equal to zero. That is, in addition to a random error term, the time series is expected to increase or decrease by a constant amount each period. A random walk with a drift can be described as:

$x_t = b_0 + b_1x_{t-1} + \varepsilon_t$
where:
b_0 = the constant drift
$b_1 = 1$

Covariance Stationarity. Neither a random walk nor a random walk with a drift exhibits covariance stationarity. To show this, let's start by expressing a random walk as:

$x_t = b_0 + b_1x_{t-1} + \varepsilon_t$
where:
$b_0 = 0$ (for a random walk without a drift)
$b_0 \neq 0$ (for a random walk with a drift)
$b_1 = 1$ (for a random walk with or without a drift)

In either case (with or without a drift), the mean-reverting level is $\frac{b_0}{1-b_1} = \frac{b_0}{0}$ (the division of any number by zero is undefined), and as we stated earlier, a time series must have a **finite mean-reverting level** to be covariance stationary. Thus, a random walk, with or without a drift, is not covariance stationary, and exhibits what is known as a **unit root** ($b_1 = 1$). For a time series that is not covariance stationary, the least squares regression procedure that we have been using to estimate an AR(1) model will not work without transforming the data. We discuss unit roots and how they are handled in the next section.

LOS 9.j: Describe implications of unit roots for time-series analysis, explain when unit roots are likely to occur and how to test for them, and demonstrate how a time series with a unit root can be transformed so it can be analyzed with an AR model.

LOS 9.k: Describe the steps of the unit root test for nonstationarity and explain the relation of the test to autoregressive time-series models.

CFA® Program Curriculum, Volume 1, page 465

As we discussed in the previous LOS, if the coefficient on the lag variable is 1, the series is not covariance stationary. If the value of the lag coefficient is equal to one, the time series is said to have a **unit root** and will follow a random walk process. Since a time series that follows a random walk is not covariance stationary, modeling such a time series in an AR model can lead to incorrect inferences.

Unit Root Testing for Nonstationarity

To determine whether a time series is covariance stationary, we can (1) run an AR model and examine autocorrelations, or (2) perform the Dickey Fuller test.

In the first method, an AR model is estimated and the statistical significance of the autocorrelations at various lags is examined. A stationary process will usually have residual autocorrelations insignificantly different from zero at all lags or residual autocorrelations that decay to zero as the number of lags increases.

A more definitive test for unit root is the Dickey Fuller test. For statistical reasons, you cannot directly test whether the coefficient on the independent variable in an AR time series is equal to 1. To compensate, **Dickey and Fuller** created a rather ingenious test for a unit root. Remember, if an AR(1) model has a coefficient of 1, it has a unit root and no finite mean reverting level (i.e., it is not covariance stationary). Dickey and Fuller (DF) transform the AR(1) model to run a simple regression. To transform the model, they (1) start with the basic form of the AR(1) model and (2) subtract x_{t-1} from both sides:

$$(1)\ x_t = b_0 + b_1 x_{t-1} + \varepsilon$$

$$(2)\ x_t - x_{t-1} = b_0 + b_1 x_{t-1} - x_{t-1} + \varepsilon \rightarrow$$

$$x_t - x_{t-1} = b_0 + (b_1 - 1)x_{t-1} + \varepsilon$$

Then, rather than directly testing whether the original coefficient is different from 1, they test whether the new, transformed coefficient ($b_1 - 1$) is different from zero using a modified *t*-test. If ($b_1 - 1$) is not significantly different from zero, they say that b_1 must be equal to 1.0 and, therefore, the series must have a unit root.

PROFESSOR'S NOTE

In their actual test, Dickey and Fuller use the variable g, which equals ($b_1 - 1$). The null hypothesis is g = 0 (i.e., the time series has a unit root). For the exam, understand how the test is conducted and be able to interpret its results. For example, if on the exam you are told the null (g = 0) cannot be rejected, your answer is that the time series has a unit root. If the null is rejected, the time series does not have a unit root.

FIRST DIFFERENCING

If we believe a time series is a random walk (i.e., has a unit root), we can transform the data to a covariance stationary time series using a procedure called **first differencing**. The first differencing process involves subtracting the value of the time series (i.e., the dependent variable) in the immediately preceding period from the current value of the time series to define a new dependent variable, *y*. Note that by taking first differences, you model the **change** in the value of the dependent variable

So, if the original time series of *x* has a unit root, the change in *x*, $x_t - x_{t-1} = \varepsilon_t$, is just the error term. This means we can define y_t as:

$$y_t = x_t - x_{t-1} \Rightarrow y_t = \varepsilon_t$$

Then, stating *y* in the form of an AR(1) model:

$$y_t = b_0 + b_1 y_{t-1} + \varepsilon_1$$

where:

$$b_0 = b_1 = 0$$

This transformed time series has a finite mean-reverting level of $\frac{0}{1-0} = 0$ and is, therefore, covariance stationary.

EXAMPLE: Unit root

Suppose we decide to model the capacity utilization data. Using an AR(1) model, the results indicate that the capacity utilization time series probably contains a unit root and is, therefore, not covariance stationary. Discuss how this time series can be transformed to be covariance stationary.

Answer:

Covariance stationarity can often be achieved by transforming the data using first differencing and modeling the first-differenced time series as an autoregressive time series.

EXAMPLE: First differencing

The next figure contains the first-differences of our manufacturing capacity utilization time series for the period 2013.1 through 2016.3. The first two columns contain the original time series. The first differences of the original series are

Study Session 3

contained in the third column of the table, and the one-period lagged values on the first-differences are presented in the fourth column of the table. Note that the first differences in this example represent the *change* in manufacturing capacity from the preceding period and are designated as y_t and y_{t-1}.

First-Differenced Manufacturing Capacity Utilization Data

Quarter	Capacity	Change in Capacity $y_t = x_t - x_{t-1}$	Lagged Change in Capacity $y_{t-1} = x_{t-1} - x_{t-2}$
2013.1	82.4		
2013.2	81.5	–0.9	
2013.3	80.8	–0.7	–0.9
2013.4	80.5	–0.3	–0.7
2014.1	80.2	–0.3	–0.3
2014.2	80.2	0.0	–0.3
2014.3	80.5	0.3	0.0
2014.4	80.9	0.4	0.3
2015.1	81.3	0.4	0.4
2015.2	81.9	0.6	0.4
2015.3	81.7	–0.2	0.6
2015.4	80.3	–1.4	–0.2
2016.1	77.9	–2.4	–1.4
2016.2	76.4	–1.5	–2.4
2016.3	76.4	0.0	–1.5

After this transformation, it is appropriate to regress the AR(1) model, $y_t = b_0 + b_1y_{t-1}$. The regression results for the first-differenced time series are presented in the next figure, where it can be seen that the estimated coefficient on the lag variable is statistically significant at 5% level of significance.

Regression Output for First-Differenced Manufacturing Capacity

Change in Capacity Utilization				
AR(1) Model $y_t = b_0 + b_1y_{t-1} + \varepsilon_t$				
R^2		0.430869388		
Adjusted R^2		0.379130241		
Standard error		0.699210366		
Observations		13		
	Coefficients	*Standard Error*	*t-Statistic*	*p-Value*
Intercept	–0.090014589	0.220409703	–0.4084	0.69082
Lag 1	0.65496839	0.226964091	2.885780	0.0148

MODULE QUIZ 9.3

To best evaluate your performance, enter your quiz answers online.

Use the following data to answer Questions 1 and 2.

The results of the estimation of monthly revolving credit outstanding (RCO) on the one-period lagged values for RCO from January 2013 through December 2015 are presented in the following table.

Regression Results for Outstanding Revolving Credit Study

Model: $RCO_t = b_0 + b_1\ RCO_{t-1} + \varepsilon_t$				
R^2	0.952643			
Adjusted R^2	0.951208			
Standard error	9.261452			
Observations	35			
	Coefficients	*Standard Error*	*t-Statistic*	*p-Value*
Intercept	–34.0019	24.19417	–1.40537	0.169255
Lag 1	1.065697	0.041362	25.76512	< 0.0001

1. What type of time-series model was used to produce the regression results in the table? A(n):
   A. AR model.
   B. heteroskedasticity (H) model.
   C. trend model with a drift.
2. An approach that may work in the case of modeling a time series that has a unit root is to:
   A. use an ARCH model.
   B. use a trend model.
   C. model the first differences of the time series.
3. Which of the following will always have a finite mean-reverting level?
   A. A covariance-stationary time series.
   B. A random-walk-with-drift time series.
   C. A time series with unit root.
4. Which of the following statements is *most accurate*? A random walk process:
   A. is nonstationary.
   B. has a finite mean-reverting level.
   C. can be appropriately fit as an AR(1) model.
5. Which of the following is not correct about the Dickey-Fuller unit root test for nonstationarity?
   A. The null hypothesis is that the time series has a unit root.
   B. A hypothesis test is conducted using critical values computed by Dickey and Fuller in place of conventional *t*-test values.
   C. If the test statistic is significant, we conclude that the times series is nonstationary.

Study Session 3

Video covering this content is available online.

MODULE 9.4: SEASONALITY

LOS 9.1: Explain how to test and correct for seasonality in a time-series model and calculate and interpret a forecasted value using an AR model with a seasonal lag.

CFA® Program Curriculum, Volume 1, page 474

Seasonality in a time-series is a pattern that tends to repeat from year to year. One example is monthly sales data for a retailer. Given that sales data normally vary according to the time of year, we might expect this month's sales (x_t) to be related to sales for the same month last year (x_{t-12}).

When seasonality is present, modeling the associated time series data would be misspecified unless the AR model incorporates the effects of the seasonality.

EXAMPLE: Detecting seasonality

You are interested in predicting occupancy levels for a resort hotel chain and have obtained the chain's quarterly occupancy levels for the most recent 40 quarters (10 years). You decide to model the quarterly occupancy time-series using the AR(1) model:

$$\ln x_t = b_0 + b_1 \ln x_{t-1} + \varepsilon_t$$

Determine whether seasonality exists using the results presented in the following example.

Autoregression Output for Log-Quarterly Hotel Occupancy

Resort Occupancy Levels			
AR(1) Model: $\ln x_t = b_0 + b_1 \ln x_{t-1} + \varepsilon_t$			
R^2	0.7929		
Standard error	0.1952		
Observations	39		
	Coefficients	*Standard Error*	*t-Statistic*
Intercept	0.0375	0.0274	1.369
Lag 1	0.5318	0.1635	3.2526

Autocorrelation of Residuals

Residual Lag	Autocorrelation	Standard Error	*t*-Statistic
1	–0.0615	0.1601	–0.3841
2	–0.0121	0.1601	–0.0756
3	–0.0212	0.1601	–0.1324
4	0.8719	0.1601	5.4460

Answer:

The bottom part of the table contains the residual autocorrelations for the first four lags of the time series. What stands out is the relatively large autocorrelation and *t*-statistic for the fourth lag. With 39 observations and two parameters, (b_0 and b_1), there are 37 degrees of freedom. At a significance level of 5%, the critical *t*-value is 2.026.

The *t*-statistics indicate that none of the first three lagged autocorrelations is significantly different from zero. However, the *t*-statistic at Lag 4 is 5.4460, which means that we must reject the null hypothesis that the Lag 4 autocorrelation is zero and conclude that seasonality is present in the time-series. Thus, we conclude that this model is misspecified and will be unreliable for forecasting purposes. We need to include a seasonality term to make the model more correctly specified.

Correcting for seasonality. The interpretation of seasonality in the above example is that occupancy in any quarter is related to occupancy in the previous quarter and the same quarter in the previous year. For example, fourth quarter 2015 occupancy is related to third quarter 2015 occupancy as well as fourth quarter 2014 occupancy.

To adjust for seasonality in an AR model, an additional lag of the *dependent* variable (corresponding to the same period in the previous year) is added to the original model as another *independent* variable. For example, if quarterly data are used, the seasonal lag is 4; if monthly data are used the seasonal lag is 12; and so on.

EXAMPLE: Correcting for seasonality in a time-series model

We continue with our resort occupancy level example, where the significant residual correlation at Lag 4 indicates seasonality in the quarterly time series. By testing the correlations of the error terms, it appears that occupancy levels in each quarter are related not only to the previous quarter, but also to the corresponding quarter in the previous year. To adjust for this problem, we add a lagged value of the dependent variable to the original model that corresponds to the seasonal pattern.

To model the autocorrelation of the same quarters from year to year, we use an AR(1) model with a seasonal lag: $\ln x_t = b_0 + b_1(\ln x_{t-1}) + b_2(\ln x_{t-4}) + \varepsilon_t$. Note that this specification, the inclusion of a seasonal lag, does not result in an AR(2) model. It results in an AR(1) model incorporating a seasonal lag term.

The results obtained when this model is fit to the natural logarithm of the time series are presented in the following. Determine whether the model is specified correctly.

Log-Resort Hotel Occupancy

AR(1) Model with a Seasonal Lag: $\ln x_t = b_0 + b_1 (\ln x_{t-1}) + b_2(\ln x_{t-4}) + \varepsilon_t$

R^2	0.948983874
Standard error	0.3754
Observations	36

	Coefficients	*Standard Error*	*t-Statistic*
Intercept	0.0085	0.0049	1.7347
Lag 1	0.2598	0.0527	4.9298
Lag 4	0.7921	0.2166	3.6570

Autocorrelation of Residuals

Residual Lag	Autocorrelation	Standard Error	*t*-Statistic
1	–0.0526	0.1667	–0.3156
2	0.0715	0.1667	0.4290
3	–0.0241	0.1667	–0.1446
4	–0.0435	0.1667	–0.2610

Answer:

Notice in the bottom of the table that the fourth-lag residual autocorrelation has dropped substantially and is, in fact, no longer statistically significant. Also notable in these results is the improvement in the R-square for the adjusted model (94.9%) compared to the R-square from the original model (79.3%). The results shown in the figure indicate that, by incorporating a seasonal lag term, the model is now specified correctly.

FORECASTING WITH AN AR MODEL WITH A SEASONAL LAG

EXAMPLE: Forecasting with an autoregressive model

Based on the regression results from the previous example and the occupancy levels over the past year (presented below), forecast the level of hotel occupancy for the first quarter of 2016.

Quarterly Hotel Occupancy Levels

Quarter	2015.1	2015.2	2015.3	2015.4
Occupancy Level	250,000	750,000	450,000	600,000

Answer:

We express the seasonally adjusted forecasting equation as:

$\ln x_t = 0.0085 + 0.2598(\ln x_{t-1}) + 0.7921(\ln x_{t-4})$

where x_t is the occupancy level for the *t*th quarter.

To forecast the occupancy level for the hotel chain for the first quarter of 2016 (i.e., 2016.1), the following computation is made:

$\ln y_{2016.1} = 0.0085 + 0.2598(\ln y_{2015.4}) + 0.7921(\ln y_{2015.1})$

$\ln y_{2016.1} = 0.0085 + 0.2598(\ln 600{,}000) + 0.7921(\ln 250{,}000)$

$\ln y_{2016.1} = 0.0085 + 0.2598(13.3047) + 0.7921(12.4292)$

$\ln y_{2016.1} = 13.3103$

Since $y = e^{\ln(y)}$, $y_{2016.1} = e^{13.3103} = 603{,}378.52$

The forecasted level of hotel occupancy for the first quarter of 2016 is 603,379, a significant increase over the same quarter the previous year.

PROFESSOR'S NOTE

Once again, the first answer you get in this calculation is the natural log of the occupancy forecast. In order to turn the natural log into an occupancy figure, you use the 2nd function of the LN key (e^x) on your BA II Plus: enter 13.3103 and press [2nd] e^x = 603,378.52.

MODULE QUIZ 9.4

To best evaluate your performance, enter your quiz answers online.

Use the following data to answer Questions 1 through 3.

Regression Results for Monthly Cash Flow Study

	Coefficients	Standard Error	*t*-Statistic	*p*-Value
Intercept	26.8625	12.15146	2.210639	0.035719
Lag 1	0.7196	0.042584	16.89837	< 0.0001

Autocorrelation of the Residual

Lag	Autocorrelation	Standard Error	*t*-Statistic	*p*-Value
12	–0.0254	0.0632	–0.4019	0.5612

1. The number of observations in the time series used to estimate the model represented in the table above is *closest* to:
   A. 16.
   B. 50.
   C. 250.
2. Based on the information given, what type of model was used?
   A. AR(1).
   B. AR(2).
   C. AR(12).

3. Does the information indicate the presence of seasonality?
   A. No, because the lag-12 autocorrelation of the residual is not significant.
   B. Yes, because the lag-12 autocorrelation of the residual is significantly different than one.
   C. There is not enough information provided; the autocorrelation for the first lag is also needed to detect seasonality.
4. A time-series model that uses quarterly data exhibits seasonality if the fourth autocorrelation of the error term:
   A. differs significantly from 0.
   B. does not differ significantly from 0.
   C. does not differ significantly from the first autocorrelation of the error term.
5. In an autoregressive time-series model, seasonality may be corrected by:
   A. excluding one or more of the lagged variables until the seasonality disappears.
   B. transforming the time series using first-differencing.
   C. adding an additional variable that reflects an appropriate lag of the time series.

MODULE 9.5: ARCH AND MULTIPLE TIME SERIES

Video covering this content is available online.

LOS 9.m: Explain autoregressive conditional heteroskedasticity (ARCH) and describe how ARCH models can be applied to predict the variance of a time series.

CFA® Program Curriculum, Volume 1, page 481

When examining a single time series, such as an AR model, **autoregressive conditional heteroskedasticity (ARCH)** exists if the variance of the residuals in one period is *dependent* on the variance of the residuals in a previous period. When this condition exists, the standard errors of the regression coefficients in AR models and the hypothesis tests of these coefficients are invalid.

Using ARCH Models

An ARCH model is used to test for autoregressive conditional heteroskedasticity. Within the ARCH framework, an ARCH(1) time series is one for which the variance of the residuals in one period is dependent on (i.e., a function of) the variance of the residuals in the preceding period. To test whether a time series is ARCH(1), the squared residuals from an estimated time-series model, $\hat{\varepsilon}_t^2$, are regressed on the first lag of the squared residuals $\hat{\varepsilon}_{t-1}^2$.

The ARCH(1) regression model is expressed as:

$$\hat{\varepsilon}_t^2 = a_0 + a_1\hat{\varepsilon}_{t-1}^2 + \mu_t$$

where a_0 is the constant and μ_t is an error term.

If the coefficient, a_1, is statistically different from zero, the time series is ARCH(1).

If a time-series model has been determined to contain ARCH errors, regression procedures that correct for heteroskedasticity, such as *generalized least squares*, must be used in order to develop a predictive model. Otherwise, the standard errors of the model's coefficients will be incorrect, leading to invalid conclusions.

Predicting the Variance of a Time Series

However, if a time series has ARCH errors, an ARCH model can be used to predict the variance of the residuals in future periods. For example, if the data exhibit an ARCH(1) pattern, the ARCH(1) model can be used in period t to predict the variance of the residuals in period t + 1:

$$\hat{\sigma}^2_{t+1} = \hat{a}_0 + \hat{a}_1 \hat{\varepsilon}^2_t$$

EXAMPLE: **ARCH(1) time series**

The next figure contains the results from the regression of an ARCH(1) model. The squared errors for periods *t* through *T* are regressed on the squared errors for periods t – 1 through T – 1. (μ_t is the error term for the model.) Determine whether the results indicate autoregressive conditional heteroskedasticity (ARCH), and if so, calculate the predicted variance of the error terms in the next period if the current period squared error is 0.5625.

ARCH (1) Regression Results

Model: $\hat{\varepsilon}^2_t = a_0 + a_1\hat{\varepsilon}^2_{t-1} + \mu_t$	Coefficients	Standard Error	*t*-Statistic	*p*-Value
Constant	5.9068	1.08631	5.4375	< 0.001
Lag 1	0.4515	0.09558	4.7238	< 0.001

Answer:

Since the *p*-value for the coefficient on the lagged variable indicates statistical significance, we can conclude that the time series is ARCH(1). As such, the variance of the error term in the next period can be computed as:

$$\hat{\sigma}^2_{t+1} = \hat{a}_0 + \hat{a}_1 \hat{\varepsilon}^2_t = 5.9068 + 0.4515(0.5625) = 6.1608$$

PROFESSOR'S NOTE

If the coefficient a_1 is zero, the variance is constant from period to period. If a_1 is greater than (less than) zero, the variance increases (decreases) over time (i.e., the error terms exhibit heteroskedasticity).

Study Session 3

LOS 9.n: Explain how time-series variables should be analyzed for nonstationarity and/or cointegration before use in a linear regression.

CFA® Program Curriculum, Volume 1, page 484

Occasionally an analyst will run a regression using two time series (i.e., time series utilizing two different variables). For example, using the market model to estimate the equity beta for a stock, an analyst regresses a time series of the stock's returns (y_t) on a time series of returns for the market (x_t):

$$y_t = b_0 + b_1x_t + e_t$$

Notice that now we are faced with two different time series (y_t and x_t), either or both of which could be subject to nonstationarity.

To test whether the two time series have unit roots, the analyst first runs separate DF tests with five possible results:

1. Both time series are covariance stationary.
2. Only the dependent variable time series is covariance stationary.
3. Only the independent variable time series is covariance stationary.
4. Neither time series is covariance stationary and the two series *are not* cointegrated.
5. Neither time series is covariance stationary and the two series *are* cointegrated.

In scenario 1 the analyst can use linear regression, and the coefficients should be statistically reliable, but regressions in scenarios 2 and 3 will not be reliable. Whether linear regression can be used in scenarios 4 and 5 depends upon whether the two time series are *cointegrated.*

Cointegration

Cointegration means that two time series are economically linked (related to the same macro variables) or follow the same trend and that relationship is not expected to change. If two time series are cointegrated, the error term from regressing one on the other is covariance stationary and the *t*-tests are reliable. This means that scenario 5 will produce reliable regression estimates, whereas scenario 4 will not.

To test whether two time series are cointegrated, we regress one variable on the other using the following model:

$$y_t = b_0 + b_1x_t + \varepsilon$$

where:
y_t = value of time series y at time t
x_t = value of time series x at time t

The residuals are tested for a unit root using the Dickey Fuller test with critical t-values calculated by Engle and Granger (i.e., the DF–EG test). If the test rejects the null hypothesis of a unit root, we say the error terms generated by the two time series are covariance stationary and the two series are cointegrated. If the two series are cointegrated, we can use the regression to model their relationship.

PROFESSOR'S NOTE

For the exam, remember that the Dickey Fuller test does not use the standard critical t-values we typically use in testing the statistical significance of individual regression coefficients. The DF–EG test further adjusts them to test for cointegration. As with the DF test, you do not have to know critical t-values for the DF–EG test. Just remember that like the regular DF test, if the null is rejected, we say the series (of error terms in this case) is covariance stationary and the two time series are cointegrated.

Figure 9.2: Can Linear Regression Be Used to Model the Relationship Between Two Time Series?

		Independent Variable Time Series	
		Is Covariance Stationary	*Is NOT Covariance Stationary*
Dependent Variable Time Series	*Is Covariance Stationary*	Yes	No
	Is NOT Covariance Stationary	No	Yes, IF the two time series are cointegrated

LOS 9.o: Determine an appropriate time-series model to analyze a given investment problem and justify that choice.

CFA® Program Curriculum, Volume 1, page 489

To determine what type of model is best suited to meet your needs, follow these guidelines:

1. Determine your goal.
   - Are you attempting to model the relationship of a variable to other variables (e.g., cointegrated time series, cross-sectional multiple regression)?
   - Are you trying to model the variable over time (e.g., trend model)?
2. If you have decided on using a time series analysis for an individual variable, plot the values of the variable over time and look for characteristics that would indicate nonstationarity, such as non-constant variance (heteroskedasticity), non-constant mean, seasonality, or structural change.

   A **structural change** is indicated by a significant *shift* in the plotted data at a point in time that seems to divide the data into two or more distinct patterns. (Figure 9.3 shows a data plot that indicates a structural shift in the time series at Point a.) In this example, you have to run two different models, one incorporating the data before and one after that date, and test whether the time series has actually shifted. If the time series has shifted significantly, a single time series encompassing the entire period (i.e., both patterns) will likely produce unreliable results.

Figure 9.3: A Structural Shift in a Time Series

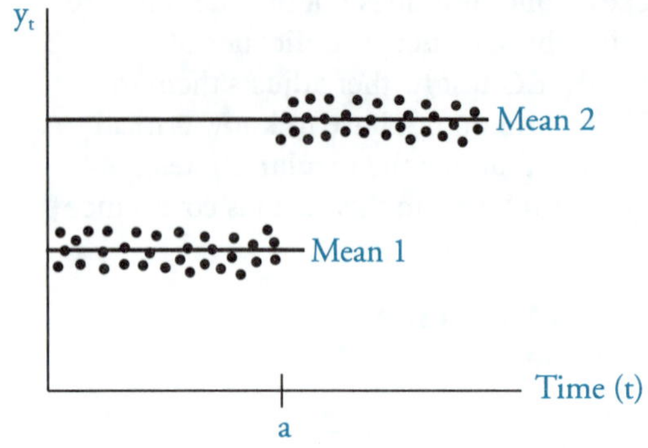

3. If there is no seasonality or structural shift, use a trend model.
   - If the data plot on a straight line with an upward or downward slope, use a linear trend model.
   - If the data plot in a curve, use a log-linear trend model.
4. Run the trend analysis, compute the residuals, and test for serial correlation using the Durbin Watson test.
   - If you detect no serial correlation, *you can use the model.*
   - If you detect serial correlation, you must use another model (e.g., AR).
5. If the data has serial correlation, reexamine the data for stationarity before running an AR model. If it is not stationary, treat the data for use in an AR model as follows:
   - If the data has a linear trend, first-difference the data.
   - If the data has an exponential trend, first-difference the natural log of the data.
   - If there is a structural shift in the data, run two separate models as discussed above.
   - If the data has a seasonal component, incorporate the seasonality in the AR model as discussed in the following.
6. After first-differencing in 5 previously, if the series is covariance stationary, run an AR(1) model and test for serial correlation and seasonality.
   - If there is no remaining serial correlation, *you can use the model.*
   - If you still detect serial correlation, incorporate lagged values of the variable (possibly including one for seasonality—e.g., for monthly data, add the 12th lag of the time series) into the AR model until you have removed (i.e., modeled) any serial correlation.

7. Test for ARCH. Regress the square of the residuals on squares of lagged values of the residuals and test whether the resulting coefficient is significantly different from zero.
    - If the coefficient is not significantly different from zero, *you can use the model.*
    - If the coefficient is significantly different from zero, ARCH is present. Correct using generalized least squares.
8. If you have developed two statistically reliable models and want to determine which is better at forecasting, calculate their out-of-sample RMSE.

MODULE QUIZ 9.5

To best evaluate your performance, enter your quiz answers online.

1. Which of the following is true of modeling a time series that contains two or more distinct periods where the data is fundamentally different?
    A. The optimal data sample period for estimating the time-series model can be calculated mathematically.
    B. To most accurately estimate the time-series model, the entire available time series data set should be used as the sample period.
    C. We have to fit two different models for each of the two distinct periods.
2. Which of the following indicates the presence of Autoregressive Conditional Heteroskedasticity (ARCH) in a time-series model?
    A. The autocorrelations of the error terms are zero at all lags.
    B. The variance of the current error depends on the variance of lagged errors.
    C. The error term shows significant serial correlation at lag 1.
3. Linear regression is least appropriate for modeling the relationship between two time series when:
    A. neither series has a unit root.
    B. one of the time series has a unit root, the other does not.
    C. both series have a unit root, and the time series are cointegrated.

KEY CONCEPTS

LOS 9.a

A time series is a set of observations for a variable over successive periods of time. A time series model captures the time series pattern and allows us to make predictions about the variable in the future.

LOS 9.b

A simple linear trend model is: $y_t = b_0 + b_1 t + \varepsilon_t$, estimated for t = 1, 2, …, T.

A log-linear trend model, $\ln(y_t) = b_0 + b_1 t + \varepsilon_t$, is appropriate for exponential data.

A plot of the data should be used to determine whether a linear or log-linear trend model should be used.

The primary limitation of trend models is that they are not useful if the residuals exhibit serial correlation.

LOS 9.c

A time series is covariance stationary if its mean, variance, and covariances with lagged and leading values do not change over time. Covariance stationarity is a requirement for using AR models.

LOS 9.d

Autoregressive time series multiperiod forecasts are calculated in the same manner as those for other regression models, but since the independent variable consists of a lagged variable, it is necessary to calculate a one-step-ahead forecast before a two-step-ahead forecast may be calculated. The calculation of successive forecasts in this manner is referred to as the chain rule of forecasting.

A one-period-ahead forecast for an AR(1) would be determined in the following manner:

$$\hat{x}_{t+1} = \hat{b}_0 + \hat{b}_1 x_t$$

A two-period-ahead forecast for an AR(1) would be determined in the following manner:

$$\hat{x}_{t+2} = \hat{b}_0 + \hat{b}_1 \hat{x}_{t+1}$$

LOS 9.e

When an AR model is correctly specified, the residual terms will not exhibit serial correlation. If the residuals possess some degree of serial correlation, the AR model that produced the residuals is not the best model for the data being studied and the regression results will be problematic. The procedure to test whether an AR time-series model is correctly specified involves three steps:

1. Estimate the AR model being evaluated using linear regression.
2. Calculate the autocorrelations of the model's residuals.
3. Test whether the autocorrelations are significant.

LOS 9.f

A time series is mean reverting if it tends towards its mean over time. The mean reverting level for an AR(1) model is $\frac{b_0}{(1 - b_1)}$.

LOS 9.g

In-sample forecasts are made *within* the range of data used in the estimation. Out-of-sample forecasts are made *outside* of the time period for the data used in the estimation.

The root mean squared error criterion (RMSE) is used to compare the accuracy of autoregressive models in forecasting out-of-sample values. A researcher may have two autoregressive (AR) models, both of which seem to fit the data: an AR(1) model and an AR(2) model. To determine which model will more accurately forecast future values, we calculate the square root of the mean squared error (RMSE). The model with the lower RMSE for the out-of-sample data will have lower forecast error and will be expected to have better predictive power in the future.

LOS 9.h

Most economic and financial time series data are not stationary. The degree of the nonstationarity depends on the length of the series and changes in the underlying economic environment.

LOS 9.i

A random walk time series is one for which the value in one period is equal to the value in another period, plus a random error. A random walk process does not have a mean reverting level and is not stationary.

LOS 9.j

A time series has a unit root if the coefficient on the lagged dependent variable is equal to one. A series with a unit root is not covariance stationary. Economic and finance time series frequently have unit roots. Data with a unit root must be first differenced before being used in a time series model.

LOS 9.k

To determine whether a time series is covariance stationary, we can (1) run an AR model and/or (2) perform the Dickey Fuller test.

LOS 9.l

Seasonality in a time series is tested by calculating the autocorrelations of error terms. A statistically significant lagged error term corresponding to the periodicity of the data indicates seasonality. Seasonality can be corrected by incorporating the appropriate seasonal lag term in an AR model.

If a seasonal lag coefficient is appropriate and corrects the seasonality, the AR model with the seasonal terms will have no statistically significant autocorrelations of error terms.

LOS 9.m

ARCH is present if the variance of the residuals from an AR model are correlated across time. ARCH is detected by estimating $\hat{\varepsilon}_t^2 = a_0 + a_1\hat{\varepsilon}_{t-1}^2 + \mu_t$. If a_1 is significant, ARCH exists and the variance of errors can be predicted using: $\hat{\sigma}_{t+1}^2 = \hat{a}_0 + \hat{a}_1\hat{\varepsilon}_t^2$.

LOS 9.n

When working with two time series in a regression: (1) if neither time series has a unit root, then the regression can be used; (2) if only one series has a unit root, the regression results will be invalid; (3) if both time series have a unit root and are cointegrated, then the regression can be used; (4) if both time series have a unit root but are not cointegrated, the regression results will be invalid.

The Dickey Fuller test with critical *t*-values calculated by Engle and Granger is used to determine whether two times series are cointegrated.

LOS 9.o

The RMSE criterion is used to determine which forecasting model will produce the most accurate forecasts. The RMSE equals the square root of the average squared error.

ANSWER KEY FOR MODULE QUIZZES

Module Quiz 9.1

1. **A** With a trend model, the independent variable is time, *t*. (LOS 9.b)

2. **A** The slope coefficient (b_1) is positive and significantly different from zero indicating an upward trend. (LOS 9.a)

3. **A** The *t*-statistic to test the statistical significance of the intercept and slope coefficient is the parameter estimate divided by its standard error. We reject the null hypothesis and conclude the coefficients are statistically significant if the absolute value of the *t*-statistic is greater than the two-tail 5% critical *t*-value with 43 degrees of freedom, which is 2.02.

$$t_{b_0} = \frac{1{,}195.6241}{8.9704362} = 133.3$$

$$t_{b_1} = \frac{12.230448}{0.3396171} = 36.0$$

Both the intercept term and the slope coefficient are significantly different from zero at the 5% level because both *t*-statistics are greater than the critical *t*-value of 2.02. (LOS 9.a)

4. **C** $\hat{Y}_{46}$ = \$1,195.6241 + \$12.230448(46) = \$1,758.225 billion. (LOS 9.a)

5. **A** The Durbin-Watson statistic is used to detect serial correlation in the residuals. The lower critical value for a DW test with one independent variable and 45 observations is 1.48 and the upper critical value is 1.57. The actual DW-statistic is 0.601, which is less than the lower critical value. This indicates the residuals are positively serially correlated. See the previous topic review for details on implementing the Durbin-Watson test. (LOS 9.b)

6. **B** A log-linear model (choice B) is most appropriate for a time series that grows at a relatively constant growth rate. Neither a linear trend model (choice A), nor an AR(1) model (choice C) are appropriate in this case. (LOS 9.b)

Module Quiz 9.2

1. **B** Time series Z has a definite upward trend, which once again suggests the expected value of the time series Z is not constant, and therefore it is not covariance stationary. (LOS 9.c)

2. **B** Given $x_{t-1} = 16.5$, $\hat{x}_t = 5 + 1.75(16.5) = 33.875$. So, $\hat{x}_{t+1} = 5 + 1.75\,\hat{x}_t = 5 + 1.75(33.875) = 64.28$. So, $\hat{x}_{t+2} = 5 + 1.75\,\hat{x}_{t+1} = 5 + 1.75(64.28) = 117.49$. (LOS 9.d)

3. **B** The seasonal (annual) lag occurs on a quarterly basis, so the appropriate model is $b_0 + b_1x_{t-1} + b_2x_{t-4} + \varepsilon_t$. The intercept b_0 should be included in the model. (LOS 9.d)

4. **B** Out-of-sample performance is the most important indicator of a model's real-world forecasting ability. In-sample forecast performance is less persuasive, because forecasting the past is not difficult. The residuals from the fitted time-series model are another name for the model's in-sample forecast errors. (LOS 9.g)

Module Quiz 9.3

1. **A** The independent variable is the dependent variable lagged one period, so the model is an AR(1) model. (Module 9.2, LOS 9.d)

2. **C** The first-differenced series usually does not have a unit root and is, therefore, covariance stationary. (Module 9.3, LOS 9.j)

3. **A** All random-walk time series have a unit root. Time series with unit root do not have a finite mean-reverting level. (Module 9.3, LOS 9.i)

4. **A** A random walk process does not have a finite mean-reverting level and hence covariance nonstationary. An AR(1) model cannot be used to fit a covariance nonstationary time series. (Module 9.3, LOS 9.j)

5. **C** For a unit root test, the null hypothesis is that the time series has a unit root. For testing for unit roots, the Dickey-Fuller (DF) test computes the conventional t-statistic, which is then compared against the revised set of critical values computed by DF. If the test statistic is significant, we reject the null hypothesis (that the time series has a unit root), implying that a unit root is not present. (Module 9.3, LOS 9.k)

Module Quiz 9.4

1. **C** The standard error of the estimated autocorrelations is $1/\sqrt{T}$, where T is the number of observations (periods). So, if the standard error is given as 0.0632, the number of observations, T, in the time series must be $(1 / 0.0632)^2 \approx 250$. (Module 9.2, LOS 9.e)

2. **A** The results in the table indicate that the prediction equation is $x_t = 26.8625 + 0.7196x_{t-1}$, which is estimated from an AR(1) model. (Module 9.1, LOS 9.a)

3. **A** The autocorrelation in the twelfth month is not statistically different from zero. (p-value: 0.5612 > 0.05) Thus, there appears to be no seasonality. (Module 9.4, LOS 9.l)

4. **A** If the fourth autocorrelation of the error term differs significantly from 0, this is an indication of seasonality. (Module 9.4, LOS 9.l)

5. **C** Adding an appropriate lag is an appropriate solution to seasonality. Excluding variables can sometimes be used to solve multicollinearity. Transforming using first-differencing can be a cure for nonstationarity. (Module 9.4, LOS 9.l)

Module Quiz 9.5

1. **C** To accurately model a time series that contains shifts, it may be necessary to strategically choose a longer or shorter sample period, or to use a first- or second-order autoregressive model. There is no accepted formula for estimating the optimal sample period (though a graphical inspection of the data may be helpful). (LOS 9.o)

2. **B** ARCH is present when the variance of the error depends on the variance of previous errors. A zero autocorrelation of the error term at all lags suggests that an autoregressive model is a good fit to the data. (LOS 9.m)

3. **B** If only one time series has a unit root, we should not use linear regression. If neither time series have unit root, or if both time series have unit root and the time series are cointegrated, linear regression is appropriate to use. (LOS 9.n)

The following is a review of the Quantitative Methods principles designed to address the learning outcome statements set forth by CFA Institute. Cross-Reference to CFA Institute Assigned Reading #10.

READING 10

Probabilistic Approaches: Scenario Analysis, Decision Trees, and Simulations

Study Session 3

EXAM FOCUS

This topic review discusses simulation as a risk-measurement tool. After studying this material, you should be able to understand the methodology used in running simulations and the limitations of simulations, recognize why and how certain constraints are introduced into simulations, and determine when simulation versus some other method (such as a decision tree or scenario analysis) is appropriate.

MODULE 10.1: PROBABILISTIC APPROACHES

Video covering this content is available online.

LOS 10.a: Describe steps in running a simulation.

LOS 10.b: Explain three ways to define the probability distributions for a simulation's variables.

LOS 10.c: Describe how to treat correlation across variables in a simulation.

CFA® Program Curriculum, Volume 1, page 520 and 522

SIMULATIONS

Imagine a capital budgeting exercise to estimate the net present value of a project. The project involves production of a new product with uncertain demand. To estimate the cash flows from the project, we need the estimated demand and selling price per unit for each of the years, as well as estimated cash expenses. All of these variables are uncertain and can only be estimated with error. Some variables are more uncertain than others; for example, cash expenses are relatively easy to estimate, but product demand is more uncertain.

Some variables (e.g., interest rates) are not limited to a few discrete outcomes; such variables can take on any number of values (within some plausible range). Simulations lend themselves to situations where the risk is continuous (e.g., uncertainty in interest rate). This flexibility helps simulations to accurately model reality and provide a full picture of the risk in an investment.

Steps in simulations

1. **Determine the probabilistic variables.** Probabilistic variables are the uncertain input variables that influence the value of an investment. While there is no limit to the number of uncertain input variables, in practice some variables are either predictable (and hence can be derived/estimated) or have an insignificant influence on the value of the investment (and hence can be assumed to be constant).
2. **Define probability distributions for these variables.** This important but sometimes-difficult step entails specifying the distribution from which to sample the uncertain variable(s). First, we must determine the appropriate distribution to characterize this uncertain variable, then we also need to specify the parameters for the distribution. For example, one uncertain variable influencing the value of a company is its estimated future revenues. To describe this variable, we might choose a uniform distribution and a specific range of possible values.

   There are three approaches to specifying a distribution:

   - *Historical data*: Examination of past data may point to a distribution that is suitable for the probabilistic variable. This method assumes that the future values of the variable will be similar to its past.
   - *Cross-sectional data*: When past data is unavailable (or unreliable), we may estimate the distribution of the variable based on the values of the variable for peers. For example, we can estimate the distribution of operating margin of a new natural-gas-fired power plant based on the known distribution of margins for other similar-sized natural gas plants.
   - *Pick a distribution and estimate the parameters*: An advantage of the above two methods is that we not only get a good idea of the appropriate distribution, but we can also estimate the relevant parameters (e.g., the mean and standard deviation of a normally-distributed variable). When neither historical nor cross-sectional data provide adequate insight, subjective specification of a distribution along with related parameters is the appropriate approach. For example, we might specify (based on insights into the industry) that the net margin for a discount retailer has a normal distribution with a mean of 3% and standard deviation of 1.2%.
3. **Check for correlations among variables.** In this step, we use historical data to determine whether any of the probabilistic input variables are systematically related. For example, net margins may not be completely random; margins may be systematically higher at higher revenues. When there is a strong correlation between variables, we can either 1) allow only one of the variables to vary (the other variable could then be algorithmically computed), or 2) build the rules of correlation into the simulation (this necessitates more sophisticated simulation packages). If we choose to pursue the first option (i.e., allow only one variable to fluctuate randomly), the random variable should be the one that has the highest impact on valuation.

4. **Run the simulation.** Running the simulation means randomly drawing variables from their underlying distributions and then using them as inputs to generate estimated values. This process may be repeated to yield thousands of estimates of value, giving a distribution of the investment's value. Because computing power is no longer a significant constraint, the cost of running higher number of simulations is not a limiting factor. The number of simulations needed for a good output is driven by:
   - *The number of uncertain variables.* The higher the number of probabilistic inputs, the greater the number of simulations needed.
   - *The types of distributions.* The greater the variability in types of distributions, the greater the number of simulations needed. Conversely, if all variables are specified by one distribution (e.g., normal), then the number of simulations needed would be lower.
   - *The range of outcomes.* The wider the range of outcomes of the uncertain variables, the higher the number of simulations needed.

LOS 10.d: Describe advantages of using simulations in decision making.

CFA® Program Curriculum, Volume 1, page 526

ADVANTAGES OF SIMULATIONS

There are two advantages of a carefully crafted simulation:

- **Better input quality.** Superior inputs are likely to result when an analyst goes through the process of selecting a proper distribution for critical inputs, rather than relying on single best estimates. The distribution selected can additionally be checked for conformity with historical or cross-sectional data.
- **Provides a distribution of expected value rather than a point estimate**. The distribution of an investment's expected value provides an indication of risk in the investment. Note that simulations do not provide *better* estimates of expected value. (Expected values from simulations should be close to the expected value obtained using point estimates of individual inputs.)

It should also be noted that simulations should not automatically be assumed to lead to better *decisions*. While simulations do provide a more complete picture of the risk in an investment, such risk measures may be misused in decision making. For example, the distribution of NPVs of a capital budgeting project gives an indication of the risk of the project. However, if the required rate of return already incorporates the underlying risk, then the risk proxy from the distribution of NPVs should not be used to evaluate competing capital budgeting projects. Competing mutually exclusive projects can be evaluated purely based on which one has a higher mean NPV; the risk is already factored in the discount rate. In other words, double counting of risk should be avoided.

LOS 10.e: Describe some common constraints introduced into simulations.

CFA® Program Curriculum, Volume 1, page 527

CONSTRAINTS

Constraints are specific limits imposed by users of simulations as a risk assessment tool. A constraint is a condition that, if violated, would pose dire consequences for the firm. For example, one constraint might correspond to the company not being able to meet its contractual debt obligations—the cost of which can be substantial. Firms employ expensive hedging tools to ensure that such constraints are not violated. Decisions about whether and how to hedge risk are made after evaluating the cost of different hedging tools versus their effectiveness in preventing violation of such constraints.

Types of constraints

There are three types of constraints:

1. **Book value constraints**

   Book value constraints are imposed on a firm's book value of equity. There are two types of restrictions on book value of equity that may necessitate risk hedging:

   – *Regulatory capital requirements*. Banks and insurance companies are required to maintain adequate levels of capital. Violations of minimum capital requirements are considered serious and could threaten the very existence of the firm.

   – *Negative equity*. In some countries, negative book value of equity may have serious consequences. For example, some European countries require firms to raise additional capital in the event that book value of equity becomes negative.

2. **Earnings and cash flow constraints**

   Earnings or cash flow constraints can be imposed internally to meet analyst expectations or to achieve bonus targets. Sometimes, failure to meet analyst expectations could result in job losses for the executive team. In such cases, executives may find it important to pursue expensive risk hedging. Risk hedging in this context is then not related to value of the firm, but rather to managerial employment contract or compensation levels.

   Earnings constraints can also be imposed externally, such as a loan covenant. Violating such a constraint could be very expensive for the firm.

3. **Market value constraints**

   Market value constraints seek to minimize the likelihood of financial distress or bankruptcy for the firm. In a simulation, we can explicitly model the entire distribution of key input variables to identify situations where financial distress would be likely. We can then explicitly incorporate the costs of financial distress in a valuation model for the firm.

LOS 10.f: Describe issues in using simulations in risk assessment.

CFA® Program Curriculum, Volume 1, page 528

There are several limitations of using simulations as a risk assessment tool:

1. *Input quality*. Regardless of the complexities employed in running simulations, if the underlying inputs are poorly specified, the output will be low quality (i.e., garbage in, garbage out). In fact, the detailed output provided in a simulation may give the decision maker a false sense of making an informed decision.
2. *Inappropriate statistical distributions*. Real world data often does not fit the stringent requirements of statistical distributions. If the underlying distribution of an input is improperly specified, the quality of that input will be poor.
3. *Non-stationary distributions*. Input variable distributions may change over time, so the distribution and parameters specified for a particular simulation may not be valid anymore. For example, based on past data, we conclude that earnings growth rate has a normal distribution with a mean of 3% and variance of 2.5%. However, the parameters may have changed to a mean of 2% and variance of 5%.
4. *Dynamic correlations*. Correlations between input variables may not be stable. To the extent that correlations between input variables change over time, it becomes far more difficult to model them. If we model the correlation between variables based on past data and such relationships amongst variables change, the output of simulation will be flawed.

Risk-Adjusted Value

An important point to remember is that cash flows from simulations are not risk-adjusted and should not be discounted at risk-free rate.

When the cash flows of an asset are discounted at a risk-adjusted discount rate (i.e., at a higher discount rate for more risky cash flows), we obtain the asset's risk-adjusted value. If we have already incorporated the risk of the asset in the discount rate, care should be taken to ensure that such risk is not double counted. For example, consider the following two stocks, which have been valued using risk-adjusted discount rates:

Stock	Price	Discount rate	Expected value using simulations	Standard deviation from simulations
X	$40	10%	$50	12%
Y	$40	12%	$50	15%

An investor should be indifferent between the two investments as they are equally underpriced relative to their risk-adjusted values of $50. Note that it would be inappropriate to choose stock X over stock Y on the basis of stock X's lower standard deviation since this would be penalizing stock Y twice; we have already accounted for stock Y's greater risk by discounting its cash flows using a higher discount rate.

LOS 10.g: Compare scenario analysis, decision trees, and simulations.

CFA® Program Curriculum, Volume 1, page 530

Simulation, decision trees, and scenario analysis are all tools used to measure risk in an investment. Scenario analysis and decision trees are used to analyze discrete risk, while simulations are used to analyze continuous risk.

Scenario analysis computes the value of an investment under a finite set of scenarios (e.g., best case, worst case, and most likely case). Because the full spectrum of outcomes is not considered in these scenarios, the combined probability of the outcomes that are considered is less than 1.

Decision trees are an appropriate approach when risk is both discrete and sequential. For example, imagine that an investment's value varies based on the uncertain outcome of a number of discrete sequential events, and at time t=0 there are two possible choices: make the investment or not. If we make the investment, the cash flow at time t=1 can be either high (C1H) or low (C1L). If the cash flow is high, we can then decide to expand capacity (expand or don't expand). If we expand capacity, the cash flow can be EC2H or EC2L, but if we don't expand capacity, the cash flow will either be DC2H or DC2L. Like simulations, decision trees consider all possible states of the outcome and hence the sum of the probabilities is 1.

If the various uncertain variables influencing the value of an investment are correlated, such correlations can be explicitly built into the simulations. We can also incorporate such correlations (albeit subjectively) into scenario analysis. It is usually not possible to model correlations in decision trees.

Figure 10.1 summarizes the risk characteristics and suitability of an appropriate risk assessment tool.

Figure 10.1: Risk Types

Appropriate method	Distribution of risk	Sequential?	Accommodates Correlated Variables?
Simulations	Continuous	Does not matter	Yes
Scenario analysis	Discrete	No	Yes
Decision trees	Discrete	Yes	No

Decision trees and simulations can be used as complements to risk-adjusted valuation or as substitutes for such valuation. Scenario analysis, because it does not include the full spectrum of outcomes, can only be used as a complement to risk-adjusted valuation. If used as a substitute, the cash flows in an investment are discounted at risk-free rate and then the expected value obtained is evaluated in conjunction with the variability obtained from the analysis. Alternatively, we can discount the cash flows using risk-adjusted discount rate and then ignore the variability of values. Regardless of the tool used, care should be taken to not double count risk.

MODULE QUIZ 10.1

To best evaluate your performance, enter your quiz answers online.

1. The first step in running a simulation is:
   A. determine the probabilistic variables.
   B. define probability distributions for key uncertain variables.
   C. check for correlations amongst variables.
2. In determining the appropriate probability distribution of an uncertain input variable in a simulation, the *least appropriate* approach is to:
   A. examine historical values of the variable.
   B. specify the same distribution as the distribution of a correlated variable.
   C. examine the values of that variable for the company's peers.
3. When two or more uncertain input variables in a simulation are correlated, the *least appropriate* approach to capturing the correlation is to:
   A. allow the variable with lower impact on valuation to vary, while the variable that has higher impact is determined algorithmically.
   B. specifically incorporate the underlying correlation in the simulation.
   C. allow the variable with higher impact on valuation to vary, while the variable that has lower impact is determined algorithmically.
4. Which of the following is *least likely* to represent an advantage of using simulations in decision making? Simulations:
   A. promote higher input quality.
   B. result in better decisions.
   C. provide a distribution of expected values.
5. Constraints imposed on simulations to maximize the likelihood of beating analyst expectations are *most likely* to take the form of:
   A. internally imposed earnings or cash flow constraints.
   B. market value constraints.
   C. externally imposed constraints.
6. Which of the following is *least likely* to represent a limitation of simulations?
   A. Specification of a distribution of inputs rather than single-best estimates.
   B. Dynamic correlations.
   C. Non-stationary distributions.
7. Which risk assessment tool is *most appropriate* when risk is discrete and sequential?
   A. Simulations.
   B. Decision trees.
   C. Scenario analysis.

KEY CONCEPTS

LOS 10.a

The steps in a simulation are 1) determine the probabilistic variables, 2) define probability distributions for these variables, 3) check for correlations among variables, and 4) run the simulation.

LOS 10.b

There are three bases to defining the probability distributions for a simulation's variables: 1) historical data, 2) cross-sectional data, or 3) rely on the analyst's subjective estimation of the appropriate distribution.

LOS 10.c

When there is a strong correlation between variables used in a simulation, we can either 1) allow only one variable to vary and algorithmically compute the other variable, or 2) build the correlation behavior into the simulation.

LOS 10.d

Advantages of using simulations in decision-making include 1) the analyst is encouraged to more carefully estimate the inputs, and 2) the expected-value output takes the form of a distribution of expected value and thus is more informative than a point estimate.

LOS 10.e

Common constraints introduced into simulations include 1) book value constraints, 2) earnings and cash flow constraints, and 3) market value constraints.

LOS 10.f

Limitations of simulations include 1) input data quality, 2) inappropriate specification of statistical distributions, 3) non-stationary distributions, and 4) non-stationary (dynamic) correlations.

Care should be taken to not double count risk: double-counting happens when we simultaneously adjust the discount rate for risk and also apply a penalty for the variability in value.

LOS 10.g

Appropriate method	Distribution of risk	Sequential?	Accommodates Correlated Variables?
Simulations	Continuous	Does not matter	Yes
Scenario analysis	Discrete	No	Yes
Decision trees	Discrete	Yes	No

ANSWER KEY FOR MODULE QUIZ

Module Quiz 10.1

1. **A** The first step in running a simulation is to determine the probabilistic variables that influence the output (for example, interest rates determine the value of a bond). (LOS 10.a)

2. **B** Examining past values of a variable (i.e., using historical data) and examining the values of numerous peers (i.e., using cross-sectional data) are two valid approaches to specifying distributions for probabilistic variables. Proxying with the distribution of a correlated variable is not a valid approach. (LOS 10.a)

3. **A** When two input variables are correlated, we can specify the distribution of the more important variable and derive the other variable algorithmically. Alternatively, we can build the rules of correlation within the simulation. (LOS 10.b)

4. **B** Better input quality and providing a distribution of expected values (rather than a single point estimate) are two advantages of simulations. However, simulations by themselves do not necessarily lead to better decisions. (LOS 10.d)

5. **A** Earnings and cash flow constraints are imposed internally to maximize the likelihood of beating analyst estimates. (LOS 10.e)

6. **A** Specification of a distribution for input variables (as opposed to a single point estimate) is generally seen as an *advantage* of using simulations rather than a disadvantage. (LOS 10.d)

7. **B** Simulations are appropriate when risk is continuous. Decision trees and scenario analysis are appropriate when risk is discrete. Decision trees are suitable when the risk is discrete as well as sequential. (LOS 10.g)

TOPIC ASSESSMENT: QUANTITATIVE METHODS

You have now finished the Quantitative Methods topic section. The following topic assessment will provide immediate feedback on how effective your study of this material has been. The test is best taken timed; allow 3 minutes per subquestion (18 minutes per item set). This topic assessment is more exam-like than a typical module quiz or QBank questions. A score less than 70% suggests that additional review of this topic is needed.

Use the following information to answer Questions 1 through 6.

Theresa Miller is attempting to forecast sales for Alton Industries based on a multiple regression model. The model Miller estimates is:

$$\text{sales} = b_0 + (b_1 \times \text{DOL}) + (b_2 \times \text{IP}) + (b_3 \times \text{GDP}) + \varepsilon_t$$

where:

sales	= change in sales adjusted for inflation
DOL	= change in the real value of the \$ (rates measured in €/\$)
IP	= change in industrial production adjusted for inflation (millions of \$)
GDP	= change in inflation-adjusted GDP (millions of \$)

All changes in variables are in percentage terms.

Miller runs the regression using monthly data for the past 180 months. The model estimates (with coefficient standard errors in parentheses) are:

$$\text{sales} = \underset{(5.4)}{10.2} + (\underset{(3.5)}{5.6} \times \text{DOL}) + (\underset{(4.2)}{6.3} \times \text{IP}) + (\underset{(5.3)}{9.2} \times \text{GDP})$$

The sum of squared errors is 145.6 and the total sum of squares is 357.2.

Miller is concerned that one or more of the assumptions underlying multiple regression has been violated in her analysis. In a conversation with Watson Crick, CFA, a colleague who is considered by many in the firm to be a quant specialist, Miller says, "Two of the key assumptions of multiple regression are:

Assumption 1: The independent variables are not random, and there is no correlation between any two of the independent variables.

Assumption 2: The variance of the residuals is constant and not related to the level of the independent variables."

Miller tests and fails to reject each of the following two null hypotheses at the 99% confidence interval:

Hypothesis 1: A 2% increase in DOL will result in an increase in sales of more than 12%.

Hypothesis 2: A 1% increase in industrial production will result in a 1% decrease in sales.

Figure 1: Partial Table of Student's *t*-Distribution (One-Tailed Probabilities)

df	p = 0.10	p = 0.05	p = 0.025	p = 0.01	p = 0.005
170	1.287	1.654	1.974	2.348	2.605
176	1.286	1.654	1.974	2.348	2.604
180	1.286	1.653	1.973	2.347	2.603

Figure 2: Partial *F*-Table Critical Values for Right-Hand Tail Area Equal to 0.05

	$df_1 = 1$	$df_1 = 3$	$df_1 = 5$
$df_2 = 170$	3.90	2.66	2.27
$df_2 = 176$	3.89	2.66	2.27
$df_2 = 180$	3.89	2.65	2.26

Figure 3: Partial *F*-Table Critical Values for Right-Hand Tail Area Equal to 0.025

	$df_1 = 1$	$df_1 = 3$	$df_1 = 5$
$df_2 = 170$	5.11	3.19	2.64
$df_2 = 176$	5.11	3.19	2.64
$df_2 = 180$	5.11	3.19	2.64

1. Are the two multiple regression assumptions proposed by Crick stated *correctly*?

Assumption 1	Assumption 2
A. Yes	No
B. No	Yes
C. No	No

2. Did Miller *correctly* interpret the results of the tests in making her reject or fail-to-reject decisions for Hypothesis 1 and Hypothesis 2?

Hypothesis 1	Hypothesis 2
A. Yes	Yes
B. Yes	No
C. No	Yes

3. The appropriate decision with regard to the *F*-statistic for testing the null hypothesis that all of the independent variables are simultaneously equal to zero at the 5% significance level is to:
   A. reject the null hypothesis because the *F*-statistic is larger than the critical *F*-value of 3.19.
   B. fail to reject the null hypothesis because the *F*-statistic is smaller than the critical *F*-value of 3.19.
   C. reject the null hypothesis because the *F*-statistic is larger than the critical *F*-value of 2.66.

4. The unadjusted R^2 and the standard error of the estimate (SEE) are *closest* to:

Unadjusted R^2	SEE
A. 59.2%	1.425
B. 59.2%	0.910
C. 40.8%	0.910

5. The multiple regression, as specified, *most likely* suffers from:
   A. heteroskedasticity.
   B. multicollinearity.
   C. positive serial correlation of the error terms.

6. What is the width of the 99% confidence interval for GDP, and is zero in that 99% confidence interval?

Width of 99% CI	Zero in interval
A. 13.8	Yes
B. 13.8	No
C. 27.6	Yes

Use the following data to answer Questions 7 through 12.

Trevor Smith, a financial analyst at the major retail chain Houseco, is working on the budget for the coming year. As an intermediate step in developing the budget, Smith would like to model the company's payroll expenses, a major variable cost for the firm.

Smith models a monthly time series of changes in payroll expenses (in millions of $) with an AR(1) model using 101 observations. The results of the regression and the first 12 lagged residual autocorrelations are shown in the next two tables.

Figure 4: Regression Results for Payroll Changes

Model: $y_t = b_0 + b_1 y_{t-1} + \varepsilon_t$

	Coefficients	Standard Error	*t*-Statistic
Intercept	1.2304	0.00923135	133.28495
Lag 1	0.1717	0.00476779	36.01249

Figure 5: Lagged Residual Autocorrelation Analysis

Lag	Autocorrelation	*t*-Statistic	Lag	Autocorrelation	*t*-Statistic
1	–0.105	?	7	0.017	0.17170
2	–0.140	–1.4139	8	–0.036	–0.36360
3	–0.044	–0.4444	9	0.163	1.64620
4	–0.032	–0.3232	10	–0.066	–0.66660
5	–0.170	–1.7169	11	0.115	1.16140
6	0.109	1.1008	12	0.021	0.21209

7. Over time, the value of this time series will show a tendency to move toward a value of:
   A. $1.050 million.
   B. $1.342 million.
   C. $1.485 million.

8. To determine whether the model is correctly specified, Smith examines the correlations of the error terms. The *t*-statistic for testing the hypothesis that the first order autocorrelation is zero is *closest* to:
   A. –1.0552.
   B. –10.710.
   C. –36.012.

9. If the change in payroll expense in June 2018 was $1 million, the forecast for the change in payroll expense in August 2018 is *closest* to:
   A. $1.402 million.
   B. $1.471 million.
   C. $1.511 million.

10. Assuming a 5% level of significance, can we conclude that the model is improperly specified?
    A. No, because the lag coefficient is significant.
    B. Yes, because most of the autocorrelations are negative.
    C. No, because none of the autocorrelations are significant.

11. To ensure that he can make valid budgeting decisions based on his model, Smith would like to check that Autoregressive Conditional Heteroskedasticity (ARCH) is not present. Which of the following would indicate the presence of ARCH in Smith's time-series model?
    A. The variance of the current error depends on the variance of previous errors.
    B. The autocorrelations of the error terms are zero at all lags.
    C. The variance of the time-series data is not constant.

12. Smith also has access to an additional time series that describes the cost of goods sold over the same period. Smith is interested in modeling the relationship between the two time series using linear regression. Linear regression would be *least appropriate* for modeling the relationship between the two time series if:
    A. both series are covariance stationary.
    B. one of the time series is covariance stationary and the other is not.
    C. neither of the two series are covariance stationary, and the two time series are cointegrated.

TOPIC ASSESSMENT ANSWERS: QUANTITATIVE METHODS

1. **B** Assumption 1 is stated incorrectly. Some correlation between independent variables is unavoidable; high correlation results in multicollinearity. An exact linear relationship between linear combinations of two or more independent variables should not exist.

   Assumption 2 is stated correctly. The assumption is that neither conditional nor unconditional heteroskedasticity is present in the residuals; in other words, the variance of the residuals is constant. Conditional heteroskedasticity occurs when the residual variance is related to the level of one or more of the independent variables. (Study Session 3, Module 8.8, LOS 8.1)

2. **A** The critical values at the 1% level of significance (99% confidence) are 2.348 for a one-tailed test and 2.604 for a two-tailed test (df = 176).

   Hypothesis 1: This hypothesis is asking whether a 2% increase in DOL will increase sales by more than 12%. This will only happen if the value of the coefficient is greater than 6, since 2 × 6 = 12. Since the regression estimate for this coefficient is 5.6, the *t*-statistic for this test is (5.6 – 6) / 3.5 = –0.114. This is a one-tailed test, so the critical value is 2.348. Miller is correct in failing to reject the null.

   Hypothesis 2: This hypothesis is asking whether the value of the coefficient is equal to –1.0, since that is the value that would correspond with a 1% increase in industrial production, resulting in a 1% decrease in sales. Since the regression estimate for this coefficient is 6.3, the *t*-statistic for this test is [6.3 – (–1)] / 4.2 = 1.74. This is a two-tailed test, so the critical value is 2.604. Miller is correct in failing to reject the null. (Study Session 3, Module 8.2, LOS 8.d)

3. **C** RSS = SST – SSE = 357.2 – 145.6 = 211.6, *F*-statistic = MSR / MSE = (RSS / k) / (SSE / n – k – 1) = (211.6 / 3) / (145.6 / 176) = 85.3. The critical value for a 5% *F*-test with 3 and 176 degrees of freedom is 2.66. Because the *F*-statistic is greater than the critical *F*-value, the null hypothesis that all of the independent variables are simultaneously equal to zero should be rejected. (Study Session 3, Module 8.3, LOS 8.g)

4. **B** $\text{SEE} = \sqrt{\dfrac{145.6}{180-3-1}} = 0.910$

   $$\text{unadjusted } R^2 = \frac{357.2 - 145.6}{357.2} = 0.592$$

   (Study Session 3, Module 8.4, LOS 8.h)

5. **B** The regression is highly significant (based on the *F*-statistic of 85.3 calculated earlier), but the individual coefficients are not. This is a result of a regression with significant multicollinearity problems. The *t*-statistics for the significance of the regression coefficients are, respectively, 1.89, 1.6, 1.5, 1.74. None of these are high enough to reject the hypothesis that the coefficient is zero at the 5% level of significance (two-tailed critical value of 1.974 from *t*-table). There is no evidence in the vignette of heteroskedasticity or serial correlation (also known as autocorrelation). (Study Session 3, Module 8.8, LOS 8.l)

6. **C** The confidence interval is 9.2 +/– (5.3 × 2.604), where 2.604 is the two-tailed 1% *t*-statistic with 176 degrees of freedom (which is the same as a one-tailed 0.5% *t*-statistic with 176 degrees of freedom). The interval is –4.6 to 23.0, which has a width of 27.6, and zero is in that interval. (Study Session 3, Module 8.2, LOS 8.e)

7. **C** The mean-reverting level is $b_0 / (1 - b_1) = 1.2304 / (1 - 0.1717) = \$1.48545$ million. (Study Session 3, Module 9.2, LOS 9.f)

8. **A** $$t = \frac{-0.105}{\frac{1}{\sqrt{101}}} = -1.0552$$

(Study Session 3, Module 9.2, LOS 9.e)

9. **B** $y_{\text{July 2018}} = 1.2304 + 0.1717(\$1) = \$1.402$ million

$y_{\text{August 2018}} = 1.2304 + 0.1717(\$1.402) = \$1.471$ million

(Study Session 3, Module 9.1, LOS 9.a)

10. **C** The critical *t*-value at a 5% level of significance with 99 degrees of freedom is approximately 1.98. At this level, none of the residual autocorrelations are significant. Were any of these residual autocorrelations significant, we could conclude that the model is improperly specified. The presence of an ARCH process, however, should also be tested. (Study Session 3, Module 9.4, LOS 9.l)

11. **A** ARCH is present if the variance of the *residuals* from the AR model are correlated across time. (Study Session 3, Module 9.5, LOS 9.m)

12. **B** If only one time series is covariance stationary, we should not use linear regression, as regression results would be invalid. If both time series are covariance stationary, or if both time series are covariance nonstationary and the time series are cointegrated, linear regression is appropriate to use. (Study Session 3, Module 9.5, LOS 9.n)

The following is a review of the Economics principles designed to address the learning outcome statements set forth by CFA Institute. Cross-Reference to CFA Institute Assigned Reading #11.

READING 11

Currency Exchange Rates: Understanding Equilibrium Value

Study Session 4

EXAM FOCUS

There's no fluff here; you need it all. Take it slow and get a good understanding of quotes, currency cross rates, triangular arbitrage, all parity conditions, and their interrelationships. Forecasting exchange rates has important applications for valuation (which is the focus of Level II). Accordingly, theories of exchange rate determination as well as factors influencing exchange rates are all important. Be prepared to identify warning signs of currency crises.

MODULE 11.1: FOREX QUOTES, SPREADS, AND TRIANGULAR ARBITRAGE

Video covering this content is available online.

LOS 11.a: Calculate and interpret the bid–offer spread on a spot or forward currency quotation and describe the factors that affect the bid–offer spread.

CFA® Program Curriculum, Volume 1, page 540

PROFESSOR'S NOTE

The "bid–offer" spread is also known as the "bid–ask" spread: the terms "ask" and "offer" mean the same thing. Accordingly, we will be using them interchangeably.

EXCHANGE RATES

An **exchange rate** is simply the price of one currency in terms of another. For example, a quote of 1.4126 USD/EUR means that each euro costs $1.4126. In this example, the euro is called the *base* currency and the USD the *price* currency. Hence, a quote is the price of one unit of the base currency in terms of the price currency.

A **spot exchange rate** is the currency exchange rate for immediate delivery, which for most currencies means the exchange of currencies takes place two days after the trade. A **forward exchange rate** is a currency exchange rate for an exchange to be done in the future. Forward rates are quoted for various future dates (e.g., 30 days, 60 days, 90 days, or one year). A forward contract is an agreement to exchange a specific amount of one currency for a specific amount of another currency on a future date specified in the forward agreement.

Dealer quotes often include both bid and offer (ask) rates. For example, the euro could be quoted as $1.4124 – 1.4128. The bid price ($1.4124) is the price at which the dealer will buy euros, and the offer price ($1.4128) is the price at which the dealer will sell euros.

FOREIGN EXCHANGE SPREAD

The difference between the offer and bid price is called the *spread*. Spreads are often stated as 'pips'. When the spot quote has four decimal places, one pip is 1/10,000. In the above example, the spread is $0.0004 (4 pips) reflecting the dealer's profit. Dealers manage their foreign currency inventories by transacting in the interbank market (think of this as a wholesale market for currency). Spreads are narrow in the interbank market.

The spread quoted by a dealer depends on:

- **The spread in a interbank market for the same currency pair.** Dealer spreads vary directly with spreads quoted in the interbank market.
- **The size of the transaction.** Larger, liquidity-demanding transactions generally get quoted a larger spread.
- **The relationship between the dealer and client.** Sometimes dealers will give favorable rates to preferred clients based on other ongoing business relationships.

The interbank spread on a currency pair depends on:

- **Currencies involved.** Similar to stocks, high-volume currency pairs (e.g., USD/EUR, USD/JPY, and USD/GBP) command lower spreads than do lower-volume currency pairs (e.g., AUD/CAD).
- **Time of day.** The time overlap during the trading day when both the New York and London currency markets are open is considered the most liquid time window; spreads are narrower during this period than at other times of the day.
- **Market volatility.** Spreads are directly related to the exchange rate volatility of the currencies involved. Higher volatility leads to higher spreads to compensate market makers for the increased risk of holding those currencies. Spreads change over time in response to volatility changes.

In addition to these factors, spreads in forward exchange rate quotes increase with maturity. The reasons for this are: longer maturity contracts tend to be less liquid, counterparty credit risk in forward contracts increases with maturity, and interest rate risk in forward contracts increases with maturity.

WARM-UP: WORKING WITH FOREIGN EXCHANGE QUOTES

Earlier, we stated that a dealer will sell a currency at the ask price and purchase it at the bid price. We need to be a bit more specific. For example, imagine that you are given a USD/AUD bid and ask quote of 1.0508-1.0510. Investors can buy AUD (i.e., the base currency) from the dealer at the ask price of USD 1.0510. Similarly, investors can sell AUD to the dealer at the bid price of USD 1.0508. Remember, investors always take a loss due to the spread. So the rule is *buy the base currency at ask, and sell the base currency at bid.*

For transactions in the price currency, we do the opposite. If we need to buy USD (i.e., the price currency) using AUD (i.e., selling the base currency), we now use the dealer *bid* quote. Similarly, to sell the price currency, we use the dealer *ask* quote. So the rule is *buy the price currency at bid, and sell the price currency at ask.*

Alternatively, it is useful to follow the *up-the-bid-and-multiply, down-the-ask-and-divide rule*. Again given a USD/AUD quote, if you want to convert USD into AUD (you are going down the quote—from USD on top to AUD on bottom), use the *ask* price for that quote. Conversely, if you want to convert AUD into USD, you are going up the quote (from bottom to top) and, hence, use the *bid* price.

EXAMPLE: Converting currencies using spot rates

A dealer is quoting the AUD/GBP spot rate as 1.5060 – 1.5067. How would we:

1. Compute the proceeds of converting 1 million GBP.
2. Compute the proceeds of converting 1 million AUD.

Answer:

1. To convert 1 million GBP into AUD, we go "up the quote" (i.e., from GBP in the denominator to AUD in the numerator). Hence, we would use the *bid* price of 1.5060 and multiply.

   1 million GBP × 1.5060 = 1,506,000 AUD

2. To convert 1 million AUD into GBP, we go "down the quote" (i.e., from AUD in the numerator to GBP in the denominator). Hence, we would use the *ask* price of 1.5067 and divide.

   1 million AUD / 1.5067 = 663,702.13 GBP

LOS 11.b: Identify a triangular arbitrage opportunity and calculate its profit, given the bid–offer quotations for three currencies.

CFA® Program Curriculum, Volume 1, page 544

CROSS RATE

The **cross rate** is the exchange rate between two currencies implied by their exchange rates with a common third currency. It is necessary to use cross rates when there is no active foreign exchange (FX) market in the currency pair being considered. The cross rate must be computed from the exchange rates between each of these two currencies and a major third currency, usually the USD or EUR.

Suppose we have the following quotes:

USD/AUD = 0.60 and MXN/USD = 10.70. What is the cross rate between Australian dollars and pesos (MXN/AUD)?

$$\frac{\text{MXN}}{\text{AUD}} = \frac{\cancel{\text{USD}}}{\text{AUD}} \times \frac{\text{MXN}}{\cancel{\text{USD}}} = 0.60 \times 10.70 = 6.42$$

So our MXN/AUD cross rate is 6.42 pesos per Australian dollar. The key to calculating cross rates is to make sure the common currency cancels out.

CROSS RATES WITH BID-ASK SPREADS

Bid-ask spreads complicate the calculation of cross rates considerably. Suppose we are given three currencies A, B, and C; we can have three pairs of currencies (i.e., A/B, A/C, and B/C).

Rules:

$$\left(\frac{A}{C}\right)_{\text{bid}} = \left(\frac{A}{B}\right)_{\text{bid}} \times \left(\frac{B}{C}\right)_{\text{bid}}$$

$$\left(\frac{A}{C}\right)_{\text{offer}} = \left(\frac{A}{B}\right)_{\text{offer}} \times \left(\frac{B}{C}\right)_{\text{offer}}$$

To compute the cross rate for A/C, given A/B and B/C, we can follow the above rules to obtain the bid and offer prices. If we are instead given A/B and C/B rates, we will have to make adjustments to obtain the B/C bid and offer rates from the C/B bid and offer rates, because A/B × C/B ≠ A/C. The process is as follows:

$$\left(\frac{B}{C}\right)_{\text{bid}} = \frac{1}{\left(\frac{C}{B}\right)_{\text{offer}}}$$

$$\left(\frac{B}{C}\right)_{\text{offer}} = \frac{1}{\left(\frac{C}{B}\right)_{\text{bid}}}$$

TRIANGULAR ARBITRAGE

Real-world currency dealers will maintain bid/ask quotes that ensure a profit to the dealer, regardless of which currencies customers choose to trade. If this was not the case, customers could earn profits through the process of triangular arbitrage. In **triangular arbitrage**, we begin with three pairs of currencies, each with bid and ask quotes, and construct a triangle where each node in the triangle represents one currency. To check for arbitrage opportunities, we go around the triangle clockwise (and later, counterclockwise) until we reach our starting point. As before, we follow the up-the-bid-and-multiply, down-the-ask-and-divide rule.

The following example will illustrate triangular arbitrage.

EXAMPLE: Triangular arbitrage

The following quotes are available from the interbank market:

Quotes:

USD/AUD 0.6000 – 0.6015
USD/MXN 0.0933 – 0.0935

1. Compute the implied MXN/AUD cross rate.
2. If your dealer quotes MXN/AUD = 6.3000 – 6.3025, is an arbitrage profit possible? If so, compute the arbitrage profit in USD if you start with USD 1 million.

Answer:

1. To compute implied cross rates, we need:

$$\left(\frac{\text{MSN}}{\text{AUD}}\right)_{\text{bid}} = \left(\frac{\text{USD}}{\text{AUD}}\right)_{\text{bid}} \times \left(\frac{\text{MSN}}{\text{USD}}\right)_{\text{bid}}$$

Since we are given USD/MXN quotes instead of MXN/USD quotes, we first invert these quotes:

$$\left(\frac{\text{MXN}}{\text{USD}}\right)_{\text{bid}} = \frac{1}{\left(\frac{\text{USD}}{\text{MXN}}\right)_{\text{offer}}} = \left(\frac{1}{0.0935}\right) = 10.70 \text{ MXN/USD}$$

and

$$\left(\frac{\text{MXN}}{\text{USD}}\right)_{\text{offer}} = \frac{1}{\left(\frac{\text{USD}}{\text{MXN}}\right)_{\text{bid}}} = \left(\frac{1}{0.0933}\right) = 10.72 \text{ MXN/USD}$$

Now, the implied cross rates:

$$\left(\frac{\text{MXN}}{\text{AUD}}\right)_{\text{bid}} = \left(\frac{\text{USD}}{\text{AUD}}\right)_{\text{bid}} \times \left(\frac{\text{MXN}}{\text{USD}}\right)_{\text{bid}} = 0.60 \times 10.70 = 6.42$$

$$\left(\frac{\text{MXN}}{\text{AUD}}\right)_{\text{offer}} = \left(\frac{\text{USD}}{\text{AUD}}\right)_{\text{offer}} \times \left(\frac{\text{MXN}}{\text{USD}}\right)_{\text{offer}} = 0.6015 \times 10.72 = 6.4481$$

2. Since the dealer quote of MXN/AUD = 6.3000 – 6.3025 falls outside of these cross rates, arbitrage profit may be possible (we have to check this). Remember to use the dealer quotes in the triangle and not the cross rates we computed.

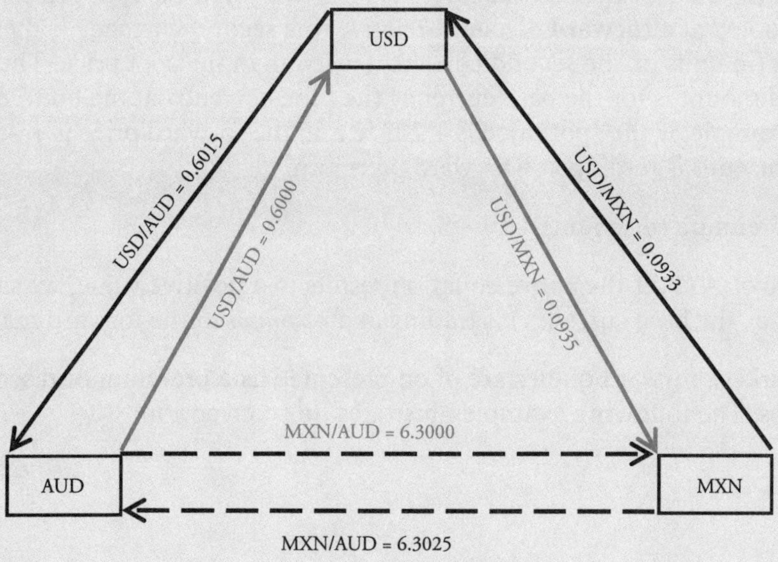

Study Session 4

To label the arrows in this triangle, we follow the "up the bid, down the offer" rule. To convert from USD to MXN, ("down" with respect to the USD/MXN quote), we use the offer rate of 0.0935.

Going clockwise and starting with USD 1 million:

1. Convert USD 1 million into MXN @ 0.0935 USD/MXN. Note that the quote is USD/MXN and hence we are going down, and thus need to use the ask. Also remember: down, divide. We get 1 million/0.0935 = 10,695,187 MXN.
2. Next, we convert 10,695,187 MXN into AUD @ 6.3025 MXN/AUD to get 1,696,975 AUD.
3. Finally, we convert AUD 1,696,975 into USD @ 0.6000 USD/AUD. Here the quote is USD/AUD and we are converting from AUD to USD, so we are going "up the quote" and need to multiply by the bid. (Remember: up, multiply.) We get 1,696,975 × 0.60 = 1,018,185 USD – a profit of 18,185 USD.

We can also check for arbitrage in the counter-clockwise direction (even though we can never earn an arbitrage profit in both directions):

1. Convert USD 1 million into AUD using 0.6015. Again, the quote is USD/AUD and we are going down, so use the ask price and divide. We get 1 million/0.6015 = 1,662,510 AUD.
2. Next, we convert 1,662,510 AUD into MXN using 6.3000 to get 10,473,814 MXN.
3. Finally, we convert MXN 10,473,814 into USD at 0.0933 to get 977,207 USD – a loss of 22,793 USD.

LOS 11.c: Distinguish between spot and forward rates and calculate the forward premium/discount for a given currency.

CFA® Program Curriculum, Volume 1, page 548

A currency is quoted at a **forward premium** relative to a second currency if the forward price (in units of the second currency) is *greater* than the spot price. A currency is quoted at a **forward discount** relative to a second currency if the forward price (in units of the second currency) is *less* than the spot price. The premium or discount is for the base currency (i.e., the currency at the bottom of the quote). For example, if the spot price is 1.20$/€ and the forward price is 1.25$/€, we say that the euro is trading at a forward premium.

$$\text{forward premium (discount)} = F - S_0$$

Given a quote of A/B, if the above equation results in a positive value, we say that currency B (i.e., the base currency) is trading at a *premium* in the forward market.

In the FX markets, forward quotes are often presented as a premium or discount over spot rates. The following example illustrates this convention.

EXAMPLE: Spot and forward quotes

Given the following quotes for AUD/CAD, compute the bid and offer rates for a 30-day forward contract.

Maturity	Rate
Spot	1.0511/1.0519
30-day	+3.9/+4.1
90-day	+15.6/+16.8
180-day	+46.9/+52.3

Answer:

Since the forward quotes presented are all positive, the CAD (i.e., the base currency) is trading at a forward *premium*.

30-day bid = 1.0511 + 3.9/10,000 = 1.05149

30-day offer = 1.0519 + 4.1/10,000 = 1.05231

The 30-day all-in forward quote for AUD/CAD is 1.05149/1.05231.

PROFESSOR'S NOTE

For an investor wishing to convert AUD into CAD in the forward market, the relevant quote would be the ask rate (remember the "down-the-ask" rule) of 1.05231. This is also known as the all-in (i.e., after adding (subtracting) the forward premium (discount) rate for the investor in question.

MODULE QUIZ 11.1

To best evaluate your performance, enter your quiz answers online.

1. All of the factors below would contribute to an increase in USD/EUR dealer spread except:
   A. increase in the volatility of EUR/USD spot rate.
   B. increase in the EUR/USD spread in the interbank market.
   C. smaller order size.
2. The bid-ask quotes for the USD, GBP, and EUR are:

   EUR/USD: 0.7000 – 0.7010

   USD/GBP: 1.7000 – 1.7010

   EUR/GBP: 1.2000 – 1.2010

   The potential arbitrage profit from a triangular arbitrage based on an initial position of 1 million USD is *closest* to:
   A. USD0.
   B. USD7,212.
   C. USD6,372.

Video covering this content is available online.

MODULE 11.2: MARK-TO-MARKET VALUE, AND PARITY CONDITIONS

LOS 11.d: Calculate the mark-to-market value of a forward contract.

CFA® Program Curriculum, Volume 1, page 554

If the forward contract price is consistent with covered interest rate parity (discussed later), the value of the contract at initiation is zero to both parties. After initiation, the value of the forward contract will change as forward quotes for the currency pair change in the market.

Mark-to-Market Value

The value of a forward currency contract prior to expiration is also known as the *mark-to-market value*. To compute the value of a forward contract prior to expiration, we take the difference between the forward price we locked-in and the current forward price, multiply that by the size of the contract, and then discount for the time period remaining until the contract settlement date.

$$V_t = \frac{(FP_t - FP)(\text{contract size})}{\left[1 + R\left(\frac{\text{days}}{360}\right)\right]}$$

where:

V_t = value of the forward contract at time *t* (to the party buying the base currency), ($t < T$) denominated in price currency
FP_t = forward price (to sell base currency) at time *t* in the market for a new contract maturing at time *T*
FP = forward price specified in the contract at inception (to buy the base currency)
days = number of days remaining to maturity of the forward contract ($T - t$)
R = interest rate of price currency

EXAMPLE: Valuing a forward contract prior to maturity

Yew Mun Yip has entered into a 90-day forward contract long CAD 1 million against AUD at a forward rate of 1.05358 AUD/CAD. Thirty days after initiation,the following AUD/CAD quotes are available:

Maturity	FX Rate
Spot	1.0612/1.0614
30-day	+4.9/+5.2
60-day	+8.6/+9.0
90-day	+14.6/+16.8
180-day	+42.3/+48.3

The following information is available (at t=30) for AUD interest rates:

30-day rate: 1.12%

60-day rate: 1.16%

90-day rate: 1.20%

What is the mark-to-market value in AUD of Yip's forward contract?

Answer:

Yip's contract calls for long CAD (i.e., converting AUD to CAD). To value the contract, we would look to unwind the position. To unwind the position, Yip can take an offsetting position in a new forward contract with the same maturity. Hence, Yip would be selling CAD in exchange for AUD and, hence, going up the bid (i.e., use the bid price). Note that after 30 days, 60 more days remain in the original contract.

The forward bid price for a new contract expiring in T – t = 60 days is 1.0612 + 8.6/10,000 = 1.06206.

The interest rate to use for discounting the value is also the 60-day AUD interest rate of 1.16%:

$$V_t = \frac{(FP_t - FP)(\text{contract size})}{\left[1 + R\left(\frac{\text{days}}{360}\right)\right]} = \frac{(1.06206 - 1.05358)(1{,}000{,}000)}{\left[1 + 0.0116\left(\frac{60}{360}\right)\right]} = 8{,}463.64$$

Thirty days into the forward contract, Yip's position has gained (positive value) AUD 8,463.64. This is because Yip's position is long CAD, which has appreciated relative to AUD since inception of the contract. Yip can close out the contract on that day and receive AUD 8,463.64.

Note: Be sure to use the AUD (price currency) interest rate.

LOS 11.e: Explain international parity conditions (covered and uncovered interest rate parity, forward rate parity, purchasing power parity, and the international Fisher effect).

CFA® Program Curriculum, Volume 1, page 557

Covered Interest Rate Parity

The word 'covered' in the context of covered interest parity means bound by arbitrage. **Covered interest rate parity** holds when any forward premium or discount exactly offsets differences in interest rates, so that an investor would earn the same return investing in either currency. If covered interest rate parity holds and euro interest rates are higher than dollar interest rates, depreciation of the euro relative to the dollar will just offset the higher euro interest rate.

Study Session 4

Formally, covered interest rate parity requires that (given A/B quote structure):

$$F = \frac{\left[1 + R_A\left(\frac{\text{days}}{360}\right)\right]}{\left[1 + R_B\left(\frac{\text{days}}{360}\right)\right]} S_0$$

where:
F = forward rate (quoted as A/B)
S_0 = spot rate (quoted as A/B)
days = number of days in the underlying forward contract
R_A = interest rate for Currency A
R_B = interest rate for Currency B

PROFESSOR'S NOTE

For all parity relations, follow the numerator-denominator rule. If you are given a USD/EUR quote, the USD interest rate should be in the numerator and the EUR interest rate in the denominator of the parity equation.

Recall that:

$$\text{forward premium (discount)} = F - S_0 = \left[\frac{1 + R_A\left(\frac{\text{days}}{360}\right)}{1 + R_B\left(\frac{\text{days}}{360}\right)} - 1\right] S_0$$

or

$$\text{forward premium (discount)} = F - S_0 = S_0\left[\frac{\left(\frac{\text{days}}{360}\right)}{1 + R_B\left(\frac{\text{days}}{360}\right)}\right](R_A - R_B)$$

EXAMPLE: Covered interest arbitrage

The U.S. dollar interest rate is 8%, and the euro interest rate is 6%. The spot exchange rate is \$1.30 per euro (USD/EUR), and the 1-year forward rate is \$1.35 per euro. Determine whether a profitable arbitrage opportunity exists, and illustrate such an arbitrage if it does.

Answer:

First, we note that the forward value of the euro is too high. Interest rate parity would require a forward rate of:

\$1.30(1.08 / 1.06) = \$1.3245

Because the market forward rate of \$1.35 is higher than that implied by interest rate parity, we should sell euros in the forward market and do the opposite (i.e., buy euros) in the spot market. The steps in the covered interest arbitrage are:

Initially:

Step 1: Borrow \$1,000 at 8%.

Step 2: Purchase 1,000 / 1.30 = 769.23 euros in the spot market.

Step 3: Invest the euros at 6%.

Step 4: Enter into a forward contract to sell the expected proceeds at the end of one year (i.e., 769.23 × 1.06 = 815.38 euros), at \$1.35 each.

After one year:

Step 1: Sell the 815.38 euros under the terms of the forward contract at $1.35 to get $1,100.76.

Step 2: Repay the $1,000 8% loan, which requires $1,080.

Step 3: Keep the difference of $20.76 as an arbitrage profit.

Uncovered Interest Rate Parity

With covered interest rate parity, arbitrage will force the forward contract exchange rate to a level consistent with the difference between the two country's nominal interest rates. If forward currency contracts are not available, or if capital flows are restricted so as to prevent arbitrage, the relationship need not hold. **Uncovered interest rate parity** refers to such a situation; uncovered in this context means not bound by arbitrage.

Consider Country A where the interest rate is 4%, and Country B where the interest rate is 9%. Under uncovered interest rate parity, currency B is expected to depreciate by 5% annually relative to currency A, so that an investor should be indifferent between investing in Country A or B.

Given a quote structure of A/B, the base currency (i.e., currency B) is expected to appreciate by approximately $R_A - R_B$. (When $R_A - R_B$ is negative, currency B is expected to depreciate). Mathematically:

$$E(\%\Delta S)_{(A/B)} = R_A - R_B$$

The following example illustrates the use of uncovered interest rate parity to *forecast* future spot exchange rates using market interest rates.

EXAMPLE: Forecasting spot rates with uncovered interest rate parity

Suppose the spot exchange rate quote is ZAR/EUR = 8.385. The 1-year nominal rate in the eurozone is 10% and the 1-year nominal rate in South Africa is 8%. Calculate the expected percentage change in the exchange rate over the coming year using uncovered interest rate parity.

Answer:

The rand interest rate is less than the euro interest rate, so uncovered interest rate parity predicts that the value of the rand will rise (it will take fewer rand to buy one euro) because of higher interest rates in the eurozone. The euro (the base currency) is expected to "appreciate" by approximately $R_{ZAR} - R_{EUR} = 8\% - 10\% = -2\%$. (Note the *negative* 2% value.) Thus the euro is expected to *depreciate* by 2% relative to the rand, leading to a change in exchange rate from 8.385 ZAR/EUR to 8.217 ZAR/EUR over the coming year.

Comparing covered and uncovered interest parity, we see that covered interest rate parity derives the *no-arbitrage forward rate*, while uncovered interest rate parity derives the *expected future spot rate* (which is not market traded). Covered interest parity is assumed by arbitrage, but this is not the case for uncovered interest rate parity.

Under uncovered interest rate parity, if the foreign interest rate is higher by 2%, the foreign currency is expected to depreciate by 2%, so the investor should be indifferent between investing in the foreign currency or in their own domestic currency. An investor that chooses to invest in the foreign currency without any additional return (the interest rate differential is offset by currency value changes) is not demanding a risk premium for the foreign currency risk. Hence, uncovered interest rate parity assumes that the investor is *risk-neutral*.

If the forward rate is equal to the expected future spot rate, we say that the forward rate is an **unbiased predictor** of the future spot rate. In such an instance, $F = E(S_1)$; this is called **forward rate parity**. In this special case, if covered interest parity holds (and it will; by arbitrage) uncovered interest parity would also hold (and vice versa). Stated differently, if uncovered interest rate parity holds, forward rate parity also holds (i.e., the forward rate is an unbiased predictor of the future spot rate).

There is no reason that uncovered interest rate parity must hold in the short run, and indeed it typically does not. There is evidence that it does generally hold in the long run, so longer-term expected future spot rates based on uncovered interest rate parity are often used as forecasts of future exchange rates.

(Domestic) Fisher Relation

Professor Irving Fisher originated the idea that the nominal rate of return is (approximately) the sum of the real rate and the expected rate of inflation.

We can write this relation (known as the Fisher relation) as:

$$R_{\text{nominal}} = R_{\text{real}} + E(\text{inflation})$$

International Fisher Relation

Under **real interest rate parity**, real interest rates are assumed to converge across different markets. Taking the Fisher relation and real interest rate parity together gives us the **international Fisher effect**:

$$R_{\text{nominal A}} - R_{\text{nominal B}} = E(\text{inflation}_A) - E(\text{inflation}_B)$$

This tells us that the difference between two countries' nominal interest rates should be equal to the difference between their expected inflation rates.

The argument for the equality of real interest rates across countries is based on the idea that with free capital flows, funds will move to the country with a higher real rate until real rates are equalized.

EXAMPLE: Calculating the real interest rate

Suppose the nominal South African interest rate is 9.0% and the expected inflation rate is 3.5%. Calculate the real interest rate.

Answer:

$$0.090 = \text{real } r_{ZAR} + 0.035$$

$$\text{real } r_{ZAR} = 0.090 - 0.035 = 0.055\text{, or } 5.5\%$$

If we move to a 2-country scenario, we will now have two nominal interest rates and two expected inflation rates. If the real rates for both countries are assumed to be equal, they drop out of the equation, and we are left with the international Fisher relation, as shown in the following example.

EXAMPLE: Using the international Fisher relation

Suppose that the eurozone expected annual inflation rate is 9.0%, and that the expected South African inflation rate is 13.0%. The nominal interest rate is 10.09% in the eurozone. Use the international Fisher relation to estimate the nominal interest rate in South Africa.

Answer:

real rate ZAR = real rate EUR ≈ (nominal interest rate in the eurozone) – (eurozone expected annual inflation rate) = 10.09% – 9% = 1.09%

R_{ZAR} = (expected South African inflation rate) + (real ZAR interest rate) = 13% + 1.09% = 14.09%

Purchasing Power Parity

The law of one price states that identical goods should have the same price in all locations. For instance, a pair of designer jeans should cost the same in Paris as they do in New York, after adjusting for the exchange rate. The potential for arbitrage is the basis for the law of one price: if designer jeans cost less in New York than they do in Paris, an enterprising individual will buy designer jeans in New York and sell them in Paris, until this action causes the price differential to disappear. Note, however, that the law of one price does not hold in practice, due to the effects of frictions such as tariffs and transportation costs.

Instead of focusing on individual products, **absolute purchasing power parity** (absolute PPP) compares the average price of a representative basket of consumption goods between countries. Absolute PPP requires only that the law of one price be correct *on average*, that is, for like baskets of goods in each country.

$$S(A/B) = CPI(A) / CPI(B)$$

In practice, even if the law of one price held for every good in two economies, absolute PPP might not hold because the weights (consumption patterns) of the various goods in the two economies may not be the same (e.g., people eat more potatoes in Russia and more rice in Japan).

Relative Purchasing Power Parity

Relative purchasing power parity (relative PPP) states that changes in exchange rates should exactly offset the price effects of any inflation differential between two countries. Simply put, if (over a 1-year period) Country A has a 6% inflation rate and Country B has a 4% inflation rate, then Country A's currency should *depreciate* by approximately 2% relative to Country B's currency over the period.

The equation for relative PPP is as follows:

$$\%\Delta S(A/B) = \text{Inflation}_{(A)} - \text{Inflation}_{(B)}$$

where:
$\%\Delta S(A/B)$ = change in spot price (A/B)

Relative PPP is based on the idea that even if absolute PPP does not hold, there may still be a relationship between changes in the exchange rate and differences between the inflation rates of the two countries.

Ex-Ante Version of PPP

The ex-ante version of purchasing power parity is the same as relative purchasing power parity except that it uses *expected* inflation instead of actual inflation.

The following example illustrates the use of the ex-ante version of the PPP relation.

EXAMPLE: Calculating the exchange rate predicted by the ex ante version of PPP

The current spot rate is USD/AUD = 1.00. You expect the annualized Australian inflation rate to be 5%, and the annualized U.S. inflation rate to be 2%. According to the ex-ante version of PPP, what is the expected change in the spot rate over the coming year?

Answer:

Since the AUD has the higher expected inflation rate, we expect that the AUD will depreciate relative to the USD. To keep the cost of goods and services the same across borders, countries with higher rates of inflation should see their currencies depreciate. The expected change in the spot rate over the coming year is inflation(USD) – inflation(AUD) = 2% – 5% = –3%. This predicts a new USD/AUD exchange rate of approximately 0.97 USD/AUD.

Because there is no true arbitrage available to force relative PPP to hold, violations of relative PPP in the short run are common. However, because the evidence suggests that the relative form of PPP holds approximately in the long run, it remains a useful method for estimating the relationship between exchange rates and inflation rates.

LOS 11.f: Describe relations among the international parity conditions.

CFA® Program Curriculum, Volume 1, page 570

It is useful to establish how all the parity relations described earlier fit together. Figure 11.1 shows the interrelationships among parity conditions. Though these relationships are not all exact, together they provide an extremely useful framework for thinking about exchange rates.

Figure 11.1: The International Parity Relationships Combined

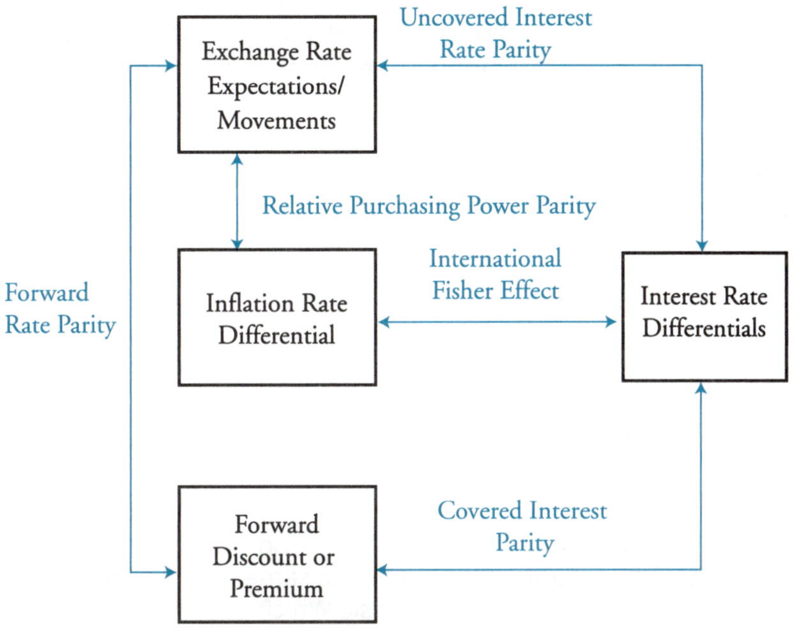

Several observations can be made from the relationships among the various parity conditions:

- Covered interest parity holds by arbitrage. If forward rate parity holds, uncovered interest rate parity also holds (and vice versa).
- Interest rate differentials should mirror inflation differentials. This holds true if the international Fisher relation holds. If that is true, we can also use inflation differentials to forecast future exchange rates—which is the premise of the ex-ante version of PPP.
- If the ex-ante version of relative PPP as well as the international Fisher relation both hold, uncovered interest rate parity will also hold.

LOS 11.g: Evaluate the use of the current spot rate, the forward rate, purchasing power parity, and uncovered interest parity to forecast future spot exchange rates.

LOS 11.h: Explain approaches to assessing the long-run fair value of an exchange rate.

CFA® Program Curriculum, Volume 1, page 560 and 566

We can use ex-ante PPP, uncovered interest rate parity, or forward rates to forecast future spot rates. As stated earlier, uncovered interest rate parity and PPP are not bound by arbitrage and seldom work over the short and medium terms. Similarly, the forward rate is not an unbiased predictor of future spot rate. However, PPP holds over reasonably long time horizons. If relative PPP holds at any point in time, the real exchange rate (i.e., the exchange rate adjusted for relative historical inflation between the currency pair) would be constant. However, since relative PPP seldom holds over the short term, the real exchange rate fluctuates around its mean-reverting equilibrium value.

The international Fisher effect (and real rate parity) assumes that there are no differences between sovereign risk premia (i.e., all countries are perceived to be equally risky by investors). This is obviously untrue as investors do demand a higher real rate of return (i.e., a risk premium) for investing in emerging market currencies that are perceived to be riskier.

MODULE QUIZ 11.2

To best evaluate your performance, enter your quiz answers online.

1. Suppose the spot exchange rate quote is 1.0120 Canadian dollars (C$) per U.S. dollar. The 1-year nominal interest rate in Canada is 3.0% and the 1-year nominal interest rate in the United States is 1.0%. The expected exchange rate at the end of the year using the uncovered interest rate parity is *closest* to:
   A. C$1.0322.
   B. C$0.9923.
   C. C$0.9918.
2. The international parity relationships indicate that the expected return on risk-free securities should be the same in all countries and exchange rate risk is really just inflation risk. Which of the following is *least likely* to be considered a practical implication of this framework?
   A. Investors will earn the same real rate of return on investments once their own currency impact is accounted for.
   B. Interest rate differentials reflect currency expectations. As a result, covered interest arbitrage will provide a return in any foreign currency that is equal to the domestic return.
   C. There are significant rewards for bearing foreign exchange risk.
3. For uncovered interest rate parity to hold, which condition is necessary?
   A. Forward rate parity holds.
   B. Covered interest rate parity holds and ex-ante relative PPP holds.
   C. Real interest rate parity and ex-ante relative PPP holds.

Use the following information to answer Questions 4 through 9.

Sally Franklin, CFA, is a financial advisor to Jamie Curtess, a U.S. citizen interested in learning more about how her investments will be affected by exchange rates and differences in interest rates internationally. Franklin has gathered the following information based on Curtess's investment interests.

The current spot exchange rate: $1 = €0.74.

	Europe	United States
Nominal 1-year interest rate:	4%	?
Expected annual inflation:	2%	1%

Franklin also gathers the following information:

	Switzerland	South Africa
Nominal 1-year interest rate:	5%	7%
Expected annual inflation:	3%	5%

4. According to the international Fisher relation, the 1-year nominal interest rate in the United States should be *closest* to:
   A. 3.00%.
   B. 4.34%.
   C. 6.00%.

5. If the relative form of the PPP holds, the expected exchange rate in one year is *closest* to:
   A. \$1.3378 per €.
   B. \$0.7463 per €.
   C. \$1.3647 per €.

6. For this question only, assume that the U.S. interest rate is 3.5%. The 1-year forward rate should be *closest* to:
   A. \$1.3647 per €.
   B. \$0.7463 per €.
   C. \$1.3449 per €.

7. Curtess wonders how spot rates are expected to change in the future and asks the following question: "What are the implications for the South African rand relative to the Swiss franc under uncovered interest rate parity, and the implications for the euro relative to the U.S. dollar under the relative form of purchasing power parity?" Franklin responds by making two statements:

   Statement 1: The South African rand is expected to depreciate relative to the Swiss franc.

   Statement 2: The euro is expected to depreciate relative to the U.S. dollar.

   Based upon the underlying parity relationships cited, are Franklin's statements accurate?
   A. No, both statements are inaccurate.
   B. Yes, both statements are accurate.
   C. One statement is accurate and one is inaccurate.

8. For this question only, imagine that the nominal interest rate in the United States is 3%. Real interest rates, using the Fisher relation, are *most likely* to be:
   A. greater in the United States than in Europe.
   B. lower in Europe than in South Africa.
   C. equal among Europe, South Africa, Switzerland, and the United States.

9. A forecasted \$/€ exchange rate in one year equal to the current 1-year forward rate is *most likely* to be based on the assumption that:
   A. absolute PPP holds.
   B. investors are risk neutral.
   C. real interest rate parity holds.

Video covering this content is available online.

MODULE 11.3: EXCHANGE RATE DETERMINANTS, CARRY TRADE, AND CENTRAL BANK INFLUENCE

LOS 11.i: Describe the carry trade and its relation to uncovered interest rate parity and calculate the profit from a carry trade.

CFA® Program Curriculum, Volume 1, page 572

FX Carry Trade

Uncovered interest rate parity states that a currency with a high interest rate should depreciate relative to a currency with a lower interest rate, so that an investor would earn the same return investing in either currency. For example, suppose that short-term interest rates are 3% in the U.K. and 1% in the United States. Uncovered interest rate parity implies that the GBP should depreciate by 2% relative to the USD over the coming year.

However, uncovered interest rate parity is not bound by arbitrage. If the GBP depreciates by less than 2% (or even appreciates), an investor who has invested in the higher yielding GBP using funds borrowed in USD will earn excess profits. In a **FX carry trade**, an investor invests in a higher yielding currency using funds borrowed in a lower yielding currency. The lower yielding currency is called the *funding currency*.

Consider the following example.

EXAMPLE: Carry trade

Interest Rates	Currency Pair	Exchange Rates	
		Today	*One year later*
U.K 3%	USD/GBP	1.50	1.50
U.S. 1%			

Compute the profit to an investor borrowing in the United States and investing in the U.K.

Answer:

return = interest earned on investment – funding cost – currency depreciation

= 3% – 1% – 0%

= 2%

The FX carry trade attempts to capture an interest rate differential and is a bet *against* uncovered interest rate parity. Carry trades typically perform well during low-volatility periods. Sometimes, higher yields attract larger capital flows, which in turn lead to an economic boom and appreciation (instead of depreciation) of the higher yielding currency. This could make the carry trade even more profitable, because the investor earns a return from currency appreciation in addition to the return from the interest rate spread.

Risks of the Carry Trade

As discussed earlier, the carry trade is profitable only if uncovered interest rate parity does not hold over the investment horizon. The risk is that the funding currency may appreciate significantly against the currency of the investment, which would reduce a trader's profit—or even lead to a loss. Furthermore, the return distribution of the carry trade is not normal; it is characterized by negative skewness and excess kurtosis (i.e., fat tails), meaning that the probability of a large loss is higher than the probability implied under a normal distribution. We call this high probability of a large loss the *crash risk* of the carry trade.

Crash risk stems from the carry trade's leveraged nature: an investor borrows a low-yielding (funding) currency and then invests in a high-yielding currency. As more investors follow and adopt the same strategy, the demand for high-yielding currency actually pushes its value *up*. However, with this herding behavior comes the risk that all investors may attempt to exit the trade at the same time. (This is especially true if investors use stop-loss orders in their carry trades.) During turbulent times, as investors exit their positions (i.e., a flight to safety), the high-yielding currency can experience a steep decline in value, generating large losses for traders pursuing FX carry trades.

LOS 11.j: Explain how flows in the balance of payment accounts affect currency exchange rates.

CFA® Program Curriculum, Volume 1, page 575

BALANCE OF PAYMENTS

Balance-of-payments (BOP) accounting is a method used to keep track of transactions between a country and its international trading partners. It includes government transactions, consumer transactions, and business transactions. The BOP accounts reflect all payments and liabilities *to* foreigners as well as all payments and obligations received *from* foreigners.

The **current account** measures the exchange of goods, the exchange of services, the exchange of investment income, and unilateral transfers (gifts to and from other nations). The current account balance summarizes whether we are selling more goods and services to the rest of the world than we are buying from them (a current account surplus) or buying more from the rest of the world than we are selling to them (a current account deficit).

The **financial account** (also known as the **capital account**) measures the flow of funds for debt and equity investment into and out of the country.

When a country experiences a current account deficit, it must generate a surplus in its capital account (or see its currency depreciate). Capital flows tend to be the dominant factor influencing exchange rates in the short term, as capital flows tend to be larger and more rapidly changing than goods flows.

INFLUENCE OF BOP ON EXCHANGE RATES

Current Account Influences

Current account deficits lead to a depreciation of domestic currency via a variety of mechanisms:

- **Flow supply/demand mechanism.** Current account deficits in a country increase the supply of that currency in the markets (as exporters to that country convert their revenues into their own local currency). This puts downward pressure on the exchange value of that currency. The decrease in the value of the currency *may* restore the current account deficit to a balance—depending on the following factors:
  - *The initial deficit.* The larger the initial deficit, the larger the depreciation of domestic currency needed to restore current account balance.
  - *The influence of exchange rates on domestic import and export prices.* As a country's currency depreciates, the cost of imported goods increases. However, some of the increase in cost may not be passed on to consumers.
  - *Price elasticity of demand of the traded goods.* If the most important imports are relatively price inelastic, the quantity imported will not change.
- **Portfolio balance mechanism.** Countries with current account surpluses usually have capital account deficits, which typically take the form of investments in countries with current account deficits. As a result of these flows of capital, investor countries may find their portfolios' composition being dominated by few investee currencies. When investor countries decide to rebalance their investment portfolios, it can have a significant negative impact on the value of those investee country currencies.
- **Debt sustainability mechanism.** A country running a current account deficit may be running a capital account surplus by borrowing from abroad. When the level of debt gets too high relative to GDP, investors may question the sustainability of this level of debt, leading to a rapid depreciation of the borrower's currency.

Capital Account Influences

Capital account flows are one of the major determinants of exchange rates. As capital flows into a country, demand for that country's currency increases, resulting in appreciation. Differences in real rates of return tend to be a major determinant of the flow of capital: higher relative real rates of return attract foreign capital. Capital flows into a country may be needed to overcome a shortage of internal savings to fund investments needed for economic growth. However, capital flows in excess of needed investment capital pose several problems. This is especially problematic for emerging markets.

Excessive capital inflows into emerging markets create problems for those countries such as:

- Excessive real appreciation of the domestic currency.
- Financial asset and/or real estate bubbles.

- Increases in external debt by businesses or government.
- Excessive consumption in the domestic market fueled by credit.

Emerging market governments often counteract excessive capital inflows by imposing capital controls or by direct intervention in the foreign exchange markets. We will discuss this further in a subsequent LOS.

LOS 11.k: Explain the potential effects of monetary and fiscal policy on exchange rates.

CFA® Program Curriculum, Volume 1, page 585

MUNDELL-FLEMING MODEL

Developed in early 1960s, the **Mundell-Fleming model** evaluates the impact of monetary and fiscal policies on interest rates—and consequently on exchange rates. The model assumes that there is sufficient slack in the economy to handle changes in aggregate demand, and that inflation is not a concern. Accordingly, changes in inflation rates due to changes in monetary or fiscal policy are not explicitly modeled by the Mundell-Fleming model.

We will look at the implications of this model for flexible exchange rate regimes as well as for fixed exchange rate regimes.

Flexible Exchange Rate Regimes

In a flexible ("floating") exchange rate system, rates are determined by supply and demand in the foreign exchange markets. We will examine the influence of monetary and fiscal policies when international capital flows are relatively unrestricted (high mobility of capital) versus when capital flows are relatively restricted (low mobility of capital), both under a flexible exchange rate system.

High Capital Mobility

Expansionary **monetary policy** and expansionary **fiscal policy** are likely to have opposite effects on exchange rates. Expansionary monetary policy will reduce the interest rate and, consequently, reduce the inflow of capital investment in physical and financial assets. This decrease in financial inflows (deterioration of the financial account) reduces the demand for the domestic currency, resulting in depreciation of the domestic currency. Restrictive monetary policy should have the opposite effect, increasing interest rates and leading to an appreciation in the value of the domestic currency.

Expansionary fiscal policy (an increased deficit from lower taxes or higher government spending) will increase government borrowing and, consequently, interest rates. An increase in interest rates will attract foreign investment, improve the financial account, and consequently, *increase* the demand for the domestic currency.

Study Session 4

Low Capital Mobility

Our discussion so far has assumed free flow of capital, which is a valid assumption with respect to developed markets. In emerging markets, however, capital flows may be restricted. In that case, the impact of trade imbalance on exchange rates (goods flow effect) is greater than the impact of interest rates (financial flows effect). In such a case, expansionary fiscal or monetary policy leads to increases in net imports, leading to depreciation of the domestic currency. Similarly, restrictive monetary or fiscal policy leads to an appreciation of domestic currency. Figure 11.2 summarizes the influence of fiscal and monetary policy on exchange rates.

Figure 11.2: Monetary and Fiscal Policy and Exchange Rates

Monetary Policy/Fiscal Policy	Capital Mobility	
	High	Low
Expansionary/Expansionary	Uncertain	Depreciation
Expansionary/Restrictive	Depreciation	Uncertain
Restrictive/Expansionary	Appreciation	Uncertain
Restrictive/Restrictive	Uncertain	Appreciation

PROFESSOR'S NOTE

Candidates are often confused by the implication under the Mundell-Fleming model that a higher-interest-rate currency will appreciate relative to a lower-interest-rate currency, because this is exactly the opposite of what we learned under uncovered interest rate parity. Note though that uncovered interest rate parity assumed that real interest rates are equal globally, and thus that nominal interest rates merely mirror expected inflation. That condition no longer holds under the Mundell Fleming model, which does not consider inflation.

Fixed Exchange Rate Regimes

Under a fixed exchange rate regime, the government fixes the rate of exchange of its currency relative to one of the major currencies.

An expansionary (restrictive) monetary policy would lead to depreciation (appreciation) of the domestic currency as stated above. Under a fixed rate regime, the government would then have to purchase (sell) its own currency in the foreign exchange market. This action essentially reverses the expansionary (restrictive) stance.

This explains why in a world with mobility of capital, governments cannot both manage exchange rates as well as pursue independent monetary policy. If the government wants to manage monetary policy, it must either let exchange rates float freely or restrict capital movements to keep them stable.

MONETARY APPROACH TO EXCHANGE RATE DETERMINATION

Monetary models only take into account the effect of monetary policy on exchange rates (fiscal policy effects are not considered). With the Mundell-Fleming model, we assume that inflation (price levels) play no role in exchange rate determination. Under monetary models, we assume that output is fixed, so that monetary policy primarily affects inflation, which in turn affects exchange rates. There are two main approaches to monetary models:

1. **Pure monetary model**. Under a pure monetary model, the PPP holds at any point in time and output is held constant. An expansionary (restrictive) monetary policy leads to an increase (decrease) in prices and a decrease (increase) in the value of the domestic currency. Therefore an x% increase in the money supply leads to an x% increase in price levels and then to an x% depreciation of domestic currency. The pure monetary approach does not take into account expectations about future monetary expansion or contraction.
2. **Dornbusch overshooting model**. This model assumes that prices are sticky (inflexible) in the short term and, hence, do not immediately reflect changes in monetary policy (in other words, PPP does not hold in the short term). The model concludes that exchange rates will overshoot the long-run PPP value in the short term. In the case of an expansionary monetary policy, prices increase, but over time. Expansionary monetary policy leads to a *decrease* in interest rates—and a larger-than-PPP-implied depreciation of the domestic currency due to capital outflows. In the long term, exchange rates gradually increase toward their PPP implied values.

   Similarly, a restrictive monetary policy leads to excessive appreciation of the domestic currency in the short term, and then a slow depreciation toward the long-term PPP value.

PORTFOLIO BALANCE APPROACH TO EXCHANGE RATE DETERMINATION

The portfolio balance approach focuses only on the effects of *fiscal* policy (and not monetary policy). While the Mundell-Fleming model focuses on the short-term implications of fiscal policy, the **portfolio balance approach** takes a long-term view and evaluates the effects of a sustained fiscal deficit or surplus on currency values.

When the government runs a fiscal deficit, it borrows money from investors. Under the portfolio balance approach, investors evaluate the debt based on expected risk and return. A sovereign debt investor would earn a return based on both the debt's yield and its currency return (When we invest in a foreign-currency-denominated security, our realized return will be comprised of the return earned on that security in its local currency, as well as a return from the performance of that foreign currency versus our domestic currency). When a government pursues a long-term stance of expansionary fiscal policy, an investor should evaluate the implications of such a policy on expected risk and return (typically the yield should increase due to a higher risk premium). If investors perceive that the yield and/or currency return is sufficient, they will continue to purchase the bonds. However, continued increases in fiscal deficits are unsustainable and investors may refuse to fund the deficits—leading to currency depreciation.

Combining the Mundell-Fleming and portfolio balance approaches, we find that in the short term, with free capital flows, an expansionary fiscal policy leads to domestic currency appreciation (via high interest rates). In the long term, the government has to reverse course (through tighter fiscal policy) leading to depreciation of the domestic currency. If the government does not reverse course, it will have to monetize its debt (i.e., print money—monetary expansion), which would also lead to depreciation of the domestic currency.

LOS 11.l: Describe objectives of central bank or government intervention and capital controls and describe the effectiveness of intervention and capital controls.

CFA® Program Curriculum, Volume 1, page 594

A combination of "push" and "pull" factors determine the flow of capital into a country. Pull factors are favorable developments that make a country an attractive destination for foreign capital. These include relative price stability, a flexible exchange rate regime, improved fiscal position, privatization of state owned enterprises etc. Push factors are largely driven by mobile international capital seeking high returns from a diversified portfolio.

As stated earlier, capital flows can lead to excessive appreciation of a currency. This can lead to several problems including loss of competitiveness of exports in the global markets, asset price bubbles, and excessive consumption fueled by credit creation. Excessive capital inflows to a country can also lead to a currency crisis when such capital is eventually withdrawn from the country. To reduce these problems, policymakers may intervene by imposing capital controls or by direct intervention in the foreign exchange market by the central bank.

Objectives

The objectives of capital controls or central bank intervention in FX markets are to:

- Ensure that the domestic currency does not appreciate excessively.
- Allow the pursuit of independent monetary policies without being hindered by their impact on currency values. For example, an emerging market central bank seeking to reduce inflation may pursue a restrictive monetary policy, increasing interest rates. However, these higher rates may attract large inflows of foreign capital, pushing up the value of the domestic currency.
- Reduce the aggregate volume of inflow of foreign capital.

Effectiveness

For developed market countries, the volume of trading in a country's currency is usually very large relative to the foreign exchange reserves of its central bank. Evidence has shown that for developed markets, central banks are relatively ineffective at intervening in the foreign exchange markets due to lack of sufficient resources. Evidence in the case of emerging markets is less clear: central banks of emerging market countries may be able to accumulate sufficient foreign exchange reserves (relative to trading volume) to affect the supply and demand of their currencies in the foreign exchange markets.

LOS 11.m: Describe warning signs of a currency crisis.

CFA® Program Curriculum, Volume 1, page 596

History has shown that market participants have failed to predict crises and typically are surprised by them. When market sentiment changes significantly, crises may occur *even for countries with sound economic fundamentals*.

The following conditions have been identified as warning signs in the period leading up to a currency crisis:

- Terms of trade (i.e., ratio of exports to imports) deteriorate.
- Fixed or partially-fixed exchange rates (versus floating exchange rates).
- Official foreign exchange reserves dramatically decline.
- Currency value that has risen above its historical mean.
- Inflation increases.
- Liberalized capital markets, that allow for the free flow of capital.
- Money supply relative to bank reserves increases.
- Banking crises (may also be coincident).

MODULE QUIZ 11.3

To best evaluate your performance, enter your quiz answers online.

1. Vilasram Deshmukh is forecasting JPY/USD exchange rates based on balance of payments analysis. He notes that the United States is running large current account deficits relative to Japan. Based on this information, he concludes that the JPY/USD rate should decrease. His conclusion is *most likely* supported by the:
   A. flow mechanism of the current account influences.
   B. portfolio composition mechanism of the current account influences.
   C. capital account influences.

2. Stephen Hall is forecasting USD/GBP exchange rates. He consults forecasts of the money supply for the United States and U.K. made by his firm's chief economist, and he notes the following statement from a report published by the chief economist: "The U.S. money supply is expected to grow at a much faster pace than the U.K. or European money supplies."

   Hall makes the following statement: "Under the pure monetary approach model, an increase in the future growth rate of the money supply would lead to an immediate depreciation in the currency's value." Hall's statement is *most likely*:

   A. correct.
   B. incorrect, as the future growth rate in the money supply would not immediately affect currency values under the pure monetary approach model.
   C. incorrect, as the future growth rate in money supply would actually increase the currency value under the pure monetary approach.

3. Chintan Rajyaguru works for a currency dealer in London. He is evaluating the implications of changes in fiscal and monetary policies occurring in Zambola, an emerging market country with low capital mobility. He concludes that Zambola's central bank is pursuing a restrictive monetary policy to curb inflation. Additionally, the Zambolan government has been reducing budget deficits to comply with new IMF lending terms. According to the Mundell-Fleming model, the change in monetary and fiscal policy is *most likely* to cause the Zambolan currency to:

   A. appreciate.
   B. depreciate.
   C. remain unchanged.

Use the following information to answer Questions 4 through 9.

Agnetha Poulsen works as an analyst in the foreign exchange overlay strategies department for CFN, a large asset management firm serving institutional clients. She is concerned about the excessive unhedged currency exposure taken on by the overlay strategies department. She makes an appointment with Alvilda Kristensen, director of risk management, to discuss this matter. Prior to the meeting, Poulsen collects information on foreign currency quotes and on interest rates as shown in Figure 11.3 and Figure 11.4.

Figure 11.3: Current Spot and Forward Exchange Rate Quotes

Quotes	USD/CHF	USD/EUR
Spot	0.9817/0.9821	1.2235/1.2238
30-day forward	–7.6/–6.9	–7.21/–6.80
60-day forward	–15.3/–13.3	–14.56/–13.76
90-day forward	–24.3/–23.05	–23.84/–22.77

Figure 11.4: Selected Interest Rates

Interest Rates	USD	EUR	CHF
30-day rate	0.20%	0.91%	1.13%
60-day rate	0.21%	0.93%	1.15%
90-day rate	0.26%	1.04%	1.25%

Poulsen also reviews the current open forward contracts. As an example, she reviews two contracts. Contract FX2001 is a 90-day forward contract initiated 60 days ago. The contract calls for purchase of CHF 200 million at an all-in rate of USD 0.9832. Contract FX2051 is a 90-day contract initiated 30 days ago to purchase 100 million EUR at an all-in rate of 1.2242.

During her meeting with Kristensen, Poulsen expresses concern about traders establishing FX carry trades in several emerging market currencies. Kristensen assures Poulsen that CFN has adequate monitoring mechanisms. She continues that these carry trades have been generating significant positive returns for the clients and Poulsen should not worry about it. Poulsen counters by stating that carry trade returns distributions are characterized by negative kurtosis and excess skewness.

Poulsen reviews her notes and decides to prepare a report on currency crises. She compiles a list of indicators of an impending currency crisis based on empirical analysis.

Poulsen then turns her attention to the firm's investments in Zambola, an emerging market. She realizes that currently the currency overlay strategy department has no trades involving the free-floating Zambolan currency, the Zu. Poulsen is concerned about significant long exposure of the portfolio in Zu. Zambola is enjoying large capital inflows drawn by Zambola's attractive yields. Her analysis indicates that Zambola has been running large current account deficits. A trend analysis on Zu indicates a steep upward trend continuing above its PPP value.

4. Based on the information provided in Exhibit 1, the 30-day forward spread on USD/CHF is *closest* to:
   A. 0.0005.
   B. 0.0007.
   C. 0.7000.
5. The current mark-to-market value of the forward contract FX2001 in USD is *closest* to:
   A. –USD460,000.
   B. –USD451,924.
   C. –USD357,940.
6. The current mark-to-market value of the forward contract FX2051 in USD is *closest* to:
   A. –USD215,900.
   B. –USD107,900.
   C. –USD216,000.

Study Session 4

7. Poulsen's description of the carry trade return distribution is *best* described as:
   A. correct.
   B. incorrect about skewness only.
   C. incorrect about both skewness and kurtosis.
8. Which of the following indicators of impending currency crises should Poulsen exclude from her report?
   A. Terms of trade improve.
   B. Increase in money supply relative to bank reserves.
   C. Increase in inflation.
9. If Zambolan government wanted to reduce the inflow of foreign capital, it should:
   A. pursue expansionary monetary policies.
   B. pursue policies consistent with currency appreciation.
   C. reduce inflation by increasing interest rates.

KEY CONCEPTS

LOS 11.a

bid-ask spread (for base currency) = ask quote − bid quote

Dealer spreads depend on spreads in the interbank market, the transaction size, and the dealer-client relationship. Interbank spreads depend on the currencies involved, time of day, and volatility in the currency pair. Forward spreads increase with maturities.

LOS 11.b

To calculate the profits from triangular arbitrage, start in the home currency and go around the triangle by exchanging the home currency for the first foreign currency, then exchanging the first foreign currency for the second foreign currency, and then exchanging the second foreign currency back into the home currency. If we end up with more money than what we had when we started, we've earned an arbitrage profit. The bid-ask spread forces us to buy a currency at a higher rate going one way than we can sell it for going the other way.

LOS 11.c

A spot exchange rate is for immediate delivery, while a forward exchange rate is for future delivery.

premium (discount) for base currency = forward price − spot price

LOS 11.d

The mark-to-market value of a forward contract reflects the profit that would be realized by closing out the position at current market prices, which is equivalent to offsetting the contract with an equal and opposite forward position:

$$V_t = \frac{(FP_t - FP)(\text{contract size})}{\left[1 + R\left(\frac{\text{days}}{360}\right)\right]}$$

where:

V_t = value of the forward contract at time *t* (to the party buying the base currency), $(t < T)$ denominated in price currency

FP_t = forward price (to sell base currency) at time *t* in the market for a new contract maturing at time *T*

FP = forward price specified in the contract at inception (to buy the base currency)

days = number of days remaining to maturity of the forward contract $(T - t)$

R = interest rate of price currency

Study Session 4

LOS 11.e

Covered interest arbitrage:

$$F = \frac{\left[1 + R_A\left(\frac{\text{days}}{360}\right)\right]}{\left[1 + R_B\left(\frac{\text{days}}{360}\right)\right]} S_0$$

Uncovered interest rate parity:

$$E(\%\Delta S)_{(A/B)} = R_A - R_B$$

International Fisher relation:

$$R_{\text{nominal A}} - R_{\text{nominal B}} = E(\text{inflation}_A) - E(\text{inflation}_B)$$

Relative PPP:

$$\%\Delta S_{(A/B)} = \text{inflation}_A - \text{inflation}_B$$

Forward rate parity:

$$F = E(S_T)$$

LOS 11.f

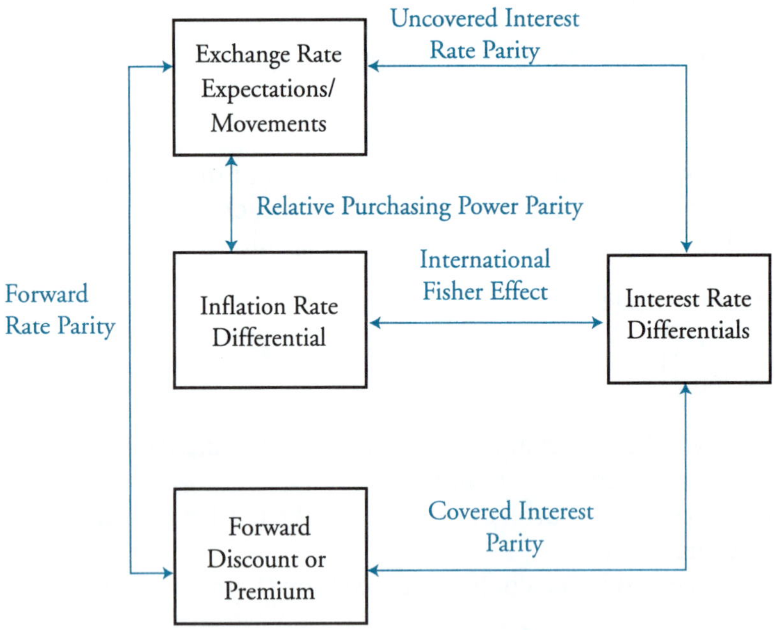

LOS 11.g, 11.h

Future spot rates can be forecasted using PPP or by uncovered interest rate parity. However, neither relationship is bound by arbitrage, nor do these relationships necessarily work in the short term. Forward exchange rates, on the other hand, can be estimated using covered interest parity, and this relationship is bound by arbitrage. If uncovered interest parity holds, then we say that the forward rate parity holds, i.e., the forward rate is an unbiased estimate of the future spot rate.

LOS 11.i

The FX carry trade seeks to profit from the failure of uncovered interest rate parity to work in the short run. In an FX carry trade, the investor invests in a high-yielding currency while borrowing in a low-yielding currency. If the higher yielding currency does not depreciate by the interest rate differential, the investor makes a profit. Carry trade has exposure to crash risk.

profit on carry trade = interest differential – change in the spot rate of the investment currency

LOS 11.j

BOP influence on exchange rate can be analyzed based on current account influence and capital account influence. Current account influences include flow mechanism, portfolio composition mechanism, and debt sustainability mechanism. Capital account inflows (outflows) are one of the major causes of increases (decreases) in exchange rates.

LOS 11.k

The Mundell-Fleming model of exchange rate determination evaluates the impact of monetary and fiscal policies on interest rates and consequently on exchange rates.

Under monetary models, we assume that output is fixed and, hence, monetary policies primarily affect inflation, which in turn affects exchange rates.

The portfolio balance (asset market) model evaluates the long-term implications of sustained fiscal policy (deficit or surplus) on currency values.

Monetary and Fiscal Policy and Exchange Rates

Monetary Policy/Fiscal Policy	Capital Mobility	
	High	Low
Expansionary/Expansionary	Uncertain	Depreciation
Expansionary/Restrictive	Depreciation	Uncertain
Restrictive/Expansionary	Appreciation	Uncertain
Restrictive/Restrictive	Uncertain	Appreciation

Under the pure monetary approach, PPP holds at any point in time.

Under the Dornbusch overshooting model, a restrictive (expansionary) monetary leads to an appreciation (depreciation) of domestic currency in the short term, and then slow depreciation (appreciation) towards the long-term PPP value.

Combining the Mundell-Fleming and portfolio balance approaches, we find that in the short term, an expansionary (restrictive) fiscal policy leads to domestic currency appreciation (depreciation). In the long term, the impact on currency values is opposite.

LOS 11.l

Capital controls and central bank intervention aim to reduce excessive capital inflows, which could lead to speculative bubbles. The success of central bank intervention depends on the size of official FX reserves at the disposal of the central bank relative to the average trading volume in the country's currency. For developed markets, the central bank resources on a relative basis are too insignificant to be effective at managing exchange rates. However, some emerging market countries with large FX reserves relative to trading volume have been somewhat effective.

LOS 11.m

Warning signs of currency crises include: deterioration in terms of trade, a dramatic decline in official foreign exchange reserves, an exchange rate substantially higher than its mean-reverting level, increases in the inflation rate, a fixed- or partially-fixed exchange rate, an increase in money supply relative to bank reserves, and banking crises.

ANSWER KEY FOR MODULE QUIZZES

Module Quiz 11.1

1. **C** Dealer spreads are lower for smaller orders as compared to larger orders. Dealer spreads are larger when spreads in the interbank market are higher. An increase in spot rate volatility will increase spreads in the interbank market. (LOS 11.a)

2. **C** Here is what the triangle looks like with the bid-ask quotes filled in:

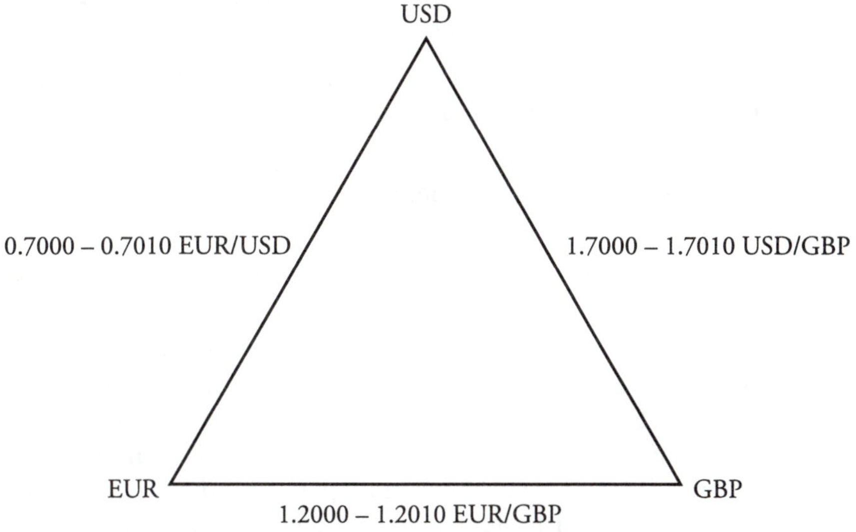

If we start with 1 million USD and move clockwise around the triangle (USD to GBP to EUR to USD), we first convert 1 million USD into GBP at the ask:

$$\frac{1 \text{ million USD}}{1.7010 \text{ USD/GBP}} = 587{,}889 \text{ GBP}$$

Then we sell the GBP for EUR at the bid:

$$587{,}889 \text{ GBP} \times \left(\frac{1.2000 \text{ EUR}}{\text{GBP}}\right) = 705{,}467 \text{ EUR}$$

Finally, we purchase USD at the ask in euros:

$$\frac{705{,}467 \text{ EUR}}{0.7010} = 1{,}006{,}372 \text{ USD}$$

Arbitrage profits are 1,006,372 USD – 1,000,000 USD = 6,372 USD. (LOS 11.b)

Module Quiz 11.2

1. **A** Because of a lower interest rate, the USD (base currency) will appreciate by 2% to $1.012 × 1.02 = C$1.0322. (LOS 11.e)

2. **C** Combining all parity relationships indicates that the expected return on risk-free securities should be the same in all countries and exchange rate risk is really just inflation risk. There are four practical implications from this framework:
    1. The real, risk-free return will be the same in all countries.
    2. Investing in countries with high nominal interest rates will not generate excess returns because the high nominal interest rates will be accompanied by local currency depreciation.
    3. All investors will earn the same expected return in their own currency on any investment denominated in a foreign currency.
    4. Exchange rate risk is simply inflation risk, so investors interested in real returns will not face exchange rate risk.

    (LOS 11.f)

3. **A** Covered interest parity is forced by arbitrage, which is not the case for uncovered interest rate parity. If the forward rate is equal to the expected future spot rate, we say that the forward rate is an unbiased predictor of the future spot rate: $F = E(S_1)$. In this special case, given that covered interest parity holds, uncovered interest parity would also hold (and vice versa). In other words, if uncovered interest rate parity (and covered interest parity) holds, the forward rate is unbiased predictor of future spot rate (i.e., forward rate parity holds). (LOS 11.e)

4. **A** According to the international Fisher relation:

    r = real r + E(I)

    From European data:

    4% = real r + 2%

    real r = 2%

    For United States:

    r = 2% + 1%

    r = 3%

    (LOS 11.e)

5. **A** Since inflation in Europe is higher than the inflation in the U.S. by 1%, the Euro is expected to depreciate by 1% annually against the dollar.

    The current spot rate is $(1/0.74) per Euro or $1.3513/€

    Expected exchange rate in 1 year = 1.3513(0.99) = $1.3378/€ (LOS 11.e)

6. **C** Using covered interest parity, the forward rate in one year (in \$ per €) can be calculated as follows:

$$\text{Spot rate} = €0.74 \text{ per } \$ = \$\left(\frac{1}{0.74}\right)\text{per } €$$

$$F = S_0 \times \left(\frac{1+r_\$}{1+r_€}\right) = \left(\frac{1}{0.74}\right) \times \left(\frac{1.035}{1.04}\right) = \$1.3449 \text{ per } €$$

(LOS 11.e)

7. **B** Franklin is correct with respect to both of his statements: the rand should depreciate relative to the franc and the euro should depreciate relative to the dollar.

   The relative form of purchasing power parity predicts that countries with higher expected inflation will experience a depreciation of their currencies. South Africa's expected inflation rate (5%) is higher than the expected inflation rate in Switzerland (3%). The expected inflation rate in Europe (2%) is higher than the expected inflation rate in the United States (1%). According to purchasing power parity, the rand should depreciate relative to the franc, and the euro should depreciate relative to the U.S. dollar.

   Uncovered interest parity makes the same predictions with regard to relative interest rates: countries with higher nominal interest rates can be expected to experience currency depreciation. The South African interest rate (7%) is higher than the Swiss rate (5%), so uncovered interest rate parity predicts that the rand will depreciate with respect to the franc. The interest rate in Europe (4%) is higher than the interest rate in the United States (3%), so the euro should depreciate relative to the U.S. dollar. (LOS 11.e)

8. **C** According to the international Fisher relation, the real interest rate is equal to the nominal interest rate minus the expected inflation rate. The real interest rate in each of the four countries is 2%. (LOS 11.e)

9. **B** The 1-year expected spot rate should be equal to the current 1-year forward rate if uncovered interest rate parity holds. One of the assumptions of uncovered interest rate parity is that investors are risk neutral. Real interest rate parity states that real interest rates are equal across countries. Uncovered interest rate parity also would hold if both (1) relative (not absolute) PPP holds and (2) the international Fisher relationship holds. (LOS 11.e)

Module Quiz 11.3

1. **A** The flow mechanism of current account influences supports the view that current account deficits lead to depreciation of currency. In this example, the reduction in the JPY/USD rate implies depreciation of the USD. Under capital account influences, current account deficits imply capital account inflows and, hence, would lead to an appreciation of USD. The portfolio

Study Session 4

composition mechanism of current account influences supports the flow mechanism if investors rebalance a portion of their portfolio out of USD assets due to gradual buildup of USD assets over time in their portfolios. The question does not provide information to support this reallocation. (Module 11.3, LOS 11.j)

2. **B** Under the pure monetary approach, growth in the money supply leads to depreciation in currency. However, the future growth rate in money supply affects the trajectory of FX rates but not the current exchange rate. (Module 11.3, LOS 11.k)

3. **A** Under the Mundell-Fleming framework, low capital mobility and restrictive monetary and fiscal policy leads to better trade balance and appreciation of the country's currency. (Module 11.3, LOS 11.k)

4. **A** (0.9821 – 0.00069) – (0.9817 – 0.00076) = 0.00047 (Module 11.1, LOS 11.c)

5. **B** The contract calls for purchase of 200 million CHF in 30 days. To compute the mark-to-market value, we would have to use the quote on 30-day forward contract to sell CHF. Given USD/CHF quote structure, we should use the bid price (going up the quote).

   all-in bid price for 30-day USD/CHF forward contract = 0.9817 – 7.6 / 10,000 = 0.98094

$$V_t = \frac{(FP_t - FP)(\text{contract size})}{\left[1 + R\left(\frac{\text{days}}{360}\right)\right]}$$

   FP_t = 0.98094 (computed above)

   FP = 0.9832 (given)

   R = 30-day USD interest rate (USD is the price currency)
   = 0.20%

$$V_t = \frac{(0.98094 - 0.9832)(200{,}000{,}000)}{\left[1 + 0.002\left(\frac{30}{360}\right)\right]} = \frac{-452{,}000}{1.000166} = -451{,}924 \text{ USD}$$

   (Module 11.2, LOS 11.d)

6. **A** The contract calls for purchase of 100 million EUR in 60 days. To compute the mark-to-market value, we would have to use the quote on 60-day forward contract to sell EUR. Given USD/EUR quote structure, we should use the bid price (going up the quote).

   all-in bid price for 60-day USD/EUR forward contract
   = 1.2235 – 14.56 / 10,000 = 1.22204

   $$V_t = \frac{(FP_t - FP)(\text{contract size})}{\left[1 + R\left(\frac{\text{days}}{360}\right)\right]}$$

   FP_t = 1.22204 (computed above)

   FP = 1.2242 (given)

   R = 60-day USD interest rate (USD is the price currency)

   = 0.21%

   $$V_t = \frac{(0.98094 - 0.9832)(200{,}000{,}000)}{\left[1 + 0.002\left(\frac{30}{360}\right)\right]} = \frac{-452{,}000}{1.000166} = -451{,}924 \text{ USD}$$

   (Module 11.2, LOS 11.d)

7. **C** Poulsen incorrectly described both the skewness as well as the kurtosis of carry trade returns. Carry trade return distributions generally have *negative skewness* and *excess kurtosis*. (Module 11.3, LOS 11.i)

8. **A** Deterioration (and not improvement) in terms of trade is an indicator of currency crisis. (Module 11.3, LOS 11.m)

9. **A** The Zu is overvalued per PPP, and Zambola is running a current account deficit. A depreciation of Zu would bring it closer to its long-run fair value. An increase in interest rates would lead to appreciation of Zu. Expansionary monetary policy would reduce interest rates and make Zambolan yields less attractive to foreign investors. (Module 11.3, LOS 11.j)

The following is a review of the Economics principles designed to address the learning outcome statements set forth by CFA Institute. Cross-Reference to CFA Institute Assigned Reading #12.

READING 12

Economic Growth and the Investment Decision

Study Session 4

EXAM FOCUS

Forecasts of economic growth rates have important implications for investment decisions. Understand the preconditions of growth, how the growth rate can be increased, and what drives economic growth. Be able to compare and contrast competing theories of growth. Finally, be able to use growth accounting equations to forecast the potential growth rate of an economy.

MODULE 12.1: GROWTH FACTORS AND PRODUCTION FUNCTION

Video covering this content is available online.

LOS 12.a: Compare factors favoring and limiting economic growth in developed and developing economies.

CFA® Program Curriculum, Volume 1, page 620

Economists measure the economic output of a country by gross domestic product (GDP). A country's standard of living, however, is best measured by GDP per capita. Of particular concern to investors is not just the level of economic output but the growth rate of output.

Historically, there have been large variations in both GDP growth rates and per capita GDP across countries. Research has identified several factors that influence both the growth of GDP and the level of GDP.

PRECONDITIONS FOR GROWTH

1. **Savings and investment** is positively correlated with economic development. For countries to grow, private and public sector investment must provide a sufficient level of capital per worker. If a country has insufficient domestic savings, it must attract foreign investment in order to grow.
2. **Financial markets and intermediaries** augment economic growth by efficiently allocating resources in several ways. First, financial markets determine which potential users of capital offer the best returns on a risk-adjusted basis. Second, financial instruments are created by intermediaries that provide investors with liquidity and opportunities for risk reduction. Finally, by pooling small amounts of savings from investors, intermediaries can finance projects on larger scales than would otherwise be possible.

   Some caution is in order, however. Financial sector intermediation may lead to declining credit standards and/or increases in leverage, increasing risk but not economic growth.
3. The **political stability, rule of law, and property rights** environment of a country also influence economic growth. Countries that have not developed a system of property rights for both physical and intellectual property will have difficulty attracting capital. Similarly, economic uncertainty caused by wars, corruption, and other disruptions poses unacceptable risk to many investors, reducing potential economic growth.
4. **Investment in human capital**, the investment in skills and well-being of workers, is thought to be complementary to growth in physical capital. Consequently, countries that invest in education and health care systems tend to have higher growth rates. Developed countries benefit the most from post-secondary education spending, which has been shown to foster innovation. Less-developed countries benefit the most from spending on primary and secondary education, which enables the workforce to *apply* the technology developed elsewhere.
5. **Tax and regulatory systems** need to be favorable for economies to develop. All else equal, the lower the tax and regulatory burdens, the higher the rate of economic growth. Lower levels of regulation foster entrepreneurial activity (startups), which have been shown to be positively related to the overall level of productivity.
6. **Free trade and unrestricted capital flows** are also positively related to economic growth. Free trade promotes growth by providing competition for domestic firms, thus increasing overall efficiency and reducing costs. Additionally, free trade opens up new markets for domestic producers. Unrestricted capital flows mitigate the problem of insufficient domestic savings as foreign capital can increase a country's capital, allowing for greater growth. Foreign capital can be invested directly in assets such as property, physical plant, and equipment (foreign direct investment), or invested indirectly in financial assets such as stocks and bonds.

LOS 12.b: Describe the relation between the long-run rate of stock market appreciation and the sustainable growth rate of the economy.

CFA® Program Curriculum, Volume 1, page 628

Equity prices are positively related to earnings growth. Economy-wide, aggregate corporate earnings can grow if GDP grows or if the share of corporate earnings in GDP grows. Therefore, the *potential GDP* of a country—the upper limit of *real* growth for an economy—is an important factor in predicting returns on aggregate equity markets.

To understand this, consider that the growth in aggregate stock market valuation is a function of GDP growth, growth in earnings relative to GDP, and growth in the price to earnings ratio:

$$\Delta P = \Delta GDP + \Delta(E/GDP) + \Delta(P/E)$$

Over the long-term, we have to recognize that *growth* in earnings relative to GDP is zero; labor will be unwilling to accept an ever decreasing share of GDP. Similarly, *growth* in the P/E ratio will also be zero over the long term; investors will not continue to pay an ever increasing price for the same level of earnings forever (i.e., the P/E ratio cannot grow indefinitely). Hence over a sufficiently long time horizon, the potential GDP growth rate equals the growth rate of aggregate equity valuation.

LOS 12.c: Explain why potential GDP and its growth rate matter for equity and fixed income investors.

CFA® Program Curriculum, Volume 1, page 630

As indicated previously, growth in potential GDP represents the main driver of aggregate equity valuation. More generally, potential GDP also has implications for real interest rates. Positive growth in potential GDP indicates that future income will rise relative to current income. When consumers expect their incomes to rise, they increase current consumption and save less for future consumption (i.e., they are less likely to worry about funding their future consumption). To encourage consumers to delay consumption (i.e., to encourage savings), investments would have to offer a higher real rate of return. Therefore, higher potential GDP growth implies higher real interest rates and higher real asset returns in general.

In the short term, the relationship between actual GDP and potential GDP may provide insight to both equity and fixed-income investors as to the state of the economy. For example, since actual GDP in excess of potential GDP results in rising prices, the gap between the two can be used as a forecast of inflationary pressures—useful to all investors but of particular concern to fixed-income investors. Furthermore, central banks are likely to adopt monetary policies consistent with the gap between potential output and actual output. When actual GDP growth rate is higher (lower) than potential GDP growth rate, concerns about inflation increase (decrease) and the central bank is more likely to follow a restrictive (expansionary) monetary policy.

In addition to predicting monetary policy, the relationship between actual and potential GDP can also be useful in analyzing fiscal policies. It is more likely for a government to run a fiscal deficit when actual GDP growth rate is lower than its potential growth rate.

Finally, because of the credit risk assumed by fixed-income investors, growth in GDP may be used to gauge credit risk of both corporate and government debt. A higher potential GDP growth rate reduces expected credit risk and generally increases the credit quality of all debt issues.

LOS 12.d: Distinguish between capital deepening investment and technological progress and explain how each affects economic growth and labor productivity.

CFA® Program Curriculum, Volume 1, page 635

FACTOR INPUTS AND ECONOMIC GROWTH

Economies are complex systems of many economic inputs. To simplify analysis, we examine a 2-factor (labor and capital) aggregate production function in which output (Y) is a function of labor (L) and capital (K), given a level of technology (T).

To examine the effect of capital investment on economic growth and labor productivity, consider a **Cobb-Douglas production function**, which takes the form:

$$Y = TK^{\alpha}L^{(1-\alpha)}$$

where:

α and $(1 - \alpha)$ = the share of output allocated to capital (K) and labor (L), respectively [α and $(1 - \alpha)$ are also referred to as capital's and labor's share of **total factor cost**, where $\alpha < 1$]

T = a scale factor that represents the technological progress of the economy, often referred to as *total factor productivity* (TFP)

The Cobb-Douglas function essentially states that output (GDP) is a function of labor and capital inputs and their productivity. It exhibits **constant returns to scale**; increasing both inputs by a fixed percentage leads to the same percentage increase in output.

Dividing both sides by L in the Cobb-Douglas production function, we can obtain the output per worker (labor productivity).

$$\text{output per worker} = Y/L = T(K/L)^{\alpha}$$

Labor productivity is similar to GDP per capita, a standard of living measure. The previous equation has important implications about the effect of capital investment on the standard of living. Assuming the number of workers and α remain constant, increases in output can be gained by increasing capital per worker (**capital deepening**) or by improving technology (increasing TFP).

However, since α is less than one, additional capital has a diminishing effect on productivity: the lower the value of α, the lower the benefit of capital deepening.

Developed markets typically have a high capital to labor ratio and a lower α compared to developing markets, and therefore developed markets stand to gain less in increased productivity from capital deepening.

PROFESSOR'S NOTE

We need to distinguish between marginal product of capital and marginal productivity of capital. Marginal product of capital is the additional output for one additional unit of capital. Marginal productivity of capital is the increase in output per worker for one additional unit of capital per labor (i.e., increasing capital while keeping labor constant).

In steady state (i.e., equilibrium), the marginal product of capital (MPK = αY/K) and marginal cost of capital (i.e., the *rental price of capital*, r) are equal; hence:

$$\alpha Y/K = r$$

or

$$\alpha = rK/Y$$

PROFESSOR'S NOTE

In the previous equation, r is rate of return and K is amount of capital. rK measures the amount of return to providers of capital. The ratio of rK to output (Y) measures the amount of output that is allocated to providers of capital. This is precisely our definition of α.

The productivity curves in Figure 12.1 show the effect of increasing capital per worker on output per worker. Capital deepening is a movement *along* the productivity curve. The curvature of the relationship derives from the diminishing marginal productivity of capital. Economies will increase investment in capital as long as MPK > r. At the level of K/L for which MPK = r, capital deepening stops and labor productivity becomes stagnant.

However, as technological progress occurs, both capital and labor can produce a higher level of output. An investment in capital leading to technological progress enhances the productivity of existing labor and capital. Technological progress, therefore, can lead to continued increases in output despite diminishing marginal productivity of capital. Technological progress *shifts* the productivity curve upward and will lead to increased productivity at all levels of capital per worker.

labor productivity growth rate

= growth due to technological change + growth due to capital deepening

Figure 12.1: Productivity Curves

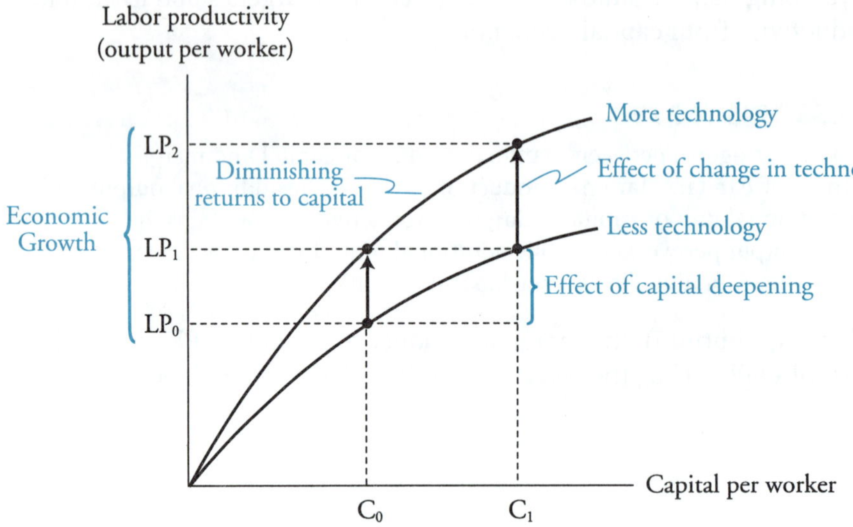

As stated earlier, for developed countries, the capital per worker ratio is relatively high (e.g., level C_1 in Figure 12.1), so those countries gain little from capital deepening and must rely on technological progress for growth in productivity. In contrast, developing nations often have low capital per worker ratios (e.g., C_0 in Figure 12.1), so capital deepening can lead to at least a short-term increase in productivity.

MODULE 12.2: GROWTH ACCOUNTING AND INFLUENCING FACTORS

Video covering this content is available online.

LOS 12.e: Forecast potential GDP based on growth accounting relations.

CFA® Program Curriculum, Volume 1, page 637

GROWTH ACCOUNTING RELATIONS

Using the Cobb-Douglas production function, the growth in potential GDP can be expressed using the **growth accounting relation** as:

$$\Delta Y/Y = \Delta A/A + \alpha \times (\Delta K/K) + (1-\alpha) \times (\Delta L/L)$$

where:

Y = output
A = technology
K = capital
L = labor
α = elasticity of output with respect to capital = share of income paid to capital
$(1 - \alpha)$ = elasticity of output with respect to labor = share of income paid to labor

or:

growth rate in potential GDP = long-term growth rate of technology
+ α (long-term growth rate of capital)
+ $(1 - \alpha)$ (long-term growth rate of labor)

In practice, levels of capital and labor are forecasted from their long-term trends, and the shares of capital and labor determined from national income accounts. The change in total factor productivity (technology) is not directly observable. Therefore, it must be estimated as a residual: the ex-post (realized) change in output minus the output implied by ex-post changes in labor and capital.

The growth accounting equation is also useful in determining the comparative effects of increasing different inputs. If labor growth accounts for the majority of economic growth, for example, analysts should be concerned with a country's ability to continue to increase its labor force. The relation can also be used to estimate potential output, as illustrated in the following example.

EXAMPLE: Estimating potential GDP growth rate

Azikland is an emerging market economy where labor cost accounts for 60% of total factor cost. The long-term trend of labor growth of 1.5% is expected to continue. Capital investment has been growing at 3%. The country has benefited greatly from borrowing the technology of more developed countries; total factor productivity is expected to increase by 2% annually. Compute the potential GDP growth rate for Azikland.

Study Session 4

Answer:

Using the growth accounting equation:

growth rate in potential GDP = 2% + (0.4)(3%) + (0.6)(1.5%) = 4.1%

Another approach to forecasting potential GDP growth is the *labor productivity growth accounting equation*, which focuses on changes in labor as follows:

growth rate in potential GDP = long-term growth rate of labor force
+ long-term growth rate in labor productivity

The long-term growth rate in labor productivity reflects both capital deepening and technological progress.

LOS 12.f: Explain how natural resources affect economic growth and evaluate the argument that limited availability of natural resources constrains economic growth.

CFA® Program Curriculum, Volume 1, page 639

Natural resources include both renewable resources, such as timber, and non-renewable resources, such as oil and gas. The role of natural resources in economic growth is complex. In some instances, countries with abundant natural resources (e.g., Brazil) have grown rapidly. Yet other countries (e.g., some of the resource-rich countries of Africa) have not. Conversely, some resource-poor countries have managed impressive growth.

One reason that limited natural resources do not necessarily constrain economic growth is that *access* to natural resources does not require *ownership* of resources. Resource-poor countries may be able to access resources via trade. Japan, for example, has managed impressive growth and high per capita GDP despite having limited ownership of natural resources.

Other theories contend that ownership of natural resources may actually inhibit growth, because the economic energy of a country rich in natural resources may be focused on recovering those resources rather than developing other industries. Furthermore, countries that own valuable resources can find their currency appreciating as the demand for those resources increases. The so-called "Dutch disease" refers to a situation where global demand for a country's natural resources drives up the country's currency values, making all exports more expensive and rendering other domestic industries uncompetitive in the global markets.

LOS 12.g: Explain how demographics, immigration, and labor force participation affect the rate and sustainability of economic growth.

CFA® Program Curriculum, Volume 1, page 641

As stated previously, an increase in the quantity of labor will increase output, but not per capita output. Quantity of labor is defined as the size of the labor force multiplied by average hours worked. **Labor force** is defined as the number of working age (ages 16–64) people available to work, both employed and unemployed.

LABOR SUPPLY FACTORS

1. **Demographics.** A country's demographics strongly influence its potential economic growth. As a country's population ages and individuals live beyond working age, the labor force declines. Conversely, countries with younger populations have higher *potential* growth. Furthermore, fertility rates drive population growth and thereby affect potential future economic output. Countries with low or declining fertility rates will likely face growth challenges from labor force declines.
2. **Labor force participation.** Labor force participation is defined as the proportion of working age population in the labor force.

$$\text{labor force participation} = \frac{\text{labor force}}{\text{working age population}}$$

   Labor force participation can increase as more women enter the workforce.
3. **Immigration.** Immigration poses a potential solution to a declining labor force. Countries with low population growth or adverse demographic shifts (older population) may find their growth constrained. Since developed countries tend to have lower fertility rates than less developed countries, immigration represents a potential source of continued economic growth in developed countries.
4. **Average hours worked.** For most countries, the general trend in average hours worked is downward. Possible explanations include legislation limiting the number of hours worked, the "wealth effect" which induces individuals to take more leisure time, high tax rates on labor income, and an increase in part-time and temporary workers.

EXAMPLE: Impact of demographics on economic growth

Data for Cangoria, a country in Asia, is shown below. Based upon this data, comment on the likely impact of Cangoria's demographic changes on its economic growth. Assume average world population growth rate is 1.2% per year.

	Population	Labor Force Participation	Median Age of Population
2000	23,400,400	60.4%	39.2
2010	28,040,300	70.3%	38.1

Answer:

Cangoria's population grew at an average annual compound growth rate of approximately 1.8% per year over the last ten years. Combined with the increase in labor force participation, labor supply growth should be above average in the future for Cangoria if those trends continue. The young median age of the population also indicates an expected increase in the labor pool in the future.

Changes in per capita GDP are difficult to predict. Output is expected to be higher due an increasing labor pool, but the larger population may mean there is no impact on per capita GDP.

LOS 12.h: Explain how investment in physical capital, human capital, and technological development affects economic growth.

CFA® Program Curriculum, Volume 1, page 647

Human capital. Human capital is knowledge and skills individuals possess. Unlike quantitative labor metrics, such as hours worked, human capital is a qualitative measure of the labor force. Increasing human capital through education or work experience increases productivity and economic growth. Furthermore, human capital may have external spillover effects as knowledgeable workers innovate. Innovations are then used by society in general creating greater efficiencies economy wide.

Physical capital. Physical capital is generally separated into infrastructure, computers, and telecommunications capital (ICT) and non-ICT capital (i.e., machinery, transportation, and non-residential construction). Empirical research has found a strong positive correlation between investment in physical capital and GDP growth rates.

This result may seem inconsistent given our previous discussion about capital deepening and diminishing marginal returns to capital. Several explanations exist to explain why capital increases may still result in economic growth. First, many countries (e.g., developing economies) have relatively low capital to labor ratios, so increases in capital may still have significant impact on economic growth. Second, capital investment can take different forms. Some capital investment actually influences technological progress, thereby increasing TFP and economic growth. For example, acceleration of spending in the IT sector has created what are termed *network externalities*. Investment in IT networks may have multiplicative effects on productivity since IT network investment actually becomes more valuable as more people are connected to the network.

Technological development. Investment in technology includes investment in both physical and human capital. Technological innovation can manifest itself in processes, knowledge, information, machinery, and software, among other things. Researchers have examined proxies for investment in technology such as research and development (R&D) spending or number of patents issued. Developed countries tend to spend the most on R&D since they rely on technological progress for growth given their high existing capital stock and slower population growth. In contrast, less developed countries often copy the technological innovations of developed countries and thus invest less in R&D as a percentage of GDP.

Ultimately, technological development should lead to increases in productivity as measured by GDP per worker. Developed countries tend to have very high levels of productivity by this measure while less developed countries tend to have greater potential for growth in productivity.

Public infrastructure. Investments in public infrastructure such as the construction of public roads, bridges, and municipal facilities, provide additional benefits to *private* investment. For example, an investment in distribution facilities by a private company would do little good without an interstate highway grid. The highway system, therefore, enhances total productivity for the economy by complementing the private investment and increasing total factor productivity.

MODULE QUIZ 12.1, 12.2

To best evaluate your performance, enter your quiz answers online.

Use the following information to answer questions 1 through 6.

Jay Smith, an analyst for Mako Capital, is evaluating investment prospects in Minikaz, an emerging market economy. Minikaz has experienced moderate growth in the past four years, after decades of stagnation. Smith is evaluating changes in government policies that would foster a higher level of growth. Figure 12.2 shows the summary of his findings.

Figure 12.2: Proposed changes in Minikaz government policies

1. Consumer protection will be at the forefront of government's agenda.
2. The government will lower the entry barriers for foreign financial institutions to operate as intermediaries in Minikaz capital markets.
3. The government will expand public domain legislation to acquire private property for public works projects.

Smith reviews a report published by the Minikaz commerce department. The report indicates that the long-term real growth rate of Minikaz GDP is 2.5%, corporate profits as a percentage of GDP increased by 2% last year, and the P/E ratio increased from 17 to 19 over the last two years. Separately, Smith also reviews World Bank reports indicating that Minikaz's potential GDP growth is 4% and that it has been experiencing actual GDP growth of approximately 2.5%. Finally, Smith reviews Minikaz's national income accounts and finds that Minikaz is experiencing both technological progress and making increased capital expenditures.

Separately, Smith evaluates the performance of Kinimaz, a neighboring republic. Kinimaz has had labor growth of 2% over the last several years and capital growth of 3%. Labor's share of total output is estimated to be 60%. Over the same period, Kinimaz's real GDP has grown by 3.7%. Comparing the two countries, Smith notes that Kinimaz has substantially higher amounts of natural resource endowments. He concludes that Minikaz's relatively lower GDP growth is due to lack of natural resources.

1. Which of the following actions by Minikaz's government would *most likely* increase their economic growth rate?
   A. Increasing regulation for consumer protection.
   B. Lowering entry barriers for foreign financial institutions.
   C. Expanding public domain legislation.

2. Based on the commerce department report, what would be the *most likely* forecast for the long-term aggregate stock market appreciation?
   A. 2.5%.
   B. 4.5%.
   C. 11.5%.

3. Based on World Bank report, which of the following conclusions is *most likely* regarding Minikaz?
   A. Inflation is 1.5%.
   B. Minikaz's government is likely to follow a restrictive fiscal policy.
   C. Minikaz's central bank is not likely to be worried about inflation.

Study Session 4

4. Using the Cobb-Douglas production function and the concepts of capital deepening and total factor productivity, which of the following outcomes is *most likely*?
   A. Minikaz will experience an increase in sustainable growth of per capita output due to the increased capital expenditures.
   B. There will be no short-term increase in per capita output.
   C. There will be both short-term and long-term increases in Minikaz's GDP growth rate.

5. Using the Cobb-Douglas relation, total factor productivity growth for Kinimaz is *closest* to:
   A. 0.5%.
   B. 1.3%.
   C. 1.7%.

6. Smith's conclusion about Minikaz's relatively lower GDP growth is *most likely*:
   A. correct.
   B. correct because in some cases, natural resources may inhibit economic growth.
   C. incorrect because access to natural resources is more important than ownership.

7. Data for the labor market of countries X and Y over the past year appears below:

Country	Unemployment Rate	% Population < Age 15	Avg. Hours Worked/Week	Immigration Growth
X	16%	16%	37	3.5%
Y	3%	10%	36.5	3.0%

   Both countries are expected to have moderate economic expansions over the next several years. Which of the following statements is *most accurate* regarding labor input of the countries in the next several years?
   A. Country X will have greater opportunities to increase labor input.
   B. Country Y will have greater opportunities to increase labor input.
   C. Neither Country X nor Country Y will be able to increase labor input.

8. Which of the following would *least likely* have externality effects on output growth for an economy?
   A. Human capital investment.
   B. ICT investment.
   C. Non-ICT investment.

MODULE 12.3: GROWTH AND CONVERGENCE THEORIES

Video covering this content is available online.

LOS 12.i: Compare classical growth theory, neoclassical growth theory, and endogenous growth theory.

CFA® Program Curriculum, Volume 1, page 658

Theories of economic growth are largely separated into three models with differing views on the steady state growth potential of an economy.

CLASSICAL GROWTH THEORY

Based on Malthusian economics, classical growth theory posits that, in the long-term, population growth increases whenever there are increases in per capita income above subsistence level due to an increase in capital or technological progress. Subsistence level is the minimum income needed to maintain life. Classical growth theory contends that growth in real GDP per capita is not permanent, because when real GDP per capita rises above the subsistence level, a population explosion occurs. Population growth leads to diminishing marginal returns to labor, which reduces productivity and drives GDP per capita back to the subsistence level. This mechanism would prevent long-term growth in per capita income. Classical growth theory is not supported by empirical evidence.

NEOCLASSICAL GROWTH THEORY

Neoclassical growth theory's primary focus is on estimating the economy's long-term **steady state growth rate** (sustainable growth rate or equilibrium growth rate). The economy is at equilibrium when the output-to-capital ratio is constant. When the output-to-capital ratio is constant, the labor-to-capital ratio and output per capita also grow at the equilibrium growth rate, g*.

PROFESSOR'S NOTE

Steady state growth rate for the purpose of neoclassical growth theory does not assume a constant level of technology and hence differs from the definition of steady state discussed earlier.

Based on the Cobb-Douglas function discussed earlier, neoclassical growth theory states that:

- Sustainable growth of output per capita (or output per worker)(g*) is equal to the growth rate in technology (θ) divided by labor's share of GDP (1 – α).

$$g^* = \frac{\theta}{(1-\alpha)}$$

Study Session 4

- Sustainable growth rate of output (G*) is equal to the sustainable growth rate of output per capita, plus the growth of labor (ΔL).

$$G^* = \frac{\theta}{(1-\alpha)} + \Delta L$$

PROFESSOR'S NOTE

In the equations for sustainable growth (per capita or total), growth rate is not affected by capital (K). Hence, we say that capital deepening is occurring but it does not affect growth rate once steady state is achieved.

EXAMPLE: Estimating steady state growth rate

An analyst is forecasting steady state growth rates for Country X and Country Y and has collected the following estimates:

Country	TFP growth rate	Labor force growth rate	Labor cost as a proportion of total factor cost
X	2.0%	1.2%	0.60
Y	1.0%	2.6%	0.52

Calculate and comment on sustainable growth rates for the two countries.

Answer:

Sustainable growth rates:

Country X = (2.0% / 0.60) + 1.2% = 4.53%

Country Y = (1.0% / 0.52) + 2.6% = 4.52%

Sustainable growth rates for the two countries are comparable. Country X's sustainable growth rate is primarily driven by higher growth rate in TFP. Country Y's sustainable growth rate is mostly driven by a higher population growth rate.

Under Neoclassical theory:

- Capital deepening affects the *level* of output but not the *growth rate* in the long run. Capital deepening may temporarily increase the growth rate, but the growth rate will revert back to the sustainable level if there is no technological progress.
- An economy's growth rate will move towards its steady state regardless of the *initial* capital to labor ratio or level of technology.
- In the steady state, the growth rate in productivity (i.e., output per worker) is a function only of the growth rate of technology (θ) and labor's share of total output ($1 - \alpha$).
- In the steady state, marginal product of capital (MPK) = $\alpha Y/K$ is constant, but marginal productivity is diminishing.

- An increase in savings will only temporarily raise economic growth. However, countries with higher savings rates will enjoy higher capital to labor ratio and higher productivity.
- Developing countries (with a lower level of capital per worker) will be impacted less by diminishing marginal productivity of capital, and hence have higher growth rates as compared to developed countries; there will be eventual convergence of per capita incomes.

ENDOGENOUS GROWTH THEORY

In contrast to the neoclassical model, **endogenous growth theory** contends that technological growth emerges as a *result* of investment in both physical and human capital (hence the name *endogenous* which means coming from within). Technological progress enhances productivity of both labor and capital. Unlike the neoclassical model, there is no steady state growth rate, so that increased investment can permanently increase the rate of growth.

The driving force behind the endogenous growth theory result is the assumption that certain investments increase TFP (i.e., lead to technological progress) from a societal standpoint. Increasing R&D investments, for example, results in benefits that are also external to the firm making the R&D investments. Those benefits raise the level of growth for the entire economy.

The endogenous growth model theorizes that returns to *capital* are constant. The key implication of constant returns to capital is the effect of an increase in savings: unlike the neoclassical model, the endogenous growth model implies that an increase in savings will permanently increase the growth rate.

The difference between neoclassical and endogenous growth theory relates to total factor productivity. Neoclassical theory assumes that capital investment will expand as technology improves (i.e., growth comes from increases in TFP not related to the investment in capital within the model). Endogenous growth theory, on the other hand, assumes that capital investment (R&D expenditures) may actually improve total factor productivity.

LOS 12.j: Explain and evaluate convergence hypotheses.

CFA® Program Curriculum, Volume 1, page 674

Empirical evidence indicates that there are large differences between productivity (output per capita) of different countries, with less developed countries experiencing much lower output per capita than their developed counterparts. The economic question is whether productivity, and hence, living standards tend to converge over time. Will less developed countries experience productivity growth to match the productivity of developed nations?

The **absolute convergence** hypothesis states that less developed countries will achieve equal living standards over time. The neoclassical model assumes that every country has access to the same technology. This leads to countries having the same growth rates but not the same per capita income. The **conditional convergence** hypothesis states that convergence in living standards will only occur for countries with the same savings rates, population growth rates, and production functions. Under the conditional convergence hypothesis, the growth rate will be higher for less developed countries until they catch up. Under the neoclassical model, once a developing country's standard of living converges with that of developed countries, the growth rate will then stabilize to the same steady state growth rate as that of developed countries.

An additional hypothesis is **club convergence**. Under this hypothesis, countries may be part of a 'club' (i.e., countries with similar institutional features such as savings rates, financial markets, property rights, health and educational services, etc.). Under club convergence, poorer countries that are part of the club will grow rapidly to catch up with their richer peers. Countries can 'join' the club by making appropriate institutional changes. Those countries that are not part of the club may never achieve the higher standard of living.

Empirical evidence shows that developing economies often (but not always) reach the standard of living of more developed ones. Over the past half century, about two-thirds of economies with a lower standard of living than the United States grew at a faster pace than the United States. Though they have not converged to standard of living of the United States, their more rapid growth provides at least some support for the convergence hypothesis. The club convergence theory may explain why some countries that have not implemented appropriate economic or political reforms still lag behind.

LOS 12.k: Describe the economic rationale for governments to provide incentives to private investment in technology and knowledge.

CFA® Program Curriculum, Volume 1, page 673

Firms accept projects when they provide an expected return greater than their risk-adjusted cost of capital. Under endogenous growth theory, private sector investments in R&D and knowledge capital benefit the society overall. For example, a new technology may initially benefit the firm that developed it but may also boost the country's overall productivity. The effects of 'social returns' or externalities are captured in the endogenous growth theory model, which concludes that economies may not reach a steady state growth but may permanently increase growth by expenditures that provide both benefits to the company (private benefits) and benefits to society (externalities).

When the external benefits to the economy (the social returns) of investing in R&D are not considered, many possible R&D projects do not have expected returns (private benefits) high enough to compensate firms for the inherent riskiness of R&D investments. From an aggregate, economy-wide viewpoint, the resultant level of R&D investment will be sub-optimal or too low. Government incentives that effectively subsidize R&D investments can theoretically increase private spending on R&D investments to its optimal level.

LOS 12.l: Describe the expected impact of removing trade barriers on capital investment and profits, employment and wages, and growth in the economies involved.

CFA® Program Curriculum, Volume 1, page 678

None of the growth theories that we have discussed account for potential trade and capital flows between countries. Removing trade barriers and allowing for free flow of capital is likely to have the following benefits for countries:

- Increased investment from foreign savings.
- Allows focus on industries where the country has a comparative advantage.
- Increased markets for domestic products, resulting in economies of scale.
- Increased sharing of technology and higher total factor productivity growth.
- Increased competition leading to failure of inefficient firms and reallocation of their assets to more efficient uses.

The neoclassical model's predictions in an open economy (i.e., an economy without any barriers to trade or capital flow) focus on the convergence. Since developing economies have not reached the point of significant diminishing returns on capital, they can attract capital through foreign investment and experience productivity growth as a result. Eventually, these economies will develop; their growth will slow and will converge to the steady state growth rate of developed economies.

The endogenous growth model also predicts greater growth with free trade and high mobility of capital since open markets foster increased innovation. As foreign competition increases, more efficient and innovative firms will survive. Those firms permanently increase the growth rate of the international economy by providing benefits beyond those simply captured by the firm. Economies of scale also increase output as firms serve larger markets and become more efficient.

In terms of convergence, removing barriers on capital and trade flows may speed the convergence of standard of living of less developed countries to that of developed countries. Research has shown that as long as countries follow outward-oriented policies of integrating their industries with the world economy and increasing exports, their standard of living tends to converge to that of more developed countries. Countries following inward-oriented policies and protecting domestic industries, can expect slower GDP growth and convergence may not occur.

MODULE QUIZ 12.3

To best evaluate your performance, enter your quiz answers online.

1. Country X has output elasticity of capital of 0.6 and population growth of 2%. If total factor productivity growth is 1%, what is the sustainable growth rate in output according to neoclassical theory?
   A. 2.0%.
   B. 2.7%.
   C. 4.5%.

2. Which of the following is the *most accurate* description of club convergence?
   A. Less developed countries will converge to living standards of other less developed countries.
   B. More developed countries may see their standard of living drop due to competition from less developed countries.
   C. Some less developed countries may converge to developed country living standards while others may not.
3. A chief economist argues that government policy should include an additional tax break for research and development expenses. The economist *most likely* agrees with:
   A. endogenous growth theory.
   B. neoclassical theory.
   C. classical theory.

Use the following information to answer questions 4 through 5.

Jignesh Sangani, an economist with a large asset management firm, makes the following statements about removal of barriers to trade and capital flows:

Statement 1: Removal of barriers is likely to lead to permanently higher global economic growth under the neoclassical theory.

Statement 2: Removal of barriers is likely to lead to permanently higher economic growth for developing countries only under the endogenous growth theory.

4. Sangani's statement 1 is *most likely*:
   A. correct.
   B. incorrect due to economic growth being permanent.
   C. incorrect due to economic growth being global.
5. Sangani's statement 2 is *most likely*:
   A. correct.
   B. incorrect due to economic growth being permanent.
   C. incorrect due to economic growth being limited to developing countries only.
6. Which of the following is *least likely* to be associated with the law of diminishing returns?
   A. Investment in labor.
   B. Investment in knowledge capital.
   C. Investment in physical capital.

KEY CONCEPTS

LOS 12.a

Significant differences in growth rates exist between economies. The following factors are positively related to growth rate:

- Sufficient level of savings and investment.
- Development of financial markets and financial intermediaries.
- Political stability, sound laws, and property rights.
- Investment in education and health care systems.
- Lower taxes and regulatory burdens.
- Free trade and unrestricted capital flows.

LOS 12.b

In the long-run, the rate of aggregate stock market appreciation is limited to the sustainable growth rate of the economy.

LOS 12.c

Potential GDP represents the maximum output of an economy without putting upward pressure on prices. Higher potential GDP growth increases the potential for stock returns but also increases the credit quality of all fixed-income investments, all else equal.

In the short term, the difference between potential GDP and actual GDP may be useful for predicting fiscal and monetary policy. If actual GDP is less than potential GDP, inflation is unlikely and the government may follow an expansionary monetary/fiscal policy.

LOS 12.d

Capital deepening is an increase in the capital stock and the capital to labor ratio. Due to diminishing marginal productivity of capital, capital deepening will lead to only limited increases in output and labor productivity if the capital to labor ratio is already high.

Technological progress enhances the productivity of both labor and capital but not the relative productivity of either. The long-term growth rate can be increased by technological progress (also called total factor productivity) since output and labor efficiency are increased at all levels of capital to labor ratios.

LOS 12.e

$$\begin{aligned}\text{growth rate in potential GDP} &= \text{long-term growth rate of technology}\\ &+ \alpha\,(\text{long-term growth rate in capital})\\ &+ (1-\alpha)\,(\text{long-term growth rate in labor})\end{aligned}$$

or

$$\begin{aligned}\text{growth rate in potential GDP} &= \text{long-term growth rate of labor force}\\ &+ \text{long-term growth rate in labor productivity}\end{aligned}$$

LOS 12.f

Natural resources are essential to economic growth. Empirical evidence has shown, however, that *ownership* of natural resources is not necessary for growth. As long as nations can acquire natural resources through trade, they can experience substantial growth. In some cases, ownership of natural resources may even inhibit growth since countries with abundant natural resources may not develop other industries.

LOS 12.g

Quantity of labor is a function of population growth, workforce participation, immigration, and average hours worked. All else equal, countries with higher population growth, higher workforce participation, younger working-age populations, higher average hours worked, and higher net immigration can grow faster due to higher labor input.

LOS 12.h

The economic growth rate of a country is positively correlated with investments in both physical and human capital. Furthermore, technological development (as evidenced by spending on R&D) is critical for economic growth. This is especially true for developed countries that already have large capital stock and a slower population growth rate.

LOS 12.i

Classical growth theory states that growth in real GDP per capita is temporary—when the GDP per capita rises above the subsistence level, a population explosion occurs, and GDP per capita is driven back to the subsistence level.

Neoclassical growth theory states that the sustainable growth rate of GDP is a function of population growth, labor's share of income, and the rate of technological advancement. Growth gains from other means such as increased savings are only temporary.

Endogenous growth theory includes the impact of technological progress within the model. Under endogenous growth theory, investment in capital can have constant returns, unlike neoclassical theory that assumes diminishing returns to capital. This assumption allows for a permanent increase in growth rate attributable to an increase in savings rate. Research and development expenditures are often cited as examples of capital investment that increase technological progress.

LOS 12.j

Absolute convergence states that the standard of living of less developed countries will converge to the standard of living of developed countries. The conditional convergence hypothesis assumes that convergence in living standards will only occur for countries with the same savings rate, population growth, and production functions.

The club convergence hypothesis contends that living standards in some less developed countries may converge to living standards of developed standards if they are in the same "club." A club comprises countries with similar institutional structures (such as property rights and political stability). Countries outside of the club (without the appropriate institutional structures) will not see their living standards converge.

LOS 12.k

Under the endogenous growth theory, investments in R&D, though risky, often enhance the productivity of the entire economy. Since the private investor only reaps part of the benefit of those investments, it is likely that private sector investments in R&D will be less than what would be optimal for the economy. Government subsidies can make these investments more attractive to private businesses.

LOS 12.l

Economies grow faster in an environment of no trade barriers and free capital flows. Higher growth rates are possible because foreign investment can provide capital to less developed countries (neoclassical theory). The larger markets and greater opportunity to take advantage of innovation will also increase the growth rate in open economies (endogenous growth theory).

Finally, convergence of living standards is likely to be quicker in an open economy.

ANSWER KEY FOR MODULE QUIZZES

Module Quiz 12.1, 12.2

1. **B** Financial intermediary development helps foster economic growth by allowing more efficient allocation of capital and risk. (Module 12.1, LOS 12.a)

2. **A** Long-term growth in the stock market is a function of GDP growth. The other factors—profits as a percentage of GDP and P/E ratios—will have a long-term growth rate of approximately zero and will not impact a forecast of long-term growth in the stock market. (Module 12.1, LOS 12.a)

3. **C** Potential GDP can be interpreted as the highest growth that can be obtained without pressure on prices. Since actual GDP is lower than potential, there is little risk of inflation. (Module 12.1, LOS 12.b)

4. **C** Since Minikaz is a developing country, it is likely to have a low capital base. With a low capital base, increased capital expenditures will still have an impact on output per worker. Technological progress always has a positive impact on output per worker. (Module 12.1, LOS 12.d)

5. **B** Use the growth accounting relations and solving for growth in TFP.

   $3.7\% = \Delta TFP + 0.4(3\%) + 0.6(2\%)$

   $\Delta TFP = 1.3\%$ (Module 12.2, LOS 12.e)

6. **C** Empirical evidence has shown that for economic growth, access to natural resources is more important than ownership. Natural resources may inhibit growth if countries that own them do not develop other industries. However, that is not the conclusion Smith reaches. (Module 12.2, LOS 12.f)

7. **A** Country X will have the greater opportunity due to the younger workforce, potential labor input from unemployed workers, and immigration. (Module 12.2, LOS 12.g)

8. **C** Both human capital and ICT investment tend to have societal benefits. This spillover effect enhances overall growth rate. (Module 12.2, LOS 12.h)

Module Quiz 12.3

1. **C** Using the equation from neoclassical theory, 1% / (1 – 0.6) + 2% = 4.5%. (LOS 12.i)

2. **C** The notion of the club is that some nations are not in the club and will not converge. (LOS 12.j)

3. **A** Endogenous growth theory includes the concept that R&D may have external benefits, and, therefore, should be subsidized by the government. (LOS 12.i)

4. **B** Under the neoclassical growth theory, the benefit of open markets is temporary. (LOS 12.i)

5. **C** Under the endogenous growth theory, open markets lead to higher rate of growth permanently for all markets. (LOS 12.i)

6. **B** Knowledge capital is a special type of public good that is not subject to the law of diminishing returns. Investment in labor and physical capital do exhibit diminishing returns, which are reflected in the shape of the productivity curve. (LOS 12.k)

READING 13

Economics of Regulation

Study Session 4

EXAM FOCUS

Regulations have important implications for economic growth and for valuation of companies. Understand the implications of regulations on financial markets, the cost-benefit analysis of regulation, regulatory interdependence and implications for valuation. There is a lot of new terminology introduced in this topic review that needs to be memorized.

MODULE 13.1: ECONOMICS OF REGULATION

Video covering this content is available online.

LOS 13.a: Describe classifications of regulations and regulators.

CFA® Program Curriculum, Volume 1, page 702

Regulations have important implications on businesses and the overall economy. Regulations can be classified as *statutes* (laws made by legislative bodies), *administrative regulations* (rules issued by government agencies or other bodies authorized by the government), or *judicial law* (findings of the court).

REGULATORS

Regulators can be government agencies or independent regulators. Figure 13.1 shows the different types of regulators. Independent regulators are given recognition by government agencies and have power to make rules and enforce them. However, independent regulators are usually not funded by the government and hence are politically independent. Some independent regulators are self-regulating organizations (SROs) that regulate as well as represent their members. Not all SROs are independent regulators (i.e., have government recognition). Also, not all independent regulators are SROs. Some independent regulators such as the Public Company Accounting Oversight Board (PCAOB) are not SROs.

It should be noted that SROs may have inherent conflicts of interest. These conflicts of interest may deter the recognition of SROs especially in the presence of a more formal and effective regulatory structure. SROs nonetheless are attractive in that they increase the overall level of regulatory resources, utilize the industry professionals with the requisite expertise, and allow regulators to devote resources to other priorities.

Outside bodies are not regulators themselves but their product is referenced by regulators. Examples of outside bodies include FASB and IASB.

Figure 13.1: Types of Regulators

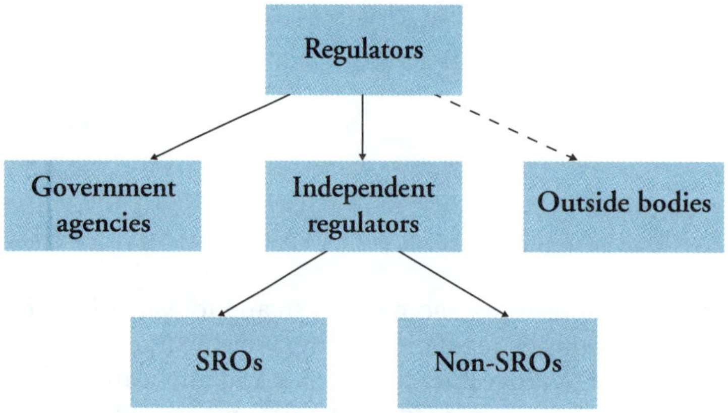

LOS 13.b: Describe uses of self-regulation in financial markets.

CFA® Program Curriculum, Volume 1, page 703

SROs without government recognition are not considered regulators. Self-regulating organizations, while independent of the government and relatively immune from political pressure, may still be subject to pressure from their members. Independent SROs when properly supervised by regulatory agencies have been effective in carrying out the objectives of the regulation.

FINRA is an SRO recognized by the SEC in the United States. FINRA's primary objective is to protect investors by maintaining the fairness of the U.S. capital markets. FINRA has the authority to enforce security laws and regulations. Similar SROs can be found globally.

However, the use of independent SROs in civil-law countries is not common; in such countries, formal government agencies fulfill the role of SROs. In these civil-law countries, non-independent SROs may support the regulatory framework via guidelines, codes of conduct, and continuing education.

In common-law countries such as the U.K. and the United States, independent SROs have historically enjoyed recognition.

LOS 13.c: Describe the economic rationale for regulatory intervention.

CFA® Program Curriculum, Volume 1, page 705

ECONOMIC RATIONALE FOR REGULATION

Regulations are often required when markets cannot provide efficient solutions for all problems. Regulations are needed in the presence of:

- Informational frictions.
- Externalities.

Informational frictions occur when information is not equally available or distributed. A situation where some market participants have access to information unavailable to others is called *information asymmetry*. Regulations are put in place in an attempt to ensure that no participant is treated unfairly or is at a disadvantage.

Externalities are costs or benefits that affect a party that did not choose to incur that cost or benefit. One externality issue commonly addressed by regulation is the provision of public goods. A public good is a resource, like parks or national defense, which can be enjoyed by a person without making it unavailable to others. Since people share in the consumption of public goods but don't necessarily bear a cost that is proportionate to consumption, regulations are necessary to ensure an optimal level of production of such public goods.

LOS 13.d: Describe regulatory interdependencies and their effects.

CFA® Program Curriculum, Volume 1, page 706

REGULATORY INTERDEPENDENCIES

Regulation does not always conflict with the interests of the regulated. The *regulatory capture theory* is based upon the assumption that, regardless of the original purpose behind its establishment, a regulatory body will, at some point in time, be influenced or even possibly controlled by the industry that is being regulated. The rationale behind the theory is that regulators often have experience in the industry, and this affects the regulators' ability to render impartial decisions. Regulatory capture is often cited as a concern with the commercialization of financial exchanges.

Regulatory differences between jurisdictions can lead to *regulatory competition*, in which regulators compete to provide the most business-friendly regulatory environment. *Regulatory arbitrage* occurs when businesses shop for a country that allows a specific behavior rather than changing the behavior. Regulatory arbitrage also entails exploiting the difference between the economic substance and interpretation of a regulation.

To avoid regulatory arbitrage, cooperation at a global level to achieve a cohesive regulatory framework is necessary. For example, regulations limiting greenhouse gas emissions should be consistent globally; otherwise polluters would simply relocate to less restrictive jurisdictions and the objectives of the regulations will not be achieved. Similarly, efforts to reduce the risk of a global financial crisis have been hampered by the lack of a cohesive global regulatory framework.

Even within a country, there may be a conflict between the objectives of different regulatory bodies, leading to an inconsistent overall regulatory framework. For example, regulations seeking higher fuel efficiency standards for automobiles may conflict with regulations from another agency seeking to make the automobiles safer.

LOS 13.e: Describe tools of regulatory intervention in markets.

CFA® Program Curriculum, Volume 1, page 708

TOOLS OF REGULATORY INTERVENTION

Three **regulatory tools** are available to regulators:

1. **Price mechanisms.** Price mechanisms such as taxes and subsidies can be used to further specific regulatory objectives; for example, sin taxes are often used to deter consumption of alcohol. Conversely, subsidies such as those on green energy can encourage specific economic behavior.
2. **Restricting/requiring certain activities.** Regulators may ban certain activities (e.g., use of specific chemicals) or require that certain activities be performed (e.g., filing of 10-k reports by publicly listed companies) to further their objectives.
3. **Provision of public goods or financing of private projects.** Regulators may provide public goods (e.g., national defense) or fund private projects (e.g., small business loans) depending on their political priorities and objectives.

It should be noted that often more than one regulatory approach may be possible and desirable. For example, in deterring consumption of junk foods, regulators may both tax the product category and require nutritional labeling for food.

The effectiveness of regulatory tools depends on the enforcement abilities (e.g., sanctioning violators) of the regulators. Furthermore, the enforcement should have the desired effect of compliance with the regulations. For example, regulations seeking to protect investors in a public company may specify sanctions for violations. If the sanctions are borne by the company (and ultimately the shareholders) and not the individuals perpetrating the violations (i.e., management), then the sanctions end up hurting those that the regulation was intending to protect in the first place.

LOS 13.f: Explain purposes in regulating commerce and financial markets.

CFA® Program Curriculum, Volume 1, page 713

1. **Regulating commerce.** Government regulations provide an essential framework to facilitate business decision making. Examples of regulations covering commerce include company laws, tax laws, contract laws, competition laws, banking laws, bankruptcy laws, and dispute resolution systems.

   Regulations may facilitate or hinder commerce. For example, protections of intellectual property facilitate long-term investments in research. Similarly, trade agreements promote commerce internationally.

2. **Regulating financial markets.** Financial market regulations include regulation of securities markets and regulation of financial institutions. Regulation of financial markets is critical to prevent failures of the financial system. The objectives of securities regulations include three interrelated goals: protecting investors, creating confidence in the markets, and enhancing capital formation.

REGULATION OF SECURITY MARKETS

Ensuring the fairness and integrity of capital markets and thereby protecting investors is a key role of financial markets regulators. Several observations can be made about security markets regulations:

- Disclosure requirements are a key element of security markets regulations. Disclosures provide transparency in financial markets and hence promote investor confidence.
- Many securities regulations are directed towards mitigating agency problem. In the financial markets, investors often work through intermediaries (agents) whose interests often diverge from the interests of investors. Regulations imposing fiduciary duties seek to mitigate such agency problems.
- Regulations have historically focused on protecting small (retail) investors, hence the relatively lax regulatory coverage of hedge funds and private equity funds that are marketed only to qualified investors.

REGULATION OF FINANCIAL INSTITUTIONS

Prudential Supervision

Prudential supervision refers to the monitoring and regulation of financial institutions to reduce system-wide risks and to protect investors. Prudential supervision is important because the failure of one financial institution can have a far-reaching impact and may result in a loss of confidence. Due to high mobility of capital across the developed world, shocks in one part of the system can affect the whole system, leading to global contagion.

The cost-benefit analysis of financial market regulations should also include hidden costs. For example, FDIC insurance for banks may provide excessive risk-taking incentives for banks (a moral hazard problem).

LOS 13.g: Describe anticompetitive behaviors targeted by antitrust laws globally and evaluate the antitrust risk associated with a given business strategy.

CFA® Program Curriculum, Volume 1, page 716

ANTITRUST REGULATION

In a global context, regulatory frameworks often conflict. While regulations often hinder foreign competition (to protect domestic businesses), they seek to promote competition among domestic businesses. Antitrust laws work to promote domestic competition by monitoring and restricting activities that reduce or distort competition.

Regulators often block a merger that leads to excessive concentration of market share. Anticompetitive behavior such as discriminatory pricing, bundling, and exclusive dealing is often also prohibited. Internationally, companies need to evaluate their product and marketing strategies in the context of multiple (and varying) regulatory regimes. For example a multinational company may be subject to U.S. antitrust laws as well as to EU antitrust laws.

When evaluating an announced merger or acquisition, an analyst should consider the anticipated response by regulators as part of the analysis.

LOS 13.h: Describe benefits and costs of regulation.

CFA® Program Curriculum, Volume 1, page 718

COST BENEFIT ANALYSIS OF REGULATION

A regulatory framework needs to be assessed in terms of the cost of the framework relative to the benefit it provides. U.S. federal regulatory agencies are required to conduct a cost-benefit analysis prior to issuing a regulation.

The costs and benefits of regulations may be easy to view but difficult to quantify. The cost of regulation is not limited to the implementation cost (i.e., the cost of operating a government agency to provide monitoring and supervision); an analyst should also consider the cost of the regulation to the private sector.

Regulatory burden (also known as government burden) refers to the cost of compliance for the regulated entity. Regulatory burden minus the private benefits of regulation is known as the *net regulatory burden.*

Regulators should be aware of unintended consequences of regulations. For example, regulations mandating an increase in automobile fuel efficiency standards may encourage consumers to drive more, reducing the effectiveness of the regulation. Regulatory burden is generally difficult to measure as it includes the indirect costs related to changes in economic behavior.

Regulatory costs are difficult to assess before a regulation is put in place. For this reason, many regulatory provisions include a '*sunset clause*' that requires regulators to revisit the cost-benefit analysis based on actual outcomes before renewing the regulation.

LOS 13.i: Evaluate how a specific regulation affects an industry, company, or security.

CFA® Program Curriculum, Volume 1, page 722

Regulations can help or hinder a company or industry. Regulations may shrink the size of one industry (e.g., if it is heavily taxed) while increasing the size of another (e.g., an industry receiving subsidies). Analysts should review the impact of current and proposed regulations on an industry or company, as regulation can have a large impact on valuation.

Regulations are not necessarily always costly for those that end up being regulated. If the regulator is captive, regulations may end up benefiting the regulated entities.

Regulations may introduce inefficiencies in the market. For example, past government bailout of financial institutions has conveyed a message of future implicit guarantees. For this reason, the credit spreads on bonds issued by the financial sector may not fully reflect their risk.

Some regulations may be specifically applicable to certain sectors while others may have broad implications affecting a number of sectors. Certain industries have more exposure to certain types of regulations. For example, environmental laws have higher implications for mining, oil, and gas sectors. Similarly, labor laws are more relevant for labor intensive industries.

MODULE QUIZ 13.1

To best evaluate your performance, enter your quiz answers online.

Use the following information to answer Questions 1 through 7.

Gyaneshwar Dharampal, CFA, is one of the newer analysts at Paramus Funds and has been assigned to cover the global financial services industry. Dharampal is currently reviewing the Zambolan financial services industry. Zambola is a rapidly growing emerging market country. The Zambolan currency is known as the Zu.

The governance of commercial banks in Zambola is covered by the Zambola Financial Institutions Act as amended (2018) (the act). The act provides the regulatory framework for security markets, commercial banks, and other financial intermediaries.

The Zambolan Finance Commission (ZFC) has enforcement and supervisory powers over commercial banks. In its regulatory role, ZFC specifies minimum capital requirements and underwriting standards for loans and investments for commercial banks in Zambola. Currently, the minimum credit rating for bonds eligible for investment by commercial banks is stipulated to be 'B' as rated by JBL Services, an independent rating agency.

The act also provides that the operation of the Zambolan stock exchange be supervised by the Exchange Association (an independent SRO). To promote independence of the Exchange Association, the act exempts it from supervisory review by ZFC.

To curb predatory lending, the act imposes a ceiling on interest rates that banks can charge on consumer loans. However, a recent decision by a Zambolan high court overturned that provision of the act. In response, in the new revenue bill, the Zambolan government included punitive taxes on earnings of commercial banks that are attributable to interest rates higher than the previously-specified ceiling.

Dharampal notes that a new regulation would impose additional taxes on Zambolan manufacturers and require them to make certain workplace safety related modifications. He estimates that the tax revenue from the new regulations would be 100 million Zu. The tax revenue will be used to cover the salaries of newly-hired personnel at the government agency in charge of enforcement of the regulation. The aggregate cost to the manufacturing sector of compliance with the new regulation is estimated to be 300 million Zu. It is also estimated that the aggregate benefit to private sector builders as a result of the new regulations would be 30 million Zu.

Finally, Dharampal notes that Zambola is in the process of introducing a national health care system wherein taxes on tobacco and alcohol will fund government-subsidized health care.

1. The removal of the interest rate ceiling on consumer loans is *most likely* an example of a(n):
   A. judicial law.
   B. statute.
   C. administrative regulation.
2. JBL services is *best* described as a(n):
   A. SRO.
   B. independent regulator.
   C. outside body.

3. Which of the following is *NOT* a good reason to delegate supervisory authority to the Exchange Association?
   A. Increase in overall regulatory resources.
   B. Exemption from supervisory review by ZFC.
   C. Additional knowledge and expertise of industry professionals.
4. Which of the following is *most likely* to be a concern related to the regulatory authority of the Exchange Association?
   A. Regulatory arbitrage.
   B. Regulatory capture.
   C. Regulatory competition.
5. Zambolan government's action of charging punitive taxes on interest earnings of commercial banks is *best* described as a:
   A. price mechanism.
   B. restriction on certain activities.
   C. provision of a public good.
6. The net regulatory burden of new workplace safety regulation is *closest* to:
   A. 170 million Zu.
   B. 270 million Zu.
   C. 430 million Zu.
7. Based on the information provided, which sector of the Zambolan economy is *most likely* to grow?
   A. Commercial banks.
   B. Health care.
   C. Alcoholic beverage producers.
8. Which of the following would *least accurately* be described as regulation of commerce?
   A. Antitrust regulations.
   B. Dispute resolution regulations.
   C. Prudential supervision regulations.

KEY CONCEPTS

LOS 13.a

Regulations can be classified as statutes, administrative regulations, or judicial law.

Regulators can be government agencies or independent regulators. Independent regulators can be self-regulating organizations (SROs) or non-SROs. Outside bodies are not regulators themselves but their product may be referenced by regulators.

LOS 13.b

Independent self-regulating organizations, when properly supervised by regulatory agencies, have been effective in carrying out the objectives of regulation. Use of independent SROs is more prevalent in common-law countries than in civil-law countries.

LOS 13.c

Regulations are needed in the presence of informational frictions and externalities. Informational frictions arise in the presence of information asymmetry. Externalities deal with the provision of public goods.

LOS 13.d

The regulatory capture theory is based upon the assumption that a regulatory body will be influenced or even controlled by the industry that is being regulated. Regulatory differences between jurisdictions can lead to regulatory competition wherein regulators compete to provide the most business-friendly regulatory environment. Firms may use regulatory arbitrage to exploit the difference between the substance and interpretation of a regulation.

LOS 13.e

Regulatory tools include price mechanisms, restrictions on or requirement of certain activities, and provision of public goods or financing of private projects.

LOS 13.f

Examples of regulations covering commerce include company law, tax law, contract law, competition law, banking law, bankruptcy law, and dispute resolution system. Governments may facilitate or hinder commerce.

Financial market regulations seek to protect investors and to ensure stability of financial system. Securities market regulations include disclosure requirements, regulations to mitigate agency conflicts, and regulations to protect small investors.

Prudential supervision is the regulation and monitoring of financial institutions to reduce system-wide risks and to protect investors.

LOS 13.g

Regulators often block a merger that would lead to excessive concentration of market share. Additionally, anticompetitive behavior such as discriminatory pricing, bundling, and exclusive dealing is often prohibited.

LOS 13.h

Regulatory burden refers to the cost of compliance for the regulated entity. Regulatory burden minus the private benefits of regulation is known as the net regulatory burden. Indirect costs of regulations need to be included in the cost-benefit analysis of regulation but are difficult to measure ex-ante. Sunset clauses require a cost-benefit analysis to be revisited before the regulation is renewed.

LOS 13.i

Regulations can have material impacts on industries and companies. Certain industries have more exposure to certain types of regulations. Analysts should review the impact of current and proposed regulations as regulations can have a large impact on valuations for a particular company or industry.

ANSWER KEY FOR MODULE QUIZ

Module Quiz 13.1

1. **A** Judicial law is findings of the court and is applicable in this case. Statutes are laws made by legislative bodies while administrative regulations are rules issued by government agencies or other bodies authorized by the government. (LOS 13.a)

2. **C** JBL Services is neither a regulator nor an SRO and is best described as an outside body. The work of such outside bodies is sometimes referenced by regulatory authorities in their regulations. (LOS 13.a)

3. **B** The Exchange Association is an SRO and hence increases overall regulatory resources. Its members also bring knowledge and expertise of industry professionals. However, due to inherent conflict of interest in an association regulating its own members, adequate regulatory oversight would be necessary. (LOS 13.d)

4. **B** The Exchange Association is exposed to conflict of interest in regulating its members. Hence regulatory capture (where a regulatory body is influenced or controlled by the industry that is being regulated) is a concern. Regulatory differences between jurisdictions can lead to regulatory competition; regulators compete to provide a business-friendly regulatory environment. Firms may also resort to regulatory arbitrage to exploit the difference between the substance and interpretation of a regulation. Neither regulatory competition nor regulatory arbitrage is applicable in this case. (LOS 13.d)

5. **A** Taxes and subsidies as regulatory tools are examples of price mechanisms. (LOS 13.e)

6. **B** Net regulatory burden is the cost of compliance for the regulated entity minus the private benefits of regulation.

   net regulatory burden = 300 – 30 = 270 million Zu

   (LOS 13.h)

7. **B** Everything else held constant, sectors being taxed (i.e., commercial banks, alcohol and tobacco) would be expected to shrink while sectors that are subsidized (i.e., health care) would be expected to grow. (LOS 13.i)

8. **C** Prudential supervision deals with regulating financial markets rather than regulating commerce. Antitrust regulations and dispute resolution regulations are elements of regulation of commerce. (LOS 13.f)

TOPIC ASSESSMENT: ECONOMICS

You have now finished the Economics topic section. The following topic assessment will provide immediate feedback on how effective your study of this material has been. The test is best taken timed; allow 3 minutes per subquestion (18 minutes per item set). This topic assessment is more exam-like than a typical module quiz or QBank questions. A score less than 70% suggests that additional review of this topic is needed.

Use the following information to answer Questions 1 through 6.

Teresa Young, CFA, is the head of research for a large financial services firm based in New York City. The company's clients include pension funds, endowments, and large foundations. Members of the research department include economists that perform short- and long-range forecasting, as well as analysts who follow industry trends and the various individual companies within the industry.

Many of the firm's clients have globally diversified portfolios, and one of the responsibilities of Young's group is to provide appropriate support to the firm's portfolio managers. One of the European equities managers approaches Young for assistance with a longtime client based in Dallas, Texas. The client's existing portfolio is well-diversified, with approximately 60% in domestic securities and 40% in global investments (primarily in Europe and Asia). The client is unhappy with the portfolio's recent performance and is convinced that there is too much exchange-rate exposure because of the large foreign allocation. The portfolio manager would like to provide evidence to the contrary to the client and believes the client is lacking a fundamental understanding of foreign exchange parity relations.

Young compiles some basic information regarding the theoretical relationships among exchange rates, interest rates, and inflation rates. She also obtains information on some of the client's key non-U.S. holdings. Young observes that the client currently has a large position in Banyo, a Japanese manufacturer and distributor of consumer electronics with a strong global market share. The client also has a substantial investment in Seine Industries, a French producer of paper products whose primary market is Western Europe.

Current spot rates:

- 1.3200 USD ($) per EUR (€).
- 95 JPY (¥) per USD ($).

Expected inflation rates:

- United States: 4.00%.
- Euro: 6.50%.
- Japan: 8.00%.

Young is concerned about changes in Japanese monetary and fiscal policies. Japan has been well integrated in global capital markets, and she expects that the policymakers in Japan will tighten monetary policy while adopting an expansionary fiscal policy for the coming three to five years. She is also concerned about changes in the regulatory environment in Japan: Young's analysis of Japanese budgets leads her to conclude that Japan is increasing funding to primary education, while the United States is increasing funding for post-secondary education.

Young then directs her attention to the French economy. She collects several macroeconomic variables for the past 20 years. The information is provided in Figure 1.

Figure 1: The French Economy: Historical Data

GDP growth rate	1.8%
Labor cost / total factor cost	0.36
Growth rate of labor	1.2%
Growth rate of capital	1.67%

Young then collects projections for France as follows:

- The rate of technological change is expected to be lower by 0.1% going forward.
- The growth rate of labor will be similar to historical values.
- The growth rate of capital will increase by 0.1% going forward.

1. Utilizing the spot exchange rate and the inflation rate information provided, the calculated JPY/USD exchange rate predicted six months from today by relative purchasing power parity (relative PPP) is *closest* to:
   A. JPY/USD 90.28.
   B. JPY/USD 96.90.
   C. JPY/USD 98.65.

2. When Young discusses the International Fisher Relation with her client, she should explain that it is based on real interest rate parity, which implies that:
   A. forward rates already reflect any difference in expected real interest rates between countries.
   B. any expected inflation differential between countries will be brought back to equilibrium by consumers' demands for the least expensive goods and services.
   C. any difference in real interest rates between countries will result in capital flows that cause real interest rates in those countries to converge to the same level.

3. Under the Mundell-Fleming model, the planned changes in Japanese monetary/fiscal policy are *least likely* to result in:
   A. a depreciation of the Japanese yen.
   B. an appreciation of the Japanese yen.
   C. a capital account surplus.

4. Regulations are *least likely* to be needed in the presence of:
   A. externalities.
   B. informational frictions.
   C. symmetrical information.

5. Compared with the impact of the incremental spending on primary education in Japan, the planned incremental spending on post-secondary education in the United States is *most likely* to result in:
   A. a higher growth in GDP.
   B. a lower growth in GDP.
   C. a similar growth in GDP.

6. Using the Cobb-Douglas production function, France's growth rate of potential GDP is *closest* to:
   A. 1.76%.
   B. 1.80%.
   C. 1.92%.

TOPIC ASSESSMENT ANSWERS: ECONOMICS

1. **B** Relative PPP hypothesizes that changes in nominal exchange rates over time are equal to national inflation rate differentials.

   The equation for relative PPP is:

   $$\%\Delta S(A/B) = \text{inflation}(A) - \text{inflation}(B)$$

   Since the ¥ has the higher inflation rate, the ¥ should depreciate by 4% per year or 2% over 6 months. Therefore, $E(S_1)$ = ¥95 × 1.02 = ¥96.90. (Study Session 4, Module 11.2, LOS 11.e)

2. **C** The real interest rate parity condition is the theory that real interest rates will converge to the same level across different markets. If real interest rate parity holds, then the level of real interest rates in one country will be identical to the level of real interest rates in a second country. (Study Session 4, Module 11.2, LOS 11.e)

3. **A** Under the Mundell-Fleming model, a restrictive monetary/expansionary fiscal policy in the presence of high capital mobility would lead to a capital account surplus (due to inflow of capital) and domestic currency appreciation. Note that the question is asking for the "least likely" result. (Study Session 4, Module 11.3, LOS 11.k)

4. **C** Regulations are needed in the presence of externalities and informational frictions. One example of a friction is asymmetrical information, which allows one market participant to have an advantage over another. (Study Session 4, Module 13.1, LOS 13.c)

5. **A** Allocation of education spending among primary, secondary, and post-secondary education can be an important determinant of growth. In developed countries like the United States and Japan, incremental spending on post-secondary education will encourage innovation and growth to a greater degree than will spending on primary and secondary education. (Study Session 4, Module 12.1, LOS 12.a)

6. **A** Growth rate of output = (rate of technological change) + α(growth rate of capital) + $(1 - \alpha)$(growth rate of labor)

   $(1 - \alpha)$ = labor cost / total factor cost = 0.36 (given)

   $\alpha = 1 - 0.36 = 0.64$

   Plugging the data given and solving for rate of technological change gives:

   1.8% = (rate of technological change) + (0.64)(1.67%) + (0.36)(1.2%)

   rate of technological change = 0.3%

   Going forward, E(rate of technological change) = 0.3% – 0.1% = 0.2%.

   E(growth in capital) = 1.67% + 0.1% = 1.77%

   Growth in labor is expected to be unchanged at 1.2%.

   Growth in potential GDP = E(GDP growth rate)

   = E(technology growth) + α[E(growth in capital)] + $(1 - \alpha)$ [E(growth in labor)]

   = 0.2% + (0.64)(1.77%) + (0.36)(1.2%)

   = 1.76%

   (Study Session 4, Module 12.2, LOS 12.e)

FORMULAS

Study Session 3: Quantitative Methods

Covariance and Correlation

sample covariance: $\text{cov}_{XY} = \dfrac{\sum_{i=1}^{n}(X_i-\overline{X})(Y_i-\overline{Y})}{n-1}$

sample correlation coefficient: $r_{XY} = \dfrac{\text{cov}_{XY}}{(s_X)(s_Y)}$

t-test for correlation coefficient: $t = \dfrac{r\sqrt{n-2}}{\sqrt{1-r^2}}$ with n − 2 df

Simple Linear Regression

slope coefficient: $\hat{b}_1 = \dfrac{\text{cov}_{XY}}{\sigma_X^2}$

intercept term: $\hat{b}_0 = \overline{Y} - \hat{b}_1\overline{X}$

confidence interval for coefficient:

$$\hat{b}_1 \pm \left(t_c \times s_{\hat{b}_1}\right), \text{or} \left[\hat{b}_1 - \left(t_c \times s_{\hat{b}_1}\right) < b_1 < \hat{b}_1 + \left(t_c \times s_{\hat{b}_1}\right)\right]$$

coefficient *t*-test: $t_{b_1} = \dfrac{\hat{b}_1 - b_1}{s_{\hat{b}_1}}$ with n − 2 df

predicted value of the dependent variable: $\hat{Y} = \hat{b}_0 + \hat{b}_1 X_p$

confidence interval for a predicted value (simple linear regression only):

$$\hat{Y} \pm (t_c \times s_f) \Rightarrow \left[\hat{Y} - (t_c \times s_f) < Y < \hat{Y} + (t_c \times s_f)\right]$$

ANOVA Table Information (Simple Linear Regression)

total sum of squares (SST): $\text{SST} = \sum_{i=1}^{n}\left(Y_i - \overline{Y}\right)^2$

regression sum of squares (RSS): $\text{RSS} = \sum_{i=1}^{n}\left(\hat{Y}_i - \overline{Y}\right)^2$

sum of squared errors (SSE): $\text{SSE} = \sum_{i=1}^{n}\left(Y_i - \hat{Y}\right)^2$

coefficient of determination: $R^2 = \dfrac{\text{total variation} - \text{unexplained variation}}{\text{total variation}}$

$$= \frac{\text{SST} - \text{SSE}}{\text{SST}}$$

standard error of estimate (SEE): $\sqrt{\dfrac{\text{SSE}}{n-2}} = \sqrt{\text{MSE}}$

$F\text{-statistic} = \frac{MSR}{MSE} = \frac{RSS/k}{SSE/(n-k-1)}$ with n − 2 df

Multiple Regression

predicted *y*-value: $\hat{Y}_i = \hat{b}_0 + \hat{b}_1 X_{1i} + \hat{b}_2 X_{2i} + \ldots + \hat{b}_k X_{ki}$

t-test for regression coefficient: $t = \frac{\hat{b}_j - b_j}{s_{\hat{b}_j}}$ with n − k − 1 df

confidence interval for regression coefficient:

$$\hat{b}_1 \pm \left(t_c \times s_{\hat{b}_1}\right), \text{or} \left[\hat{b}_1 - \left(t_c \times s_{\hat{b}_1}\right) < b_1 < \hat{b}_1 + \left(t_c \times s_{\hat{b}_1}\right)\right]$$

ANOVA: total variation (SST) = explained variation (RSS) + unexplained variation (SSE)

mean squared error: $MSE = \frac{SSE}{n-k-1}$

mean regression sum of squares: $MSR = \frac{RSS}{k}$

F-test for multiple regression: $F = \frac{MSR}{MSE} = \frac{RSS/k}{SSE/(n-k-1)}$, with k and n − k − 1 df

adjusted R^2: $R_a^2 = 1 - \left[\left(\frac{n-1}{n-k-1}\right) \times \left(1 - R^2\right)\right]$

Breusch-Pagan Chi-square test for heteroskedasticity:

$$BP = n \times R^2_{resid} \text{ with k degrees of freedom}$$

Durbin-Watson test for serial correlation: $DW = \frac{\sum_{t=2}^{T} (\hat{\varepsilon}_t - \hat{\varepsilon}_{t-1})^2}{\sum_{t=1}^{T} \hat{\varepsilon}_t^2} \approx 2(1 - r)$

Time-Series Analysis

AR model of order *p*, AR(*p*): $x_t = b_0 + b_1 x_{t-1} + b_2 x_{t-2} + \ldots + b_p x_{t-p} + \varepsilon_t$

Mean reverting level of AR(1): $x_t = \frac{b_0}{(1 - b_1)}$

ARCH(1) model: $\hat{\varepsilon}_t^2 = a_0 + a_1 \hat{\varepsilon}_{t-1}^2 + \mu_t$

Study Session 4: Economics

Where applicable, ALL notation assumes A/B currency quote convention.

bid-ask spread (for base currency) = ask quote − bid quote

cross rates with bid-ask spreads:

$$\left(\frac{A}{C}\right)_{bid} = \left(\frac{A}{B}\right)_{bid} \times \left(\frac{B}{C}\right)_{bid} \qquad \left(\frac{A}{C}\right)_{offer} = \left(\frac{A}{B}\right)_{offer} \times \left(\frac{B}{C}\right)_{offer}$$

forward premium = (forward price) − (spot price) = $F - S_0$

value of a forward currency contract prior to expiration:

$$V_t = \frac{(FP_t - FP)(\text{contract size})}{\left[1 + R\left(\frac{\text{days}}{360}\right)\right]}$$

covered interest rate parity:

$$F = \frac{\left[1 + R_A\left(\frac{\text{days}}{360}\right)\right]}{\left[1 + R_B\left(\frac{\text{days}}{360}\right)\right]} S_0$$

uncovered interest rate parity:

$$E(\%\Delta S)_{(A/B)} = R_A - R_B$$

Fisher relation:

$$R_{\text{nominal}} = R_{\text{real}} + E(\text{inflation})$$

international Fisher relation:

$$R_{\text{nominal A}} - R_{\text{nominal B}} = E(\text{inflation}_A) - E(\text{inflation}_B)$$

relative purchasing power parity:

$$\%\Delta S_{(A/B)} = \text{inflation}_{(A)} - \text{inflation}_{(B)}$$

where:

$\%\Delta S_{(A/B)}$ = change in spot price (A/B)

labor productivity:

output per worker $Y/L = T(K/L)^{\alpha}$

growth accounting relation:

growth rate in potential GDP = long-term growth rate of technology
+ α(long-term growth rate of capital)
+ $(1 - \alpha)$(long-term growth rate of labor)

or

growth rate in potential GDP = long-term growth rate of labor force
+ long-term growth rate in labor productivity

neoclassical growth theory:

sustainable growth of output per capita (g^*) equals growth rate in technology (θ) divided by labor's share of GDP ($1 - \alpha$)

$$g^* = \frac{\theta}{(1 - \alpha)}$$

sustainable growth rate of output (G^*) equals sustainable growth rate of output per capita plus growth of labor (ΔL)

$$G^* = \frac{\theta}{(1 - \alpha)} + \Delta L$$

APPENDIX A: STUDENT'S T-DISTRIBUTION

STUDENT'S T-DISTRIBUTION

	Level of Significance for One-Tailed Test					
df	**0.100**	**0.050**	**0.025**	**0.01**	**0.005**	**0.0005**

	Level of Significance for Two-Tailed Test					
df	**0.20**	**0.10**	**0.05**	**0.02**	**0.01**	**0.001**
1	3.078	6.314	12.706	31.821	63.657	636.619
2	1.886	2.920	4.303	6.965	9.925	31.599
3	1.638	2.353	3.182	4.541	5.841	12.294
4	1.533	2.132	2.776	3.747	4.604	8.610
5	1.476	2.015	2.571	3.365	4.032	6.869
6	1.440	1.943	2.447	3.143	3.707	5.959
7	1.415	1.895	2.365	2.998	3.499	5.408
8	1.397	1.860	2.306	2.896	3.355	5.041
9	1.383	1.833	2.262	2.821	3.250	4.781
10	1.372	1.812	2.228	2.764	3.169	4.587
11	1.363	1.796	2.201	2.718	3.106	4.437
12	1.356	1.782	2.179	2.681	3.055	4.318
13	1.350	1.771	2.160	2.650	3.012	4.221
14	1.345	1.761	2.145	2.624	2.977	4.140
15	1.341	1.753	2.131	2.602	2.947	4.073
16	1.337	1.746	2.120	2.583	2.921	4.015
17	1.333	1.740	2.110	2.567	2.898	3.965
18	1.330	1.734	2.101	2.552	2.878	3.922
19	1.328	1.729	2.093	2.539	2.861	3.883
20	1.325	1.725	2.086	2.528	2.845	3.850
21	1.323	1.721	2.080	2.518	2.831	3.819
22	1.321	1.717	2.074	2.508	2.819	3.792
23	1.319	1.714	2.069	2.500	2.807	3.768
24	1.318	1.711	2.064	2.492	2.797	3.745
25	1.316	1.708	2.060	2.485	2.787	3.725
26	1.315	1.706	2.056	2.479	2.779	3.707
27	1.314	1.703	2.052	2.473	2.771	3.690
28	1.313	1.701	2.048	2.467	2.763	3.674
29	1.311	1.699	2.045	2.462	2.756	3.659
30	1.310	1.697	2.042	2.457	2.750	3.646
40	1.303	1.684	2.021	2.423	2.704	3.551
60	1.296	1.671	2.000	2.390	2.660	3.460
120	1.289	1.658	1.980	2.358	2.617	3.373
∞	1.282	1.645	1.960	2.326	2.576	3.291